The media's watching Vault!
Here's a sampling of our coverage.

"For those hoping to climb the ladder of success, [Vault's] insights are priceless."
– *Money magazine*

"The best place on the web to prepare for a job search."
– *Fortune*

"[Vault guides] make for excellent starting points for job hunters and should be purchased by academic libraries for their career sections [and] university career centers."
– *Library Journal*

"The granddaddy of worker sites."
– *US News and World Report*

"A killer app."
– *The New York Times*

One of Forbes' 33 "Favorite Sites"
– *Forbes*

"To get the unvarnished scoop, check out Vault."
– *Smart Money Magazine*

"Vault has a wealth of information about major employers and job-searching strategies as well as comments from workers about their experiences at specific companies."
– *The Washington Post*

"A key reference for those who want to know what it takes to get hired by a law firm and what to expect once they get there."
– *New York Law Journal*

"Vault [provides] the skinny on working conditions at all kinds of companies from current and former employees."
– *USA Today*

VAULT
> the most trusted name in career information™

W9-BOM-247

VAULT GUIDE TO THE TOP

FINANCIAL SERVICES EMPLOYERS

© 2007 Vault, Inc.

VAULT GUIDE TO THE TOP
FINANCIAL SERVICES EMPLOYERS

**DEREK LOOSVELT
AND THE STAFF OF VAULT**

© 2007 Vault, Inc.

Copyright © 2007 by Vault Inc. All rights reserved.

All information in this book is subject to change without notice. Vault makes no claims as to
the accuracy and reliability of the information contained within and disclaims all warranties.
No part of this book may be reproduced or transmitted in any form or by any means,
electronic or mechanical, for any purpose, without the express written permission of Vault Inc.

Vault, the Vault logo, and "the most trusted name in career information™" are trademarks of
Vault Inc.

For information about permission to reproduce selections from this book, contact Vault Inc.,
150 West 22nd St, New York, New York 10011, (212) 366-4212.

Library of Congress CIP Data is available.

ISBN 13: 978-1-58131-506-6

ISBN 10: 1-58131-506-6

Printed in the United States of America

ACKNOWLEDGEMENTS

This book could not have been written without the extraordinary efforts of Sara Calabro, Chris Huen, Richard Larson, Mary Sotomayor, Marcy Lerner, Laurie Pasiuk, Ed Shen and Matt Thornton. Thanks also to Hussam Hamadeh, Samer Hamadeh, Danielle Koza, Todd Kuhlman, Mark Oldman and Kristy Sisko.

Special thanks to all of the recruiting coordinators and corporate communications representatives who helped with the book. We appreciate your patience with our repeated requests and tight deadlines.

The *Vault Guide to the Top Financial Services Employers* is dedicated to the financial services professionals who took time out of their busy schedules to be interviewed or complete our survey.

Table of Contents

Visit the Vault Finance Career Channel at **www.vault.com/finance** — with
insider firm profiles, message boards, the Vault Finance Job Board and more.

VAULT CAREER LIBRARY

ix

Visit the Vault Finance Career Channel at **www.vault.com/finance** — with
insider firm profiles, message boards, the Vault Finance Job Board and more.

VAULT CAREER LIBRARY

xi

Get the BUZZ on Top Schools

Read what STUDENTS and ALUMNI have to say about:

- Admissions
- Academics
- Career Opportunities
- Quality of Life
- Social Life

Surveys on thousands of top programs
College • MBA • Law School • Grad School

VAULT

> the most trusted name in career information™

Go to www.vault.com

INTRODUCTION

VAULT CAREER LIBRARY © 2007 Vault, Inc.

A Guide to this Guide

All of our profiles follow the same basic format. Here's a guide to each entry.

Firm facts

• **Departments:** The firm's major divisions.

• **The Stats:** Basic information about the firm, usually information that's available to the general public. This includes the firm's leadership (generally, the person responsible for day-to-day operations, though it can include the chairman and relevant department heads), employer type (e.g., public, private, or subisdiary), ticker symbol and exchange (if public), 2005 revenue and net income (usually only for public companies; we do have some estimates from third-party sources for private companies and in some cases, the firm has confirmed that information), number of employees and number of offices.

• **Key Competitors:** The firm's main business rivals. Size, business lines, geography and reputation are taken into account when evaluating rivals.

• **Uppers and Downers:** The best and worst things, respectively, about working at the firm. Uppers and downers are taken from the opinions of insiders based on our surveys and interviews.

• **Employment Contact:** The person (or people) that the firm identifies as its contact(s) for submitting resumes or employment inquiries. We've supplied as much information as possible, including names, titles, mailing addresses, phone or fax numbers, e-mail addresses and web sites. Because companies process resumes differently, the amount of information may vary. For example, some firms ask that all employment-related inquiries be sent to a central processing office, while other firms mandate that all job applications be submitted through the company web site.

The profiles

Most profiles are divided into three sections: The Scoop, Getting Hired and Our Survey Says; (some profiles have only Scoop and Getting Hired sections).

Visit the Vault Finance Career Channel at **www.vault.com/finance** – with
insider firm profiles, message boards, the Vault Finance Job Board and more.

VAULT CAREER LIBRARY   3

- **The Scoop:** The company's history, a description of the business, recent clients or deals and other significant developments.

- **Getting Hired:** An overview of the company's hiring process, including a description of campus recruiting procedures, the number of interviews, questions asked and other tips on getting hired.

- **Our Survey Says:** Quotes from surveys and interviews done with employees or recent employees at the company. Includes information on culture, pay, hours, training, diversity, offices, dress code and other important company insights.

© 2007 Vault, Inc.

Industry Overviews

State of the Industry

Come one, come all ...

Like a bazaar that offers something to satisfy every customer's potential needs, the financial services industry presents a little bit of everything to prospective clientele. But while the trade is a vast one, its subdivisions are specialized to meet individuals' fiscal needs. Many of these specialized financial categories are covered in this guide.

We chose to profile as the top financial services firms primarily operate in one of the following categories: credit cards, insurance, mortgages, auto financing, ratings, financial data services or diversified financials. (Noticeably missing categories include accounting, investment banking, commercial banking and investment management—all of which are covered in other Vault guides.)

Although the evolution of the financial services business has been a long and storied one, its development and expansion continues well into this century. The following gives a brief overview of the financial services sectors covered in this guide.

Credit Cards

Looming large

Issuing credit cards is one of the most common ways in which financial services firms provide credit to individuals. Via the credit card, firms provide individuals with the funds required to purchase goods and services, and in return, individuals repay the full balance at a later date, or make payments on an installment basis. Via the debit card, people avoid debt by withdrawing the purchase amount from their bank accounts and transferring it to the seller. Though you're most likely familiar with a how credit and debit cards work, you might not be aware of just how large the industry is today.

According to *The New York Times*-sponsored documentary *The Secret History of the Credit Card*, approximately 641 million credit cards are in

Visit the Vault Finance Career Channel at **www.vault.com/finance** – with insider firm profiles, message boards, the Vault Finance Job Board and more.

VAULT CAREER LIBRARY

5

circulation in the U.S. in 2006 and account for about $1.5 trillion in consumer spending. And worldwide, the number of credit cards in circulation hit 2.5 billion in 2006, with Visa leading the way with a 64 percent market share. The most popular card is the Visa credit, followed by MasterCard credit, then Visa debit, American Express credit, MasterCard debit and Discover credit.

Heavy metal

The credit card traces its roots back to 1914 when Western Union began doling out metal cards, called "metal money," which gave preferred customers interest-free, deferred-payment privileges. A decade later, General Petroleum Corporation issued the first metal money for gasoline and automotive services, and by the late 1930s, department stores, communication companies, travel and delivery companies had all began to introduce such cards. Then, companies issued the cards, processed the transactions and collected the debts from the customer. The popularity of these cards grew until the beginning of World War II, when "Regulation W" restricted the use of cards, stalling their growth.

After the war, though, cards were back on track. Modes of travel were more advanced and more accessible, and more people were beginning to buy expensive modern conveniences such as kitchen appliances and washing machines. As a result, the credit card boomed in popularity, as consumers could pay for these things on credit that otherwise they couldn't afford to buy with cash.

Charge-It

In 1951, New York's Franklin National Bank created a credit system called Charge-It, which was very similar to the modern credit card. Charge-It allowed consumers to make purchases at local retail establishments, with the retailer obtaining authorization from the bank and then closing the sale. At a later date, the bank would reimburse the retailer and then collect the debt from the consumer. Acting upon the success of Franklin's Charge-It, other banks soon began introducing similar cards. Banks found that cardholders liked the convenience and credit line that cards offered, and retailers discovered that credit card customers usually spent more than if they had to pay with cash. Additionally, retailers found that handling bank-issued cards was less costly than maintaining their own credit card programs.

© 2007 Vault, Inc.

The association and the Master

Bank of America masterminded credit card innovations in the 1960s with the introduction of the bank card association. In 1965, Bank of America began issuing licensing agreements that allowed other banks to issue BankAmericards. To compete with the BankAmericard, four banks from California formed the Western States Bankcard Association and introduced the MasterCharge. By 1969, most credit cards had been converted to either the MasterCharge (which changed its name to MasterCard in 1979) or the BankAmericard (which was renamed Visa in 1977).

Cutting the cost of transaction processing and decreasing credit card fraud were the next innovations introduced to the industry. Electronic authorizations, begun in the early 1970s, allowed merchants to approve transactions 24 hours a day. By the end of the decade, magnetic strips on the backs of credit cards allowed retailers to swipe the customer's credit card through a dial up terminal, which accessed the issuing bank cardholder's information. This process gave authorizations and processed settlement agreements in a matter of minutes. In the 1980s, the ATM (automatic teller machine) began to surface, giving cardholders 24-hour access to cash.

The debut of the debit, the climb of the cobrand

The 1990s saw the debit card rise in popularity. The debit card grew from accounting for 274 million transactions in 1990 to 8.15 billion transactions in 2002. (And according to 2006's *A Guide to the ATM and Credit Card Industry*, a report compiled by the Federal Reserve Bank of Kansas City, the amount of debit card transactions rose to 2.6 trillion in 2006.) The 1990s also witnessed the surge of cobranded and affinity cards, which match up a credit card company with a retailer to offer discounts for using the card (think Citibank's AAdvantage cards and American Express' Mileage Rewards program). Although cobranded cards took a dip in the late 1990s—according to some industry experts, this was because issuers had exhausted the most lucrative partners—they've recently returned in full force. Consider that in 2003 alone, MBNA, which *BusinessWeek* has called "King of the Plastic Frontier," struck some 400 new deals with various companies such as Merrill Lynch, Royal Caribbean and Air Canada. Additionally, it renewed deals with another 1,400 organizations, including the National Football League and the University of Michigan. And in 2004, MBNA signed agreements with numerous other companies and organizations such as A.G. Edwards & Sons, the Massachusetts Institute of Technology, Arsenal Football Club (U.K.), Starwood Hotels and Resorts, and Charles Schwab.

Visit the Vault Finance Career Channel at **www.vault.com/finance** – with insider firm profiles, message boards, the Vault Finance Job Board and more.

VAULT CAREER LIBRARY   7

And then there were four

In September 2003, a federal court upheld a lower court ruling that cost credit card powerhouses Visa and MasterCard a combined $3 billion. The court found Visa and MasterCard rules preventing the companies' member banks from also issuing American Express and Morgan Stanley's Discover cards to be illegal and harmful to competition. MasterCard was forced to pay $2 billion in damages and Visa paid $1 billion.

In October 2004, the U.S. Supreme Court decided not to hear Visa and MasterCard's appeal in the government's antitrust suit against them, effectively ending the two companies' rules that have prevented banks from issuing cards on rival networks. As a result, Amex and Discover became free to partner with the thousands of banks that issue Visa and MasterCard, which should allow These two companies to gain ground on the two credit powerhouses.

Upon the initial ruling in September 2003, Amex CEO Kenneth I. Chenault said, "We plan to add more partnerships with other issuers on a selective basis, ensuring they are a strategic fit for our brand and can drive more high-spending customers to the merchants on our network." In 2004, David W. Nelms, chairman and CEO of Morgan Stanley's Discover Financial Services unit, told *BusinessWeek* that the ruling "will create competition in our industry for the first time."

That competition is expected to be intense, say insiders. According to *BusinessWeek*, U.S. consumers use cash or checks to pay for about 59 percent of their $8.2 trillion in transactions each year. That leaves $4.8 trillion in cash outlays for credit card companies to capture. *The Nilson Report* estimates that debit and credit card spending will grow 13 percent a year from 2005 to 2008. "You're talking about the most profitable retail banking product in the world," Nilson publisher David Robertson told *BusinessWeek* in August 2004. "The competition among the titans is going to be fierce." He added, "They are already clobbering each other."

Re-Discovering the possibilities

In the midst of Morgan Stanley's great personnel exodus of March 2005, the firm announced plans to spin off its Discover credit card unit. The reason for the plan, according to former Morgan Stanley CEO Philip Purcell, was Discover "will be more properly valued as a stand-alone entity" than as a piece of Morgan Stanley. Soon after the announcement, analysts began estimating the Street value of the huge credit card unit. The range fell

© 2007 Vault, Inc.

anywhere between $9 billion and $16 billion. Analysts also disagreed over whether or not the spin-off would maximize shareholder value.

However, new CEO John Mack's first big move at the helm after taking over the reins in mid-2005 was to reverse course on the Discover business, which predecessor Purcell had talked of selling off. "Discover is not only a strong business, but also an attractive asset for Morgan Stanley," Mack said in a statement. "It is a unique, successful franchise with growth opportunities that gives Morgan Stanley a consistent stream of stable, high-quality earnings and substantial cash flow, diversifies the company's earnings and broadens our scale and capital base."

But despite the kind words, there was ultimately a change of heart for Morgan Stanley. Although Discover delivered record before-tax earnings of $16 billion in 2006, Morgan Stanley announced that year that it plans to spin off Discover, which some analysts say will allow both businesses to grow more quickly.

The big buy

In June 2005, BofA went big again, following its $49 billion purchase of FleetBoston Financial in 2003 with the announcement that it would acquire credit card behemoth MBNA in a deal worth $35 billion. The purchase made Bank of America one of the largest card issuers in the U.S., with $143 billion in managed outstanding balances and 40 million active accounts. Bank of America will add more than 20 million new customer accounts as well as affinity relationships with more than 5,000 partner organizations and financial institutions. Bank of America expects to achieve overall expense efficiencies of $850 million after tax, which would be fully realized in 2007, and anticipates a restructuring charge of $1.25 billion after tax. Cost reductions will come from a range of sources, including laying off 6,000 employees. And in November 2006, BofA announced that it had agreed to acquire US Trust, the wealth management subsidiary of Charles Schwab Corporation. In February 2007, the parties said the deal would close later than expected (in the third quarter of 2007, not the second), because BofA and Charles Schwab need more time to coordinate their computer systems. The $3.3 billion acquisition will help BofA strengthen its capabilities in serving high-net-worth clients, and will also increase its assets under management.

Visit the Vault Finance Career Channel at **www.vault.com/finance** – with insider firm profiles, message boards, the Vault Finance Job Board and more.

VAULT CAREER LIBRARY   9

The big IPO

At the end of August 2005, MasterCard, which became a private share corporate in 2002, announced that it planned to become a publicly traded company. On May 25, 2006, MasterCard went public, and began trading on the New York Stock Exchange under the ticker MA.

As part of the IPO, the firm adopted new corporate governance and an open ownership structure that included the appointment of a new board of directors, comprised mostly of independent directors, and the establishment of a charitable foundation. Under the new corporate governance and ownership structure, MasterCard's former shareholders, approximately 1,400 financial institutions worldwide, retained a 41 percent equity interest in MasterCard through their ownership of nonvoting Class B common stock. In addition, shareholders received Class M common stock that have no economic rights but provide them with certain rights, including the right to elect several directors from financial institutions around the world.

"Listing on the NYSE marks a major milestone for MasterCard and reinforces our commitment to continued growth and building value for our customers and stockholders," Robert Selander, the company's president and chief executive officer, told Associated Press. The market had expected the issue to open in the $40 to $43 range, but MasterCard was at $39 after a series of setbacks delayed the process. By most accounts, though, the IPO has been a huge success. Since the firm went public, the stock has zoomed to over $140 per share as of June 2007, making MasterCard one of the most successful IPOs of 2006.

No contact credit

"Contactless" cards and finger-swiping systems are the latest advances in the world of plastic purchasing. By the end of 2006, banks had issued 27 million debit and credit cards that do not need to be run through a machine but simply scanned via a radar-like beam. Already, these cards can be used at retailers like McDonald's, 7-Eleven and CVS.

The popularity of contactless credit and debit cards is only expected to skyrocket—according to market research firm Packaged Facts, there will be approximately 109 million in circulation by 2011. Other than not having to run the cards through a machine, a benefit is for purchases less than $25, signing isn't required.

© 2007 Vault, Inc.

Another no contact credit payment system is now in place: the pay-by-finger system, in which individuals' fingers are scanned and linked to their payment information. All you have to do is press your finger (its print) against a device, enter some personal information, such as your phone number, on a keypad and your payment is made; fingerprints are linked up with credit or debit cards. The system is already in place at hundreds of U.S. supermarkets such as Albertsons and Piggly Wiggly.

An eye to the future

But the credit card industry has also been forced to confront a few profitability issues as of late. The exponential cost of credit cards offering rewards programs is concerning the industry, especially with the burgeoning popularity of debit card use, according to a 2006 Booz Allen Hamilton report. The industry is also dealing with the problem of sluggish receivables growth, the report said. To continue to attract customers, card issuers have employed a variety of strategies, including mergers and acquisitions and rewards across cards that tend to trigger more customer spending. Ultimately, the report said, companies need to examine their most profitable sectors, and develop cost allocations and new incentives for customers from there.

Risky business

The insurance industry combines to form a multitrillion-dollar market dealing in risk. In exchange for a premium, insurers promise to compensate, monetarily or otherwise, individuals and businesses for future losses, thus taking on the risk of personal injury, death, damage to property, unexpected financial disaster and just about any other misfortune you can name.

The industry often is divided into categories such as life/health and property/casualty. Life insurance dominates the mix, making up about 60 percent of all premiums. The bigger categories can be subdivided into smaller groups; property insurance, for instance, may cover homeowner's, renter's, auto and boat policies, while health insurance is made up of subsets including disability and long-term care.

But these days, you can find insurance for just about anything—even policies for pets (a market that grew 342 percent from 1998 to 2002, with sales of up to $160 million in 2005 and expected to increase at least 25 percent through 2007, according the industry publication *Small Business Trends*), weddings and bar mitzvahs, and the chance of weather ruining a vacation. Even insurance companies themselves can be insured against extraordinary losses—by

Visit the Vault Finance Career Channel at **www.vault.com/finance** – with
insider firm profiles, message boards, the Vault Finance Job Board and more.

VAULT CAREER LIBRARY   **11**

companies specializing in reinsurance. Celebrity policies always get a lot of press—while rumors that Jennifer Lopez had insured her famous asset (sorry) for $1 billion proved to be unfounded, other such policies do indeed exist. In fact, the phrase "million-dollar legs" comes from Betty Grable's policy for that amount (a similar policy is held by TV's Mary Hart); other notable contemporary policies include Bruce Springsteen's voice, reportedly covered at around $6 million.

The world's top five

Though the U.S. is well ahead of the rest of the world in terms of insurance coverage, insurance is a truly global business. The industry is the biggest in the world, raking in about $3.4 trillion in revenue per year, according to a 2006 report written by industry experts. Ranked by sales, the top-five insurance companies are Germany's Allianz, the Netherlands' ING, New York-based American International Group (AIG), France's AXA and Nippon Life Insurance Company, of Japan. Other leading U.S. insurers include State Farm, MetLife, Allstate, Prudential, Aetna and Travelers.

Consolidation is the name of the game—Hoovers reports that the top-10 property/casualty insurers account for nearly half of all premiums written. Perhaps the most notable example of the mergers and acquisitions mania in the industry was the $82 billion merger in 1998 between Citicorp and the Travelers Group, which created Citigroup (now known as Citi). Some insurance companies have also begun to reconfigure themselves from mutual insurers, or those owned by policyholders (e.g., State Farm), to stock insurers, or those held by shareholders (e.g., Allstate). This process, known as "demutualization," promises to raise even more capital for insurance companies to indulge in more acquisitions.

The last 25 years have seen a shift in the industry away from life insurance toward annuity products, focusing on managing investment risk rather than the (inevitable) risk of mortality. With increasing deregulation in the U.S. and Japan, these insurers are moving ever closer to competition with financial services firms. Indeed, the business of the insurance industry doesn't end with insurance. The world's top insurance companies have broadened their array of financial services to include investment management, annuities, securities, mutual funds, health care management, employee benefits and administration, real estate brokerage, and even consumer banking. The move towards financial services follows the 1999 repeal of the Glass-Steagall Act, which barred insurance companies, banks and brokerages from entering each other's industries, and the Gramm Leach-Bliley Act of 1999, which further defined permissible acts for financial holding companies. Now insurance companies are

    © 2007 Vault, Inc.

free to partner with commercial banks, securities firms and other financial entities.

At the speed of the Internet

Like many other industries, the insurance market has been transformed in recent years by the Internet. Traditionally, insurance products have been distributed by independent agents (businesspeople paid on commission) or by exclusive agents (paid employees). But insurers who sell over the Web reap the benefits of lower sales costs and customer service expenses, along with a more expedient way of getting information to consumers is transforming those traditional methods by cutting costs and increasing the amount of information available to consumers. Communications estimates that the online insurance market takes in over $200 billion in sales each year. Of course, an automated approach to doing business means fewer salespeople are needed—Celent reports that insurance giant Cigna, for instance, eliminated 2,000 jobs in 2002 because of increased efficiencies.

With more IT comes a greater need for IT security—Celent estimates that U.S. insurers spent around $770 million on security alone in 2006. Aside from the threat of viruses, hackers, and the like, regulations have made security a top priority—the Health Information Portability and Accountability Act (HIPAA), for instance, which went into effect in 2003, sets strict standards for the privacy and security of the patient information transferred between health insurers and providers.

Recovering from September 11

The September 11 terrorist attacks sent shockwaves through the industry. Not only did they constitute perhaps the largest insured loss in U.S. history-with estimates ranging between $40 billion and $50 billion in claims for loss of life and property, injuries and workers' compensation—but they also caused insurers and reinsurers to take a hard look at how they would handle the risks associated with possible future terrorist acts. The Terrorism Risk Insurance Act, signed into law by President Bush in November 2002, aimed to deal with the nearly incalculable risk posed by this threat. Among other things, the law defines a terrorism-related event as one with a minimum of $5 million in damages. It provides for the sharing of risk between private insurers and the federal government over a three-year period, with each participating company responsible for paying a deductible before federal assistance is available. If losses are incurred above the insurer's deductible, the government is obliged to pay 90 percent. While the measure met with a considerable amount of grumbling from all parties involved, for the most part the industry acknowledged that the plan at least allows for the potential risk to insurers from terrorism-related disasters to be quantified.

Property insurance stalemate?

In parts of the U.S. such as California and Louisiana, which have dealt with rampant wildfires and Hurricane Katrina in recent years, another trend has arisen. More and more, property insurers are requiring homeowners to take precautions to protect their houses—or confront the possibility of being dropped. Some insurance companies in California are requiring homeowners to replace their roofs with fire-resistant ones and other companies in hurricane-prone coastal areas are requiring policyholders to install storm-resistant shutters. Still, since the requirements are following three years of record profits for the property insurance industry, the Associated Press reported in June 2007, many homeowners are up at arms about the potential cost. The insurance industry isn't backing down on the requirements, either—and some companies have even decided to pull out of certain states altogether. But for now, at least, it looks like there are no certainties when it comes to loss.

Unhealthy health care

Medical malpractice is another hot topic. Health insurers generally get a bad rap from the public, and the media and politicians give plenty of air time to horror stories about managed care companies slighting critically ill patients, and insurers refusing to cover necessary treatments or technologies. Is this reputation deserved? Depends on who you ask, but the industry has its own battles in health care—for example, it sees medical malpractice claims, which have skyrocketed in recent years, as a true crisis. Indeed, according to the Insurance Information Institute, some insurers have quit writing malpractice policies entirely rather than shoulder the risk (the median malpractice award in 2001, the latest year for which this figure is available, was $1 million). Insurance company Farmers, which racked up more than $100 million in malpractice-related losses in 2003, finally got out of malpractice overage in September of that year.

Working in insurance

The insurance industry employs around 2.3 million people, according to the *Seattle Times*. Of these jobs, 62 percent are with insurance carriers, while the

© 2007 Vault, Inc.

remainder are with insurance agencies, brokerages, and providers of other insurance-related services, the U.S. Bureau of Labor Statistics reported. Most insurance agents specialize in life and health insurance, or property and casualty insurance. But a growing number of "multiline" agents sell all lines of insurance. An increasing number of agents also work for banking institutions, non-depository institutions, or security and commodity brokers.

Ratings

Making the grade

Credit ratings are another sector of the financial services industry that serve a highly specific purpose. Founded by John Knowles Fitch as the Fitch Publishing Company in 1913, Fitch was one of the early leaders in providing financial statistics. The Fitch rating system of "AAA" to "D," introduced in 1924, has become the standard for the financial community. Fitch, one of the four major credit-rating agencies (the others are Moody's, Standard & Poor's and DBRS), is the leader in providing ratings on debt issued by companies, covering entities in more than 80 countries.

Moody's Investors Service, founded in 1900, is one of the most prominent and widely utilized sources for credit ratings, research and risk analysis on debt instruments and securities. In addition, Moody's provides corporate and government credit assessment and training services, credit training services and credit software to financial institutions, with 9,000 accounts at 2,400 institutions worldwide. The firm's ratings and analyses track 100 sovereign nations, 11,000 company insurers, 25,000 public finance issuers and 70,000 structured finance obligations. Moody's ratings business consists of four groups: structured finance, corporate finance, financial institutions and sovereign risk, and public finance. The firm's primary clients include corporate and government issuers as well as institutional investors, banks, creditors and commercial banks.

Standard & Poor's operates through six main divisions: credit ratings, data services, equity research, funds, indices and risk solutions. Over $1 trillion in investor assets is directly tied to S&P indices, more than all other indices combined. The firm has the world's largest network of credit ratings analysts, and its equity research division is the world's largest producer of independent equity research. More than 1,000 institutions—including 19 of the top-20 securities firms, 13 of the top-20 banks, and 11 of the top-20 life insurance companies—license its research for their investors and advisors.

Visit the Vault Finance Career Channel at **www.vault.com/finance** – with
insider firm profiles, message boards, the Vault Finance Job Board and more.

VAULT CAREER LIBRARY   15

DBRS, an international ratings agency, is headquartered in Toronto and gives ratings to borrowing entities. The company is split into corporate, financial institutions, public finance and structured finance divisions. The firm prides itself on being "the leading rating agency in Canada" as well as being the first rating agency to have a full-service web site for customers.

Auto Financing

Revving up the payments?

Essentially the first on the scene, Ford Motor Credit was the forerunner when it came to auto financing. An indirect, wholly owned subsidiary of Ford Motor Company, Ford Motor Credit was incorporated in Delaware, in 1959, so that Ford dealers could provide competitive financing services to individuals and businesses interested in buying cars. The company's true origins, however, were about 40 years earlier, when founder Henry Ford sought to discourage excessive consumer borrowing by devising layaway plans to keep his $265 Model Ts rolling off the lot; this tactic sowed the seeds for Ford Motor Credit to later make ownership possible for customers unable or unwilling to meet the entire up-front cost of a car.

Other giants in the business include Chrysler Financial and GMAC, which have been making headlines lately. Cerberus Capital Management announced in 2007 its plans to buy Chrysler and take control of GMAC. But Chrysler and GMAC are hardly the only big fish in the industry. GE Capital Auto Financial Services (the financing unit of General Electric) and Honda Financial Services are contenders as well-along with a plethora of banks' auto financing divisions, such as HSBC Auto Finance, Wells Fargo Auto Financing and Capital One Auto Financing.

The auto financing business has existed for decades, but some recent new developments have caused some raised eyebrows. Particularly, the drawn-out costs involved in the sector has drawn some criticism as of late. *The Wall Street Journal* reported in June 2007 that loan financing plans for car owners have been extended longer and longer, due mostly to the rise of small monthly payments and arrangements that involve no money down. The *Journal* reported that this trend is resulting in consumers becoming blind to the full cost of a product, looking only at the monthly payments involved instead of the overall cost of the vehicle—often adding thousands of dollars to the overall cost.

The Consumer Banking Association reported the same trend in 2006, adding that loans continue to get longer as consumers keep deciding to refinance the

© 2007 Vault, Inc.

outstanding balance of their old car loan in order to lock in low monthly payments—but lengthening their loan term in the process.

Mortgages

Life in the sub-prime sector

Home mortgages were initially the turf of commercial banks at the outset of the century. But shortly after the Depression, the government created the Federal Housing Administration, which offered insured home loans. Fannie Mae, originally part of the FHA, was established in 1938 to help provide affordable homeownership. In 1968, it officially became a shareholder-financed company, but its mission remains the same. Similarly, Freddie Mac, founded in 1970, helps Americans finance homes and also provides assistance in financing rental housing. Other major mortgage providers in the U.S. include Regions, Capital Home Loans and SunTrust. And on the Internet, online companies such as LendingTree connect potential homeowners with hundreds of lenders.

While it's not exactly dismal quite yet, the mortgage industry has suffered a few setbacks as of late, especially with sub-prime lending figures finally surfacing in federal employment reports. (Sub-prime lending is when lenders loan money to customers who aren't eligible for loans from more mainstream lenders.) Mortgage companies have felt the pinch in several different ways, one being the waning of staff. Employees in the mortgage banking/brokerage are on the decline—along with mortgage brokers. And the overall state of affairs in sub-prime lending paints a decidedly grim picture—between 2006 and 2007, approximately 20 sub-prime mortgage in the U.S. have either quit or ended up penniless.

Mortgage fraud has also become a major issue for the industry. According to *National Mortgage News*, it's "one of the fastest growing white-collar crimes in the U.S." And the issue has advanced in such a way that at least one state has sought to legislate against it. In June 2007, Arizona state legislators announced that they planned to make mortgage fraud a felony. How? Specifically, the proposed law would focus on wiping out deals where buyers receive loans for more than the worth of a home and then pocket the extra money. Such deals fiscally harm lenders and usually result in the inflated value of other homes.

Visit the Vault Finance Career Channel at **www.vault.com/finance** – with
insider firm profiles, message boards, the Vault Finance Job Board and more.

VAULT CAREER LIBRARY   17

Financial Data Services

Coulda been contenders ...

The financial data services industry provides services ranging from retirement services and payroll to screening services and credit monitoring. And there's been a lot of buzz business recently. According to *Fortune* magazine's Most Admired Companies for 2007, the top-six most admired firms in the financial data services sector are Dun & Bradstreet, DST Systems, MasterCard, Automatic Data Processing, Paychex and Equifax. (Contenders, they say, are Ceridian, First Data, SunGard Data Systems and Fiserv.) And in terms of top financial data services companies according to profits, First Data is No. 1, followed by Fiserv, Western Union, SunGard Data Systems, MasterCard, DST Systems and Alliance Data Systems.

© 2007 Vault, Inc.

EMPLOYER
PROFILES

Aflac (American Family Life Assurance Company)

1932 Wynnton Road
Columbus, GA 31999
Phone: (706) 323-3431
Fax: (706) 324-6330
www.aflac.com

DEPARTMENTS

Aflac Information Technology,
  Incorporated
Aflac International, Incorporated
Aflac Insurance Service Company,
  Ltd. (Japan)
Aflac Payment Service Company,
  Ltd. (Japan)
American Family Life Assurance
  Company of Columbus (Aflac)
Aflac Japan
Aflac U.S.
American Family Life Assurance
  Company of New York

THE STATS

Employer Type: Public Company
Ticker Symbol: AFL (NYSE)
Chairman & CEO: Daniel P. (Dan) Amos
President, CFO & Director: Kriss Cloninger III
Revenue: $14.6 billion (FYE 12/06)
Net Income: $1.48 billion
No. of Employees: 7,411

KEY COMPETITORS

MetLife
UnumProvident

UPPERS

- "Embraces diversity, offering many opportunities for advancement"
- "The best support and training available in the insurance industry"

DOWNERS

- "Family-like" culture is "good and bad"— it feels like "everyone is constantly in your business"
- "Hours can be long in certain departments"

EMPLOYMENT CONTACT

See "careers" at www.aflac.com

© 2007 Vault, Inc.

THE SCOOP

The innovator

Founded in Columbus, Georgia, in 1955 by the Amos brothers—John, Paul and William—the American Family Life Assurance Company (Aflac) began offering life, health and accident insurance. Today, the company focuses on marketing and selling of supplemental health and life insurance policies for special health conditions, most notably cancer treatment. In fact, Aflac is one of the largest supplemental insurance providers in the U.S., and is a dominant force in Japan. Recently, Aflac was ranked No. 164 on the Fortune 500. And in 2007, for the seventh consecutive year, Aflac was named one of *Fortune*'s America's Most Admired Companies. *Fortune* has also named the company as one of the Top 50 Employers for Women and Top 50 Companies for Minorities.

Goodbye Columbus

The Amos brothers opened their doors for business in November 1955 in a one-room office in downtown Columbus, Ga. As the brothers sought out untapped markets, they were inspired by premiums written especially for polio in the 1940s and 1950s. So, the Amos' chose to sell cancer insurance following their father's death from the disease. The company created the world's first cancer-expense policy in 1958, and after one year, Aflac had sold upwards of $1 million in policies, expanding beyond Georgia state lines. By 1971, Aflac operated in 42 states. The 1980s found American sales lagging but the Japanese market grew into the centerpiece of Aflac's revenue stream.

After building a multinational company on cancer insurance, John Amos succumbed to the disease in 1990. His nephew Dan Amos took the reins, and dubbed the company Aflac two years later. Amos explained the move was an attempt to promote the company's profile, taking into account so many other companies use the word "American."

FLEXibility

For individuals, Aflac U.S. offers a number of voluntary benefit policies, including accident and disability, dental, life, vision, long-term care, short-term disability, and coverage for indemnity and hospital intensive care. The company also offers care plans, general medical expense plans, medical/sickness riders and a living benefit life plan. Aflac services include many programs for employers looking for coverage for their staff. The FLEX

ONE plan allows employees to contribute pre-tax dollars towards qualified benefits, such as health insurance and child care, while the company's Single-Point Billing option consolidates billing and financial requirements from multiple insurance carriers into a single overall benefits group.

Turning Japanese

John Amos first considered Japan to be a prime market for Aflac's products after a trip to the 1970 World's Fair in Osaka. Noting that the country's national health care system neglected to protect its citizens from the enormous financial burden of cancer treatment, Amos spent the next four years seeking approval to enter into the Japanese market, finally getting licensing after convincing government officials that his policies did not compete with existing products. He also gained backing from prominent investors in the insurance and medical industries. In 1974, Aflac officially opened for business in Japan, only the second foreign company licensed to sell insurance policies there.

By 2004, Japan accounted for nearly 75 percent of the company's revenue. However, Aflac reported that net income in the third quarter of 2006 dropped to $408 million, compared to $336 million in the same period the previous year, which the company attributed to competition in Japan. New annualized premium sales in Japan fell 12 percent during the quarter, and Aflac said it expected sales in Japan to decline for the rest of the year. U.S. revenue for the fourth quarter 2006 was strong, though, offsetting weaknesses in Japan. For the quarter, revenue increased 3.4 percent versus the fourth quarter 2005 to $3.7 billion, but net income fell 8.8 percent to $332 million. For the year ended December 31, 2006, total revenue was $14.6 billion, an increase of 1.8 percent versus 2005, while net earnings were flat, at $1.5 billion. The firm said that the modest year versus 2005 was largely a result of a weaker yen/dollar exchange rate.

The Japanese market has been beneficial to the company, as the firm insures one in four households in Japan. To be more competitive within the Japanese market, Aflac formed a marketing alliance with Dai-ichi Mutual Life, one of Japan's biggest life insurers. The company is seeking to introduce new products: One example is the Japanese "living benefit," which includes lump sum payments for heart attacks and strokes.

Duck walk of fame

In September 2005, the Aflac duck was added to Madison Avenue's Walk of Fame during an induction ceremony paying homage to America's most beloved advertising icons. The duck is one of the most successful corporate

© 2007 Vault, Inc.

icons in memory, prompting an increase in brand recognition from 12 percent to over 90 percent, according to Aflac. The duck has been a generous performer over its career, sharing screen time with such luminaries as Melania Trump, Yogi Berra and Chevy Chase. The duck has also appeared in the film *Lemony Snicket's A Series of Unfortunate Events*, and has appeared on the *Tonight Show with Jay Leno* and *Saturday Night Live*.

Just ducky

As a means of retaining personnel, Aflac offers employees an array of benefits, including flextime and telecommuting, and the firm has the largest on-site child care facility in the state of Georgia. There are also professional and personal development courses that help employees drive their career and personal life to the next level. For the ninth consecutive year, Aflac was named to *Fortune* magazine's list of the 100 Best Companies to Work For in America. *Working Mother* magazine also named it one of the 100 Best Companies for Working Mothers in October 2006. In June 2006, *Black Enterprise* magazine named the company to its list of Best Companies for Diversity. And in February 2006, *Hispanic* magazine added it to its list of 100 Companies Providing the Most Opportunities to Hispanics.

GETTING HIRED

Looking for passion

According to Aflac, the company is looking for applicants who are "truly passionate" about their work to join its team. The careers section of Aflac's web site offers information for sales positions and corporate employment. Those in the sales force manage their own time and schedule. New agents are encouraged to participate in specialized programs, including orientation, training and earning the proper certifications. For more information on becoming an independent sales agent, call Aflac at (800) 448-1771.

Corporate jobs are searchable on the Aflac web site and are separated into several job categories, including actuarial, aviation, administrative, facilities, government relations/legal, printing/press operations, communications, finance and accounting, human resources, management, information technology, sales support and administration, operations and project management. Interested candidates can post a resume on the site and create a user profile. Potential corporate applicants

Visit the Vault Finance Career Channel at **www.vault.com/finance** – with
insider firm profiles, message boards, the Vault Finance Job Board and more

VAULT CAREER LIBRARY

23

can call Aflac at (800) 522-0011 if they have any specific questions. The company also recruits through career fairs and lists future events on its web site.

OUR SURVEY SAYS

Going swimmingly

Sources are effusive when it comes to their enthusiasm for the company. "Working for Aflac has been an awesome experience," raves one insider, adding that staffers are "highly valued as the driving force behind the success of the company." Another contact calls the corporate culture "one of teamwork and professionalism." And the good feelings regarding corporate culture may just have something to do with the duck. One insider notes that "over the last 12 years, Aflac has gone through a major transition," adding that "the introduction of the advertising duck in 2000 has greatly increased our corporate recognition, and because of that, it has become easier to sell for Aflac."

One respondent calls the culture "very family-like, which is good and bad," adding that although it's "really nice that people come together to do things for co-workers who have had death in the family or have a new baby."

Depends on the day

For Aflac staff, the dress code is business casual, insiders report. One calls the dress code "business casual to business attire, depending on the type of client seen" and another notes that "we dress day-to-day according to our activities for the day." Hours are flexible, too, an insider reports, commenting that "we make our own hours around what the client's demands are." Another concedes, "Some areas, such as core business units, work a lot of overtime," and "the hours can be long in certain departments."

Training gets good feedback. One insider says the company offers "the best support and training available in the insurance industry." Training programs seem to have improved tremendously over the years. Another contact says, "The state and local training are also getting better and improving the retention of associates."

The "income potential is extreme," notes a source, who adds that "for sales associates, the income varies depending on the level of commitment." Be ready

© 2007 Vault, Inc.

to hit the ground running. "Less committed associates make less money," adds the contact.

Get the skills

Diversity gets good marks from insiders. One says the firm "embraces diversity and offers many opportunities for advancement." Another adds that Aflac "targets a diverse group of cultures," and because the firm is "lacking in bilingual associates," there are "fantastic opportunities for candidates with these skills," and the firm notes it's "always" on the lookout for such candidates.

Visit the Vault Finance Career Channel at **www.vault.com/finance** – with
insider firm profiles, message boards, the Vault Finance Job Board and more

VAULT CAREER LIBRARY

25

Alliance Data Systems Corporation (Alliance Data)

17655 Waterview Pkwy.
Dallas, TX 75252
Phone: (972) 348-5100
Fax: (972) 348-5335
www.alliancedata.com

THE STATS

Employer Type: Public Company
Ticker Symbol: ADS (NYSE)
Chairman & CEO: J. Michael (Mike) Parks
President & COO: John W. Scullion
Revenue: $2.0 billion (12/06)
Net Income: $189.6 million
No. of Employees: 9,000 worldwide
No. of Offices: 60 worldwide

EMPLOYMENT CONTACT

See "careers" at
www.alliancedata.com

© 2007 Vault, Inc.

THE SCOOP

Alliance takes off

Alliance Data is the result of a 1996 merger of JC Penney's transaction services business and The Limited Inc.'s credit card bank operation, both of which were acquired by venture capital firm Welsh, Carson, Anderson and Stowe; the two businesses were combined to then create Alliance Data. When the company was freed from its ties to its parent companies, Alliance was able to court outside business.

Today, the company provides transaction, credit and marketing services to over 600 clients, including retailers, oil companies, utilities, supermarkets and financial services companies. Alliance Data is the second-largest outsourcer of retail private label credit cards, with approximately 90 million accounts. Ranked on the S&P 400, Alliance Data's sales have tripled since it went public in 2001. Limited Brands was the second-largest stockholder until it sold its stake in 2003, but it remains Alliance Data's biggest customer. Welsh, Carson, Anderson and Stowe currently holds approximately 17 percent of the company. Alliance boosted revenue 29 percent in 2006 to $2 billion, and net income by 36.6 percent to $189.6 million.

Recently, Alliance was ranked No. 859 on the Fortune 1000, was named one of the 100 Fastest Growing Tech Companies 2005 by *Business 2.0*, and ranked No. 99 in *BusinessWeek*'s Infotech 100 Companies in 2006.

Outsourcing hat trick

Alliance Data's main focus is managing and facilitating interactions between retailers and consumers through the three segments of its business: transaction, credit and marketing services. Transaction services include processing of sales transactions, account processing and billing services. Its credit services business involve private label credit card programs and gift card services. In addition to the processing of these financial transactions, Alliance Data stands out by providing marketing services, thereby allowing clients to outsource management of the entire financial relationship. The company's marketing services includes creating and managing loyalty programs.

Alliance Data's private label credit card business has been the biggest profit generator for the company, with finance charges being a major source of income. This sector has stayed profitable with the addition of new retail

Visit the Vault Finance Career Channel at **www.vault.com/finance** – with
insider firm profiles, message boards, the Vault Finance Job Board and more

V/\ULT CAREER LIBRARY   **27**

contracts, and the renewal of existing ones. In late 2006, the company signed a long-term agreement with Cruise Management International to provide co-branded credit card services for cruise industry customers. Also this year, it has signed a multiyear renewal agreement with American Signature Inc., a major furniture retailer. Its longtime clients include every division of Limited Brands, Abercrombie & Fitch, Lane Bryant and Value City Furniture.

Alliance stands apart from the pack in its ability to provide marketing services. Most of its closest competitors simply serve as the outsourcing solution for the processing of financial transactions, such as payment and billing processing between companies and its customers. Alliance Data differs in that it handles loyalty programs and marketing strategies.

Alliance Data also runs the Canadian AIR MILES® Reward Program, which is a coalition loyalty program that more than two-thirds of all Canadian households participate in.

Growth story

A key source for Alliance Data's growth has been through acquisitions. Over the last two years in particular, Alliance Data has acquired companies in its marketing services segment, which has now become the company's largest source of revenue.

Epsilon Data Management Inc., a provider of database marketing and customer loyalty programs, was acquired in 2004. Epsilon then agreed to buy e-mail marketing and services company Bigfoot Interactive. Epsilon also announced in September 2006 that it agreed to acquire CPC Associates, a provider of data products for direct marketing programs. And in late 2006, Alliance Data's Epsilon also acquired Abacus, a leading provider of data and direct mail marketing services.

Other previous deals included acquiring Orcom Solutions, provider of customer and billing services for utilities in 2003; Atrana Solutions, provider of point-of-sale transaction software; and Frequency Marketing , marketing software maker, in 2002. In 1998, the company acquired the Loyalty Group, which operated Canada's AIR MILES Reward Program.

Columbus (not Calcutta) calling

It's a well-known fact that call-center employment has declined in the past few years in the U.S., as jobs have been outsourced to India and other low-wage nations. However, one of Alliance Data's big bragging points is the fact

© 2007 Vault, Inc.

that it does not outsource call centers. Its largest is in Columbus, Ohio, but it also has call centers in Texas, Nebraska, Louisiana and Oklahoma. In addition to keeping its call centers in the U.S., Alliance has proven its commitment to helping its community. The Alliance Data School Partnership program provides mentoring and tutoring. Alliance also sponsored Latinos READ, a literary initiative that brought Latino celebrities together to promote literacy in the Dallas/Ft. Worth area. In addition, Alliance received the 2005 Corporate Caring award from Columbus Business First.

GETTING HIRED

Keep apace

Alliance Data says it has a "fast-paced, friendly environment that supports career advancement," and prides itself in the "diversity of its associates." Also according to the firm, it's looking for "talented people who are eager to contribute ideas and take action to keep our momentum strong." If you think you're up to the challenge, go to www.alliancedata.com/careers.html and start building your resume through its system. The firm posts job openings with detailed descriptions of duties.

Visit the Vault Finance Career Channel at www.vault.com/finance – with
insider firm profiles, message boards, the Vault Finance Job Board and more

VAULT CAREER LIBRARY   29

The Allstate Corp.

2775 Sanders Road
Northbrook, IL 60062-6127
Phone: (847) 402-5000
Fax: (847) 326-7519
www.allstate.com

DEPARTMENTS

Allstate Bank
Allstate Distributors, LLC
Allstate Insurance Company
Allstate Insurance Company of
  Canada
Allstate Life Insurance Company
Ivantage Group, LLC

THE STATS

Employer Type: Public Company
Ticker Symbol: ALL (NYSE)
Chairman: Edward M. Liddy
Presidents & CEO: Thomas J. Wilson
Revenue: $35.8 billion (FYE 12/06)
Net Income: $5 billion
No. of Employees: 36,800

KEY COMPETITORS

Farmers Group
Progressive Corp.
State Farm

UPPERS

- "Great, supportive culture"

DOWNERS

- "Very bureaucratic"

EMPLOYMENT CONTACT

www.allstate.com/careers

© 2007 Vault, Inc.

THE SCOOP

Starting at Sears

Insurance broker Carl Odell and Sears & Roebuck Chairman Robert Wood came up with the idea for Allstate, now the second-largest U.S. personal lines insurer behind State Farm, during a 1930 bridge game on a Chicago commuter train. Named after a popular brand of Sears tires, Allstate followed Sears into the retail world and sold its insurance policies next to Sears furniture and clothing. In 1950, a company sales manager came up with the "You're in good hands with Allstate" slogan, which is still used today. Sears began to drop out of the financial services business in 1993 and spun off Allstate as a separate company in 1995. Suffering $4 billion in combined losses from the Northridge, Calif., earthquake and Hurricane Andrew in Florida in the early 1990s, Allstate passed off some of its riskiest policies to other companies in 1996. The company also sold off its real estate portfolio for nearly $1 billion to a private investment fund.

The "good hands" people

As the nation's largest publicly held personal lines insurer, Allstate insures more than 17 million households, selling auto, homeowners, life insurance and investment products, such as fixed and variable annuities in the U.S. and Canada. Other products offered include mutual funds and 529 college savings plans, which are available through the broker-dealer Allstate Financial Services, LLC.

In addition, Allstate Workplace Division, a subsidiary of The Allstate Corporation, offers supplemental insurance products such as disability, cancer, critical illness and accident insurance. The company has also launched a web-based bank, Allstate Bank, which targets its parent company's existing customers, and offers checking and savings accounts, CDs, ATM/debit cards, residential mortgages, home equity loans and lines of credit. Altogether, the company employs almost 40,000 people in the U.S. and Canada and has 14,100 independent exclusive agencies and financial specialists.

The company booked revenue of $35.8 billion in 2006, a slight increase from the $35.38 billion it booked in 2005. Net income was up drastically versus 2005, due mostly to the costs incurred by Hurricane Katrina in 2005. Allstate booked net income of $5 billion in 2006 versus $1.77 billion in 2005.

Visit the Vault Finance Career Channel at www.vault.com/finance – with
insider firm profiles, message boards, the Vault Finance Job Board and more

VAULT CAREER LIBRARY

31

Free agents

In 1999, as the company announced a $600 million cost-cutting program, it also announced that it was eliminating its employee agent program. Going forward, agents who wished to represent the company exclusively could do so only as independent contractors. The plan was criticized by some agents because the company would no longer have to pay for health insurance or pension benefits on behalf of these agents.

Several agents filed a lawsuit against Allstate in August 2001, alleging age discrimination and illegal denial of benefits. The Equal Employment Opportunity Commission (EEOC) filed a separate lawsuit on their behalf in December 2001. A third lawsuit, on behalf of those agents who became independent contractors, was also filed in 2001. In December 2002, Allstate won a ruling from the National Labor Relations Board stating that its exclusive agents are independent contractors rather than employees, thereby ending any attempts by the agents at collective bargaining. The NLRB regional director ruled that agents are contractors because they hire their own employees, advertise themselves and determine how much work they will take on. But the agents pressed on with their bid to unionize, only to be denied once again in March 2003, when the NLRB denied their appeal.

But the company's legal troubles continued in 2003, when the EEOC filed a suit against it, on behalf of Allstate's agents, charging age discrimination. The AARP (formerly known as the American Association of Retired Persons) jumped into the fray as well, assigning two lawyers to the case. In May, a federal judge in Philadelphia agreed to certify the agents' lawsuit as a class action. Then in March 2004, the United States District Court for the Eastern District of Pennsylvania ruled in favor of Allstate, determining that it did not discriminate against its agents.

The company also streamlined operations by forming Allstate Protection by combining Allstate Property and Casualty with independent distributor Ivantage Group. The company has sold off most of its operations outside North America to focus on the U.S. and Canadian markets.

About 1,000 employees accepted a voluntary buyout in April 2006 as part of a deal offered to all 6,800 salaried employees at the company's Northbrook, Ill., headquarters. The company offered the as part of an expense reductions effort to strengthen its competitive position.

© 2007 Vault, Inc.

Post Katrina

Katrina cost Allstate $1.55 billion in the third quarter of 2005 due to the catastrophic hurricane that struck the Gulf Coast. Besides offering employees buyouts, the company also denied storm renewals in some parts of Florida and New York, and bought $2 billion in reinsurance to help cover possible future losses from storms, earthquakes and fires. The company also dropped earthquake insurance to most of its 407,000 quake customers nationwide. In April 2006, a federal judge in Mississippi ruled that Allstate's policies that excluded damage from flooding caused by Katrina were allowed, saying the policies that excluded damage from "tidal waters" are "clear and unambiguous." Unfortunately for Allstate customers affected by the hurricane, damage from a "storm surge" isn't covered under flood insurance. For the third quarter of 2006, the company posted a profit of $1.16 billion, compared to a loss of $1.55 billion in the third quarter of 2005 because of the hurricane.

In March 2006, Allstate entered into a transaction with Prudential Financial that would implement Allstate's decision to exit the manufacturing of variable annuities. On June 1, 2006, that transaction closed when Allstate and Prudential entered into a number of other agreements, including agreements for Prudential to reinsure and administer Allstate's in-force VA business and to work with Allstate to deliver VA products in the Allstate Agency and Financial Institutions Division (FID) channels.

Helping hands

Initially established in 1952, The Allstate Foundation is an independent corporation, funded by contributions from the company, that awards grants to nonprofit organizations working toward improving the quality of life in local communities across the country. The Allstate Foundation funds more than 1,000 national and local programs each year that support Allstate's three key focus areas: safety and vitality of communities; tolerance, inclusion and diversity; and economic empowerment.

Allstate has won numerous awards and honors for its commitment to diversity, especially when it comes to women. In October 2006, *Working Mother* magazine named Allstate as one of its 100 Best Companies for Working Mothers for the 16th straight year. The magazine rates companies on their child care support, leave for new parents, flexible work arrangements, work/life balance, advancement opportunities and the percentage of women in the workplace. *Working Mother* also named Allstate Best Company for Women of Color in May 2006.

Visit the Vault Finance Career Channel at www.vault.com/finance – with
insider firm profiles, message boards, the Vault Finance Job Board and more

VAULT CAREER LIBRARY   33

Leadership change

At the end of 2006, Edward M. Liddy, chairman and CEO of the company since 1999, stepped down as CEO. Allstate's president and COO, Thomas J. Wilson, took on the CEO role. Liddy will retire from the company in spring 2008. Wilson said that under his leadership Allstate would continue to grow its property insurance business.

GETTING HIRED

They're serious about exploring

"Whether you're serious about finding a new position or just exploring the job market," the firm encourages candidates to check out the positions posted on its web site. Allstate accepts resumes into a database, where they remain for a minimum of 12 months. Allstate recruiters utilize a candidate tracking system allowing them to create profile/skill searches for matches against the database. Positions are regularly open in the sales, information technology, finance and marketing, and claims departments. Specific information on a wide variety of openings can be found on Allstate's employment web page, located at www.allstate.com/careers, which offers applicants the opportunity to fill out an online resume form and submit it for positions that interest them.

Finding your way in the door

Allstate recruits at universities across the country. "Employees are encouraged to refer individuals," says a contact. Rewards are available in some areas to those who refer candidates. According to one insider, "They include a behavior analysis as part of the interview process. You will usually talk to three managers on three different occasions before you are hired, plus take a standardized test." Of course, experiences in terms of the number of interviews and the need to take a test are likely to vary depending on location and the type of position a candidate is seeking. The company does confirm that assessment tests are used in many areas in addition to a behavioral-based interview, and that candidates should expect a number of interviews during the process.

The interview method "focuses on what candidates have done in the past, not on what they say they might do in the future," says an insider, adding that "before the interview, our recruitment team identifies core competencies and

© 2007 Vault, Inc.

skills required to succeed in a particular role, and then builds a structured pattern of questions around these." Another contact says that the interview involved questions such as "why I left my last job and what I could offer the company. They also asked what kind of clerical/PC skills I had."

The firm also offers internship positions through its web site. Interested candidates can apply online, but, like with regular positions, you may have a leg up if you happen to have a friend in the company—Allstate notes that "employees are encouraged to submit internship candidates through the employee referral process."

OUR SURVEY SAYS

Nicer at the top

The dress code, says one source, is "business casual, so most people wear slacks and polo-type shirts," while "the officers generally are in button-down shirts and slacks with nicer shoes than us non-officers." Moreover, Allstate has long ago relaxed its "famously formal" dress code (which required "dresses or modest skirts and nylons for women, while men had to wear coats and ties"), and staffers now "commonly" dress in business casual attire, although "jeans, skirts that are extremely short, and shirts without collars or with printed slogans or advertising on them" are prohibited. The decentralized structure allows for "some office autonomy," but many sources comment on the company's "inflexible response" to suggestions for changing corporate procedures. Says one claims department insider, "The corporate culture is very bureaucratic, so you must learn to go with the flow." Another contact shares, "As an agent, you make as much money as the time, money and effort you put into the business."

Several respondents weigh in on what they call a "top-down management style." One insider notes that it's a guiding principle within the firm that's taken "to the extreme." Another says that "you are assigned tasks, you complete them, and then move on to the next task."

No BS here

"Allstate prides itself in a diverse workforce," says an insider. Another comments that "diversity here is very much encouraged." Yet another puts it succinctly; "I have not seen any discrimination." To be sure, sources give

Visit the Vault Finance Career Channel at www.vault.com/finance – with
insider firm profiles, message boards, the Vault Finance Job Board and more

VAULT CAREER LIBRARY   35

Allstate high marks for hiring women managers and being committed to diversity. Allstate is also involved with community service programs, including its Helping Hands program which allows employees to volunteer in soup kitchens, revitalize neighborhoods and help the elderly.

Good support

The firm has a "great, supportive culture," says an insider, and an "excellent work/life balance." On the whole, Allstate sources are "proud" to be in the "business of helping people." The "above-average" pay earns praise, and working parents laud perks such as scholarships for employees' children and on-site child development centers. Respondents praise Allstate for treating its staff like "family." "This past year I underwent liver surgery," says one insider, "and everyone was very supportive. The policies regarding sick leave and opportunities to work at home made my recovery and return to work very comfortable and not all rushed."

© 2007 Vault, Inc.

American Express

World Financial Center
200 Vesey Street
New York, NY 10285
Phone: (212) 640-2000
www.americanexpress.com

DEPARTMENTS*

Global Network Services &
  Merchant Services
International Card & Global
  Communication Services

Primary Operating Segements

THE STATS

Employer Type: Public Company
Ticker Symbol: AXP (NYSE)
Chairman & CEO: Kenneth I. Chenault
Revenue: $27.136 billion (FYE 12/06)
Net Income: $3.707 billion
No. of Employees: 65,800

KEY COMPETITORS

Discover
JPMorgan Chase
Mastercard
Visa

UPPERS

- "Company values"
- "Good culture"
- "The focus on employee development and satisfaction"

DOWNERS

- Compensation
- "Work isn't as challenging as other financial services jobs"
- Need to "push and promote" diversity programs

Visit the Vault Finance Career Channel at **www.vault.com/finance** — with
insider firm profiles, message boards, the Vault Finance Job Board and more

VAULT CAREER LIBRARY   37

THE SCOOP

The master of reinvention

American Express is more than a blue, green, gold or platinum plastic card. With annual revenue of $27 billion, Amex offers customers a wide variety of products and services, including travelers cheques, expense management services, travel services, publishing and more.

Founded in 1850, American Express has evolved from a freight forwarding company to a leading global payments, network and travel company. Today, the company is engaged in businesses that fall into three operating segments. The U.S. card services group issues a wide range of card products and services to U.S. consumers and small businesses, provides consumer travel services to cardmembers and other consumers, and issues travelers cheques and other prepaid products around the world. International card and global commercial services issues proprietary consumer and small business cards outside the U.S., offering global corporate payment and travel-related products and services and international banking services through American Express Bank. Global network and merchant services signs up merchants to accept cards as well as processing and settling card transactions for those merchants.

In 2005, American Express ended a 21-year relationship with the spin-off of Ameriprise, formerly American Express Financial Advisors. Amex shareholders received all of the common shares of Ameriprise under the terms of the spin-off, with one share of Ameriprise common stock for every five shares of Amex common stock outstanding.

American Express benefited from the spin-off. In 2006, the firm reported full-year net revenue of $27.14 billion, up from $24.1 billion in 2005. Net income declined slightly, to $3.707 billion in 2006 from $3.734 billion in 2005. Net income from continuing operations increased to $3.7 billion from $3.2 billion in 2005. In a press release, Kenneth I. Chenault, chairman and CEO of Amex, said that in 2006, "overall credit quality was excellent and key indicators improved from a year ago."

A firm commitment

In May 2002, American Express moved back into its lower Manhattan headquarters, which was damaged eight months earlier in the September 11 World Trade Center terrorist attacks. (As a result of the attacks, employees

© 2007 Vault, Inc.

had been forced to relocate to seven different offices in New York, Connecticut and New Jersey.) Many praised Amex for its return and commitment to rebuilding the downtown New York area, which included becoming the founding sponsor of the Tribeca Film Festival and title sponsor of the River to River Festival.

Amex 's commitment to its employees has also been recognized in the past few years. *Working Mother* magazine named Amex one of the top 100 firms in its 2006 list of the 100 Best Companies for Working Mothers. It has consistently ranked on *Fortune*'s list of the 100 Best Companies to Work For in America. Also in 2006, the National Association for Female Executives said American Express is among the Top 30 Companies for Female Executives. The company was also ranked No. 23 in *DiversityInc*'s annual list of Top Companies for Diversity.

Buffalo '41

Back in 1841, Buffalo, N.Y., was a wild and thriving frontier town. It was the Western terminus of the Erie Canal and a bridge for people and goods between the developed Eastern states and the wide-open Northwest Territory. A man named Henry Wells recognized a need in the boomtown for a service that would provide safe transport of permit goods, valuables and bank remittances in and out of Buffalo. Wells started an express service, first carrying precious metals and securities between Albany and Buffalo (the trip took four days). Wells merged his service with two competitors in 1850 to form American Express. The leadership of the new firm proved accommodating, even though the company's directors nixed an idea for expansion into the then-gold rush state of California, where President Wells and Secretary William G. Fargo started a new firm in 1852—Wells Fargo—while continuing their responsibilities at American Express.

Plastics

American Express merged with a competing company in 1868. That year, William Fargo took over the presidency of American Express from Henry Wells. His younger brother, J.C. Fargo, succeeded him. Under the younger Fargo's 33-year tenure, the American Express Money Order was developed. In 1891, the famed American Express Travelers Cheque arrived, and by 1901 over $6 million of the checks had been purchased. The firm created a travel department in 1915. When the U.S. government nationalized all express services after WWI, American Express concentrated on its money and travel businesses.

American Express services enjoyed a boost during the increased overseas activity of World War II and its aftermath. By the 1950s, it became apparent that an American Express charge card would be a logical extension of the company's services. Introduced in 1958, the card enjoyed immediate popularity. Within three months, half a million people wouldn't leave home without their American Express card. In the 1960s, when the globalization of markets picked up, sales of American Express Travelers Cheques increased exponentially, and the company established a firm presence in overseas markets.

The supermarket idea

Envisioning itself as a one-stop financial supermarket, the firm began to diversify during the 1960s and 1970s by acquiring subsidiary businesses. In 1968, the company purchased an insurance company called the Fireman's Fund, a publishing concern that went on to produce the popular *Travel and Leisure* magazine, and Equitable Securities. The acquisition bandwagon picked up steam during CEO James Robinson's reign (1977 to 1993). In the 1980s, American Express acquired three brokerage firms (Shearson Loeb Rhoades, Investors Diversified Services, and E.F. Hutton), two banks (the Boston Company and Lehman Brothers), and one real estate company (Balcor).

The financial supermarket strategy never took off. American Express was inexperienced in offering revolving debt credit cards, and the other financial services units did poorly. All of them, except for IDS (renamed American Express Financial Advisors in 1995), were combined as Shearson Lehman Brothers. Declining earnings in the early 1990s caused Amex to promote Harvey Golub, formerly CEO of IDS, to head the entire company. Golub immediately cut costs, restructured the company and introduced new credit card products. American Express sold Shearson to Travelers and spun off Lehman Brothers as an independent investment bank in 1994.

Key to the Citi

In September 2003, a federal court upheld a lower court ruling that found Visa and MasterCard rules, which prevented the credit card companies' member banks from also issuing cards run by American Express and Morgan Stanley's Discover, were illegal and harmful to competition. The following year, the U.S. Supreme Court decided not to hear Visa and MasterCard's appeal in the government's antitrust suit against them, which effectively

© 2007 Vault, Inc.

ended Visa and MasterCard rules that have prevented banks from issuing cards on a rival network. Separately, Amex filed suit against Visa and MasterCard, which also included major U.S. banks that are members of the two card associations.

This is the power Amex had been waiting for: It's now free to partner with the thousands of banks that issue Visa and MasterCard, which was supposed to allow Amex to gain ground on the two credit powerhouses. In December 2005, Amex inked a deal with Bank of America to issue a group of American Express-branded credit cards. Bank of America acquired MBNA in a $35-billion deal in June 2005. Citicorp also began offering Amex-branded cards in late 2005. The two companies have long been rumored to merge.

Investing in the East

In March 2006, Amex sold its Brazilian operations to Banco Bradesco SA for $490 million. The deal included credit card portfolios, travel and foreign exchange services and consumer credit units.

But when one market closes another opens. Amex teamed up with Goldman and Allianz AG to invest $3.8 billion for a stake in China's largest mainland bank, the Industrial and Commercial Bank of China (ICBC), expected to go public in late October 2007 in a $19 billion offering in Hong Kong and Shanghai, in what will be the world's biggest IPO.

GETTING HIRED

Browse and learn

Under "Careers @ American Express" at www.americanexpress.com, applicants can search for international opportunities and learn about the company culture. But be aware—"The selection process is fairly stringent," says an insider in recruiting. "Ultimately, only one applicant out of 25 gets hired." Generally, the recruiting process begins at www.americanexpress.com, where a detailed career section is maintained. Applicants can search for jobs by function and location or create a job search agent that sends an e-mail when promising openings pop up. "Jobs are posted for one or two weeks," notes a source. "Online applicants are sent notification of receipt of application. Applicants of interest will be contacted rather quickly, once posting ends."

Visit the Vault Finance Career Channel at www.vault.com/finance – with
insider firm profiles, message boards, the Vault Finance Job Board and more

VAULT CAREER LIBRARY   41

The company also recruits at a broad range of colleges and universities in various regions around the world, including top-tier MBA programs and undergraduate institutions. The campus selection and assessment process involves several rounds of structured interviews, which are focused on candidates answering specific questions based on American Express core competencies.

One insider reports a fairly streamlined interview process, noting that "I first applied online, was interviewed by a panel of three that included the head of HR, and then had a final interview with the president." Another describes going through "two interviews, meeting with a manager, a director and a VP." But the interview process can vary somewhat, according to department, though as one insider reports, "Most people interview with between three and five people, including the hiring manager, the hiring manager's boss, peers of the hiring manager and possibly would-be peers of the interviewee." Another contact reports a stress-free process, noting, "I think the reason why I was hired quite easily was because of my experience."

One contact gives a blow-by-blow of his experience landing at American Express. " All available job listings are located on the company web site," he says that "Upon online application I was contacted by the human resources department for a preliminary phone-based interview. After the initial weed out, resumes are forwarded to the hiring manager who directly contacts the candidates they want to interview. The second-round interview is directly with the hiring manager and the third round is with senior management." The interview questions vary. "At the lower levels, the interview process is basically a test-your-knowledge sort of interview combined with personality matching. No particular questions stand out in my mind, but the general sense of the interview was comfortable and low stress. Just make sure you're very familiar with Excel and PowerPoint, and possibly writing macros," says that financial analyst. One customer service representative remembers getting "behavioral questions" such as "'Describe a situation in which you gave outstanding customer service' or 'Describe a situation where you had to work with a difficult co-worker.'" Another says that the interviews questions center around four areas: "customers, implementation, results and communication."

The more you know

One source who started with the firm as an intern in the risk management department praises the program, adding, "I gained so much valuable knowledge both in the technical area as well as financial." Indeed, veterans of the internship program say that internships help the company try out potential full-time employees—and helps interns try out the company for

© 2007 Vault, Inc.

size. "Many interns have special projects during their summers, but I worked in a regular line position in card retention," says a former summer (and now permanent) employee. "I believe it was easier to get a full-time position after having interned here because I demonstrated that I was a good fit. It was also easier for me to get hired at other companies after interning here." In the firm's summer internship, "pay is competitive," and a source says, "It's much easier to get hired after an internship—if you perform well."

OUR SURVEY SAYS

Your opinion may vary

Insiders call the corporate culture everything from "conservative" to "employee-focused." One notes that the "corporate culture is quite good" and although sources have "culture conflicts," "people are all nice to each other," "with no bias at all." Another contact says, "The most positive aspect of my tenure has been the quality of the people I have worked with," adding, "My current group is comprised of some of the most intelligent and genuinely decent people that I have ever worked with." One insider agrees, saying, "You can develop good friendships with the people at the company, and you're always in a position to move around and try new things. There are many opportunities at Amex." While the company has "some groups can be much more political and have high school-like cliques," "this is not universal and even in those groups, you can find a few fantastic people." Another source says the culture is "extremely supportive and conducive to professional and personal growth."

But in a company as large as American Express, it comes as no surprise that insiders have conflicting views of the company's culture. (Amex has operations in all 50 states plus the District of Columbia, so aspects such as pay, benefits and even culture will vary from region to region.) One source uses a slew of adjectives—"smart, analytical, consensus-based, respectful, diverse [and] competitive"—to praise the company. Others paint the picture of a company that's "bureaucratic and closed to new ideas unless those ideas come from upper management," and that's trying to pull off impossibilities like "changing four tires on a car moving at 90 miles per hour." One former insider from the Midwest region says the "corporate culture was mostly Midwest in nature with a very strong emphasis on understanding diversity and cultural differences as a positive to the workforce." "I was very impressed with the people at American Express from top managers on down to my team members," says another source.

Visit the Vault Finance Career Channel at **www.vault.com/finance** – with
insider firm profiles, message boards, the Vault Finance Job Board and more

VAULT CAREER LIBRARY

43

"We were a very diverse group and all groups were very well represented and their needs were addressed in a very professional and caring way." One contact says the company "wants to win in the marketplace," but notes, "conflicting and overlapping efforts in separate business units often causes silo mentality and passive aggressive behaviors." Another critic calls American Express "a very poorly managed organization" with "narrow-minded managers who are unwilling to learn from mistakes" and who "preach the latest buzzwords about diversity and teamwork but manage the old-fashioned way." However, the contact admits the firm is "making some progress towards reengineering its processes and systems." Another lauds the office's open seating arrangement, where managers are "visible and contactable at all times," and "are there to help and answer questions—and it's is common knowledge that the managers sit below us on the corporate pyramid and are there to support us. Our customers are above us."

Another company, who has only positive things to say about the firm, brags that "working for Amex is great, especially in the finance department." The source explains, "The finance group consists of some of the best people I have worked with, all dedicated to their jobs, and leading innovation and business profitability using some of the most current theories in finance."

The company allows for year-round business casual dress in most, but not all offices. "Dress code is casual except when clients visit," says a source. You'll have to do it by the book, though. "We have a dress policy with specifics on what is acceptable 'business casual' and what is not," says one insider. Another says it's "formal always" where she works (in Minneapolis). Still another adds that the dress code is "flexible" and "every Friday and the day before any public holidays are casual days, where we can wear jeans and T-shirts." One source calls the code "generally casual" and adds that "although women aren't supposed to wear flip-flops in the summer, that rule is never enforced." As far as the aesthetics of the firm's offices, one contact notes that it "varies by location," but says, "generally, they're above average."

Pretty accommodating

While working hours "depend on your team leader and your clients," they are "flexible," says one insider, adding that "you don't need to come in at 9 a.m. strictly, and if you're late, you can leave late to make it up." And "the needs of employees are very much attended to," so "if you need to pick up your child early, arrangements are willingly made to accommodate all your needs." Staffers also have the "ability to work from home and teleconference into

© 2007 Vault, Inc.

meetings. Amex prides itself on maintaining a good work-life balance, and it shows."

And although the company expects an honest day's work, respondents say they aren't locked in the office indefinitely. "Most jobs don't have any pressure to bill, and there is no requirement to stick around for 'face time,'" says a source. "However, jobs are meaty and often require long hours. I generally work 55 to 60 hours a week." Others put the target a little lower, and most report never having to work weekends. "Although there were times when extra hours were needed, for the most part the leadership model dictates that employees should be able to perform their weekly job functions within 35 hours," remembers one former insider. Special arrangements can be accommodated. "The culture is fairly supportive of flexible work schedules," says one source who takes advantage of the company's generosity in this regard. "Individuals are accountable for themselves."

The skinny on salaries

Insiders have different takes when it comes to compensation. One New York contact says that while "salaries are slightly lower than average for financial services," employees still receive "four weeks vacation, plus holidays, plus four summer flex days, so it's not too bad." Another source reports that "the salary is competitive with other major firms. Bonuses are paid out on a bell curve so that only so many people will receive the highest possible." Sometimes it pays to come in from the outside. "For experienced hires, salary ranges are wide for similar positions," says an insider. "This is because Amex has to pay market rates for external hires but pays less to people who transfer internally. The result is that external hires make $10,000 to $12,000 more per year in the same position as an internal transfer." Pay is standard for entry-level hires and is based on competitive regional salary ranges. Though one source comments that "employee benefits should be given more emphasis," the company offers a variety of perks and benefits, which include "tuition reimbursement; a variety of health care options, life insurance, stock options, vacation purchase plan, pensions, 401(k), many employee programs with large retailers, and the opportunity to win tickets to Amex-sponsored events."

Take the opportunities

American Express is trying to quicken the pace when it comes to training. "For several years, training was sparse," reports one contact. "It is picking up again,

Visit the Vault Finance Career Channel at **www.vault.com/finance** – with
insider firm profiles, message boards, the Vault Finance Job Board and more

VAULT CAREER LIBRARY

45

mainly because many of the midlevel managers haven't ever attended appropriate training and it's needed." Another insider says, "You are given endless opportunities to better your leadership skills and it is encouraged that you take part in a variety of training sessions. Opportunities for advancement depend on the leadership teams working together but, there are always other areas that consider your knowledge and years of experience a bonus to the organization." Another notes that "opportunities for advancement seem hard" and when it comes to promotions, superiors "only consider your management skills, but never consider how long you've been working here." One contact says that while "opportunities for advancement easily exist for analysts, there are not as many once you get to the director level, and vice president positions are very hard to come by." But another insider says, "Amex encourages you to move to a new position approximately every year, if you so desire," and "they recognize that things may become stale and a new environment and new challenges can help you grow as an employee," adding that they encourage staffers to explore international opportunities as well. To advance, an MBA might be a good investment. "An MBA is not required for upward movement," says an insider. "However, it seems anyone under 35 has one. So do the math."

Push those programs

American Express generally gets good diversity marks, though one insider notes that "it should push and promote programs and initiatives that will give equal treatment to women and minorities," and adds that the firm should "support and encourage our lawmakers to pass bills that will guarantee employment and security of tenure to women." Another notes that the firm is "receptive to all people," and others praise the company's efforts. "My particular office consists of many foreign nationals of both genders," says one finance professional. "Some of the highest ranking finance officers in the company are women." Things can be different at a specific location. "Overall, Amex is very diverse, but not necessarily in all locations," notes a source. Another insider notes that "there are many nationalities and people, many different religions and backgrounds." But one insider says that while there is "good diversity in terms of race and sex, you don't see a lot of different opinions or ideas because almost everyone comes from upper-middle-class or upper-class families and the same few business schools, banks and consulting firms."

© 2007 Vault, Inc.

American International Group Inc. (AIG)

70 Pine Street
New York, NY 10270
Phone: (212) 770-7000
Fax: (212) 509-9705
www.aig.com

DEPARTMENTS

AIG American General Life
  Companies
AIG Annuity Insurance Company
AIG Star Life Insurance Co., Ltd.
AIG SunAmerica Life Assurance
  Company
Life Insurance & Retirement
  Services

THE STATS

Employer Type: Public Company
Ticker Symbol: AIG (NYSE)
Chairman: Robert Willumstad
President & CEO: Martin Sullivan
Revenue: $113.19 billion (12/06)
Net Income: $14.05 billion
No. of Employees: 97,000

KEY COMPETITORS

Allianz
AXA
Zurich Financial Services

UPPERS

- "Great place to learn"
- Good benefits

DOWNERS

- Diversity efforts could be better
- "The bar needs to be raised for hiring"

EMPLOYMENT CONTACT

See "careers" at www.aig.com

Visit the Vault Finance Career Channel at **www.vault.com/finance** — with
insider firm profiles, message boards, the Vault Finance Job Board and more

VAULT CAREER LIBRARY

47

THE SCOOP

Made in China

New York-based American International Group (AIG), one of the world's largest insurance firms and the second-largest U.S. life insurer, was founded in 1919 in Shanghai, China, by Cornelius Vander Starr, a former U.S. Army veteran. At first, the company offered only fire and marine insurance. In 1936, it opened a New York office specializing in insuring risks incurred outside the country by U.S. companies. World War II forced the company to move its headquarters to the U.S. and focus on the life insurance markets in North and South America. In 1967, Maurice "Hank" Greenberg replaced Starr as the head of AIG. Two years later, the insurer went public. Greenberg's policy on underwriting profits is credited for much of the company's success, preventing AIG from suffering during the insurance industry price wars in the early 1980s. During the 1990s AIG became the first established insurance agency to enter the Vietnamese market, the first foreign company in Pakistan in two decades and the first major foreign investor in the Russian insurance industry. In 2001, AIG established life and general insurance operations in India.

AIG operates in 130 countries around the world, and foreign premiums account for more than a third of its revenue. The company also provides financial services and asset management, as well as auto insurance, mortgage guaranty, annuities and aircraft leasing. In August 2001, it bought American General Corporation for $23 billion, by far its largest acquisition. More recently, in November 2006, AIG agreed to acquire London City Airport, with Credit Suisse Group and General Electric Co. Under terms of the deal, AIG will own 50 percent of the airport's equity. Insider's speculated that the value of the deal was about $1.4 billion.

AIG's stock is traded on the New York Stock Exchange, as well as stock exchanges in London, Paris, Switzerland and Tokyo.

Help from Uncle Sam

In November 2002, insurers received a helping hand from the president and Congress when the Terrorism Insurance Bill was signed into law. The action was a major victory for companies like AIG and others in the industry, which had lobbied Congress tirelessly for such a backstop since the 2001 World Trade Center attacks cost the industry more than $40 billion in insured losses.

    © 2007 Vault, Inc.

Part of the legislation included an amendment offered by U.S. Senator George Allen (R-Va.) and Senator Tom Harkin (D-Iowa) that used the frozen assets of terrorists and terrorist states to compensate victims who had been awarded court judgments for damages they caused, and who had been otherwise denied satisfaction of those judgments.

A history of acquisitions

In 1998, AIG beefed up its variable annuity business when it bought California-based financial services company SunAmerica for $18.3 billion. Two years later, it bought specialty property insurer HSB Group for $1.2 billion. That deal helped AIG broaden its property-casualty business and expand even more overseas. These pricey purchases only served to whet AIG's appetite for bigger game, and in August 2001, AIG closed its whopping $23 billion acquisition of insurance giant American General. The deal was the largest ever between two U.S.-based insurers and made AIG the second-largest life insurer, and the biggest provider of fixed and variable annuities in the U.S. The transaction almost didn't go through for AIG, however, as the company had to slug it out in a bidding war with Britain's Prudential plc. The deal led to the termination of roughly 1,500 employees, or 1.8 percent of the combined company's workforce of 85,000 employees at the time.

It's not easy being Greenberg

In March 2005, Maurice "Hank" Greenberg, who had been with AIG for over four decades, was forced out of his CEO position by the company's board of directors, due to state and federal investigations into the company's accounting practices. He was replaced by Martin J. Sullivan, another longtime AIG veteran. Also pushed out was former CFO Howard Smith, who was replaced by Steven J. Bensinger, formerly a senior VP, treasurer and comptroller at AIG. In November 2006, former top Citigroup official Robert Willumstad was elected chairman of AIG.

Greenberg's departure was only part of the fallout related to a spate of bad publicity AIG has endured. An ongoing investigation by then-New York State Attorney General Eliot Spitzer and the Securities and Exchange Committee revealed that a reinsurance deal with Berkshire Hathaway's general reinsurance unit in 2001 led to an artificial boost in AIG's balance sheet. In May 2005, Spitzer's team of state insurance regulators filed civil charges against AIG, Greenberg and Smith, accusing the men of engaging in fraud to falsely inflate stock price; Greenberg continues to deny the allegations.

AIG restated its earnings in 2005 because of questions raised by these transactions, and in February 2006 agreed to pay $1.64 billion to resolve allegations that it used deceptive practices to mislead investors. That settlement required that the company amend its business procedures to guarantee proper behavior in the future: AIG has thus retained an independent consultant to review its internal controls as part of the 2006 settlement. The settlement did not cover Greenberg, who still faces civil action.

Starr Wars: The Greenberg Strikes Back

On August 7, 2006, Hank Greenberg sued three AIG employees alleging that they tried to destroy the four companies he now heads under C.V. Starr & Co-Starr Tech, Starr Aviation, C.V. Starr & Co., and American International Marine Agency. He charged that the staffers misappropriated confidential information, stole employees and tried to discredit Starr. While Greenberg was chairman of AIG, there was a cozy relationship with the Starr agencies, and Starr had all of its policies underwritten by AIG. When Greenberg left AIG, that relationship was severed. C.V. Starr owns about 47 million shares of AIG, while affiliate Starr International Co. owns more than 300 million. Starr's complaint is in response to a July 2006 suit filed by AIG against two former AIG Avaiation employees now working for by Starr. AIG alleges the two staffers used confidential information to recruit more than 20 AIG staffers to Starr Aviation.

After the flood

After Katrina, insurers, including AIG, raised premiums on coastal properties by as much as 500 percent. That, and a relatively quiet 2006 hurricane season, helped insurers boost third-quarter earnings more than any other industry. AIG had $1.57 billion in after-tax catastrophe costs in the third quarter of 2005 thanks to Katrina.

As expected, financial results looked very good in 2006 versus 2005. Net income increased 34 percnt to $14.05 billion, while total revenue increased 4 percent to $113.19 billion. In an earnings release, AIG President and CEO Martin J. Sullivan said results were led by the firm's general insurance businesses and improved performance in its foreign life insurance business.

© 2007 Vault, Inc.

GETTING HIRED

Discover the culture

Learn about AIG's culture, benefits, diversity hiring policies and career development efforts at www.aig.com/careers. Job openings are available on the site, too, and applicants can send or e-mail resumes to addresses listed in the "career opportunities" sections. Qualifications and requirements for applicants vary by department. For more information, applicants can call AIG's job hotline. Potential hires should be pleased to know that the company offers a variety of benefits, including extensive medical, life and disability insurance (naturally), as well as work/life benefits such as public transportation subsidies, parental leave, back-up child care and for the children of employees, assistance in choosing and applying to colleges. One insider says that AIG "rarely" recruits from schools, and usually culls candidates from recruiting firms instead. Interviews are "conducted by HR, the hiring manager and usually another manager."

OUR SURVEY SAYS

Pretty intense

While the corporate culture is "several notches below investment banking" in terms of intensity, it's still "intense for the insurance field." Sources note that "working at AIG has its benefits and drawbacks like any other global financial services firm." One insider calls the culture "very results-oriented," but another says the culture is "starting to get like Wal-Mart in the sense of 'How cheap and how fast can it be done?'" The source adds, "Like any shop that uses this thinking, you get short-term gains, but in the long run, the process and product suffer."

In part due to the decentralized organized structure, insiders say, that AIG engenders an entrepreneurial environment. "AIG encourages entrepreneurship and rewards it," reports one contact. "If you made a wrong decision, and if you had AIG's best interest in mind, there will be no adverse consequences. But don't make the same mistake twice." Another respondent concurs that "as a very strong company, AIG can permit you to create something by yourself if you play the game."

Visit the Vault Finance Career Channel at www.vault.com/finance – with
insider firm profiles, message boards, the Vault Finance Job Board and more

VAULT CAREER LIBRARY

51

The loose environment unfortunately doesn't extend to AIG's dress code, which "is corporate—men in suits, women in suits and dresses." Not everyone is comfortable working for a large global corporation however, with one source saying, "It's obviously a very large company, and in a lot of ways it seems way too structured." But where one sees too much structure, another sees opportunity. A contact notes, "AIG is a large company with a diverse workforce and offers lots of work locations for business types." Another notes that while "the company is an ideal place if you are mid-career ... if you are young, motivated, bright, ambitious and want to develop a career, this might not be the best place for you."

Putting in the time

Face time required depends largely on your location. One insider says, "Hours are very good—at the home office in New York it is 9 to 5, and by 5:01 p.m., you could hear a pin drop since everybody has left for the day." The source adds, "Many people come in late and take one-and-a-half- or two-hour lunches, and nobody seems to notice or say anything." Another, though, says, "AIG is not a 9-to-5 company. If you want to be really successful, you must be willing to go the extra mile." One contact says that the company has a "Work 'til you drop" culture. And yet another says that he and his colleagues "work hard," but management "will often buy lunch for employees if under deadline." An insider reports that the New York offices offer a perk in the form of the company cafeteria "which is cheaper than most of the restaurants in the area." Another gives the "stock purchase plan" a thumbs-up.

Reports yet another worker, "Since AIG's headquarters are in New York, the environment is a little more tense and intense than it might be otherwise." But there is a method to this system. AIG employees are willing to work hard, because, well, they can get rich doing so. "They do pay well, and there's a lot of room for growth," says one. Adds another, "There are a lot of very rich people working for AIG. I'm not talking about the get-rich-quick thing you hear about Silicon Valley. You may not see instant gratification for your efforts, but in the long run, the rewards can be great." Several respondents report that there's an unspoken rule at the firm—"if you make it to two years and want to continue, then you are a lifer. A perfect fit."

Needs some polish

Insiders report that the company's diversity efforts leave quite a bit to be desired, especially diversity efforts with respect to women. One respondent

© 2007 Vault, Inc.

reports that "like at most companies, diversity is just an HR-driven program," and "as a male, even I found the jokes to be crude, reflecting a lack of emphasis on education and polish found at other financial firms." A female source admits that she feels "angry, frustrated and upset" regarding her treatment with the firm, adding that AIG "is the only place I have ever experienced discrimination." The contact goes on to say that she and several female colleagues "were made conscious of my age and sex on more than one occasion."

Pretty perky

AIG offers its staff the usual array of benefits, including medical, dental and life insurance, as well as a retirement plan, tuition reimbursement program and a stock purchase plan where employees can buy the company's stock at a discounted rate. The company also offers college coaching for employees' college-bound children and scholarship programs. One contact notes, "My son got a $12,000-a-year scholarship from the company." In addition, AIG offers its staff an adoption assistance program and a pre-tax dependant care reimbursement account, which enables eligible employees to use pre-tax dollars to pay for certain expenses related to caring for dependent children, parents or other family members. And for those in New York in the summer, these rewards include a "blast" of a company picnic.

Although the company is one of the largest insurance providers in the world, some contacts think the plan it offers could be better. "They actually offer surprisingly poor insurance benefits, especially in light of AIG being one of the world's largest insurance companies," says one source. "There's a good 401(k), though, and an OK stock option plan."

AIG also provides a few innovative award programs like its Service Award Program that offers gifts to staffers dedicated to service after specified periods of continuous employment, the Big Idea Program that grants financial awards for ideas outside of an individual's job responsibilities that result in a solution/potential benefit to the company, and the Talent Search award that offers financial rewards to employees for the referral of individuals who are hired for full-time employment.

Visit the Vault Finance Career Channel at www.vault.com/finance – with
insider firm profiles, message boards, the Vault Finance Job Board and more

V/\ULT CAREER LIBRARY

53

AmeriCredit

801 Cherry St., Ste. 3900
Fort Worth, TX 76102
Phone: (817) 302-7000;
800-284-2271
www.americredit.com

DEPARTMENTS

ACF Investment Corp.
AFS Conduit Corp.
AFS Funding Corp.
AFS Funding Trust
AFS Management Corp.

THE STATS

Employer Type: Public Company
Ticker Symbol: ACF (NYSE)
Chairman: Clifton H. Morris Jr.
President & CEO: Daniel E. (Dan) Berce
Revenue: $1.81 billion (FYE 6/06)
Net Income: $306.2 million
No. of Employees: 4,087 (at FYE 06/2006)
No. of Offices: 80

KEY COMPETITORS

Capital One
Consumer Portfolio
Credit Acceptance

EMPLOYMENT CONTACT

See "career seekers" at
www.americredit.com

© 2007 Vault, Inc.

THE SCOOP

Used cars

Cash America pawnshop executives Jack Daugherty, Clifton Morris and a group of investors created the country's first used-car chain in 1986. UrCarco also offered financing to customers with bad credit ratings, and from these humble beginnings a company that would eventually appear on the S&P 400 was born. After a splashy IPO in 1989, the company got into financial trouble due to bad loans and a slumping market. After landing $10 million from Rainwater Management in 1991 and restructuring, the company changed its name to AmeriCredit in 1992.

The company sold off its used cars and beefed up its lending business by teaming up with credit-scoring firm Fair Issac to develop a credit risk scorecard to avoid making bad loans. The company branched out in 1996 by buying Rancho Vista Mortgage, which became AmeriCredit Corp. of California. The Rancho Vista buy allowed the company to build a home equity lending business. But three years later it pulled the plug on its mortgage business and began focusing on car loans. The company launched an online network that allows dealer to send loan applications to lenders, called DealerTrack, in 2001.

The company hit choppy waters again in 2003, cutting its quarterly loan origination volume, closing more than 100 branch office and cutting more than 1,000 positions. Its loan portfolio declined by 20 percent. The company made changes, such as slowing its growth rate, that righted the shop and now have it moving ahead again.

Dan Berce took on the additional role of CEO in August 2005, after serving as the company's president since 2003. Berce replaced Clifton H. Morris Jr., who remains chairman. Shortly thereafter, Hurricane Katrina devastated the Gulf Coast. In response, AmeriCredit reached out to customers affected by the storms who needed help with their auto loans.

Betting on Bay View and the Great White North

In November 2005, AmeriCredit inked a deal to buy Bay View Capital's auto finance unit for $63.6 million. Bay View offers specialized financing for customers with prime credit scores.

Visit the Vault Finance Career Channel at www.vault.com/finance – with
insider firm profiles, message boards, the Vault Finance Job Board and more

VAULT CAREER LIBRARY   55

The company moved back into the Canadian market in May 2006 by establishing AmeriCredit Financial Services of Canada in Mississauga, Ontario. The company's underwriters will be based in Mississauga with sales reps located across the country. The company plans further Canadian expansion. AmeriCredit actually operated in the country from 1998 to 2003, but left due to restructuring.

For the first quarter of fiscal 2007, ended September 2006, the company reported net income of $74 million, up from $54 million in the same period the previous year. Automobile loan purchases increased to $1.68 billion, compared to $1.52 billion last year. "Our September quarter was a solid beginning to fiscal year 2007, with new loan volume and credit performance improved from a year ago," said president and CEO Dan Berce. "We have further developed our core subprime business as we continued to roll out a broader credit spectrum of product offerings through our Bay View platform."

The firm also had a strong second quarter of fiscal 2007, increasing revenue to $575.6 million from the $448.1 million it booked the previous year's second quarter, and net income to $95.4 million from $86.6 million. At the beginning of the fiscal third quarter, AmeriCredit Financial Services, a subsidiary of AmeriCredit's subsidiary, completed its $282.5 million acquisition of Long Beach Acceptance Corp., the auto finance subsidiary of ACC Capital Holdings.

Promoting volunteering

AmeriCredit offers its staff eight hours of paid time off to volunteer each quarter. The company has worked with a variety of charities, including March of Dimes, Salvation Army, United Way, American Red Cross, Habitat for Humanity, Make A Wish Foundation, Meals on Wheels and Special Olympics.

GETTING HIRED

Play matchmaker

Under the "career seekers" section of www.americredit.com, those interested can view positions by location or position. And through the firm's online

PeopleMatch Career Center, applicants can check out potential matches. If you prefer to give the firm a ring, you're in luck. Job seekers can call "The HR Connection" for additional information about positions at 1-866-411-HR4U.

OUR SURVEY SAYS

No cure for AmeriCredit

The company says it bases its culture around "four fundamental principles: integrity, investment, innovation and information." It seems to be working. One insider says the company "really values its employees and sincerely cares about team member involvement." Another calls the culture "not only evident, but also contagious."

AmeriCredit offers a full array of benefits, from standard options like medical and dental coverage to "floating holidays" and "paid time off for volunteer work through AmeriCredit's Community Investment program."

Visit the Vault Finance Career Channel at **www.vault.com/finance** – with
insider firm profiles, message boards, the Vault Finance Job Board and more

VAULT CAREER LIBRARY

57

Aon Corp.

Aon Center
200 E. Randolph St.
Chicago, IL 60601
Phone: (312) 381-1000
Fax: (312) 381-6032
www.aon.com

DEPARTMENTS

Aon Consulting Worldwide
Aon Risk Services, Inc.
Aon Re, Inc.
Combined Insurance Company of
  America

THE STATS

Employer Type: Public Company
Ticker Symbol: AOC (NYSE)
Executive Chairman: Pat Ryan
President, CEO & Director: Greg Case
Revenue: $8.954 billion (FYE 12/06)
Net Income: $720 million
No. of Employees: 43,600
No. of Offices: 500

KEY COMPETITORS

Arthur J. Gallagher
Marsh & McLennan
Willis Group

UPPERS

- "Corporate culture is very laid-back"
- "Good benefits"

DOWNERS

- "Can be bureaucratic at times"
- "The many acquisitions" have "still not been well integrated"

EMPLOYMENT CONTACT

See "careers" at www.aon.com

© 2007 Vault, Inc.

THE SCOOP

Aon flux

Aon, which means "oneness" in Gaelic, is the world's largest commercial insurance broker. Aon focuses on three areas: commercial brokerage/risk management, human capital consulting services and specialty insurance underwriting. Risk and insurance brokerage services increased 5 percent to $5.6 billion in 2006. The company's brokerage operations include retail and wholesale insurance for groups and businesses. In the late 1980s, the company launched Aon Consulting, which focuses on employee benefits, M&A and outsourcing. Aon also offers supplementary health, accident and life insurance through its older and smaller insurance underwriting division, which includes its original underwriting business, Combined Insurance.

Aon was one of the most unprofitable insurance brokers in the industry and embarked on a mission to change that in 2005 under the leadership of new CEO Greg Case. Aon put its credit, warranty, and property and casualty underwriting business on the block, selling Aon Warranty Group, which included Virginia Surety, to Onex for $710 million in a deal announced in July 2006. That October, the company also agreed to unload the Construction Program Group (CPG), part of its property and casualty operations, to Old Republic Insurance for $85 million. "We have placed the remainder of the specialty property and casualty programs in runoff, and will continue to explore disposition alternatives for other portions of the book," Case said in a statement. "We believe this will enable us to focus our attention and resources on our core businesses."

Aon also launched a restructuring program in summer 2005 and set out to cut 1,800 positions worldwide. The company said its restructuring plan is expected to result in pre-tax charges of about $300 million and is projected to result in annualized savings of $210 million by 2008.

Mean streets of Chicago

Aon is celebrating its 20th anniversary in 2007. The Aon and its predecessor companies can actually trace their origins back to the 1680s, when the world's first commercial insurance brokerage company was established in the Netherlands. The company, Hudig-Langeveldt, was the largest broker in continental Europe when Aon acquired it in 1991. The contemporary Aon was started by Patrick Ryan, who merged his insurance company, Ryan

Visit the Vault Finance Career Channel at www.vault.com/finance – with
insider firm profiles, message boards, the Vault Finance Job Board and more

VAULT CAREER LIBRARY   59

Insurance, with W. Clement Stone's Combined Insurance Co. of America in 1987.

Under Ryan's leadership, the company focused on insurance brokering and added more upscale insurance products. In 1987, he changed the company's name to Aon. The company sold off its remaining direct life insurance holdings to focus on risk management in 1995.

Post-September 11

Aon's largest office was in the south tower of New York's World Trade Center. The company lost 175 employees in the September 11 terrorist attacks. Aon inked a deal in early 2006 to sublease 200,000 square feet of office space from Wachovia at 199 Water Street in lower Manhattan, moving all of it's staff downtown once again.

In Spitzer's sight

Former New York attorney general Elliot Spitzer began investigating the business practices of the major insurance brokers in 2004. At issue were processes relating to the legal practice of brokers receiving contingent commissions from insurance carriers, which function as service providers to broker clients. The attorney general considered the payments a conflict of interest because commissions could influence brokers to favor carriers instead of their customers. Spitzer argued that brokers should represent the interests of their clients who buy the insurance, not insurers, and commissions led to bid rigging. Aon agreed to settle for $190 million. The brokers involved in the case never admitted any wrongdoing, however they agreed not to accept undisclosed payments from the insurers and to inform their clients in writing how their compensation packages worked.

In 2004, the company announced CEO Ryan would step down and in 2005, Case, a former McKinsey & Co. consultant who had led McKinsey's global insurance practice, took the helm. Total revenue for 2006 rose 5 percent to $9 billion. Since Case has been chief executive officer, Aon's stock price has risen by 70 percent. Case called the company's 2006 performance "fully on track with the first year of our three-year improvement plan."

© 2007 Vault, Inc.

GETTING HIRED

World of opportunity

Check out job openings in 120 countries when you log on to the firm's web site at www.aon.com/about/careers.jsp. But don't send general inquiries through the site. If you have questions about listed positions, the firm directs candidates to "contact the office listed—all hiring is done locally."

Get referred

The difficulty of the interview process may depend on how you get in the door. One insider with connections notes that the "interview process very easy if you were referred by another employee." The interview consisted of "basic questions" and a source says that is your basic "couple of rounds of interviews with different people." One insider explains that Aon puts "a lot of emphasis on personality and interaction with others, i.e., I was taken to lunch and observed [for] how I interacted with the team." Another source says, "We typically look for applicants that will not melt down under the pressure. Computer skills are essential. We often give an Excel test, a general balance sheet question and answer quiz, and a case study torture session." One source says that his interview consisted of questions such as "what I believed the most important strengths are in a person and behavioral questions where I had to give specific examples regarding certain situations I had encountered in the past."

OUR SURVEY SAYS

Unit to unit

"The corporate culture is very laid-back," says an insider. Another says the work environment "varies highly from business unit to business unit." One consultant says he finds the company made up of "nice people with a rather laid-back attitude." But even with this casual atmosphere, go-getters and out-of-the-box thinkers reap the rewards. An insider reports, "Good and innovative ideas are valued and do receive attention." Another says that "one common thread is a big focus on client happiness, which can mean going way out of the way and working long hours to shield the client from any distress or difficulty." Being a self-starter helps, too. One accounting specialist says the firm is "a good

Visit the Vault Finance Career Channel at **www.vault.com/finance** – with insider firm profiles, message boards, the Vault Finance Job Board and more

VAULT CAREER LIBRARY

61

environment for people who take the initiative to advance in their career. Aon has an entrepreneurial culture where you are in charge of your own career path and, depending on the type of manager you have, lots of training opportunities available to take advantage of." Another insider says that "professional advancement is dependent on your ability to attract new clients, expand existing client relationships and retain clients—this is a very sales-driven firm."

Disjointed units

One oft-mentioned downside to the company is its size. One insider complains that "Aon is very large and can be bureaucratic at times." It also seems that various groups within the firm are not tightly knit, with quite a heterogeneous mix of offices and working groups. A consultant says, "Aon has so many subsidiaries and so many different departments and specialties so it's really hard to describe each one. I find that different offices' departments operate pretty autonomously," while another states that "morale within Aon varies widely among various locations and business units. There is great variance even within my business unit. High-performing units are great to work in, underperforming units are a drag. Hours also·vary pretty widely depending on business units."

As far as workers' compensation, staffers aren't jumping up and down for joy over their paychecks, but are pleased that "Aon has good benefits, including 401(k), stock purchase plans and bonuses." In addition, a source claims that "the vacation time is competitive."

Looking to integrate

The company's outlook is "decent," says an insider, adding that its weakness is that "the many acquisitions that created it are still not well integrated, and thus there is a lot of deep institutional knowledge that can not be easily spread to other parts of the firm." Other sources do see some problems to be overcome at Aon, but in general are positive on the company's future. An assistant VP says, "Aon's overall outlook is quite good. Given the recent shake up in the insurance brokerage industry, Aon has emerged stronger. Our new CEO is doing a fantastic job and our stock has been rising steadily over the past few months. It's a great time to join Aon." A VP sees the situation similarly: "The firm grew exclusively through acquisitions, without any business strategy in place for years. All new management has just been put in place in the past year, most from McKinsey, so the long-term outlook is quite good, as reflected in the recent stock upswing."

© 2007 Vault, Inc.

Arthur J. Gallagher & Co.

The Gallagher Centre
2 Pierce Place
Itasca, IL 60143-3141
Phone: (630) 773-3800
Fax: (630) 285-4000
www.ajg.com

DEPARTMENTS

Employee Benefits Consulting
Insurance Brokerage
Investment Management
Risk Management Services

THE STATS

Employer Type: Public Company
Ticker Symbol: AJG (NYSE)
Chairman, President & CEO: J. Patrick Gallagher Jr.
Revenue: $1.534 billion (FY 12/06)
Net Income: $128.5 million
No. of Employees: 8,800
No. of Offices: 250+

KEY COMPETITORS

Aon
Marsh
Willis Group

UPPERS

- "Relaxed atmosphere"

DOWNERS

- Diversity efforts could be improved

EMPLOYMENT CONTACT

At www.ajg.com see "job opportunities" under "company facts"

Visit the Vault Finance Career Channel at **www.vault.com/finance** — with insider firm profiles, message boards, the Vault Finance Job Board and more

VAULT CAREER LIBRARY   63

THE SCOOP

Midwest giant

Founded by its namesake in 1927 in Itasca, Ill., Arthur J. Gallagher & Co. is the world's fourth-largest insurance brokerage and risk management services firm, working through a network of subsidiaries in the U.S., Australia, Bermuda, Canada, Singapore and the U.K. The company, which went public in 1984, also manages employee benefits programs; and its Gallagher Bassett Services subsidiary offers risk management consulting and services, including claims management, information management and loss control services.

The financial services unit handles the company's investment portfolio, which includes tax-advantaged investments and an alternative investment fund manager. The company's clients include businesses of all sizes, not-for-profits, associations and municipal and governmental entities.

Gallagher, named one of *Forbes* magazine's Platinum 400 Best Big Companies in America and listed on the Fortune 1000 in 2004, conducts business in about 120 countries and has grown through a feeding frenzy, gobbling up small insurance brokers and benefits consultants. Gallagher acquired 19 companies in 2004, 10 companies in 2005, 11 companies in 2006, and completed seven acquisitions in the first quarter of 2007.

Legal wrangling

In 2005, the company lost a jury trial over licensing royalties that South Jordan, Utah-based alternative energy company Headwaters claimed it was owed by Gallagher's investment unit. Gallagher's synthetic fuel facilities used the technology to make synthetic fuel from coal. The companies agreed to settle all litigation for $50 million and inked a deal to let Gallagher use the technology for $70 million plus pay Headwaters an annual royalty. Gallagher took a $131 million pre-tax charge in the first quarter of 2006 related to the settlement. The company was also sued by its former CFO for $13 million in June 2006. Michael Cloherty, who resigned as CFO in 2002 after 21 years on the job and then served as an advisor to Gallagher, claims the company owes him his salary and a $2.5 million bonus. The company has not commented on the case.

Gallagher launched a lawsuit of its own in 2006, claiming rival firm Palmer & Cay holdings, acquired by Wachovia Insurance Services in 2005, illegally

© 2007 Vault, Inc.

hired the head of Gallagher's St. Louis brokerage operation in 2003. The suit alleges that Palmer & Cay improperly recruited Jeffrey Combs and encouraged him to solicit his former clients and co-workers to move to the rival broker. Combs had a two-year noncompete clause in his contract that Gallagher claims was violated.

End of an era

The company's chairman, Bob Gallagher, died in August 2006 at 83 years of age, after almost 60 years with the company his father founded. His nephew Patrick, who was serving as president and CEO, took over as chairman in October. To stay true to its Midwestern values, Bob Gallagher composed a list in 1984 of 25 shared values for the company and its culture that he dubbed "The Gallagher Way," which is still taught to employees. The firm reported $1.534 billion in revenue for full-year 2006, up from $1.484 billion in 2005. Net income in 2006 rose considerably to $128.5 million from $30.8 million the year before.

GETTING HIRED

Looking for leadership

Like a potential suitor rhapsodizing about the characteristics of its perfect mate, Arthur J. Gallagher & Co. lists an assortment of qualifications for itsideal candidate on the career section of its web site, noting that it's looking for "strong leadership potential," "flexibility," "exceptional drive," "good interpersonal and communication skills" and the "ability to learn and retain new information." Don't pin your hopes on browsing the firm's current openings, however; instead of cataloging specific job opportunities on the site, the firm encourages candidates to contact individual offices to learn about possible open positions.

Think fast

Once you're called into the office for a meeting, expect "team interviews" and "quick decisions," says an insider. Another interviewing for an account manager position says that he went through a "first interview with the division vice president that went on for about 30 minutes" and that involved

Visit the Vault Finance Career Channel at **www.vault.com/finance** – with
insider firm profiles, message boards, the Vault Finance Job Board and more

VAULT CAREER LIBRARY   **65**

"a Q&A format that was easy to respond to." The second round with HR was "relaxed" and included two tests—a "personality test along with a short general knowledge test."

Learn the ropes

Gallagher offers a summer internship program, where interns get the chance to learn "basic insurance concepts," "what a broker does" and "where Gallagher fits in the world of insurance." Interested parties can fill out an application online, or direct any specific questions to SIP_Info@ajg.com.

OUR SURVEY SAYS

Good support

One insider notes experiencing "a lot of support from staff members," adding that the firm promotes "a professional and relaxed atmosphere." Another calls Gallagher "a good company in many ways." Management receives high marks, too. One contact says, "I felt comfortable around upper management, who were personable and approachable." In addition, hours are "outstanding and flexible," and the dress code is "business casual and usually not abused by the staff." And climbing up the corporate ladder seems to be a matter of grabbing the right rung. One insider says that "opportunities for advancement were there if you worked for it."

More inclusion needed

The firm's diversity efforts could stand to be improved, sources report. The company "does not encourage, recruit, promote or retain qualified diverse employees," says one insider, adding that he had one "profoundly antebellum experience" where "stereotypical comments and actions" occurred. The contact goes on to suggest that "to move beyond the firm's equal opportunity statement to achieve true diversity, senior management should be required to participate in mandatory diversity training." Another insider agrees that there is a "lack of qualified diverse talent at AJG and a culture that is not inclusive" within the firm.

© 2007 Vault, Inc.

Berkshire Hathaway Inc.

1440 Kiewit Plaza
Omaha, NE 68131
Phone: (402) 346-1400
Fax: (402) 346-3375
www.berkshirehathaway.com

DEPARTMENTS

GEICO Corp.
Insurance Re
McLane Co.
National Idemnity

THE STATS

Employer Type: Public Company
Ticker Symbol: BRK (NYSE)
Chairman, President & CEO: Warren Buffett
Revenue: $98.539 billion (FYE 12/06)
Net Income: $11.0 billion
No. of Employees: 192,000

KEY COMPETITORS

HM Capital Partners
KKR
Onex

Visit the Vault Finance Career Channel at **www.vault.com/finance** — with insider firm profiles, message boards, the Vault Finance Job Board and more

VAULT CAREER LIBRARY

67

THE SCOOP

Omaha stakes

The Oracle of Omaha founded Buffett Partnership in 1956 with $105,000 when he was still 25 and fresh from studying under investing guru Benjamin Graham at Columbia University. Averaging annual returns of more than 22 percent over the next 48 years, Warren Buffett is now the second richest man in the world (behind his close friend Bill Gates. Buffett is a major contributor to the Bill & Melinda Gates Foundation) and his company is now valued at $136 billion. The Oracle holds about 40 percent of the company's shares. Not bad for a kid from Nebraska. A buck invested in Berkshire Hathaway in 1965 would be worth about $2,500 today.

Although Berkshire Hathaway's investment strategy has been incredibly successful, it's quite simple: The company takes the "float"—cash income prior to claims payouts—from its major interest, the insurance companies it owns, and uses the money to buy undervalued businesses, cheap but promising stock and even simple bonds. Potential profit is the sole determining factor in Berkshire's investment decisions, however, it's well known that Buffett views profitability as being intrinsically linked to intelligent, responsible management. Refusing to invest in Internet stocks during the 1990s boom, Buffett had the last laugh during the dot-com implosion. Berkshire Hathaway's subsidiaries employ more than 192,000, but only 16 people, all personal friends and family of the founder, work at BH's world headquarters.

Lizard king

Berkshire Hathaway's core holdings are its insurance companies, of which the most significant are GEICO and Gen Re. GEICO is one of the largest auto insurers in the U.S. The company prefers low-risk clients, particularly government and military employees, but has in recent years begun taking on greater numbers of average drivers.

Gen Re is among the four-largest reinsurers worldwide. Reinsurers sell insurance to insurance companies, helping spread the risks incurred by their customers. Gen Re also operates a North American property and casualty insurance subsidiary and a life and health insurance division. In October 2006, General Re received a letter from the U.S. attorney for the Eastern District of Virginia in Richmond saying the reinsurer is not a target in the government investigation of collapsed insurer Reciprocal of America. Government investigators hadwanted to know if General Re participated in an alleged program to deceive state regulators and Reciprocal policyholders that led to a jail sentence for the former president of Reciprocal. Four former and current General Re employees who had been subpoenaed were also cleared.

Berkshire Hathaway has been successful in minimizing risk, which means that for most of its 36 years in the industry, income has exceeded claims outlays, fueling the company's acquisitions. Buffett has backed blue-chip stocks and select newcomers with spectacular results. However, the chaos in the market in the last decade, due mostly to dot-com debacles, has reduced the number of stocks that meet his criteria: favorable economic characteristics, sound management and reasonable prices. In response, Berkshire Hathaway has turned to buying businesses outright.

Berkshire Hathaway tends to buy companies that make practical products, such as underwear, paint, steel beams, carpet and hamburgers. The company owns Dairy Queen and is a major shareholder in Coca-Cola and Anheuser-Busch (5.8 percent), a larger stake than even chairman Auggie Busch, who holds 1.2 percent. Berkshire Hathaway is also a shareholder in American Express, Moody's, The Washington Post Co. and Wells Fargo.

2006 was another busy year. The company acquired press release distributor Business Wire, workers' compensation products specialist Applied Underwriters, sportswear company Russell, and 80 percent of Iscar Metalworking, an Israel-based maker of metal-cutting tools.

Practical diversification

Berkshire's holdings can be grouped into four rough categories. The first and largest is the building materials group, which includes carpet maker Shaw Industries, Benjamin Moore, Johns Manville, MiTek Inc. and Acme Building Materials.

Fruit of the Loom, Justin Brands, H.H. Brown and Dexter make up the bulk of the second category—the clothing and footwear manufacturers. All are among the leading brands in their respective fields; they account for some 27,000 workers. Berkshire Hathaway also has significant holdings in the furniture industry, including Jordan's, Nebraska Furniture Mart and R.C. Willey Home Furnishings. This group employs 7,000. Lastly, the company has a sizeable number of food industry holdings. The aforementioned Dairy Queen is theirs; so is McLane Industries, a national food distributor

Visit the Vault Finance Career Channel at **www.vault.com/finance** – with insider firm profiles, message boards, the Vault Finance Job Board and more

VAULT CAREER LIBRARY   69

purchased from Wal-Mart in 2003. The company also owns FlightSafety International, one of the pioneers of fractional ownership of private airplanes.

But Buffett's strategy does have its critics, who claim that much of Berkshire Hathaway's profitability comes from cost-cutting and downsizing after purchasing a company. Buffett has also named union-busting Wal-Mart his most-admired company in *Fortune* magazine's poll for several years running.

The Oracle's future

At the company's annual 2006 shareholder meeting in Omaha, a/k/a "Woodstock for Capitalists," Buffett told the faithful that he's working on another blockbuster acquisition in the $15 billion range. Analysts estimate that the company has about $40 billion to invest. In 2006, Buffett also announced that he has chosen his successor as CEO, but has refused to disclose who it was. However, his son Warren will become chairman and Louis Simpson will be director of investments. In 2006, the firm reported net income of $11.015 billion, up from $8.528 billion a year earlier. The company's insurance businesses made an underwriting profit of $917 million in 2006 versus an underwriting loss of $1.17 billion the prior year. BH sold plenty of expensive hurricane reinsurance after 2005's storms, when rivals were cutting their storm exposure and demand was high. The gamble paid off, as there were no big storms in 2006.

GETTING HIRED

Sink or swim

Getting in at a Berkshire Hathaway company may be difficult, but as noted earlier, employment at Berkshire Hathaway headquarters is virtually impossible. The company's homepage doesn't even list openings. To find a position at a Berkshire Hathaway company, job seekers should visit the individual companies' web sites. Also, as noted above, dead wood doesn't float in Buffett's ocean. Employees, particularly managers, are expected to get results wherever possible, whenever possible, even against industry trends. Those who do will be rewarded with the usual perks and benefits; those that don't will be shown the door. One insider with more than "20 years of experience as a workers' compensation adjuster" reports one such experience, commenting that he was "interviewed and hired by a manager"

© 2007 Vault, Inc.

for a senior adjuster position in Georgia and "asked to come to work as soon as possible." Upon starting at the position, the contact says that technical issues and "password problems" led to spotty "access to the company's computer system" for two days. On the third day, the contact says he was told "by that manager that I was 'not a senior adjuster and needed to find another job.'"

Visit the Vault Finance Career Channel at **www.vault.com/finance** – with
insider firm profiles, message boards, the Vault Finance Job Board and more

VAULT CAREER LIBRARY   71

Capital One Financial

1680 Capital One Drive
McLean, VA 22012
Phone: (703) 720-1000
www.capitalone.com

DEPARTMENTS

Capital One Bank
Capital One, F.S.B.
Capital One Auto Finance
Capital One, N.A.
North Fork Bank

THE STATS

Employer Type: Public Company
Ticker Symbol: COF (NYSE)
Chairman, President & CEO: Richard
D. Fairbank
Revenue: $12.1 billion (FYE 12/06)
Net Income: $2.4 billion
No. of Employees: approx 32,000
No. of Offices: 12 (U.S., UK and
Canada)

KEY COMPETITORS

American Express
Bank of America
Countrywide Financial
Discover Financial Services
Freddie Mac
Wells Fargo

UPPERS

- "Collegial, collaborative and very smart" co-workers
- "Culture focused on getting work done, not on how many hours you spend doing it"

DOWNERS

- "Slow advancement opportunities"
- "Diverse at the lower levels, but not at the senior levels"

EMPLOYMENT CONTACT

See "careers" at www.capitalone.com

© 2007 Vault, Inc.

THE SCOOP

Gaining ground

Based in McLean, Va., Capital One is the nation's fifth-largest issuer of MasterCard and Visa credit cards and has over 50 million customers. In addition to its card services, the firm provides savings and consumer lending products. Its main subsidiaries are Capital One Bank, Capital One, N.A., Capital One, F.S.B., Capital One Auto Finance and North Fork Bank. Capital One Services, another subsidiary, provides operating and back-office services to the company and its other subsidiaries. Capital One has been recognized for its employee training, speed in authorizing credit card transactions, education programs and fundraising, and for its leadership in the IT space. In September 2006, *Working Mother* magazine named Capital One to its list of 100 Best Companies for Working Mothers, and in 2007, *Fortune* magazine ranked Capital One No. 84 on its Best Companies to Work For List.

The company offers a full range of credit cards, including platinum cards, secured cards and cards for small businesses. Capital One's savings products include certificates of deposit, money market accounts and individual retirement accounts; the firm's lending unit helps consumers purchase everything from cars to homes.

In 2006, the firm delivered another year of solid results and made a transformational move in banking with the acquisition of North Fork. Earnings per share grew 13 percent, and assets continued to grow. Managed loans increased 39 percent during the year to $146.2 billion (including $31.7 billion of loans from North Fork), while organic loan growth was 10 percent for the year.

More personal plastic

In the late 1980s, consultants Richard Fairbank and Nigel Morris met at Strategic Planning Associates (which became Mercer Management Consulting) and devised a new way to market and structure credit cards. They felt that most credit card issuers were too bland in the way they conceived of their products and that the companies didn't completely understand that individual customers require customized products. They shopped their idea from bank to bank, getting no takers until Virginia-based Signet Banking Corp. expressed interest. Capital One was spun off by Signet in 1995.

Visit the Vault Finance Career Channel at **www.vault.com/finance** – with insider firm profiles, message boards, the Vault Finance Job Board and more

VAULT CAREER LIBRARY

73

Knowing what's in your wallet

Capital One's success derives from its pioneering efforts in data collection via its proprietary information-based strategy. The company collects and analyzes credit data on more than 100 million potential customers in order to determine which products might be the right one for each. It then tailors its offerings to fit a potential customer's unique financial background. The company was also the first to entice new customers by offering to let them transfer balances at low introductory rates, a strategy quickly imitated by competitors.

Bowling for dollars

Capital One is by no means an anonymous financial conglomerate, on account of its creative marketing and advertising efforts. In addition to its ubiquitous television spots featuring the popular Visigoth characters, Capital One also sponsors financial seminars and quirky promotions. The company also sponsors a college bowl game, as well as its annual Capital One Mascot of the Year contest to target college students and sports fans.

The firm has also launched a number of initiatives aimed at increasing financial literacy and responsibility. Capital One and Consumer Action jointly introduced the MoneyWi$e program in March of 2003, designed to educate investors on making better financial choices, and to sponsor financial education seminars for community and nonprofit groups. In August 2005, the MoneyWi$e partnership between Capital One and Consumer Action awarded stipends totaling $75,000 to community groups in 10 states.

In 2006, Capital One and JA Worldwide (Junior Achievement) won the Corporate Citizenship Award from the U.S. Chamber of Commerce in September 2006 for their work in providing financial literacy training to students through Capital One's Finance Park. The award acknowledges businesses and chambers of commerce that have demonstrated ethical leadership and corporate stewardship, and that have made a difference in their communities.

Branching out

The year 2006 was a defining one for Capital One. With the acquisition North Fork, Capital One became the 11th-largest bank in the U.S. based on deposits, with a growth platform in one of the best banking markets in the country—the greater New York region. And with the integration of Hibernia

© 2007 Vault, Inc.

largely complete, the company now has the leading market share in Louisiana, a top-three position in the New York region, and a solid presence in Texas. Currently, the company has more than 720 locations in New York, New Jersey, Connecticut, Texas and Louisiana.

In 2006, Capital One Auto Finance delivered net income of $233.5 million, up 77 percent. Origination volumes were strong with managed loans at the end of 2006 of $21.8 billion, up $5.4 billion from a year ago. Capital One's Global Financial Services division also had a strong year, with net income of $274 million, up 47 percent from 2005. Managed loans grew $3.6 billion, or 15 percent. GFS continues to provide growth and diversification to the company.

GETTING HIRED

Exam time

If you're thinking of applying to Capital One, but you're not sure about which position to apply for, never fear—the firm is one step ahead of you. The career section of its site contains tests that "help us predict your fit with different roles" within the firm. Or if you already have an idea of what you'd like to apply for, just check out the site for information on the company's college, MBA and military recruiting process—Capital One looks for former military personnel to fill a diverse array of jobs from fraud investigators to senior managers.

Underlining the variety of schools at which the firm recruits, one insider says the firm recruits from "colleges all over." "We look for the ultimate best and the brightest," says another insider. The interviews can be tough—one insider says "the process can be rigorous." "We put our applicants through an intense testing, followed by a series of 'power days' to interview," says a source. "Interviews are primarily behavioral-based. Questions are specific to past experiences and 'how would you handle' situations." Another agrees, adding that the firm will "test your skills" and might give you "a case study relevant to the position." "A test is given first, then several interviews," says another contact. One source expands on that description, saying, "You must pass a math test on interpretation of graphs to be given an offer. Interviews are case and behavioral. Case interviews are about calculating outcomes, not about developing strategies."

Visit the Vault Finance Career Channel at **www.vault.com/finance** – with insider firm profiles, message boards, the Vault Finance Job Board and more

VAULT CAREER LIBRARY

75

Yet another respondent says, "The interviews are a combination of cases and behavioral questions. You can expect the cases to closely mirror the type of analyses that are done routinely at the company." One insider notes that the written test "centers around quantitative and data interpretation skills." He admits, "This test was pretty simple for me due to my background, but I guess one needs good numerical skills as well as fast calculation and data comprehension skills." The case interviews, which most but not all candidates will go through, "can be difficult, especially if you're not a math wiz." Case interviews are "quantitative" and "have a clear solution rather than some of the consulting cases where the answer depends on the approach."

OUR SURVEY SAYS

Capital ideas

The Capital crew is "collegial, collaborative and very smart," notes an insider. Another calls the firm a "fairly young company with a very young workforce." It has "long been known for its entrepreneurial environment and very collegial work culture," says a contact. "This also came with fast-track career development. However, the company is maturing very fast into a big bank-type workplace, which has a lot to do with the industry they are in and the big banks they're competing with." "Our culture is very collaborative," says an insider. "The company's primary motive is for its employees to enjoy coming to work every day, ensuring a daily challenge and a fun place to work." Others say that the firm has "a culture of encouraging great analysis, and allowing all employees to participate in decision making through good arguments." The culture is also called "consensus-based and genteel," full of colleagues who are "warm, friendly and inclusive."

But others say that Capital One's culture has been changed by growth. "With the rapid expansion, the company is definitely trying to keep up the internal organization with that pace," observes one source, who adds, "The culture within the firm is strong and apparently favors people who can speak loud and make their voices heard." One pleased credit card insider calls the firm "very entrepreneurial." Another happy contact says, "People here are very smart and have a very high level of analytical ability and quantitative skill." One complaint seems to be the "slow advancement opportunities."

   © 2007 Vault, Inc.

As for managers, one respondent says, "I've had some great managers and some not-so-great managers." He adds, "Regular feedback is encouraged and will help you grow. I've learned a lot. The key to success is to network at the level more senior than yours." "In general," comments another contact, "the working atmosphere is fun and pleasant, and collaboration is essential for success."

Depends on where you look

The company has a "diverse culture," notes an insider. But that may not be an attribute that occurs throughout the entire firm. Although Capital One is "very diverse at the lower levels, once you get to the senior levels, it's not," notes an insider. "It's very much a frat boy culture in some departments, as well. The company is working to address this, but they have a long way to go." Another calls the firm "preppy and white bread," saying, "It's perfect for the typical Ivy-Leaguer or MBA who wants to work in a straightforward, hierarchical environment. Your day will be scheduled down to the minute and you'll learn to follow process." However, another source says, "The culture is very open, with associates at all levels able to challenge the status quo and to push on our strategies and latest thinking."

You have great freedom to move horizontally and try out different roles that interest you." And according to Capital One, the firm "works to create an atmosphere of inclusion" through hosting diversity forums with presenters such as Geraldine Ferraro, the first female vice presidential nominee, and Betty DeGeneres, mother of actress and comedienne Ellen DeGeneres. The firm says it has also established associate networks that provide support in the form of programs, resources and tools "enabling Capital One's diverse associates to achieve their full potential in an environment that values the differences everyone brings to the workplace."

All down the line

You may get paid the same rate regardless of the area in which you work, some insiders say. One notes, "It seemed like the D.C. and Richmond areas paid the same even though it's cheaper to live in Richmond." The contact adds, "It's easier to get hired if you are willing to work in Richmond." Another source says of his offer, "The base salary was barely enough [but] Capital One interviewers and HR staff will repeatedly tell you how inexpensive Richmond is. The key is Richmond was inexpensive at one time."

Visit the Vault Finance Career Channel at **www.vault.com/finance** – with insider firm profiles, message boards, the Vault Finance Job Board and more

VAULT CAREER LIBRARY

77

Benefits include a generous 401(k) that "matches half of employee contributions up to 6 percent," a "stock purchase plan for employees" and an "on-site fitness center" in some locations. Additionally, the firm offers "educational reimbursement provided for bachelor's or graduate degrees." There is also a "free on-site health center with a doctor in Richmond," "concierge service," "good food service," "discounts to retailers and theaters," "quarterly social events" and "lots of community events." One source points to another nice perk: "three weeks of vacation, and four weeks after five years" with the firm. And it doesn't hurt that the dress code is "business casual."

Capital One isn't keeping anybody in the office or demanding face time. "Culture is focused on getting the work done, not how many hours you spend doing it," says an insider. Even so, some sources admit "work hours can be long." Others say hours are "dependent on the current projects you're working on." One contact says that though "hours are very reasonable and mostly you're working 40 to 50 hour weeks, once in a while there could be spikes where you're working 60 to 80 hours per week, depending on projects and roles." The insider adds that "flexible work arrangements are increasingly being encouraged."

Nice outlook

Things are looking rosy for the firm lately. "The company has been doing great lately and I would expect it to continue growing at a healthy rate," one source enthuses. There's a "positive outlook" among staff and "morale is generally good, though it varies by department." One insider notes that "the morale of the people was hurt when the company started establishing tighter corporate governance policies and sharpening control of the policies following a memorandum of understanding signed with the Federal Reserve." But others say that the company "continues to manage its credit card business very well and has embarked on an aggressive new product development plan." And it's been "actively acquiring new businesses to ensure that it is fully diversified and continues to have growth opportunities." A contact agrees, for the most part, saying, "Overall business outlook is good, but challenging. The core credit card business is slowing, but Capital One is diversifying into highly fragmented business areas—auto, home equity, retail banking—with excellent growth and consolidation prospects." Indeed, the firm has a "rock solid strategy to expand and diversify," and "very strong leadership and analyst teams."

© 2007 Vault, Inc.

CB Richard Ellis Group, Inc.

100 N. Sepulveda Blvd., Ste. 1050
El Segundo, CA 90245
Phone: (310) 606-4700
Fax: (949) 809-4357
www.cbre.com

DEPARTMENTS

Asset Services • Brokerage—
Tenant & Landlord Representation •
Capital Markets • Consulting •
Debt & Equity Finance (CBRE |
Melody) • Development &
Investment (Trammell Crow
Company) • Facilities
Management • Global Corporate
Services • Government & Public
Sector • Healthcare • Industrial •
Investment Brokerage/Agency •
Investment Management (CBRE
Investors) • Office • Project
Management • Research &
Investment Strategy (Torto
Wheaton Research) • Retail •
Specialty Services • Transaction
Management • Valuation &
Advisory Services

THE STATS

Employer Type: Public Company
Ticker Symbol: CBG (NYSE)
Chairman: Richard C. Blum
President & CEO: Brett White
Revenue: $4.032 billion (FYE 12/06)
Net Income: $318.6 million
No. of Employees: 24,000
No. of Offices: 300

KEY COMPETITORS

Cushman & Wakefield
Jones Lang LaSalle

EMPLOYMENT CONTACT

www.cbre.com/careers

Visit the Vault Finance Career Channel at **www.vault.com/finance** — with
insider firm profiles, message boards, the Vault Finance Job Board and more

VAULT CAREER LIBRARY   79

THE SCOOP

Breaker, Breaker, we're No. 1

Founded in 1906 in San Francisco, CB Richard Ellis Group is the world's largest commercial real estate services company. Its offerings include brokerage services, corporate services, consulting, project management, market research, mortgage banking, and asset management and advisory services. With the acquisition of Insignia Financial in 2003, CBRE became the world's largest commercial property manager. CBRE's three geographic segments are the Americas; Europe, the Middle East and Africa (EMEA); and Asia-Pacific.

The company was taken private in 2001 by a group of investors led by Richard Blum (now CBRE's chairman) and Ray Wirta. Blum Capital Partners bought the 60 percent of publicly traded CBRE that it did not already own. In 2003, CBRE merged with top commercial real estate broker and property manager Insignia Financial. The next year the company changed its name to CB Richard Ellis Group and went public once again. In February 2004, CBRE filed for a $150 million initial public stock offering. Richard Blum maintains a nearly 15 percent stake in CBRE through Blum Capital Partners.

Banking of the banker

Colbert Coldwell and Albert Tucker started real estate brokerage Tucker, Lynch, & Coldwell in 1906 in San Francisco. In 1962, it was incorporated as Coldwell Banker, which went public in 1968. Sears, Roebuck & Co. bought the company in 1981 for 80 percent above its market price. But by 1991, Sears sold Coldwell Banker's commercial operations to The Carlyle Group as CB Commercial Real Estate Services Group. In 1998, the company acquired REI Limited, the non-U.K. operations of Richard Ellis; it was renamed CB Richard Ellis Services.

Growth through acquisitions

CB Richard Ellis has used acquisitions as a key method for growth in recent years. In July 2006, the company acquired The Polacheck Company, a commercial real estate services firm in Wisconsin, for approximately $20 million. Also in July 2006, it acquired Holley Blake, an industrial real estate

© 2007 Vault, Inc.

services specialist in the United Kingdom, for approximately $22 million in cash.

In August 2006, CBRG and Alfa Capital Partners announced that CB Richard Ellis acquired the remaining outstanding shares (49 percent) in CB Richard Ellis Noble Gibbons, one of Russia's leading real estate services firms, from ACP's investors and other shareholders. CB Richard Ellis had acquired a 51 percent ownership interest in Noble Gibbons in April 2006, and the entity was renamed CB Richard Ellis Noble Gibbons at that time. The acquisition reflects CB Richard Ellis' strategy of buying affiliate firms that are leaders in their regional markets.

And in one of its biggest deals, the company entered into an agreement to acquire its rival, Trammell Crow Company for $2.2 billion in cash. The deal closed in December 2006. The deal increased the company's total number of employees to more than 24,000, and the firm now counts approximately 85 percent of the Fortune 100 among its clients.

Looking up

The firm reported $4.032 billion in revenue for 2006, up from $2.911 billion in 2005. Net income also saw an increase—2006 total net income came in at $318.6 million, up from $217.3 million the year prior. CEO Brett White attributed 2006's performance to "the powerful client-focused platform we have built and continue to enhance."

CB Richard Ellis is currently ranked 520 on the Fortune 1000 list of the largest U.S. corporations. However, the acquisition of Trammel Crow would allow CBRE to be the first commercial real estate services company to qualify for the Fortune 500 list. Also, in 2006, for the sixth year in a row, CBRE was ranked No. 1 on the Lipsey Co.'s list of Top Commercial Real Estate Brands. In September 2006, the company was named the overall winner of *Euromoney* magazines Global Real Estate Awards. CBRE also became the only commercial real estate services firm on the S&P 500 index.

Visit the Vault Finance Career Channel at **www.vault.com/finance** – with
insider firm profiles, message boards, the Vault Finance Job Board and more

VAULT CAREER LIBRARY   81

GETTING HIRED

Take your pick

Resumes can be sent to opps@cbre.com, or alternately, applicants can try their luck emailing the head of corporate human resources at jack.vanberkel@cbre.com. Women interested in working at CBRE will find themselves in good company. A breakfast for female employees organized by Senior Vice President Lisa Konizeczka at the CBRE annual conference in 2001 led to the creation of the Women's Network, now 250 members and growing. The network's main tasks these days are to establish company-wide initiatives for the recruitment, retention and advancement of women. For its efforts in recruiting female employees, CBRE won the Organization of the Year award in October 2004, presented by the Commercial Real Estate Women Network.

The firm operates offices in "virtually all of the world's key business centers," and recruits from "universities and the industry," so candidates can expect interviewing experiences to run the gamut, but one insider says he went through "three interviews, including "two with the president."

OUR SURVEY SAYS

All around the world

The firm's international reach ensures that clients and employees alike have access to every possible resource they might require. "Working for CB Richard Ellis is an awesome experience," says an insider, adding that "the company offers great customer service." One thing that's the same across the board is the dress code, which sources call "formal always" and "business professional." One insider notes, "We have an appearance to uphold." The contact goes on to say that "opportunities do exist for advancement for sales negotiators," and "many of the company's directors have been promoted from within the company over the past 14 years."

© 2007 Vault, Inc.

The Chubb Corporation

15 Mountain View Road
Warren, NJ 07059
Phone: (908) 903-2000
Fax: (908) 903-2027
www.chubb.com

DEPARTMENTS

Chubb Commercial Insurance
Chubb Personal Insurance
Chubb Specialty Insurance

THE STATS

Employer Type: Public Company
Ticker Symbol: CB (NYSE)
Chairman, President & CEO: John D. Finnegan
Vice Chairman & COO: Thomas F. Motamed
Vice Chairman & CFO: Michael O'Reilly
Revenue: $14.0 billion (FY 12/06)
Net Income: $2.5 billion
No. of Employees: 10,800
No. of Offices: 120

UPPERS

- "Relationship"-driven culture
- "Easy" hourse

DOWNERS

- Tough to get promoted
- Diversity efforts need improvement

KEY COMPETITORS

AIG
The Hartford
Travelers

EMPLOYMENT CONTACT

See "careers" at www.chubb.com

Visit the Vault Finance Career Channel at **www.vault.com/finance** — with
insider firm profiles, message boards, the Vault Finance Job Board and more

VAULT CAREER LIBRARY   83

THE SCOOP

Focusing on the rich

Based in Warren, N.J., The Chubb Corporation, is a holding company for a group of property and casualty insurance firms known as the Chubb Group of Insurance Companies. The company offers three kinds of insurance: commercial, specialty and personal. The commercial insurance segment offers a range of insurance products, including workers' compensation, casualty and property insurance. Chubb's specialty insurance includes executive risk protection and professional liability insurance for private and public companies, financial institutions, nonprofits and health care organizations. Chubb's personal insurance is generally geared toward the rich, offering coverage to those with expensive homes and possessions, such as yachts, who are in need of higher limits and broader coverages than those in standard insurance policies. For example, Chubb's Masterpiece Valuable Articles Coverage includes "mysterious disappearance" and accidental breakage. Chubb is also a leader in insuring yachts valued at over $1 million. Additionally, Chubb's surety business offers bid, performance and payment bonds for construction and financial companies.

In 2005, Chubb sold its reinsurance unit to Harbor Point. Chubb received $200 million of 6 percent convertible notes and warrants, which represented approximately 16 percent of the new company, and will continue to receive cash payments through 2007.

Getting Chubby

In 1882, Thomas C. Chubb and his son Percy formed Chubb & Son in New York to underwrite marine insurance. The company became the U.S. manager for Sea Insurance Co. and launched New York Marine Underwriters, which became Chubb's chief property/casualty affiliate, eventually known as Federal Insurance Co. In 1939, Chubb bought Vigilant Insurance Co. Twenty years later, the company bought Colonial Life, and then later Pacific Indemnity in 1967. That same year, Chubb Corp. was formed as a holding company. In 1991, three subsidiaries were combined to form Chubb Life Insurance Co. of America.

In the 1970s, Chubb worked on expanding its real estate portfolio by acquiring Bellemead Development. In 1997, Chubb sold its life and health

© 2007 Vault, Inc.

insurance operations and parts of its real estate business, and focused instead on its lucrative property/casualty market.

After the flood

2005 was a bad year for insurance companies and Chubb was no exception. The company took some heavy hits from the year's record-breaking hurricane season, as Katrina slammed it with pre-tax costs of $511 million. However, due to a milder hurricane season, 2006 has been a much different story. Although revenue was down slightly in 2006—$14.003 billion from $14.082 billion a year prior—the firm's net income fared better. In 2006, Chubb reported $2.528 billion in income, up from $1.826 billion in 2005.

Sign of the times

In November 2005, Chubb partnered with Identity Theft 911 to help customers recover or recreate missing personal identification and documentation after a disaster or other calamity. Homeowing customers receive free access to the service, which gives them identity authentication and verification as well as access to investment and bank accounts. Theft 911 will also help members replace birth certificates, driver's licenses and passports, Social Security cards, and check and credit cards.

In 2006, Chubb announced that will provide group benefits customers with the option to purchase financial protection for child abductions and home invasions. Customers can elect optional coverage of up to $50,000 for medical expenses and wages lost while recovering from the trauma associated with a home invasion or abduction of a child. It can also cover the costs of temporary relocation or security enhancements. Chubb first introduced a broader version of this one-of-a-kind policy to its personal insurance customers a few years earlier.

Also in 2006, Chubb broadened its kidnap/ransom and extortion insurance policy in its specialty commercial lines packages for companies, as well as for high-net-worth individuals. The policy helps pay for ransoms, negotiators and security expenses. The policy even includes cyber extortion.

Visit the Vault Finance Career Channel at **www.vault.com/finance** – with
insider firm profiles, message boards, the Vault Finance Job Board and more

VAULT CAREER LIBRARY   85

GETTING HIRED

Let Chubb invest in you

The firm's careers site offers a searchable database of employment opportunities in a variety of different job categories, including accounting, actuarial, appraisal, claims, human resources, information technology, loss control operations services and underwriting. Job opportunities are available in 20 states and the District of Columbia as well as internationally.

Broadening their horizons

The firm's chief diversity officer cites what could be the firm's credo: "We believe that talent comes in many packages." And it seems that the firm practices what it preaches. The HRC rates Fortune 500 companies on a 100-point scale based on seven key indicators of fair treatment for GLBT employees, including policies prohibiting discrimination based on sexual orientation, gender identity and equal health care benefits. Chubb received the highest possible score on the Human Rights Campaign Foundation 2006 annual report card on corporate America's GLBT employees for the fourth year in a row. It was also named one of the 50 best U.S. employers for Latinas by *Latina Style* magazine in September 2006.

Chubb received one of three 2006 Catalyst Awards for the development and advancement of women in business. Catalyst honored Chubb for the company's Reach Up, Reach Out, Reach Down program, which encourages employees to take charge of their own careers in an inclusive atmosphere while reaching out to and advising their co-workers. The award emphasized Chubb's employee resource groups such as the Minority Development Council, Women's Development Council, Gay & Lesbian Employee Network and Asian-American Business Network, all of which have access to executive leadership.

© 2007 Vault, Inc.

OUR SURVEY SAYS

Relationships matter

The firm is "a good place to work," notes an insider, and while "its culture is a bit hard to describe, it's generally very rooted in relationships." The contact adds that "this is the sort of company that employs people who, by and large, love the firm."

Sources report that the dress code is "business attire from Labor Day until Memorial Day" and "business casual in the summer." Plus, the hours are "easy," notes an insider, adding that "the place is empty after 4:30 p.m. every day." Another contact says that the hours "vacillate between eight- and 12-hour shifts." But as far as advancing within the firm, things might not be so cut and dried. One insider notes that there's a "greater pressure on titles than in the past." Another agrees, adding that there's "no advancement unless you seriously luck out." One contact says that there's "no chance of being promoted" within the firm and that "in order to get promoted, you have to be a robot and not an independent thinker."

Strides to make

Despite the firm's accolades for its diversity efforts, one respondent notes that not every office is forward-thinking, adding that while "diversity is good in L.A.," "my own bosses have made a lot of disparaging remarks about different ethnic groups, gay people and so forth. I requested sensitivity training on many occasions, but our super-blond and blue-eyed boss is like, 'What?'" Another insider says, "As a woman, advancement is much harder to achieve."

Visit the Vault Finance Career Channel at **www.vault.com/finance** – with
insider firm profiles, message boards, the Vault Finance Job Board and more

VAULT CAREER LIBRARY   87

CIT Group

505 Fifth Avenue
New York, NY 10017
Phone: (212) 771-0505
www.cit.com

DEPARTMENTS

Consumer & Small Business
  Lending
Corporate Finance
Trade Finance
Transportation Finance
Vendor Finance

THE STATS

Employer Type: Public Company
Ticker Symbol: CIT (NYSE)
Chairman & CEO: Jeffrey (Jeff) M.
Peek
Revenue: $6.94 billion (FYE 12/06)
Net Income: $1.05 billion
No. of Employees: 7,200
No. of Offices: 50 in North America

KEY COMPETITORS

Citigroup
FINOVA
GECF

UPPERS

- Flexible hours

DOWNERS

- Training needs improvement

EMPLOYMENT CONTACT

See "careers" section of www.cit.com

© 2007 Vault, Inc.

THE SCOOP

All inclusive

CIT Group provides financing and related services to just about everybody, from small businesses to the world's largest multinational corporations. With finance products ranging from acquisition financing and asset management to venture capital and vendor financing, CIT operates across 30 industries in 50 countries, including North America, Europe, Latin America, Asia, Australia and New Zealand. The company does business with 80 percent of the Fortune 1000 companies, and by the end of 2006, managed over $74.16 billion in assets.

Founded in 1908, CIT has weathered a somewhat rocky past under the ownership of numerous companies. It is probably best known for its affiliation with Tyco, which in 2002, embroiled in corporate scandals, spun off CIT. Out from under its beleaguered owner, CIT has grown over the past few years through acquisitions, including units from GE Commercial Services, HSBC Bank and CitiCapital. Today, it is a healthy global commercial and consumer finance company, providing financing solutions, leasing products and advisory services to commercial and consumer clients around the world. Especially strong in factoring, vendor financing, equipment and transportation financing, Small Business Administration loans and asset-based lending, CIT is a Fortune 500 company and member of the S&P 500 Index.

Five pillars

CIT's business can be broken down into five main segments. Corporate finance provides lending, leasing, and other financial and advisory services to middle-market companies, with a focus on specific industries, including health care, energy, communications, media and entertainment. At the end of 2006, the unit had $21.33 billion in assets. The trade finance division, worth $6.975 billion in assets at the end of 2006, provides factoring and other trade and financial products to companies in the retail supply chain. Transportation finance, with $12.1 billion in assets, provides lending, leasing and other banking services to the rail and aerospace and defense industries. Vendor finance provides financing solutions to manufacturers, distributors and other intermediaries, including Avaya, Dell, Microsoft, Snap-on and Toshiba. The unit had $12.66 billion in managed assets at the end of 2006. Finally, consumer/small business lending, with $21.13 billion in assets at the end of

Visit the Vault Finance Career Channel at www.vault.com/finance – with
insider firm profiles, message boards, the Vault Finance Job Board and more

VAULT CAREER LIBRARY   89

2006, provides collateralized and government-secured loans to consumers and small businesses (SBA, student loans and home mortgages) leveraging broker and other intermediary relationships.

Small business, big rewards

In November 2006, CIT's Small Business Lending Corporation unit was recognized for the fourth consecutive year as the No. 1 Small Business Administration (SBA) 7(a) volume lender to women- veteran- and minority-owned businesses nationwide. The ranking is based on SBA 7(a) loan volume for the 2006 SBA fiscal year (October 1, 2005 to September 30, 2006). CIT provided $440,672,900 in these kinds of loans to 862 women-minority- and veteran-owned small businesses nationwide. And in October 2006, CIT small business lending corporation unit pulled in another consecutive award, this time the seventh in a row, as the No. 1 Small Business 7(a) volume lender overall. In total, CIT provided $872,595,495 in SBA 7(a) loans to 1,487 small businesses nationwide between October 1, 2005 and September 30, 2006.

Mounting new business

CIT expanded its Canadian operations in November 2006, with three senior appointments in the region: Mark Hart as chief sales officer and senior vice president for CIT Commercial Finance, Canada; Peter Kinkartz as managing director and head of CIT Capital Markets, Canada; and Bruce Smith as senior vice president of CIT vendor finance, Canada. "These senior appointments reflect CIT's commitment to growing our business and expanding our relationships throughout Canada," said J. Daryl MacLellan, president of CIT Canada, in a company press release. "Canada represents an important area of growth for CIT's overall business strategy with above average investment and growth in key lending areas, such as vendor finance, natural resource development and corporate finance."

From sun comes ... Snow?

The company made another important hire in October 2006, naming Kris Snow president of its vendor Americas business. In this role, Snow is responsible for growing CIT's vendor financing business throughout Canada, Latin America and the U.S. She oversees office products and technology/systems leasing, health care vendor and diversified vendor business segments. Snow joined CIT from Sun Microsystems, where she

© 2007 Vault, Inc.

held significant management roles over the past 16 years. Most recently she was the general manager for Sun's captive finance arm, global financial services.

Mingling with big banks

In October 2006, CIT announced plans to acquire the U.K. and German vendor finance businesses of Barclays Bank. The gross assets of the acquired vendor finance businesses totaled approximately $2 billion as of June 30, 2006, or 12 percent of the gross assets of Barclays Asset & Sales Finance, the specialist commercial asset finance provider within Barclays' U.K. Business Banking. According to a company press release, the acquisition represents a significant step for CIT in its effort to increase its presence in key European markets. The businesses to be acquired provide asset finance to customers of industrial equipment and technology manufacturers and suppliers throughout the U.K. and Germany. Approximately 60 percent of the purchased assets come from Barclay's U.K. business, with the balance in Germany. As part of the acquisition, CIT will take on the vendor finance sales and administration staff in the U.K. and Germany.

CIT is being advised by JPMorgan on the Barclays deal. According to *Financial News*, "JP Morgan last advised CIT on the lender's $381 million acquisition of Education Lending Group in January 2005, which brought CIT a $4 billion-plus portfolio of loans. The only other bank CIT has used on a publicly disclosed deal in the past two years is Lazard, which advised on CIT's acquisition of Healthcare Business Credit for an undisclosed amount in July 2005." CIT does not lack the savvy to deal with big investment banks, however. CEO Jeff Peek held top executive posts at both Merrill Lynch and Credit Suisse before taking over at CIT.

Bigger and bigger

The firm went through some new expansion efforts in early 2007. CIT announced plans to open offices in Shanghai and Singapore, and it bought Barclays' vendor finance business in England and Germany. It's managed to keep busy in other ways, too. In April 2007, the firm filed an IPO of $275 million for the real estate investment trust Care Investment Trust. Within the same month, CIT Chairman and CEO Peek told *Investment Dealers' Digest* about a few other new developments the firm has on tap for the future, such as an agreement to finance Microsoft's software sales and the recent hiring of

Visit the Vault Finance Career Channel at **www.vault.com/finance** – with insider firm profiles, message boards, the Vault Finance Job Board and more

VAULT CAREER LIBRARY   **91**

a loan specialist team "to look for distressed debt when we find something that is of value."

GETTING HIRED

Sit down and discover CIT

On the CIT Group's career web site (www.cit.com/main/careers), potential employees can check out the firm's benefits program (which CIT says ranks "either first or second in total value provided among prominent financial services organizations"), learn about the firm's focus and values, and even read firsthand testimonials from current employees. Or just skip the frills and go straight to the site's job postings, which are divided into subsections for professionals and graduating seniors.

OUR SURVEY SAYS

Good times

"I like working here," says one respondent simply, adding that "the employees are very close and get along pretty well." On top of that, the firm offers flexible hours. One insider comments that the flexibility "fits in well with my young family," adding that "sometimes I will start work at 7 a.m. and sometimes 10 a.m. Basically, I need to be available when a new or existing customer needs to see me to discuss a new acquisition." Another says that while work hours "are officially 8:30 a.m. to 5 p.m.," "in departments like new business and audit that require travel, much more flexibility is allowed."

Not quite the fast lane

One insider from the Charlotte office says that "valuable training opportunities are available for recent graduates in the management training program," adding that "individuals who are selected for the program are provided the opportunity to rotate through the various departments such as customer credit, client credit, audit and new business for up to 18 months and

© 2007 Vault, Inc.

learn firsthand how these departments function. In so doing, they gain a broad overview of the company's function and business dealings." But this doesn't seem to necessarily put trainees on the fast track. The contact continues that "unfortunately, although this is called a management training program, most of these individuals will end up as rank-and-file employees in one of these departments when the training is completed."

But there are opportunities to move up. One calls the firm a "large expanding business and there are many opportunities for advancement," and says that "the opportunities within CIT are really only restricted by your ambition."

No complaints

The dress code is "relaxed," says an insider. Another calls it "business casual, although sometimes on visits to clients and customers, employees will dress more formally." Yet another employee says that it "varies," adding that "the rule is to dress up for first meetings in a shirt and tie, and then dress at the customers' level for subsequent meetings."

Company perks receive high marks. One insider says, "CIT encourages continued education, and will pay 100 percent tuition reimbursement for grades of B or higher." Another enjoys that the firm "participates in a lot of charity work and helping less fortunate people."

Initiating diversity

The company also gets decent diversity marks from employees when it comes to women. One insider notes that the company "has recently implemented a women's initiative," in which the firm "actively seeks to promote and advance qualified women within the company." Committees made up of "senior women have been assembled in each region that meet periodically" to discuss issues related to women in the workplace. But there's definitely room for improvement. One source notes, "Beyond this, CIT does not demonstrate a significant focus in the area of diversity."

Visit the Vault Finance Career Channel at **www.vault.com/finance** – with
insider firm profiles, message boards, the Vault Finance Job Board and more

VAULT CAREER LIBRARY   93

Citigroup

399 Park Avenue
New York, NY 10043
Phone: (800) 285-3000
Fax: (212) 793-3946
www.citigroup.com

DEPARTMENTS

Alternative Investments
Global Consumer Group
Global Wealth Management
Markets and Banking

THE STATS

Employer Type: Public Company
Ticker Symbol: C (NYSE)
Chairman and CEO: Charles (Chuck) O. Prince III
Net Revenue: $89.615 billion (FYE 12/06)
Net Income: $21.54 billion
No. of Employees: 327,000 (as of 12/06)
No. of Offices: 7,500

KEY COMPETITORS

Bank of America
Deutsche Bank
JPMorgan Chase

UPPERS

- "Market leaders on many of our products"
- "Smart and fun people; challenging and exciting projects"
- "Career mobility: the opportunities made available by the sheer size, global presence and diversity of operations"

DOWNERS

- "At such a large organization, many decision are politically motivated"
- "I don't think we're compensated well enough"
- "If you have a problem with your technology it may take days or even weeks for the problem to get resolved"

EMPLOYMENT CONTACT

See "careers" section of www.citigroup.com

© 2007 Vault, Inc.

THE SCOOP

No. 1

Citigroup is the largest bank in the U.S. and the No. 8 company on the 2006 Fortune 500. It offers seemingly every financial service under the sun to consumer and corporate customers, catering to some 200 million customer accounts and doing business in more than 100 countries. Citigroup is managed along the following four segment lines: global consumer, market and banking and global wealth management, and alternative investments.

Citigroup's global consumer group typically accounts for over half of Citigroup's profits. In September 2005, the group reorganized its businesses along client lines to capitalize on the different opportunities within the retail market. The U.S. consumer business is organized as follows: U.S. retail distribution composed of branch-based consumer businesses and Primerica Financial Services; U.S. consumer lending, which includes mortgage, auto and student loan businesses; U.S. cards; and U.S. commercial business.

As part of this sharpened focused on its consumer business in 2005, Citigroup decided to give asset management the heave ho. "The asset management industry is an extremely competitive one," said CEO Charles Prince, in a conference call. "Frankly, our performance in asset management has not been what we had hoped for it to be. We are not a leader today in that business." On December 1, 2005, the firm completed the sale of its asset management business to Legg Mason, in a deal estimated at $3.7 billion, $2.1 billion of which Citigroup reaped after taxes. And in July 2005, Citigroup made another huge sale, handing over Travelers Life & Annuity to MetLife for approximately $1 billion in MetLife common stock and $10.8 billion in cash. The sale, which included nearly all of Citigroup's international insurance businesses, resulted in an after-tax gain of about $2 billion.

Traveling along

Citigroup's roots lie in the City Bank of New York, which was founded in 1812 by Samuel Osgood, the first commissioner of the U.S. Treasury. By the 1900s Citibank (as it came to be known) it had expanded overseas, then moved beyond commercial banking to provide personal loans.

The modern era of Citigroup began in 1988 when a Baltimore-based loan company called Commercial Credit bought Primerica and assumed its name. Five years later Primerica merged with insurance company Travelers Corp.

(and took its name); in 1997 Travelers acquired the Salomon Brothers investment bank and merged it with subsidiary Smith Barney to form Salomon Smith Barney. In 1998 Travelers, headed by former Commercial Credit Chairman Sandy Weill, made the merger of its life, joining Citicorp to become Citigroup. Weill became CEO of Citigroup, but was replaced in 2003 by its current chief, Charles O. Prince III. The bank Weill built was a sprawling giant, and is still the largest bank in America. Under Prince's reign, Citigroup has been showing signs of change: instead of making as many acquisitions as possible, the focus has been on consolidating and emphasizing core sectors, while making a few targeted purchases to strengthen existing businesses.

Clients first

In September 2006, CEO Charles Prince came up with another plan to improve customer service that he hopes will make the bank more money. The program, "Client First," was rolled out across all businesses and regions, and Citigroup set up a designated advisory board to monitor progress of the initiative; an internal web site also was set up for employees to voice their concerns or make suggestions. The plan marked the second time Prince has tried to implement company-wide changes at the bank. The first, when Prince outlined a Five Point Plan to get Citigroup on track after a series of scandals, resulted in the Federal Reserve in April 2006 lifting a yearlong ban on big acquisitions. Prince has equally high hopes for the Client First plan, which was announced amid not only scrutiny about his own pay package, but also Prince's decision to increase bankers' pay to keep up with other Wall Street investment banks.

Smart buys

An example of Citigroup's focused buying plans came in December 2006 when it purchased Quilter, one of the United Kingdom's biggest wealth advisory firms, with over $10.9 billion of assets under management. Citigroup bought Quilter from Morgan Stanley, who was selling the firm as part of its own streamlining measures. The buy gave Citigroup access to Quilter's 18,000 clients and 300 staff in 10 offices throughout the United Kingdom—making Citigroup one of the region's top-10 wealth managers.

Another purchase that complemented Citigroup's core was the December 2006 acquisition of Capmark Financial Group's affordable housing debt business. Capmark Affordable Housing Debt (CAHD) is America's leading

© 2007 Vault, Inc.

affordable housing underwriter and banker, with over $1.2 billion in assets. It merged into Citigroup's municipal securities practice, which was already a leader in the municipal secondary market and in government debt markets.

Record revenue, lower net income

In 2006, the firm reported record full-year revenue of $89.5 billion, a 7 percent increase from the year before. However, net income dropped to $21.54 billion in 2006 from $24.59 billion in 2005. Chairman and CEO Prince said the results "were highlighted by double-digit revenue growth in our corporate and investment banking, wealth management and alternative investment businesses." For 2007, Prince said the firm plans to be "focusing sharply on expense management."

The company's global consumer group, Citigroup's largest driver of revenue, saw its net income go up in 2006, to $12.06 billion from $10.9 billion a year earlier. Citigroup's consumer net income also increased—to $8.39 billion from $7.17 billion in 2006. Within the consumer net income group, cards drew the most net income for the group, coming in at 46 percent. Net income for the firm's international consumer group dipped slightly in 2006, however, to $4.017 billion from $4.098 billion in 2005.

Management shake-up

In December 2006, Citigroup named the firm's head of investment banking, Robert Druskin, chief operating officer. In a sign that Prince recognizes Citigroup's expenses had spiraled out of control, the CEO said in a press release announcing the appointment that one of Druskin's first assignments would be to look into the matter. "Bob will greatly assist us in achieving our goals of driving increased revenue and earnings growth throughout our businesses, while improving our operating efficiency. In that regard, one of his first tasks is to undertake a comprehensive review of our expense base." Citigroup's COO post had been open since July 2005, when Robert Willumstad resigned and Prince said he was doing away with the position.

The appointment of Druskin came just two days before Prince took the stage at the firm's annual Investor Day meeting, at which investors were hoping for some concrete proof that the firm was on track to improve shareholder value. Days before the event—and Druskin's new job announcement—industry watchers were speculating about Citigroup CFO Sallie Krawcheck, a well-known female executive who has been tossed around as a possible successor to Prince. But, according to *The Wall Street Journal*, "Some investors have

Visit the Vault Finance Career Channel at **www.vault.com/finance** – with insider firm profiles, message boards, the Vault Finance Job Board and more

VAULT CAREER LIBRARY   97

expressed displeasure with her performance and have questioned whether she should continue to hold the dual roles of finance chief and head of strategy, as she has for the past two years. She has taken heat for Citigroup's failing to successfully navigate the tricky financial environment facing banks recently: Recent trends in interest rates, known as a flattened yield curve, have cut into the profit margins that banks can earn between the interest rate at which they borrow money and the interest rate they get when lending it out."

So far, Krawcheck's people insist that she is not leaving the company, although speculation abounds that the decision to promote Druskin, which slid Michael Klein and Thomas Maheras into the top investment banking posts, is a sign that she may be out of the running to succeed Prince.

Closing the umbrella

The "leaner, thinner" Citigroup will have a new look and a new name. In February 2007, the firm retired its famous red umbrella logo. In the second quarter of 2007, the firm also sliced the 'group' from its brand, going forward with the lone "Citi" as its brand name (although 'Citigroup' will remain the "umbrella" term for Citi businesses). Markets and banking will use the brand name Citi; wealth management will use the names Citi Smith Barney, Citi Investment Research and Citi Private Bank; and Citigroup Alternative Investments will become Citi Alternative Investments. The new logo features a simple red arc over the word Citi in silver.

Reducing and relocating

More recently, in April 2007, Citigroup's announced its long-awaited, large-scale restructuring, going public with its plans to cut or relocate more than 26,500 of its jobs—8 percent of its workforce—in an effort to reduce expenses by $4.6 billion within the next three years. Citigroup intends to eliminate about 17,000 jobs in addition to moving approximately 9,500 positions to India and other lower-cost locations. Its headquarters in New York City alone will lose 6 percent of its 27,000 employees. Citigroup COO Druskin said that approximately 57 percent of eliminated positions will be jobs that are located outside of the U.S. The firm anticipates that managerial jobs and positions in trading and prime brokerage units will be heavily affected, as will many positions in U.S. consumer operations.

Citigroup CEO and Chairman Prince announced in a statement, "These changes will streamline Citi and make us leaner, more efficient and better

© 2007 Vault, Inc.

able to take advantage of high revenue opportunities." The cuts are designed to bring expenses in line with rival banks. They're also designed to appease stockholders. Since Prince stepped in as CEO in 2003, Citigroup's stock had increased only 15 percent at the time of the announcement, and shareholders had recently put pressure on the bank to raise the stock price and shrink expenses.

As part of the costs of the reorganization, Citi plans to record a $1.38 billion pre-tax charge in the first quarter of 2007 and about $200 million spread over the rest of the year. Citigroup expects to reap the benefits quickly—a reduction of $2.1 billion in expenses for the year, increasing to a $4.8 billion savings by 2009—but financial analysts are unsure just how the cuts and improved efficiency will translate to increased opportunities for revenue.

GETTING HIRED

High demand, low supply

It's not easy to land a job at Citigroup, and the firm takes recruiting seriously. There's a "very high demand for only a handful of positions," say insiders, and the firm "recruits at many schools." Sources say Citi does an "excellent job of selecting intelligent candidates through the interview process." "Personality, common sense and a strong desire to learn are important qualities that need to come through during interviews." One respondent says, "Those selected to conduct interviews are careful to distinguish between one candidate's 'fluff' and another's genuine interest in the position."

Citi visits "top undergraduate and graduate business schools," but "also welcomes applications from schools where we do not recruit." Schools where the firm recruits include Boston College, Georgetown, Duke, Penn, NYU, Columbia, Morehouse, Spellman, Cornell Harvard, Stanford, Texas and Notre Dame. The interview process will vary depending on which unit you interview with, but typically, for the campus recruiting process, "first-round interviews are held on campus, and final-round interviews are held on-site in New York."

"Round one consisted of a 30-minute interview with two employees," explains one insider. "And round two was three 30-minute interviews, each also with two employees." Another source who had four interviews, which included "one with HR," says he was asked questions such as "What are your

Visit the Vault Finance Career Channel at **www.vault.com/finance** – with
insider firm profiles, message boards, the Vault Finance Job Board and more
VAULT CAREER LIBRARY
99

strengths and weaknesses? Are you are team player? Give us an example of when you faced a problem, and what you did to solve it. Discuss your work experience. Why did you attend your school? What do you know about Citigroup?"

Another source, who didn't go through the campus recruiting process, had a "first-round phone interview with a VP, and then had two in-person interviews with directors during the second round." He adds, "There was one case question, and the rest were behavioral. They asked a lot about my past work experience and how I've handled various situations."

Summer in the Citi

Citi also has its eyes peeled for summer interns. Paid interns are part of "a very structured program, with an individual manager, as well as a group summer project with the other summer interns." "The work was the same that full-time analysts were doing," says a source in finance who worked as an intern before being hired full time. "It made coming back easier because it was a simple readjustment." Indeed, says another former intern, an internship "certainly makes it easier to be hired directly for the full-time program."

OUR SURVEY SAYS

Honest and open

Insiders say Citi has an honest, open and free-speaking culture." People are "encouraged to share ideas and contribute to the team." There are "high levels of support for the junior level, and managers keep an "open-door policy." The culture is also "very entrepreneurial," but it's also "a bit bureaucratic." Sources note that if you want the work, it's there for the taking. "People can always take on more responsibility if they want more challenging assignments." As for its people, Citi is diverse with staff from all different backgrounds and nationalities." And sources say Citi's folks have a "business professional attitude in business casual attire." Though, the dress code depends on department, as some must be "formal always" and others have a "business-casual-except-for-client-contact" code.

Even so, an insider notes, "Citi's culture is more laid-back than other firm's. Despite our more casual culture, we take our work and our values very

© 2007 Vault, Inc.

seriously." Another contact says, "You also have the possibility to move around the firm into different businesses, positions and locations around the world."

As for managers, "each has their own style of teaching," says a source, "because they only know how they themselves became successful. Therefore, I think managers here respect subordinates who work hard and strive to do their best even when they don't feel like it." The contact admits, "There will always be those managers who make outlandish requests, but it generally means they are looking to see if you'll go the extra mile. I have never seen hard work go unrewarded." Another insider says that while there is "a definite hierarchy, everyone gets along well. On certain floors within the office, senior management is interspersed within the rank and file, which creates an interesting dynamic." Says yet another source, "Managers are all very friendly and easy to talk to."

Average comp but good hours

Compensation gets average marks by insiders. Insiders, for the most part, say salaries are "mediocre" compared to other firms. However, perks and benefits are plentiful. "Citi recently changed the 401(k) matching program to include all income levels and allow for immediate vesting." Also, "associates and up can invest in Citi's private equity funds." There is "a gym and cafeteria in the building" in New York, meal allowance is $25 for dinner for weekdays and $25 for both lunch and dinner on the weekends." "Car services are provided after 9 p.m., and cabs can be comped after 8:30 pm." Staffers get "free access to museums in New York, and are allowed to travel "business class if the flight is over four hours, and first class if over 10 hours." Other perks include "employee discounts at certain stores and health clubs, and MetroCard and cell phone discounts."

Hours get better marks from sources. Of course, hours vary by department, but most report "rarely to never" having to work weekends. Still, some insiders say they work quite a few hours. "The days can be long," says one source, "but they tend to go by extremely fast. Fortunately, the extra time I spend in the office serves the purpose of learning more." Another insider notes that there's "no pressure to be in the office late night if there's not a business need," adding, "We have a good work/life balance, and are given flexibility for personal issues such as doctor appointments, etc." And yet another contact says, "Standard work hours are roughly 50 per week, with virtually no weekend work."

Visit the Vault Finance Career Channel at **www.vault.com/finance** – with
insider firm profiles, message boards, the Vault Finance Job Board and more

VAULT CAREER LIBRARY   **101**

Class time

Training gets high marks, too. "Training programs exist in several departments," says one source, "and the mentor/mentee relationships within those programs are key to development." Beyond formal training, "there are weekly product information sessions," in some groups, "but these don't go into as much detail as I'd like," says a contact. Another notes, "With cost controls, you'd need to make a strong case for external training." Still, overall, insiders generally call training opportunities "excellent," "comprehensive" and "useful."

Aesthetically speaking

Insiders nearly unanimously call the firm's offices "sufficient." "There is nothing unpleasant about the offices," says a source, "though I would not consider them particularly luxurious or exciting." Indeed, the office space is OK. The facilities in 388 Greenwich Street are nice and definitely better than 390 Greenwich Street." Another contact notes, "My space has room for my four screens, three drawers and a small work area. It's all I need." Another believes, "The lobby is very nice, but the floors where we work are drab and could be better decorated."

A diverse force

Citi is a "very diverse and international organization." "The Women's Council has various events related to career progression and mobility," says one respondent. "But I still encounter managers who don't work well with women." Still, "senior managers participate in the development of woman at the firm." The firm "does a good job at hiring, but not retaining women in senior positions," says one source. With respect to minorities, "there is a respect for the firm's diversity in terms of monthly celebrations for Hispanic heritage, Black history, etc.," says another. "And sometimes there are cultural/musical performances in the cafeteria during lunch." One contact notes, "I visibly see the initiative to facilitate the hiring and promotion of minorities in the workplace." While another adds, "The minorities that are here care about each other's progress and development."

© 2007 Vault, Inc.

Countrywide Financial Corp.

4500 Park Granada
Calabasas, CA 91302-1613
(818) 225-3000
Fax: (818) 225-4051
www.countrywide.com

DEPARTMENTS

Banking
Capital Markets
Countrywide Home Loans &
  LandSafe, Inc.
Global Operations
Insurance

THE STATS

Employer Type: Public Company
Ticker Symbol: CFC (NYSE)
Chairman & CEO: Angelo R. Mozilo
President: David Sambol
Revenue: $24.88 billion (FYE 12/06)
Net Income: $2.67 billion
No. of Employees: 54,655
No. of Offices: 800

KEY COMPETITORS

Bank of America
Fannie Mae
Washington Mutual
Wells Fargo

UPPERS

- "Financially sound"
- "Projected to grow like crazy"
- "Team-oriented"

DOWNERS

- "A lot of work"
- "They don't care about anything but the bottom line"
- "Morale can be low"

EMPLOYMENT CONTACT

www.countrywidecareers.com

Visit the Vault Finance Career Channel at **www.vault.com/finance** — with
insider firm profiles, message boards, the Vault Finance Job Board and more

VAULT CAREER LIBRARY   103

THE SCOOP

Big Countrywide

Countrywide Financial Corporation is the largest U.S. mortgage lender, providing mortgage banking and diversified financial services through its family of companies. Founded in 1969, Countrywide is a member of the S&P 500, Forbes 500 and Fortune 500.

The firm is organized into five major divisions: mortgage banking, capital markets, banking, insurance and global operations (a joint venture in the U.K. launched in 1999). The mortgage banking segment is comprised of three divisions: loan production, loan servicing and loan closing services. Loan production originates prime and non-prime mortgage loans through a national distribution system. Loan servicing services mortgage loans on behalf of Fannie Mae, Freddie Mac, Ginnie Mae and various private and public investors in return for an annual fee. By March 31, 2007, Countrywide's mortgage loan-servicing portfolio surpassed $1.4 trillion, up $199 billion from the previous year. Loan closing services provides credit reports, appraisals, title reports and flood demonstrations to the loan production sector and other third parties.

The banking segment's operations are made up of Countrywide Bank, N.A. and Countrywide Warehouse Lending. Countrywide Bank offers depository and home loan products to consumers. Total assets at Countrywide Bank reached $200 billion as of year-end 2006, an increase from $175 billion in 2005. Countrywide Warehouse Lending provides temporary financing secured by mortgage loans to third-party mortgage bankers.

The capital markets segment is a fixed income investment banking firm comprised mainly of the operations of Countrywide Securities Corporation (CSC), a registered broker-dealer and primary-dealer of U.S. treasury securities. CSC primarily engages in the sales, trading and underwriting of mortgage, U.S. treasury and other asset-backed securities, as well as related research and advisory activities. Securities trading volume in March 2007 reached $397 billion, up 7 percent versus 2006.

Insurance activities are conducted through Balboa Life and Casualty Group, whose companies are national providers of property, life and casualty insurance; and Balboa Reinsurance, a captive mortgage reinsurance company. Global operations' primary unit is Global Home Loans, a majority-owned

© 2007 Vault, Inc.

joint venture that provides loan origination processing and loan sub-servicing in the U.K.

Humble beginnings

In 1969, Angelo Mozilo, who began his career as a 14-year-old messenger for a Manhattan mortgage company, and David Loeb launched their own mortgage company, Countrywide Credit Industries. Before the year's end, Countrywide went public, trading at less than $1 per share. The offering did not raise much capital but, undeterred, the two New York bankers left the Big Apple thereafter and opened an office in Los Angeles amidst a booming housing market.

During its initial years in business, the company offered Federal Housing Administration (FHA) and the Veterans Administration (VA) loans through a commissioned sales force. Countrywide has always focused on the multicultural community and is the largest lender to minorities, including being the top lender to African-Americans, Hispanics and Asians, as well as the leading lender in low- to moderate-income communities. The company became the first mortgage lender to surpass $1 trillion in servicing in 2006.

However, the firm's founders believed that its existing business model did not provide the proper type of customer service, and decided they needed to move in a new direction. Over lunch one day, the two came up with a model that would revolutionize the way they do business. Namely, the company would open branch offices without sales people, where customers could receive retail bank-like service. The first branch was opened in 1974 in Whittier, California. Over the next 10 years, loan production and branches grew steadily, and by 1980, there were 40 Countrywide branches in nine states. Eventually, the firm further expanded lending operations into conventional loans that could be sold to Fannie Mae and Freddie Mac.

Capital markets efforts began in 1981, with the creation of Countrywide Securities Corporation, a broker-dealer subsidiary formed in line with the development of the mortgage-backed securities market to facilitate the pooling and sale of loans to investors as production levels increased and secondary market liquidity became more readily available. In the late 1970s, the firm had already begun looking into ways to increase efficiency and, in doing so, developed the industry's first PC-based loan servicing system. Within a year, the data in 12,000 loan files was computerized and available in real time to computer users throughout the company, dramatically reducing the cost to service a loan.

During the mid-1980s, the firm further expanded its loan production capabilities to include the wholesale (loans sourced from a network of independent mortgage brokers) and correspondent (closed loans purchased from smaller financial institutions) channels.

The big chill

Countrywide has long been one of the country's best performing stocks. Riding a booming housing market, 2005 was the second best in Countrywide's history, exceeded only by 2003 numbers, which were driven by the record level of industry-wide mortgage refinance activity. According to *Inside Mortgage Finance*, Countrywide was the largest residential mortgage originator and servicer in 2005. With a 16 percent origination market share for 2005, the company funded nearly one of every six mortgages. One of the most important milestones of the year was reaching $491 billion in mortgage loans, a single-company record and $99 billion more then the second-biggest lender, Wells Fargo. The company said that it planned to control almost 30 percent of the home loan production market and 20 percent of the mortgage servicing market by 2010. As part of its plans for further market domination, the company bought Hopkinton, Mass.-based Marathon Mortgage Corp. in early 2006.

However, in 2006 the market began to cool, and in September 2006, the company announced it planned to sell up to $4.5 billion in new debt. With Wells Fargo catching up and trying to regain its position as the country's top home lender, Mozilo warned investors that he had to prepare the company for the "worst that could happen in the market," adding that he had never seen a soft landing in 53 years. Prices of new homes fell in 2006 for the first time since 1991; and Countrywide has offered many nontraditional loans, including payment-option adjustable-rate mortgages (ARMs) that allow borrowers to make minimal payments by deferring part of the interest. The company reported mortgage loan fundings for March 2007 as $43 billion, up 5 percent from a year earlier.

As a result of a turbulent market, the company said it would cut up to 10 percent of its general and administrative workforce, but would continue to grow its sales staff. The cuts could affect up to 2,300 workers and began in fall 2006. Meanwhile, Countrywide's Indian unit opened a second office in Bombay in February 2006, and the firm said it plans to almost double the staff in the country by adding 1,700 employees. But in April 2007, the company announced that it plans to cut 108 positions in its wholesale lending unit's sub-prime division.

© 2007 Vault, Inc.

In September 2006, without giving a reason or a departure date, the company's president and COO for more than a decade, Stanford L. Kurland, said he was leaving the company. Kurland was believed to be the heir apparent to Mozilo, who was expected to step down as CEO at the end of the year, but remain as chairman. The company then named David Sambol, who served as executive managing director of business segment operations, as Kurland's replacement, and Mozilo renegotiated his contract with the board to stay on. Industry insiders are betting Sambol will eventually replace Mozilo when he decides, again, to leave. Mozilo also drew the ire of AFSCME Employees Pension Plan at the annual stockholder's meeting. The union claimed that Mozilo's compensation ($160 million in total compensation in 2005) was excessive. The company countered that attracting and retaining top staff is a critical function for the board.

GETTING HIRED

No snail mail

Submitting a resume online is the "fastest and most efficient way to express interest in job opportunities," according to the firm, as it "no longer accept resumes via e-mail, mail or fax." Insiders say the firm recruits "nationally," but there seems to be a focus out West. One source cites "UCLA, Stanford, USC and Pepperdine" as major hunting grounds. Even so, the firm does go coast to coast, as it visits schools such as Boston University, the University of Illinois at Chicago, Kent State (in Ohio), Arizona State University, UNLV and the University of North Texas, among others. On-campus recruits could have as many as five interviews. One risk management insider who went through that many adds, "It took about three months to get the offer." Another, who works in sales, only went through "three interviews" and ranks the firm about average when it comes to selectivity.

At the firm's careers site, www.countrywidecareers.com, candidates can search for openings by job category and location. They can also read about the firm's programs in tuition reimbursement, career development, mentoring and diversity. There's also a link to the firm's on-campus recruiting events and a place for candidates to sign up to be reminded about events in their area.

Visit the Vault Finance Career Channel at **www.vault.com/finance** – with
insider firm profiles, message boards, the Vault Finance Job Board and more

VAULT CAREER LIBRARY   **107**

Background info

"One thing to note is extensive and time-consuming background checks are done on every employee regardless of the job," warns an insider, adding that "offers will not be made until the background check is successfully completed." Depending on position and location, the rest of the interview process tends to vary. "I was contacted directly by the hiring manager who found my resume online," says one contact. "I was surprised that the hiring manager didn't want to do a phone screen prior to bringing me in." The source adds that when he did go in, "the interview was fairly pleasant. The hiring manager spent several minutes describing his department and the various functions in it, as well as the function he wanted me to perform. We had some very basic Q&A and it went quite well." The source does admit that he felt "very uneasy about the fact that I was fairly isolated during the entire interview process. I was not even casually introduced to anybody in the halls."

Another respondent says that it "was one of the easiest interviews I've ever had," adding, "I met the hiring manager for lunch on a Saturday, then met with his manager the following Wednesday for about an hour and received my offer letter the following week. During the interview, there were no tough questions, just the standard, 'Where do you see yourself in five years?' 'What are your strengths?' and 'Tell me about a time when ...'"

An insider who went through several interviews says, "I was interviewed by a senior recruiter in HR, the EVP of sales, the EVP and SVP of operations, the EVP of compliance, and the director of the division at the corporate office. I was also interviewed by the regional sales manager and the regional operations manager in the hiring location." In addition, he was "interviewed via telephone twice and in person four times," adding that when applying for a senior vice president-level position, candidates will be asked questions "primarily directed at management style and experiences in other organizations similar to the position. The interview process seemed more like they were selling the company to me than vice versa."

As for specific questions at other levels, one insider who went through two interviews to land her job was asked, "If you could describe yourself in one word, what would it be?" Another reports going through an "easy interview with two people who would become my bosses" before landing the job. A business analyst lays out a four-tier process: "The first interview with a recruiter who asks you why you want to work here and the basic behavioral questions. The second one was with the head of the group who was also the hiring manager and who asked questions about work experience. The third was with the same person as the second and it was a technical interview with a written exam. The last interview was with an executive who asked behavioral questions."

OUR SURVEY SAYS

Pick up the pace

"The culture is a bit rigid, but fast-paced," says one respondent. Other insiders are split on Countrywide's culture. One calls the firm's culture "excellent" and "ethics driven, with focus on productivity." Another agrees, saying, "It's a culture of accountability where employees are expected to work hard." Underscoring the love for the culture, yet another source says, "I really enjoy my job and co-workers." "Nice people and great co-workers," says a contact describing the culture. "And my group is very diverse." Others, though, are less pleased. "This is a good company and it tries to institute a noble culture, but with some of the managers in place, the culture cannot take hold." The contact adds that for advancement "it depends on who you know." Another source says, "I was promised training and never received it. They are full of broken promises." Yet another says, "For a long time, I really enjoyed our work environment. My co-workers were fun, and our branch manager fostered an open, friendly environment. Then the regional sales manager got involved, and everything went downhill." Manager relations, though, generally receive good marks. "My manager is great," says one source, who concedes, though, that "it does all depend on the individual manager."

The comp and the extras

Sources give compensation and benefits average ratings. "Stock options, 401(k) with matching, and an on-site gym and cafeteria" are among the extras provided. Others include two weeks of vacation per year for the first five years (higher-ups receive more), increasing to three weeks after that, eight paid holidays, one floating paid holiday and six sick days. An employee stock purchase plan is also available.

The dress code is "nice business dress," "with some unique rules." For women, shoes "must be closed in either the front or the back— no dress sandals allowed" and "if you wear a sleeveless blouse, you must keep your

Visit the Vault Finance Career Channel at **www.vault.com/finance** – with
insider firm profiles, message boards, the Vault Finance Job Board and more

VAULT CAREER LIBRARY **109**

jacket on all day." Another insider says that staffers are allowed to wear "jeans only on the last day of the month."

Hours are more or less set in stone, sources report. "All employees are expected to be at their desks by 8 a.m. every morning and not leave until after 5 p.m.," says one. And "if lunch is taken, it should not be more than an hour." A risk manager puts his normal hours as "50 to 60" per week and, during crunch times, as "60 to 70." He adds, "Even if you're here until 1 a.m. working on something, you're still expected to be in first thing in the morning." He does, though, report "rarely" coming in on the weekends.

The office space is just average, report insiders. One says that "only VPs receive offices, and the cube walls are very, very low," making it "difficult at best to have any type of a private conversation or view anything private on your computer." And one respondent notes that while "diversity efforts are big, it's not a top priority."

© 2007 Vault, Inc.

DaimlerChrysler Financial Services

Eichhornstraße 3
10875 Berlin, Germany
Phone: +49-30-2554-0
Fax: +49-30-2554-2525
www.daimlerchrysler-
financialservices.com

27777 Inkster Road
Farmington Hills, MI 48334
Phone: (248) 427-6300
Fax: (248) 427-6600
www.daimlerchrysler-
financialservices.com/na

DEPARTMENTS

Business Vehicle Financing
Consumer Leasing
Credit Cards
Dealer Financing
Fleet Financing
Municipal Financing
Owner-Operator Financing
Personal Insurance
Vocational Financing

THE STATS

Employer Type: Subsidiary of
DaimlerChrysler AG*
Chairman: Jürgen H. Walker
President & CEO, Americas: Klaus D.
Entenmann
Revenue: €17.154 billion (FYE 12/06)
No. of Employees: 11,000
No. of Offices: 100

KEY COMPETITORS

Ford Motor Credit
GMAC
JPMorgan Chase

UPPERS

• "The people"

DOWNERS

• "Increasing competition and
pressure"

EMPLOYMENT CONTACT

See "careers" section of
www.daimlerchrysler-
financialservices.com/na

Visit the Vault Finance Career Channel at **www.vault.com/finance** — with
insider firm profiles, message boards, the Vault Finance Job Board and more

VAULT CAREER LIBRARY   111

THE SCOOP

Financial driver

A global financial services provider within DaimlerChrysler AG, DaimlerChrysler Financial Services is one of the world's largest financial services providers outside the banking and insurance industries. Headquartered in Berlin, Germany, it offers flexible financial solutions customized to suit the requirements of individual customers of all vehicle brands within the DaimlerChrysler Group, as well as cross-brand fleet management. Its subsidiary, DaimlerChrysler Financial Services Americas LLC, serves as headquarters for the company's operations in the U.S., Canada, Mexico, Argentina, Brazil, Venezuela and Puerto Rico. Globally, the company manages a portfolio of approximately $147 billion through its operations in more than 40 countries; every third DaimlerChrysler vehicle sold is financed or leased by DaimlerChrysler Financial Services. DaimlerChrysler Financial Services Americas LLC has approximately 5,600 employees who manage a portfolio of more than $106 billion with nearly five million contracts.

As an entity, DaimlerChrysler Financial Services Group-which formerly just went by DaimlerChrysler Services-also shares financial service duties with Chrysler Financial, Mercedes-Benz Financial and DaimlerChrysler Truck Financial. Together, the division serves DaimlerChrysler-branded car dealer inventories as well as automobile purchases by customers.

Good news in 2006

In 2006, DaimlerChrysler Financial Services generated record profits for the fifth year in a row. Operating profit increased to €1.714 billion in 2006 from €1.468 billion in 2005. Revenues also increased to €17.154 billion in 2006 from €15.439 billion the year prior. The firm noted that "we made progress towards our goal of sustained profitable growth" due in part to the fact that the automotive finance company provided value to its automotive brand partners, its dealer body and consumers.

Socially responsible

DaimlerChrysler Financial Services strives to be a good corporate citizen in the communities in which it operates. The company is active in the areas of education, especially financial literacy, community advancement and arts and culture. Community relations focus on driving long-term positive social change.

© 2007 Vault, Inc.

Most important, DCFS employees give back to the community by volunteering their time, knowledge and skill sets. In 2005 alone, 90 percent of the entire workforce across the Americas engaged in hands-on activities in more than 40 communities.

Late-1980s discovery

The story of DaimlerChrysler Financial Services began in 1989, when the board of then Daimler-Benz AG decided to establish a financial arm, initially called Debis. In 1990, Debis was made official and divided into five business units: Systemhaus, Financial Services, Insurance Brokerage, Trading and Marketing Services. In 1991, together with Metro trading company and NYNEX, Debis founded Debitel, a network-independent telecommunications provider. In 1993, Debis played its hand at aviation, when it started an aircraft fund for private investors for the financing of A340 airbuses. By January 2005, Debis was generating 50 percent of its revenues with customers outside of Daimler-Benz.

Debis' focus began to become more centered in 1998, when Daimler-Benz AG and Chrysler Corporation merged, creating DaimlerChrysler. The next year, DaimlerChrysler announced that it was uniting its worldwide financial services under the umbrella of Debis. And a few years later, in 2001, the division became known as DaimlerChrysler Services. Also in 2001, the division found presence in the German banking market by changing the Mercedes-Benz Lease Finanz Group's name to DaimlerChrysler Bank.

Rebranding

In April 2005, the division renamed itself DaimlerChrysler Financial Services to better communicate its focus on automotive financial services for the DaimlerChrysler brands, which include Mercedes-Benz, Chrysler, Jeep and Dodge. Another name change came in January 2006, when DaimlerChrysler Services North America LLC announced it would be taking the moniker DaimlerChrysler Financial Services Americas LLC. "We believe that adding the word 'Financial' to the names of our enterprise and to our business units accurately reflects the services we offer to our automotive and truck dealers and their retail customers," said Klaus Entenmann, president and CEO of DaimlerChrysler Financial Services Americas. "Additionally, the new name signals that we are serving our manufacturing partners in the automotive and trucking industries throughout North and South America." In the Americas, the company conducts business as Chrysler Financial and Mercedes-Benz Financial. As DaimlerChrysler Truck Financial, it also finances commercial vehicles for affiliate products such as Freightliner, Sterling and Western Star. Doing business as DaimlerChrysler Insurance Company, the company provides dealers and consumers with a broad range of insurance products.

But the changes didn't stop there. In May 2007, DaimlerChrysler AG announced its plans to sell Chrysler Group to private equity firm Cerberus Capital Management of New York.

Cerberus will pay $7.4 billion to gain a majority stake of 80.1 percent in the group. (Once the transaction closes, Chrysler Financial will be part of the Chrysler Holding LLC.) Chrysler Group had been losing money, due largely to costs associated with rising pension and health costs, and partly because of this, Chrysler Group announced a restructuring plan that will cut approximately 13,000 jobs. With this plan, the firm isn't expected to turn a profit until 2009.

Heading East

In September 2005, DaimlerChrysler Financial Services received permission from the China Banking Regulatory Commission to establish a financing company in China. The new company, DaimlerChrysler Auto Finance (China), became the first captive financing company in China to offer a broad product portfolio of dealer and customer financing, insurance services for passenger cars and financial services for commercial vehicles. Headquartered in Beijing, the company has about 50 employees, and handled approximately 3,000 financing contracts in 2006.

Keep on truckin'

In October 2006, DaimlerChrysler Truck Financial, the financial services provider for Freightliner, Sterling and Western Star dealers and their customers, was named Lender of the Year at Paschall Truck Lines' annual Vendor Appreciation Day.

DaimlerChrysler Truck Financial was recognized for its ability to demonstrate clear, plain-language documentation; high levels of customer satisfaction; and two-way communications.

Pretexting in private

Not many people had heard the term "pretexting" before Hewlett-Packard came under investigation for using the practice to find a snitch in its boardroom. But according to a December 2006 account by The Wall Street

© 2007 Vault, Inc.

Journal, pretexting - pretending to be someone else to obtain coveted information, such as financial or phone records - is nothing new. Automotive finance companies sometimes retain outside vendors to provide contact information like telephone numbers or addresses to locate customers they cannot contact or collateral they cannot locate through their regular outreach activities.

Fraud alert!

When consumers across the United States were victimized by a lottery scam utilizing DaimlerChrysler Financial Services' name, the company sprang into action and alerted the public. After all, one of their executives, Andreas Hinrichs, serves as Chairman of the American Financial Services Association's (AFSA) Fraud and Identity Theft Committee. In November 2006, consumers received fraudulent letters from the so-called Ontario Lottery and Gaming Commission in Canada claiming they won $170,000. The letters contained counterfeit checks allegedly issued by "DaimlerChrysler Services" and "DaimlerChrysler Services Truck Finance" in the amount of $2,260. As part of the con, recipients were asked to deposit the check to cover a service charge of the same amount in order to receive their winnings. However, before the check cleared, recipients were requested to call a representative and, ultimately, to write a personal check for $2,260 to "finalize the payment process." Not surprisingly, the original check never cleared and the promised payout of $170,000 never arrived. In the meantime, the consumer's funds disappeared. "We care about the well-being and financial health of consumers," said Andreas Hinrichs, Chief Compliance Officer for DaimlerChrysler Financial Services Americas and AFSA Committee Chairman. "Therefore, we felt strongly about alerting the public to this ongoing criminal activity, especially when con artists victimize consumers by pretending to be associated with us." DaimlerChrysler Financial Services and DaimlerChrysler Truck Financial posted fraud alerts on their Web sites and assured consumers that it was taking steps to investigate the fraud.. Victims also were encouraged to file a consumer fraud complaint with the Federal Trade Commission.

Visit the Vault Finance Career Channel at www.vault.com/finance – with
insider firm profiles, message boards, the Vault Finance Job Board and more

VAULT CAREER LIBRARY   115

GETTING HIRED

What are you looking for?

"Are you the person we want? Are we the company you want?" asks the company on its Web site. Decisions, decisions. But don't feel too pressured, as the firm has lots of ways applicants can get a sense for the company culture while they consider their options. At the "careers" section of www.daimlerchrysler-financialservices.com/na, the firm's Americas unit site, candidates can check out an FAQ page that details the firm's philosophy, culture and training, among other useful information. Candidates can also search for openings by location, keyword and category (financial services, insurance, and customer service and call center). The site directs those looking for open positions in Canada to www.workopolis.com.

DaimlerChrysler recruits through events and campus visits at colleges throughout the U.S., and keeps an updated list that interested candidates can access on its web site.

One insider says the company also recruits through "the Internet, newspapers and headhunters."

Round and round

st candidates report going through at least two rounds of interviews with the firm. One insider reports going through three interviews, fielding questions that "focused on my previous experience and education." Another contact says their interview questions "centered on writing abilities-I had to provide samples-and my strategic vision for the position." Yet another insider reports an all-day interview in an "assessment center" with "six to seven group exercises as well as individual interviews."

And once you're extended an offer on the salaried side, watch out for "HR bluffs," one insider warns. "HR played the 'bad cop' and said that they were a 'first offer is the best offer' company, and the terms offered could not be changed. I found out after I was hired that this was not true."

© 2007 Vault, Inc.

OUR SURVEY SAYS

Talking culture

DaimlerChrysler is "a culture of talking and politics," says one insider. Another employee says that "it's a pretty good place to work," but the specific company culture "varies by department, since each department has the leeway to set the standards for hours, dress code, opportunities for advancement, etc." One employee agrees, adding that "hours and dress code are left up to individual department management."

The dress is "generally business casual," reports one insider, who adds that the hours are also good. "As long as you take care of the work you are responsible for in the time frame it needs to be done, flex-time is accepted." Other perks include the "Christmas bonus," "company-provided meals" and cars provided for work.

Move on up

Advancement opportunities are available, but employees "have to manage their own careers" and "take the initiative if the opportunity is there," says one insider, adding that "people rarely stay in the same job or department for their entire career." It's also expected within the firm that "you move to a different position every three years or so." Employees are "the drivers for opportunities for advancement," notes one insider. Another contact says that "opportunities for advancement are multiple, since DaimlerChrysler is a very global company and has many interesting departments." And largely, the culture seems to vary from department to department. While "some departments have totally empowered the workers to do the job and make decisions," others "have a more traditional, 'you-must-get-your-boss'-approval' type of management." But "generally speaking, any employee can express their opinion respectfully to any of the company's officers-they are visible and accessible."

More progress needed

The firm needs to move beyond lip service when it comes to diversity, some employees say. One employee says that "we have the same opportunities," but another insider says that "diversity and work-life balance are talked about as being valued by the company, but while progress is being made, there is still a ways to go for females and minorities." Another employee reports that "diversity

Visit the Vault Finance Career Channel at www.vault.com/finance – with insider firm profiles, message boards, the Vault Finance Job Board and more

VAULT CAREER LIBRARY   117

is heavily talked about, but even though one woman and one African American are officers, the top of the company is still overwhelmingly white males."

That said, according to the firm, of the 12 top leaders profiled on its corporate web site, three are women or an ethnic minority. In addition, the company is engaged in a number of diversity initiatives, such as a diversity council made up of senior executives within the firm as well as respected community and business leaders from across the U.S. The firm says. "The council serves as a sounding board as the company works toward a more diverse and inclusive workplace." The DCFS Inclusion Forum is a diverse group of middle management employees that addresses specific opportunities within the company. The firm also sponsors seven employee resource groups and a number of diversity committees, and employees and temporary workers are required to complete several diversity and inclusion training courses, through which employees learn the principles of diversity and inclusion.

© 2007 Vault, Inc.

DST Systems

333 W. 11th Street
Kansas City, MO 64105
Phone: (816) 435-1000
Fax: (816) 435-8618
www.dstsystems.com

DEPARTMENTS

Brokerage Subaccounting
Business Process Management
Distribution Support & Financial
  Intermediary Solutions
Healthcare Solutions
Integrated Customer
Communications & Output
International Asset Management &
  Portfolio Accounting
International Shareholder & Investor
  Recordkeeping Solutions
Outsourcing Solutions
Retirement Plan Solutions
U.S. Mutual Fund Shareholder
Recordkeeping
Wealth Management

THE STATS

Employer Type: Public Company
Ticker Symbol: DST (NYSE)
President & CEO: Thomas (Tom) A.
McDonnell
Revenue: $2.24 billion (FYE 12/06)
Net Income: $272.9 million
No. of Employees: 10,500

KEY COMPETITORS

Misys
PFPC
SunGard

UPPERS

• Flexible hours

DOWNERS

• Diversity hiring efforts could be
  better

EMPLOYMENT CONTACT

See "careers" section of
www.dstsystems.com

Visit the Vault Finance Career Channel at **www.vault.com/finance** — with
insider firm profiles, message boards, the Vault Finance Job Board and more

VAULT CAREER LIBRARY   119

THE SCOOP

Dippin' DST

Founded in 1969 as a division of Kansas City Southern Industries, DST Systems was established to develop an automated recordkeeping system for the mutual fund industry. Today, it is the largest provider of third-party shareholder recordkeeping services in the U.S., with over 10,000 employees and about $2.24 billion in revenue in 2006. In December 2006, a Prudential analyst downgraded DST, noting, according to the Associated Press, "There are few organic catalysts that could drive company growth, which forces the company to rely heavily on new account wins, which have been scarce."

Jack of two trades

DST Systems operates in two segments: financial services and output solutions. The financial services segment provides information processing, and computer software services and products to mutual funds, investment managers, insurance companies, health care providers, banks, brokers, financial planners, health payers, third-party administrators and medical practice groups. Its software systems include mutual fund shareowner and unit trust recordkeeping systems for U.S. and international mutual fund companies; a defined-contribution participant recordkeeping system for the U.S. retirement plan market; and investment management systems to U.S. and international investment managers, and fund accountants. This segment also provides a business process management and customer contact system to mutual funds, insurance companies, brokerage firms, banks, cable television operators, health care providers and mortgage servicing organizations; recordkeeping systems to support managed account investment products; health care processing systems and services to health payers, third party administrators and medical practice groups; and recordkeeping systems to support consumer risk transfer programs.

The output solutions segment provides integrated print and electronic statement, and billing output solutions. It also offers various related professional services, including statement design and formatting, customer segmentation and personalized messaging tools. The output solutions segment also provides electronic bill payment and presentment solutions, and computer output archival solutions.

© 2007 Vault, Inc.

Acquiring Amisys

In October 2006, DST Systems' Birmingham-based DST Health Solutions subsidiary completed the acquisition of Amisys Synertech (ASI) for an undisclosed sum. Amisys, an enterprise software developer, software applications service provider and business process outsourcer for the commercial health care industry, employs about 1,400 people at three offices in Pennsylvania, Maryland and India. The company reported 2005 revenue of $103.4 million and as of September 2006, had amassed more than $65 million year-to-date. Following the close of the deal, the integrated companies began operating as DST Health Solutions.

Healthy hires

DST Health Solutions made a different kind of investment in June 2006, when it appointed three leading health care information technology veterans: Robert Thompson, as vice president of sales, marketing and account management; Rob Kennedy, as vice president for information technology; and Joey White, as officer for strategic investment and research development.

Thompson leads efforts to enhance the DST Health Solutions information technology brand in the health care payer and provider markets, to increase sales, and to deliver extraordinary customer service to its 300-plus clients. Before joining DST Health Solutions, he managed multimillion-dollar sales and marketing operations in manufactured products, software, consulting and service industries in a sales career spanning more than 25 years. Most recently, he was vice president of McKesson's corporate solutions group.

Rob Kennedy directs DST Health Solutions' efforts to enhance and maintain the technology framework for both new and existing clients. Additionally, he provides oversight for the development of service-oriented architecture components that allow customers to leverage existing technology investments while adding new capabilities. Kennedy's 25 years of experience in the health care IT industry have included positions with Aetna, First Consulting Group, McKesson, Humana and most recently, UnitedHealth Group.

Joey White is charged with leading strategic research and development of DST Health Solutions' new products, including development of service-oriented-architecture frameworks. These frameworks include components that add functionality to administrative processing for payers transitioning to the consumer-directed healthcare market, as well as an integration platform that will facilitate the evolution from legacy to service-oriented-architecture

Visit the Vault Finance Career Channel at www.vault.com/finance – with insider firm profiles, message boards, the Vault Finance Job Board and more

VAULT CAREER LIBRARY 121

technologies. Because these components can integrate with most legacy systems, they allow health plans to upgrade at their own pace.

GETTING HIRED

Search it

The careers section of www.dstsystems.com allows applicants to search current openings for all DST groups, from DST Systems positions to DST Health Solutions and DST Realty jobs. Job seekers can also submit their resumes to the company for consideration for potential openings. The career site also lays out the training programs, advancement opportunities, benefits and diversity efforts offered.

OUR SURVEY SAYS

Anything for customer love

The culture is "relaxed," says one insider. Another says that it's a culture where "the customer is always right no matter what," adding that "we will do absolutely anything to keep the customer happy." In addition, the firm "prides itself on maintaining a flat management organization," where "promotions and transfers are achievable, but very few promotions represent an actual advancement because day-to-day responsibilities won't change." Plus, "actual advancement typically occurs without a promotion or salary change." Another says simply, "opportunities for advancement are not great."

And while the hours are "flexible," notes one respondent, "10 to 15 hours of unpaid overtime per week is the norm, and there are situations that typically last three to six months where 60 to 70 hours of unpaid overtime are required." Another says that "employee morale is often difficult to gauge," and that "during periods of high stress and overtime, morale descends deeply for several months. That said, generally only a very small section of the company is experiencing that stress and overtime. Most of the time, most of our employees are very satisfied with their jobs." Sources also laud the "business casual" dress code.

© 2007 Vault, Inc.

Developing diversity

The firm could definitely expand its diversity efforts, insiders say. One adds says that "diversity is almost nonexistent" within the company. Another says that DST "hires regardless of race, creed, color, religion or gender," but "while there are females in upper management, there are no minorities."

Visit the Vault Finance Career Channel at **www.vault.com/finance** – with
insider firm profiles, message boards, the Vault Finance Job Board and more

VAULT CAREER LIBRARY   **123**

The Dun & Bradstreet Corporation

103 JFK Parkway
Short Hills, NJ 07078
Phone: (973) 921-5500
Fax: (973) 921-6056
www.dnb.com

DEPARTMENTS

Business Development
Finance
Global Technology
Human Resources
Marketing
Product Management
Sales Operations
Strategy

THE STATS

Employer Type: Public Company
Chairman & CEO: Steven W. Alesio
Ticker Symbol: DNB (NYSE)
Revenue: $1.5 billion (FYE 12/06)
Net Income: $240.7 million
No. of Employees: 4,350

KEY COMPETITORS

Acxiom
Equifax
infoUSA

UPPERS

• Professional culture

DOWNERS

• Some managers "play favorites"

EMPLOYMENT CONTACT

See jobs @ D&B at www.dnb.com

© 2007 Vault, Inc.

THE SCOOP

D&B is B-to-B

The Dun & Bradstreet Corporation (known as D&B) mainly provides business-to-business insight on public and private companies. Its aspiration is to "be the most trusted source of commercial insight so our customers can decide with confidence." Its commercial database includes information on over 100 million companies. Information is culled from a variety of sources, including management interviews, accounts-receivable information, state filings and news services. D&B sells this business credit information, and additionally, offers marketing information and purchasing support services.

D&B's D-U-N-S (Data Universal Numbering System) system was developed and is regulated by D&B. The system assigns a unique numeric identifier to a single business entity. The number provides information about the company, including addresses, sales, number of employees, market research, mailing lists, new product development and corporate family trees. A DUNS number is required for many government transactions.

Two pioneers merge

The history of Dun & Bradstreet begins in 1841, when Lewis Tappan, a noted abolitionist, formed his Mercantile Agency in New York. This agency served as a way for wholesalers and importers to rate customer credit. In 1859, this business was taken over by Robert Dun, whose *Dun's Book* listed information on over one million businesses by 1886. The company's biggest rival at the time was the John M. Bradstreet Company. In 1933, the two companies merged, and took on the name Dun & Bradstreet in 1939.

Some of Dun & Bradstreet's notable acquisitions have included Reuben H. Donnelley Corp., publisher of the *Yellow Pages*, in 1961. In 1962, Moody's Investor Service became part of D&B. Moody's eventually developed the largest private database in the world, and this information was used to create Dun's Financial Profiles in 1979.

In the 1970s and 1980s, Dun & Bradstreet bought additional information and publishing companies, including AC Nielsen, Hoover's Inc. and McCormack & Dodge. By the 1990s, however, poor performance suggested D&B had overreached. The company began to shed its subsidiaries, including AC Nielsen, Cognizant (which included Nielsen Media Research and IMS Health and Nielsen Media Research), R.H. Donnelley and Moody's.

After spinning off subsidiaries, D&B returned to focusing on providing business insight, helping businesses manage credit exposure, find profitable clients and convert prospects to clients. Customers include over 90 percent of the Fortune 1000 companies, as well as thousands of small and medium-sized businesses.

Changing of the guard

In October 1999, Chairman and CEO Volney Taylor retired amid shareholder pressure to put the company on the block. Allen Loren was then brought in to serve as chairman and CEO and succeeded in making strong headway, which ultimately resulted in a steadily rising stock price.

In January 2005, Loren passed the CEO baton to then-president Steve Alesio and completely retired from D&B later that year. The company has started to focus heavily on web-enabled information tools. The 2003 acquisition of Hoover's, a subscription-based business information company, is one example of this strategy. D&B has also given its traditional products a stronger web presence—the company's credit reporting business is now largely web-based.

Going global

In 2005, D&B increased its risk management business when it acquired LiveCapital, a provider of online credit management software, for $16 million. International operations, both by acquisition and divestitures, are also a large part of D&B's current focus. A series of purchases in Italy, such as the 2003 acquisition of controlling interests in three Italian real estate data companies, have strengthened D&B's position in that country.

Also, D&B sold its operations in Denmark, Finland, Norway and Sweden to Bonnier Business Information in 2003. Bonnier now operates those businesses under D&B's name, and provides D&B access to its business information databases.

In November 2006, D&B announced that it signed an agreement with Huaxia International Credit Consulting Co. Ltd., a provider of business information and credit management services in China, to establish a joint venture that will trade under the name Huaxia D&B China.

Overall, D&B's strategy appears to be paying off. D&B's full-year revenue grew to $1.5 billion from $1.4 billion a year prior. Meanwhile, net income for 2006 grew to $240.7 million from $221.2 million in 2005. In addition, the

© 2007 Vault, Inc.

firm's stock price has increased 500 percent over the past six years. D&B Chairman and CEO Alesio said of the results, "we are pleased with our 2006 financial performance, as we once again met or exceeded each of our guidance metrics and delivered our sixth consecutive year of strong earnings growth."

GETTING HIRED

Pick a category, any category

Go to the Jobs at D&B link at www.dnb.com, and search job listings in categories such as sales, technology, marketing, finance, operations, customer service and human resources. While you're there, in addition to applying for positions, you can learn about the firm's company culture ("focused on winning in the marketplace and creating shareholder value," in case you were wondering) and the benefits offered.

OUR SURVEY SAYS

Home sweet home

The firm is "good with flexibility and work-at-home" options, says one New Jersey insider, and since "there are many employees commuting from New York or Pennsylvania," the culture is "very supportive" of working at home. Another source in the Greensboro, N.C., office says the culture is "very professional," adding that the office promotes a "good casual environment" and is "generally business casual" with "casual 'jeans days' when the office hits sales milestones."

Opportunities to advance vary, however. One contact says that "there have been some years where I have had no people reporting to me and my prospects seemed slim. Then, other years with a different leader, it was completely different. It also really depends on what kind of year the company is having as well as who you work for." Morale tends to get down at times, reports an insider, who explains, "The worst part of working here is that they have tremendous turnover. I have probably been though more than six rounds

Visit the Vault Finance Career Channel at www.vault.com/finance – with
insider firm profiles, message boards, the Vault Finance Job Board and more

VAULT CAREER LIBRARY   127

of layoffs and restructuring since I've worked here, and many employees are left wondering when they will be next."

Perks get generally good marks, though. One insider says that "D&B's benefit package is generous compared to similar companies in its industry." The office space gets a thumbs-up, too. The cubes are "fairly decent and everyone except the senior leadership team is in them, so it's not so bad." But the firm's diversity efforts could be better, sources say. One insider notes, "There's not a whole lot of diversity compared to other companies I have worked at."

© 2007 Vault, Inc.

Equifax

1550 Peachtree St. NW
Atlanta, GA 30309
Phone: (404) 885-8000
Fax: (404) 885-8055
www.equifax.com

DEPARTMENTS

Marketing Services
North America Information Services
Personal Solutions

THE STATS

Employer Type: Public Company
Ticker Symbol: EFX (NYSE)
Chairman and CEO: Richard (Rick) F. Smith
Revenue: $1.55 billion (FYE 12/06)
Net Income: $274.5 million
No. of Employees: 6,900
No. of Offices: Locations across 13 countries

KEY COMPETITORS

D&B
Experian Americas
TransUnion

UPPERS

• "People are very friendly"

DOWNERS

• Average salaries

EMPLOYMENT CONTACT

See "careers" under "about Equifax" section of www.equifax.com

Visit the Vault Finance Career Channel at **www.vault.com/finance** — with
insider firm profiles, message boards, the Vault Finance Job Board and more

VAULT CAREER LIBRARY   129

THE SCOOP

Securing customers for over a century

In business since 1899 and called Equifax since 1975, this Atlanta-based company enables and secures global commerce through its information management, marketing services, direct-to-consumer, commercial and authentication businesses. In plain English, Equifax is a credit-reporting agency. It gathers data, and compiles and processes them utilizing its proprietary software and systems, and distributes them to customers in various formats. Equifax's products and services include consumer credit information, information database management, marketing information, business credit information, decisioning and analytical tools, enabling technologies and identity verification services. The company's mission is to enable businesses to make informed decisions about extending credit or service, mitigate fraud, manage portfolio risk and develop marketing strategies. Equifax also helps consumers manage and protect their financial affairs through a portfolio of products that it sells directly via the Internet and in various hard copy formats. As one of the nation's largest credit reporting agencies, Equifax has information on more than 400 million credit holders worldwide. It services clients across industries, including financial services, retail, health care, telecommunications/utilities, brokerage, insurance and government industries.

Equifax reported $1.55 billion in revenue in 2006, up from $1.44 billion in 2005. Net income also rose to $274.5 million from $246.5 million a year earlier. Equifax Chairman and CEO Richard F. Smith said that the firm "met or exceeded the guidance provided in all areas." Equifax was named by *Fortune* magazine as one of America's Most Admired Companies in March 2007.

Financial techies

In November 2006, Equifax was named to the 2006 FinTech 100 list by *American Banker* and Financial Insights. The company placed 26th on this annual listing of technology companies that derive more than one-third of their revenue from the financial services industry. Companies are selected based on their primary business, key application solution or vertical industry, and 2005 total annual revenue.

© 2007 Vault, Inc.

"This accolade demonstrates our strong commitment to developing and introducing new technologies to give our customers a competitive edge in today's marketplace," said Rob Webb, Equifax's chief technology officer, in a company press release.

Equifax has earned a strong reputation in the marketplace for its continued investment in new technologies. Nearly 1,000 organizations, including some of the world's largest banks, financial institutions and many of the top utility companies use Equifax technology. In fact, 30 of the top-50 banks, and four of the top-five telecommunications companies rely on Equifax's decisioning solutions.

Adding TALX, Austin-Tetra

In May 2007, Equifax acquired TALX Corp. in a stock and cash transaction valued at approximately $1.4 billion. Based in St. Louis, TALX provides employment verification and related human resource/payroll services, serving over 9,000 clients in the U.S., including 385 companies in the Fortune 500. TALX provides a wide variety of products and services, including employment and income verification, pay reporting, hiring and employment tax management services. The company said the acquisition of TALX is aligned with its long-term growth strategy of expanding into new markets and acquiring proprietary data sources.

In October 2006, Equifax expanded its commercial information business by acquiring Fort Worth, Tex.-based Austin-Tetra, a privately held provider of business-to-business data management solutions for FORTUNE 1000 companies and government agencies, in an all-cash transaction. Austin-Tetra leverages a proprietary database of more than 30 million global businesses, with information aggregated from more than 300 information sources. In a third-quarter 2006 earnings release, Equifax CEO Rick Smith called the Austin-Tetra acquisition "an integral part of our long-term growth strategy, complementing our commercial information business."

Equifax in 2010

Rick Smith went into more detail about the company's long-term strategy at a September investor conference. At the event, Equifax brass outlined how the company plans to build on the strengths of its current core business model, and then implement a long-term strategy based on four pillars: Deepen its relationships with existing customers; provide unique and differentiated data; build on its capabilities to offer enabling technologies and predictive sciences; and target emerging opportunities, through organic growth, acquisitions or geographic expansion. The company identified initiatives with potential

Visit the Vault Finance Career Channel at www.vault.com/finance – with
insider firm profiles, message boards, the Vault Finance Job Board and more

VAULT CAREER LIBRARY   131

incremental revenue in each of those areas, and outlined the application of the corporate strategy to its North America information services, marketing services, personal solutions, Europe and Latin America business units. By 2010, the firm hopes to achieve compound annual growth in revenue of 7 to 10 percent from organic market growth, core organic growth initiatives and new markets, adjacencies and mergers/acquisitions; earnings-per-share growth in excess of 10 percent; and cumulative cash from operations in excess of $1.9 billion.

Seasoned pros

Lee Adrean was appointed Equifax's CFO in October 2006, replacing the retiring Donald T. Heroman. Adrean, who most recently was CFO for NDCHealth Corporation, joined Equifax on October 4 and will take over officially when Heroman's retirement begins on June 1, 2007. "We're delighted to welcome Lee Adrean as our new CFO," says CEO Rick Smith, in a press release. "Lee is a seasoned executive whose financial track record with Fortune 500 companies is the ideal fit for Equifax as we continue to strongly execute against our smart growth strategy." Prior to NDCHealth Corporation, Adrean held senior level positions at such companies as EarthLink, First Data Corporation, Providian Corporation, Bain & Company, and the former Peat, Marwick, Mitchell & Co. (now KPMG).

In May, 2006, Smith hired another seasoned pro, Coretha Rushing, to oversee human resources. Rushing brought 25 years of human resources experience to Equifax. She recently served as senior vice president of human resources at The Coca-Cola Company where she led all human resource functions. In addition, from BellSouth, Smith brought on board Joseph ("Trey") Loughran, to spearhead Equifax's mergers and acquisitions growth strategy. At BellSouth, Loughran held a number of leadership positions, including, most recently, managing director of the company's corporate strategy and planning department. During his five years there, he also served as executive director of marketing in BellSouth's Interconnection Services unit, a $4.1 billion wholesale division of the company.

GETTING HIRED

Get choosy

Never say you don't enough don't have enough choices in life. Equifax lists jobs ranging from decision sciences, enabling technologies and sales on the career

© 2007 Vault, Inc.

section of www.equifax.com. You can be choosy geographically as well, because the company lists an assortment of openings across the U.S. and Canada.

If asked to come in for an interview, keep in mind that it's a large firm with many offices, so there's no cookie-cutter hiring route. One insiders says that after being "contacted by a tech recruiter," a telephone interview was set up within 24 hours. "The phone interview was very simple and straightforward—mainly a screening. Then I got a face-to-face interview the following day." And though the contact says she "only interviewed with the hiring manager," the turnaround was quick. She says, "I was notified I had the job before I got home, and after taking the drug test and the reference checks," the deal was sealed.

OUR SURVEY SAYS

Fair enough

One insider in the Alpharetta, Ga., office calls the corporate culture "fair," adding that "the people are very friendly" and while it's "fairly laid-back," it may be due to the fact that there's "primarily tech folks" in that particular office. The dress code is "casual always, unless you go to headquarters at midtown, which is rare."

Salaries get average marks. One insider notes that although the "base salary for business analysts and project managers vary," the range tends to be "from mid-$60K to over $90K." The contact goes on to add, "I was offered between $85K to $90K with an annual bonus of 10 percent, which was based partly on performance incentive and partly on company incentive. But there were no signing bonuses or anything like that."

"Other kinds of diversity"

"There aren't a lot of minorities in senior management," comments one insider. Another says that "there are other kinds of diversity now that so many employees from India are at Equifax now, because of the outsourcing. So in that sense, there are other kinds of diversity."

The firm's outlook looks bright. Several sources comment positively about the relatively recent addition of CEO Richard Smith in 2005. One insider says, "The future of the company looks good," and Smith "seems to really know what he's doing."

Visit the Vault Finance Career Channel at **www.vault.com/finance** – with
insider firm profiles, message boards, the Vault Finance Job Board and more

VAULT CAREER LIBRARY   **133**

Fannie Mae

3900 Wisconsin Ave., NW
Washington, DC 20016-2892
Phone: (202) 752-7000
Fax: (202) 752-6014
www.fanniemae.com

THE STATS

Employer Type: Public Company
Ticker Symbol: FNM
Chairman: Stephen B. Ashley
President & CEO: Daniel H. Mudd
Revenue: $50.1 billion (FYE 12/05)
Net Income: $6.3 billion
No. of Employees: 6400
No. of Offices: 78

KEY COMPETITORS

Countrywide Financial
Freddie Mac
Wells Fargo

UPPERS

• "Work/life environment is excellent"

DOWNERS

• "Hierarchical" and "very
  bureaucratic" at times

EMPLOYMENT CONTACT

See the "careers" link at
www.fanniemae.com

© 2007 Vault, Inc.

THE SCOOP

Fannie's wide reach

Fannie Mae is the financial services company that likes to tug at your heartstrings. The company's slogan proclaims, "Our Business is the American Dream," and its mission is to increase opportunities for home ownership among low- and middle-income Americans. Originally a government agency under Franklin D. Roosevelt's New Deal, Fannie Mae (Federal National Mortgage Association, or FNMA) was created in 1938 to boost and replenish the supply of loan money for mortgages, thereby helping to stimulate the economy in the wake of the Great Depression. Today, Fannie Mae is a public, shareholder-owned company—and a large one at that. Fannie Mae is one of the leading sources of financing for home mortgages. Since 1968, the company has provided more than $7 trillion in financing to over 73 million families. Fannie Mae has helped finance more than one in every five home loans in the U.S.

Fannie Mae operates under a federal charter, which grants it special rights and responsibilities. Under the charter, the company is required to increase liquidity in the residential mortgage finance market and promote access to mortgage credit throughout the country. In return, Fannie Mae is exempt from SEC registration requirement and state and local income taxes, and enjoys other privileges as well. Fannie Mae and its corporate cousin Freddie Mac (created in 1970 to break Fannie Mae's monopoly) are the only two Fortune 500 companies not required to report any sort of financial difficulty to the public. In July 2002, Fannie Mae registered with the SEC voluntarily and irrevocably in response to federal pressure on corporate leaders to step up their financial disclosures. However (and partly as a result of this concession), Fannie Mae securities remain exempt from registration.

The SEC cracked down on Fannie Mae in December 2004 for accounting problems, demanding it restate three-and-a-half years of earnings reports. Federal regulators fined Fannie Mae $400 million in May 2006 for allegedly cooking the books to boost the bonuses of the firm's executives. Three months later, after millions of man hours and an army of consultants sifted through the mountains of data, the company announced that 2004 losses would be "significantly smaller" than its previous estimate. Fannie Mae completed the restatement and filed its 2004 10-K with the SEC in December 2006. Six months later, in May 2007, the company filed its 2005 10-K. Fannie Mae has posted a cautionary note on its site, noting that the firm has filed its revised 2004 and 2005 information with the SEC but "investors and others should not rely on Fannie Mae's annual and quarterly financial statements issued prior to December 2004."

First in the secondary

Fannie Mae operates in what is known as the secondary mortgage market. The primary market consists of institutions like mortgage companies, commercial banks, savings and loan associations or credit unions. These groups are the ones that conduct transactions directly with borrowers. The lending institution then has the option to either hold the mortgage in its portfolio or to sell the mortgage into the secondary market. By selling the debt to another entity, the primary lender recoups its money and is able to extend another loan. Some of Fannie Mae's rivals in the secondary mortgage market include pension funds, insurance companies, securities dealers and other financial institutions. By setting certain restrictions on the size and terms of the mortgages that it purchases, Fannie Mae encourages primary lenders to make more funds available to low- and middle-income borrowers.

Trouble brewing

Investors got jittery in October 2003, when Fannie Mae announced that it had miscalculated its mortgage equity by $1.2 billion and would have to restate its third-quarter earnings. In late 2003, the company's regulator, the Office of Federal Housing Enterprise Oversight (OFHEO), launched an investigation into the firm's accounting practices. In its report, OFHEO alleged that Fannie Mae was manipulating its figures to report steady earnings, meet targets and entitle top management to bonuses. In February 2004, then then-Federal Reserve Chairman Alan Greenspan expressed concerns about the size and power of Fannie Mae and its corporate cousin, Freddie Mac, which has been under investigation for its accounting practices since 2003.

In September 2004, the SEC launched an inquiry into Fannie Mae's accounting practices. While downplaying the issue, Fannie Mae delayed its reporting of third-quarter earnings. In addition, the Justice Department started a criminal investigation of the company, and at the request of lawmakers, the inspector general at the Department of Housing and Urban Development investigated the possibility of political influence on the OFHEO report.

The results were stunning. In December, the SEC required Fannie Mae to restate its prior financial statements dating back to 2001 to eliminate the use

© 2007 Vault, Inc.

of hedge accounting and to correct for errors in accounting for deferred purchase price adjustments. The OFHEO also raised questions about the company's accounting. That launched a complete re-audit of all aspects of the company's financial statements from January 2001 through June 30, 2004. The company hasn't reported timely results since mid-2004. In August 2006, the U.S. Justice Department discontinued its investigation and said the it does not plan to file charges against the company.

Despite the turmoil, Fannie Mae's work on behalf of the little guy continues. Over 58 percent of all multifamily units financed by Fannie Mae were reserved for special affordable (low and very low income), and over 59 percent of all loans were made in underserved markets.

Changes at the helm

Daniel H. Mudd replaced CEO Franklin Raines, who was forced to retire in December 2004. Mudd, the former president and CEO of GE Capital, Japan, was first installed as an interim replacement before being named permanently to the post in June 2005. To address the obvious problems with internal control over financial reporting, Mudd and the management team dumped KPMG as the company's auditor and replaced it with Deloitte & Touche, reorganized the company's finance area and hired a new controller, a new chief audit executive and several new senior accounting officers.

GETTING HIRED

Dream a little dream

Fannie Mae outlines its "American dream commitment" on its web site, and if your version of the American dream happens to include an interest in helping people find affordable housing, Fannie's got plenty of opportunities available for you. But beware. According to one insider, the firm is "very selective, since only looking for people with several years of experience." Expect several interviews. "The initial interview is with an HR person," says one source, "then you'll meet with a line manager, and then you'll have several interviews with peers." Another contact went through an "interview with the hiring manager in the central program management office" before landing a job. Specific questions he received included, "Describe your background in financial services and comfort using analytical tools to understand and communicate the big picture," "Describe specific examples where you led projects throughout the lifecycle," "Describe your level of expertise using Excel, MS Project and other MS Office tools for analysis and reporting," and "Describe your willingness to often work beyond 5 p.m."

A source who went through three rounds describes the process at length: "First I had a phone interview with a recruiter, who asked basic recruiting questions and was quick to the point and very resume-based. The second round, I had [a] personal interview with the recruiter followed by an interview with the prospective manager who asked about previous work experience as pertained to the job. The final interview was with a VP in HR that was more of a formality than an actual interview." The contact adds, "It seemed important that the applicant know and ask about the company and its vision, and understand their place in the mission."

At the "careers" section of the firm's web site, candidates can search for available positions and apply online. In addition, they can read extensively about the firm's career development opportunities (think lots of internal training and tuition reimbursements), health benefits, financial benefits (an equally long list with offerings such as an "employer-assisted housing benefit to help defray the cost of purchasing a home") and family benefits (i.e., "time off for new parents includes 10 to 12 weeks paid maternity leave, four weeks paid paternity leave and four weeks paid leave for adoption"). Those eligible can also take 10 hours per month to volunteer in the community. In addition, candidates can download a brochure that outlines the pluses of working at Fannie Mae, along with the benefit offerings.

OUR SURVEY SAYS

Positioned for gain

Insiders say Fannie Mae has a "strong business outlook" and a "strong competitive advantage in the mortgage securities markets due to asset size, market position, diversity of products and use of technology products that help mortgage bankers make loan decisions more quickly." Sources also note that "while it's prestigious to work for Fannie Mae," "they don't offer the most competitive salaries," and the culture can be "hierarchical" and "very bureaucratic" at times. One insider simply says that Fannie Mae is "not a well-run organization at all." However, the "new CEO, Dan Mudd, is on an

© 2007 Vault, Inc.

internal campaign to refresh the corporate culture towards an openness to bring issues to the table and make decisions, eliminating as much as possible the big-company bureaucracy." Indeed, the corporate culture is "very governmental, inflexible and consensus-oriented, but it is changing due to continual and meaningful efforts by upper management." Still, at the moment, the "corporate culture is fairly conservative, especially when it comes to challenging status quo."

But the "work/life environment is excellent," says one source," with great acceptance and understanding of family and personal time." And the dress code is "casual and relaxed, as are the hours." Indeed, the hours are "reasonable" and sources report "rarely" working weekends. Some sources, though, aren't so pleased with managers. One insider says, "Unfortunately, management is out of date with cutting-edge management techniques." Another adds that "if upper management can flush out the middle management inefficiencies within, then the company looks like an extremely promising place to work in the coming years."

Diversity with respect to women is looking pretty promising as well, and generally receives high marks. But with respect to minorities, diversity receives merely average grades. "There's lots of talk about diversity, but there's the same old group of white guys at the top."

Overall, one source says the best thing about working for Fannie Mae is definitely the "benefits." He adds, "I also personally feel good about our core business and how it affects others."

Fidelity National Financial

601 Riverside Avenue
Jacksonville, FL 32204
Phone: (888) 934-3354
www.fnf.com

DEPARTMENTS

Claims Management
Specialty Insurance
Title Insurance

THE STATS

Employer Type: Public Company
Ticker Symbol: FNF (NYSE)
Chairman & CEO: William P. Foley II
Revenue: $9.436 billion (FYE 12/06)
No. of Employees: 19,500
No. of Offices: 1,500

EMPLOYMENT CONTACT

www.fnf.com/FNF/careerops.htm

© 2007 Vault, Inc.

THE SCOOP

New name, new structure

In November 2006, Fidelity National Title Group, Inc. (FNT) changed its name to Fidelity National Financial, Inc. (FNF). Fidelity National Financial had been the name of FNT's parent holding company; the name change followed a decision to eliminate the holding company structure and create an independent company. Fidelity National Financial has approximately 1,500 offices in 49 states and the District of Columbia, plus agent operations in Guam, Puerto Rico, Canada, Mexico and the U.S. Virgin Islands.

Headquartered in Jacksonville, Fla., Fidelity National provides title insurance, specialty insurance and claims management services. Its title insurance underwriters (Fidelity National Title, Chicago Title, Ticor Title, Security Union Title and Alamo Title) make up the Fidelity National Title Group. Fidelity's specialty insurance business, Fidelity National Property and Casualty Insurance Group, offers homeowners, auto, personal and flood insurance. Its claims management services (including workers' compensation, disability and liability and claims services) are operated through its subsidiary, Sedgwick CMS, which serves corporate and public sector entities. FNF was ranked No. 248 on the 2006 Fortune 500 (up from its 2005 spot at No. 261).

Undaunted by disaster

The giant that is Fidelity National Financial was born in 1847 when a young Chicago law clerk named Edward Rucker created a system for tracking documents and legal proceedings related to real estate titles. Rucker's system saved attorneys the laborious task of searching official records in connection with transfers of real property. This service helped develop what would later become Chicago Title. One year later, over in California, a San Francisco notary public named C.V. Gillespie began the company that would eventually become Fidelity National Title Insurance.

Both men's firms played important roles in American history: Chicago Trust employees risked their lives to save records from the devastating 1871 Chicago fire (their efforts led to the creation of the Cook County land records system). And when the great earthquake struck San Francisco in 1906, Gillespie's successors and their wives rescued huge bundles of title records— a good thing, as San Francisco's own Hall of Records and City Hall were

Visit the Vault Finance Career Channel at **www.vault.com/finance** – with insider firm profiles, message boards, the Vault Finance Job Board and more

VAULT CAREER LIBRARY   141

completely destroyed. Chicago Title and Fidelity underwent a series of mergers and acquisitions in the ensuing decades; in 2000 their paths came together with Fidelity's purchase of the Chicago Title Corporation and its many subsidiaries. This merger made Fidelity the biggest title insurance entity in the world.

Top ratings

Fidelity is rated A by Standard & Poor's and Fitch Ratings, A- by A.M. Best Co. and A3 by Moody's. At the end of 2005, *Fortune* magazine placed Fidelity on its list of America's Most Admired Companies; it was ranked No. 5 in the mortgage services category. Fidelity made its debut on the Fortune 500 in 2002, and its ranking on the list has increased each year.

In 2006, Fidelity reported full-year results of $9.436 billion, down from $9.654 billion in 2005. Net income dropped, too, from $964 million in 2005 to $437 million in 2006. Total assets dipped as well, to $7.26 billion in 2006 from $11.01 billion in 2005. Chairman and CEO William Foley blamed the decline in profitability in part due to "a reduction of Hurricane Katrina-related flood claims processed, as well as an increase in fire- and weather-related claims."

Linking up

In 2005 Fidelity acquired ServiceLink, the nation's foremost provider of centralized mortgage and residential real estate title and closing services for institutional lenders and major financial institutions. ServiceLink began in 1997 with five employees and grew into the largest closing management company in the country, with over 700 employees. ServiceLink was integrated into Fidelity's title insurance business, and at the same time the firm's title business was designated Fidelity National Title Group (FNTG). Randy Quirk, former FNTG president, was named CEO of the newly-expanded FNTG.

The newest addition

Sedgwick Claims Management Services (Sedgwick CMS) is the latest addition to the Fidelity family, following a January 2006 buyout. Fidelity and two partner private equity firms acquired a controlling stake in Sedgwick, and under the terms of the deal Sedgwick became an independently organized business division under the Fidelity umbrella. With headquarters in

© 2007 Vault, Inc.

Memphis, Sedgwick boasts more than 1,200 clients (including 28 members of the Fortune 100) and an annual revenue of approximately $600 million.

GETTING HIRED

Just the facts

While the firm doesn't provide a lot of information regarding career opportunities on its web site other than a listing of open full-time and temporary slots and descriptions, candidates can check out available positions by job title as well as location at www.fnf.com/FNF/careerops.htm. And for those who prefer a slightly more personal touch, the firm has you covered—it lists its national human resources number as (800) 815-3969.

Visit the Vault Finance Career Channel at **www.vault.com/finance** – with insider firm profiles, message boards, the Vault Finance Job Board and more

V/\ULT CAREER LIBRARY   **143**

First Data Corporation

6200 S. Quebec Street
Greenwood Village, CO 80111
Phone: (303) 967-8000
Fax: (303) 967-6701
www.firstdata.com

DEPARTMENTS

First Data Commercial Services
First Data Financial Institution
  Services
First Data International

THE STATS

Employer Type: Public Company
Ticker Symbol: FDC (NYSE)
Chairman & CEO: Henry C. "Ric"
Duques
Revenue: $7.08 billion (FYE 12/06)
No. of Employees: 29,000

UPPERS

• "Wonderful benefits" and
  "competitive compensation"

DOWNERS

• Not very cohesive culture due to
  mergers

EMPLOYMENT CONTACT

www.firstdata.com/careers/index.htm

© 2007 Vault, Inc.

THE SCOOP

A child of the '60s

The Mid-America Bankcard Association (MABA), a nonprofit bank card processing cooperative, was launched in Omaha in 1969. In 1971, First Data Resources (FDR), a for-profit processing service made up of 110 employees, was created to serve MABA. FDR was bought by American Express Information Services Corporation in 1980; First Data was spun off from Amex and went public in 1992. Three years later it merged with First Financial Management Corporation (FFMC). This new entity had three business units: card issuers' services, merchant services and consumer services. Western Union, the famed wire transfer and telegram company, became part of First Data in conjunction with the FFMC merger.

First Data expanded rapidly from 2001 to 2005, engaging in a series of acquisitions overseas and in the U.S. A 2004 merger with Concord EFS brought the STAR Network (with 1.9 million ATM and retail locations) under the First Data umbrella. The company also grew its international businesses, launching operations in Europe, Asia and Latin America. Today First Data is based in Colorado with offices in 35 states, plus employees who telecommute and work at vendor sites. Its international operations are conducted in 61 global locations.

The nature of the businesses

First Data's business in the U.S. is conducted through two core groups, First Data Commercial Services (FDCS) and First Data Financial Institution Services (FDFIS). FDCS offers credit card processing, debit card processing (through the STAR Network), gift and pre-paid card issuing (through ValueLink), electronic check guarantee and verification services (through TeleCheck), payroll cards (through MoneyNetwork) and Internet commerce and mobile terminal solutions.

FDFIS is made up of eight separate product lines: First Data Resources (which offers comprehensive card transaction processing), Output Services (responsible for mailing company offers and reports, as well as plastic card printing and embossing), First Data Debit Services, Integrated Payment Systems, REMITCO (remittance processing, including electronic deposit services), First Data Voice Services (which develops and implements speech

Visit the Vault Finance Career Channel at **www.vault.com/finance** – with insider firm profiles, message boards, the Vault Finance Job Board and more

VAULT CAREER LIBRARY   **145**

recognition software), First Data Health Care Services and First Data Utilities.

First Data's clients include grocery stores and pharmacies, gas stations and convenience stores, restaurants, retailers, financial institutions, travel and entertainment companies, e-businesses, automotive companies, professionals, government agencies, health care companies and utilities.

Big, bigger, bigger

In 2005 and 2006, First Data continued its path of growth by acquisition. In 2005, it bought FinecoBank's credit card processing unit. It also purchased EuroProcessing International and Korea Mobile Payment Services, thereby greatly extending its global reach. First Data kept rolling into 2006, developing a partnership with ABN AMRO to provide global payment processing. It also acquired German firm GZS and a new check processing company called ClearCheck Services.

The (temporary) return of Ric

Henry C. "Ric" Duques originally joined First Data's board of directors in 1989, going on to serve as the firm's chairman from 1989 to 2003 and as CEO from 1989 to 2002, leading the firm through its 1992 IPO. In November 2005, First Data CEO Charles T. Fote (who was also the president and chairman of the board) resigned abruptly, having come under fire for falling stock prices. His replacement? Ric Duques, who agreed to take the top spot for two years while First Data sought a permanent replacement. The executive changeover was accompanied by a cut of nearly 1,000 employees in the firm's card issuing business, which had been lagging behind its other sectors.

Telegrams: stop

On January 26, 2006, First Data announced that it would spin off Western Union, allowing it to become an independent publicly traded company. The next day Western Union announced that it would no longer provide telegraph and communications services: e-mail and fax services had put a dent in that century-old business. Instead, it would focus on its money transfer businesses, which reap nearly $3 billion in revenue each year.

© 2007 Vault, Inc.

Liked on the lists

First Data won plenty of recognition in 2006, ranking No. 2 in the financial services industry on *Fortune*'s Most Admired Companies list. It also ranked No. 224 on the Fortune 500 list and No. 99 on Standard & Poor's 500. The Forbes 2000 ranked First Data No. 248 based on its scores in sales, profits, assets and market value.

GETTING HIRED

It's all in who you know

If you happen to have contacts within the company, milk 'em—insiders say the best way to get an interview with First Data is to name drop. One respondent reports applying "several times for positions, but I failed to get even one interview or callback until I had someone that I knew who worked there intercede on my behalf." The tactic seems to work wonders. "Once they had my name, they pursued me actively." Another source reports being "recruited by the sales manager who knew me when we had worked together previously" and therefore, "there was no interview." One insider (without a friend within the firm) reports going through three interviews, "one with the application and a test, and then later, two interviews with two different HR coordinators," adding, "All were very professional."

Another contact paints a different picture of the hiring process, calling the interviews "very informal" and the process "loose and disorganized." Ultimately, says the insider, the company "took forever to make a decision," and "then the offer letter had a different amount than the verbal offer, and we had to work through that." Yet another reports having gone through a "phone interview first, then an in-person panel interview was scheduled, but only one of the panel interviewers showed up. I was also warned by the interviewer how difficult the 18-month probationary period would be."

Visit the Vault Finance Career Channel at **www.vault.com/finance** – with
insider firm profiles, message boards, the Vault Finance Job Board and more

VAULT CAREER LIBRARY   147

OUR SURVEY SAYS

Running the gamut

The firm culture "really varies by location," one insider notes, adding that "First Data has purchased so many companies and has not done a very good job of blending the cultures." A source says, "Because of the poor job of combining their many 'companies' into a cohesive 'team,' many employees feel neglected, not treated with equal respect, and pressured to work long hours and to not take their paid time off days." Another says, "The job is extremely stressful due to the nature of our business of credit and debit card processing," adding, "If one of the merchants is down and cannot process, we have a time-critical situation on our hands." One contact gives kudos to the culture, however, calling it "a flexible environment and a corporate culture that cares about employee satisfaction."

The "wonderful benefits," "competitive compensation" and "lax" dress code all get high marks. But insiders have a beef with the "limited advancement opportunities." One insider expounds, saying there's "not much opportunity for advancement," but "lots of opportunities to learn." The hours, however, are long. An insider who works from home reports working "at least 12-hour days." Others say there are "lots of over 40-hour weeks for all levels," and "overtime for exempt salaried employees is expected without question." And one insider notes that staffers are "frequently assigned to new positions without consultation." Diversity efforts could also stand a little work, employees say. Although one insider reports that there's a "diverse workforce," another calls the culture "male-dominated."

© 2007 Vault, Inc.

Fiserv

255 Fiserv Drive
Brookfield, WI 53045
Phone: (262) 879-5000
Fax: (262) 879-5013
www.fiserv.com

DEPARTMENT

Depository Institution Processing
Financial Institutions
Investment Support Services
Payments & Industry Products
  Insurance

THE STATS

Employer Type: Public Company
Ticker Symbol: FISV (NASD)
President & CEO: Jeffery W. Yabuki
Revenue: $4.54 billion (FYE 12/06)
Net Income: $450 million
No. of Employees: 23,000
No. of Offices: 261

UPPERS

• Entrepreneurial culture

DOWNERS

• More diversity needed

EMPLOYMENT CONTACT

www.fiserv.com/careers.htm

Visit the Vault Finance Career Channel at **www.vault.com/finance** — with
insider firm profiles, message boards, the Vault Finance Job Board and more

VAULT CAREER LIBRARY   149

THE SCOOP

From small banks to big business

Founded in 1984, Fiserv began as a provider of financial service data processing for small banks. The company went public two years later and grew into a regional processor, serving larger banks and credit unions. By the 1990s, Fiserv's clients included some of the country's biggest financial institutions, and its services expanded to include electronic funds services, card fulfillment, securities transaction processing, insurance, business process outsourcing (BPO), software and systems solutions and health benefits. Fiserv is headquartered in Wisconsin with approximately 245 offices nationwide and more than 16 offices internationally. International operations are carried out through its Fiserv CBS Worldwide unit, which serves clients in 50 countries.

As of 2007, Fiserv reported serving more than 18,000 clients worldwide and was ranked No. 486 on the Fortune 500 list. Fiserv operates in three segments: financial institution services, insurance services and investment support services.

Buy, buy, Fiserv

Fiserv embarked on a "growth-by-acquisition" path in 2005, snapping up mortgage banking software business Del Mar Database, the U.S. e-lending business of Emergis, electronic bill services firm BillMatrix and underwriting software provider VerticalPoint, among others. This trend continued in the first half of 2006 with Fiserv's purchases of CareGain, a consumer health plan software provider; the Missouri-based Jerome Group LLC, a provider of critical business communications solutions; Insurance Wholesalers, a California company that generates leads for mortgage and life insurance sales; and the assets of CT Insurance Services & CCH Wall Street. In the second half of 2006, Fiserv purchased InsureWorx and Innovative Cost Solutions. In 2007, Fiserv purchased antifraud and compliance company NetEconomy to delve deeper into the risk, compliance and antifraud financial services area.

Get on Traxx

Who wants to deal with piles of paper bills? Fiserv responded to client demand for better online bill payment systems in August 2006 with the

© 2007 Vault, Inc.

launch of its proprietary Paytraxx system, designed to help financial institutions manage online payments quickly and securely. A 2006 study by Forrester Research showed that 27 million American households pay bills online; that number is expected to grow to 47 million by the year 2010. With Paytraxx, Fiserv's clients can implement and customize online billing-or revamp an outdated online billing system—all financial information processed through Fiserv's dedicated TruServ certified data center. Through Paytraxx, nearly all of the firm's financial units work with the same system to serve clients.

Paytraxx is an example of changes occuring firmwide at Fiserv described as Fiserv 2.0, a company initiative to make its 75 business units work more closely together to serve clients' needs. Fiserv President and CEO Jeff Yabuki spearheded Fiserv 2.0. Yabuki, who came on board in November 2005, was the first CEO from outside the original four companies that came together to launch Fiserv. Yabuki spent six months reviewing the firm's business, policies and culture before unveiling Fiserv 2.0 in September 2006. According to the firm, Fiserv 2.0 "changing the way we do business. We're breaking down internal silos, and focusing on our clients' needs. We have restructured our divisions, and hired a number of top executives in the last year from outside the firm."

Tops in tech

In November 2006, Fiserv announced that it had been ranked No. 1 in the *American Banker* and Financial Insights FinTech 100 for the third consecutive year. This annual list ranks companies by revenue earned by providing technology services to the financial services industry, and is the only such ranking of its kind in the world. Companies that earn more than one-third of their total annual revenue from technology services sales to financial clients are eligible for consideration.

The MISMO seal of approval

Two of Fiserv's key software programs, easyLENDER and UniFi PRO Loan Origination Software, received certification from automated underwriting systems by the Mortgage Industry Standards Maintenance Organization (MISMO) in the fall of 2006. Both products had previously been certified for credit and mortgage insurance, and are designed to help reduce mortgage costs and increase speed and accuracy in underwriting approvals. According to the Mortgage Banking Association, MISMO ratings are a critical part of data standard-setting in the mortgage industry, ensuring fewer errors and better connectivity between lenders and borrowers.

Taking care of claims

Fiserv's health care practice is one of its fastest-growing segments. The October 2006 purchase of Innovative Cost Solutions (ICS), a health care claims resolution company, further increased Fiserv's heath cost management capabilities (Fiserv already had a division called ppoONE that specialized in repricing in-network PPO claims). Under the terms of the deal ICS would operate as a company within Fiserv's health specialty solutions practice, and would continue to be based in its Chicago offices. Fiserv's health care practice includes plan and benefits management, business process outsourcing services and software products.

An Allegient alliance

In November 2006, Fiserv formed a strategic alliance with Allegient Systems, a Connecticut-based firm that pioneered the use of legal expense and performance management systems for law firms and corporate law departments. The partnership will give Fiserv clients access to Allegient's legal bill auditing and business analysis services. Fiserv's existing claims applications will be integrated with Allegient's bill review applications. Fiserv clients will also be able to use Allegient's auditing interfaces and tools used to analyze legal spending patterns.

GETTING HIRED

Industry insight

Insiders report that the hiring process at the firm "varies by position," but has one thing in common—having "financial services industry experience is an important criteria." Another says that "the interview process itself was fine, but the information provided to me over the phone from the HR office in California was different from the actual information, such as the place I was to show up for my interview." And after the interview, "it took a very long time for HR to get back to me on the decision, and even longer to get the necessary paperwork mailed back and forth." According to Fiserv, a new

© 2007 Vault, Inc.

executive vice president of human resources came on board in April 2007, with plans to update the HR practices and streamline the hiring process.

OUR SURVEY SAYS

Entrepreneurial culture

The company culture is "very entrepreneurial." "I really enjoyed working with my specific co-workers," notes one contact, "and enjoyed the actual work we produced, even though the hours were horrid." Another source says he has an "outstanding" relationship with his manager, and one respondent says the best aspects about the firm are "the great co-workers" and "opportunity for advancement." Not everyone feels the same, though. One insdier says the firm "does not like 'new blood,'" and "there are opportunities for advancement only through longevity and being a favorite." And others say the firm needs to best up its diversity efforts. But according to the firm, with the introduction of its Fiserv 2.0 initiative in September 2006, it's "ramping up our diversity efforts," and two recent hires (Rahul Gupta, group president of payments, and Bridie Fanning, executive vice president of HR) are "great examples of it."

Fitch Ratings

1 State Street Plaza
New York, NY 10004
Phone: (212) 908-0500
Fax: (212) 480-4435
www.fitchratings.com

DEPARTMENTS

Algorithmics
Derivative Fitch
Fitch Training

THE STATS

Employer Type: Subsidiary of Fimalac
President & CEO: Stephen W. Joynt
No. of Employees: 2,400 (worldwide)
No. of Offices: 50 (worldwide)

KEY COMPETITORS

DBRS
Moody's
Standard & Poor's

UPPERS

• Great perks, such as "subsidized
  membership at New York Health &
  Racquet"

DOWNERS

• Might be more "title-oriented in its
  structure and more bureaucratic"
  than its predecessor firms

© 2007 Vault, Inc.

THE SCOOP

Making the grades

Founded by John Knowles Fitch as the Fitch Publishing Company in 1913, Fitch was one of the early leaders in providing financial statistics. The Fitch rating system of "AAA" to "D," introduced in 1924, has become the standard for the financial community. Fitch, one of the four major credit rating agencies (the others are Moody's, Standard & Poor's and DBRS), is the leader in providing ratings on debt issued by companies, covering entities in more than 80 countries. The firm is dual-headquartered in New York and London.

In 1997, Fitch became a subsidiary of Fimalac, a large French business support services company, when it merged with London-based IBCA Limited, Europe's largest rating agency. In 2000, Fitch acquired both Duff & Phelps Credit Rating Co. and Thomson BankWatch, thereby boosting its coverage and international personnel.

Fitch Ratings currently maintains coverage of more than 5,900 financial institutions, including 3,194 banks and 2,430 insurance companies. Finance and leasing companies, broker-dealers and managed funds make up the remainder of Fitch's financial institution coverage universe. Additionally, Fitch rates over 1,400 corporate issuers, 100 sovereigns, and 140 sub-sovereigns and maintains surveillance on over 86,000 U.S. municipal transactions.

In addition, the company currently has over 5,900 U.S. structured finance transactions under surveillance, comprising 3,597 RMBS pools, 470 CMBS and 1,897 ABS deals. Fitch also maintains surveillance on more than 890 European and 250 Asia-Pacific structured finance transactions.

Derivatives, risk and training

In October 2006, Fitch established Derivative Fitch, a rating agency dedicated to providing ratings and services for the CDO and credit derivatives markets. Derivative Fitch, a wholly owned subsidiary of Fitch Ratings, has over 1,700 global credit derivatives under surveillance.

Algorithmics, a member of the Fitch Group, is the world's leading provider of enterprise risk solutions. More than 300 financial institutions rely on Algorithmics' software, analytics and advisory services to make risk-aware

Visit the Vault Finance Career Channel at **www.vault.com/finance** – with
insider firm profiles, message boards, the Vault Finance Job Board and more

VAULT CAREER LIBRARY **155**

business decisions, maximize shareholder value and meet regulatory requirements. Supported by a global team of risk experts based in major financial centers, Algorithmics offers solutions for market, credit and operational risk, as well as collateral and capital management.

Based in London, Fitch Training provides financial analytic training with a specialization in credit, corporate and structured finance.

The Enron surprise

After the Enron scandal of 2001, the three main rating agencies came under close scrutiny for their failure to expose the crisis. The rating agencies, in turn, claimed that Enron had provided them with misleading information. In 2002, during the Senate hearing on the crisis, the SEC announced plans to launch a thorough investigation into the practices of the three agencies. And later in 2002, similar scandals erupted at WorldCom and Global Crossing, and the agencies were once again questioned for their failure to expose the problems. In late 2004, corporate CFOs, as well as lawmakers, were putting pressure on the SEC to increase governmental oversight of credit rating agencies. Pressure on rating agencies has increased in Europe as well, in response to a crisis at Parmalat and other companies.

Some think competition could help regulate the agencies. Until 2003, the only firms authorized by the SEC to provide credit ratings for companies were Fitch Ratings, Moody's and Standard & Poor's. But in February 2003, the SEC approved a fourth: Toronto-based Dominion Bond Rating Service (DBRS), whose CEO, Walter Shroeder, has a reputation for outspokenness and had already blown the whistle on several firms, including Bombardier, Telus Corp. and Roger Communications.

Zeroing in

At the beginning of 2005, Fitch Group, Fitch Ratings' parent company, paid $175 million to acquire Algorithmics, an enterprise risk management company. With the purchase, Fitch's top brass is hoping to expand the customer base and product offerings of its existing risk management services. Algorithmics merged with Fitch Risk Management when it was acquired. In August 2005, Fitch further expanded its risk expertise when it acquired ValuSpread, a credit derivative pricing data business, from Lombard Risk Management.

© 2007 Vault, Inc.

On a corporate level, the deals reflect Fimalac's strategy of turning Fitch Group into its primary source of growth, development and earnings. Fitch Group, which includes Fitch Ratings and Algorithmics, represents approximately $600 million in revenue. In June 2005, Fimalac sold off home furnishing subsidiary Cassina. Fimalac also has plans to divest its Facom Tools and Beissbarth units, which primarily manufacture tools and tool cabinets for the automotive industry.

Breaking out with Prism

Fitch had a busy 2006. In May, the firm launched a commercial real estate collateralized debt obligation group headed by Jenny Story, a senior executive in the commercial mortgage-backed securities group. The company rolled out a dynamic economic capital model, called Prism, in July that it will start using in 2008. Fitch will initially use Prism in its analysis of life, nonlife and health insurers in the U.S., U.K., France and Germany before expanding into other countries. Prism uses simulations to create thousands of economic scenarios. The key selling point of the system is that it can compare companies in different regions and businesses.

In October 2006, the company launched a new credit derivatives focused agency, Derivative Fitch, to focus on structured finance securities and collateralized debt obligations, which are bonds backed by other bonds or derivatives. Derivatives are one of the fastest growing segments of the capital markets. The company wanted to provide users with a package of portfolio analytics that is broader than traditional credit ratings, said CEO Stephen Joynt. The new venture was also launched to facilitate joint ventures, acquisitions or mergers with other financial data providers, Joynt added.

GETTING HIRED

Get the lowdown

Discover detailed job descriptions for job listings in eight countries when you log on to the "careers" section of www.fitchratings.com. Applicants can browse a list of current openings by location, along with contact information for each job. The site also provides a link to information on the firm's U.K. Graduate Recruitment Program, a two-year rotational program in corporate finance, structured finance or financial institutions in London. According to

Visit the Vault Finance Career Channel at **www.vault.com/finance** – with insider firm profiles, message boards, the Vault Finance Job Board and more

VAULT CAREER LIBRARY   157

the firm, program participants "will be provided with extensive formal and informal training and development, given the opportunity to study for the Chartered Financial Analyst qualification, and participate fully in the day-to-day operations of the company." Additionally, depending on a participant's progress, "advancement into an analytical role on completion of the program may be available."

Prospective candidates for the program can download an application online. According to one insider, analysts can expect to go "through three rounds of interviews: the first with the department head, then with other analysts and finally with a managing director." Another reports going through a "phone interview, then in-office interviews with five people holding different positions within the firm, from analyst to managing director."

OUR SURVEY SAYS

Taking it easy

The company culture is "very easygoing," says one respondent. Others note that the firm is steadily staking its own claim on the ratings frontier. "Since Fitch is the result of mergers and acquisitions of four smaller rating agencies, the corporate culture is only now starting to become more unified." Insiders say the new Fitch might be more "title-oriented in its structure and more bureaucratic" than its predecessor firms, but "as a much larger organization now, Fitch is paying more attention to in-house training." The firm "provides tuition reimbursement for relevant course work and covers the costs associated with taking the CFA" exam. The working hours are "reasonable," with some saying they put in the "occasional late night," but "not usually more than once a week.

The company dress code also gets high marks, with insiders calling it "casual always except for client contact" and "business casual unless you have a meeting or are traveling outside of the office for meetings." Additionally, the firm offers all the standard benefits, and then some. "One great special perk is a very subsidized membership at New York Health & Racquet," says a source, "which is across the street from Fitch's offices." Insiders say "as a worldwide organization, Fitch has a diverse workforce," and "among analysts, Asians are probably the most prominent minority group."

 © 2007 Vault, Inc.

As for advancement opportunities, "there are a lot of really qualified, great analysts at Fitch, and advancement depends on having the opportunities to excel in various situations, and these opportunities vary from department to department."

Visit the Vault Finance Career Channel at **www.vault.com/finance** – with
insider firm profiles, message boards, the Vault Finance Job Board and more

VAULT CAREER LIBRARY

159

Ford Motor Credit Company

The American Road
Dearborn, MI 48126
Phone: (313) 322-3000
Fax: (313) 323-2959
www.fordcredit.com

THE STATS

Employer Type: Subsidiary of Ford Motor Company
Chairman & CEO: Michael Bannister
Revenue: $17.25 billion (FYE 12/06)
Net Income: $1.3 billion
No. of Employees: 13,000

EMPLOYMENT CONTACT

See www.mycareer.ford.com/main.asp

© 2007 Vault, Inc.

THE SCOOP

Financing solutions

An indirect, wholly owned subsidiary of Ford Motor Company, Ford Motor Credit was incorporated in Delaware, in 1959, so that Ford dealers could provide competitive financing services to individuals and businesses interested in buying cars. The company's true origins, however, took place about 40 years earlier, when founder Henry Ford sought to discourage excessive consumer borrowing by devising layaway plans to keep his $265 Model Ts rolling off the lot; this tactic sowed the seeds for Ford Motor Credit to later make ownership possible for customers unable or unwilling to meet the entire up-front cost of a car. The company finances cars and trucks for buyers through Ford, Lincoln, Mercury, Jaguar, Land Rover, Mazda, Aston Martin and Volvo dealerships, making it one of the world's largest auto financing companies. It finances new, used and leased vehicles and provides wholesale financing, mortgages and capital loans for dealers. The company also offers individual and business fleet financing, and its insurance operations offer extended service contracts, automobile insurance, wholesale inventory insurance, and credit, life and disability insurance.

But times have been tough for Ford Motor Company, and it's been throwing ballast overboard in order to stay afloat. On November 28, 2006, Ford Motor Company announced its intention to mortgage nearly all of its North American operations to raise loans of $18 billion; for the first time in its 103-year history, it offered its manufacturing equipment, cars and subsidiaries as a guarantee in return for financing. Its cash call will bring in $15 billion of secured loans to replace an existing unsecured borrowing facility of $6.3 billion, and it will raise an additional $3 billion of loans on the capital markets that could include notes transferable into shares. The money will be spent on implementing a radical restructuring, including 45,000 job cuts and the closure of 16 plants in the U.S.; analysts said the move was indicative of the depth of the company's financial problems, and the company was downgraded by the three major credit rating agencies. Persistently high gas prices and changing consumer preferences also took their toll on the company throughout 2006, though a recent drop in gasoline prices has somewhat revived flagging interest in new SUVs.

According to Dow Jones in late 2006, "Ford Motor Credit is in a much better position to ride out its credit rating downgrade than it would have been several years ago. The [company] tightened its lending policies and improved loan servicing as part of a turnaround at the beginning of the decade. And it is no longer dependent on commercial paper and other unsecured debt to raise the money it lends."

North American restructuring

In September 2006, Ford Motor Credit announced that 59 branches would be merged with six existing service centers to consolidate U.S. originations, dealer credit, wholesale operations and servicing functions. Dealers will continue to be served by sales personnel located in their markets, and consolidated operations will provide dealers with extended hours of service and faster contract approvals. In addition, operating costs will be reduced through global cost reductions, North American restructuring and salaried personnel reductions of about 2,000 positions. The move was a continuation of the company's decade-long global business transformation. In the 10 years, Ford Motor Credit had restructured operations in Australia, Germany, Japan, Mexico, North America and the U.K. Since 2003, the company has closed nearly 110 branches in the U.S. and Canada.

Down but making progress

Ford Motor Credit booked net income of $1.3 billion in 2006, down from $1.9 billion in 2005. The decline was largely due to higher borrowing costs and depreciation expenses, as well as lower average receivables. Despite the drop in earnings, Chairman and CEO Mike Bannister said in a press release that the firm "made good progress on several fronts this year, notably our solid funding and strong liquidity, our focus on global cost reduction and our plans to restructure our North American operations." He did, though, add that the firm also expects lower earnings in 2007 "due to margin and volume pressures, and lower credit loss reserve reductions."

GETTING HIRED

Pop quiz

For those who may not know what area they're an ideal fit for, the company provides a detailed questionnaire on its career web site that, upon completion, will "show you jobs that match your interest." Or if you're looking for

© 2007 Vault, Inc.

something a little more general, you can read about the training and development programs that Ford runs, get a full list of benefits offered to staff, read about requirements to land a job, look for open positions and submit a resume. For the Ford Motor Credit College Recruiting and Development Program, which the firm calls an "entry-level professional position," the firm says it's looking for "bright, enthusiastic, team-oriented individuals who fully understand modern business principles and quality-conscious consumers." The program lasts 18 to 24 months and "prepares you for supervisory positions in business centers," according to Ford Motor Credit. "You will receive a solid foundation, working with customers in one of our business centers, with training that includes classroom instruction and on-the-job training in different functions and positions, culminating in leadership training and experience."

The company also hires recent graduates as dealer services analysts or team leaders at business centers throughout the U.S. and Canada. According to Ford Motor Credit, "These are positions where you will not only learn the basics of the automotive finance business, but you will also be given tremendous responsibility and empowerment." Ford says the requirements for these jobs include "a bachelor's degree, preferably in finance, marketing, management, business administration or economics; a minimum GPA of 3.0; and a willingness to relocate."

The firm's benefits are plentiful and include "comprehensive medical," "dental," "life insurance and disability plans," "company-participating savings plans," "pay-for-performance programs" and a "retirement investment program." Ford Motor Credit also offers "employee discounts" on its products, "tuition assistance" and "group rates on auto, home and liability insurance." In addition, the company says it offers staff "the opportunity to relocate to challenging jobs in exciting locations throughout North America and around the globe," recommending candidates "make sure your passport is up-to-date."

OUR SURVEY SAYS

Tough to move up

Though one insider calls the firm "a very good company to work for," others give different feedback. One warns that "you can stay with the company and be a top performer for eight years with no promotions at all." The contact goes on to advise "I do not recommend working for them as benefits have also been considerably reduced." However, the firm notes, "Our benefits continue to be competitive with, or better than, the leading companies in the nation."

And while salary increases "are OK to start," "as soon as you start making over $40,000, they will tell you that your raise is only 1 or 2 percent because you are at the upper salary of your pay grade level, which means no pay by performance anymore." That said, according to the firm, "Employees are eligible for incentive pay, in addition to their base pay, which reflects their performance." There are different job classifications and pay grade categories, and staffers can move up through those levels based on their performance. "Most employees are in a higher grade," says the firm, "including participants in the Ford Credit College Recruitment and Development Program."

© 2007 Vault, Inc.

Freddie Mac

8200 Jones Branch Drive
McLean, VA 22102-3110
Phone: (703) 903-2000
www.freddiemac.com

THE STATS

Employer Type: Public Company
Ticker Symbol: FRE (NYSE)
Chairman & CEO: Richard F. Syron
Revenue: $5.2 billion (FYE 12/06)
Net Income: $2.2 billion
No. of Employees: 5,398 (full time)
No. of Offices: 12

KEY COMPETITORS

Citigroup
Countrywide Financial
Fannie Mae

UPPERS

• "Very friendly, intelligent and easygoing" culture

DOWNERS

• "Environment is highly political"

EMPLOYMENT CONTACT

www.freddiemac.com/careers/index.html

Visit the Vault Finance Career Channel at **www.vault.com/finance** — with insider firm profiles, message boards, the Vault Finance Job Board and more

VAULT CAREER LIBRARY   165

THE SCOOP

Big Mac

You would be hard-pressed to find a company with more power on Capitol Hill than Freddie Mac. The firm was born out of Congressional legislation in 1970 and remains a government-sponsored enterprise with a heavy hand in the U.S. residential market. The firm is a publicly traded enterprise that purchases conventional mortgages from mortgage banks, mortgage companies, credit unions, online lenders and thrifts (including savings banks and savings and loan associations), and then securitizes these mortgages. By doing so, the firm transfers the financial risk from those lending institutions, and as a result, helps increase homeownership in the U.S. This, in turn, lowers mortgage rates across the board, increases the number of mortgage finance options to homebuyers and attracts investors to support America's mortgage lending needs.

The firm enjoys many advantages that go along with being chartered by the government, including implied federal government guarantee of its debt and exemptions from some state and local taxes. Further contributing to its success is the perception that Freddie Mac would receive federal bailout if it ran into dire financial straits. Additionally, the firm has a back-up credit line with the U.S. Treasury for $2.25 billion, which Freddie Mac has never used.

The birth of Fannie Mae's "little" brother

In the late 1960s, the U.S. mortgage market was highly volatile, due to a wide disparity in interest rates from city to city. Also, due to the risky nature of mortgage loans, banks were conservative in their underwriting of properties, making mortgage loans harder for the average citizen to get. Neither the government nor the private banking sector alone could address the nation's housing finance needs.

In 1970, just two years after chartering the Federal National Mortgage Association (Fannie Mae), Congress chartered The Federal Home Loan Mortgage Corporation (Freddie Mac), both loosely named after their acronyms. Freddie Mac, along with its sister company, was formed "to provide stability in the secondary market for residential mortgage, to respond appropriately to the private capital market, to provide ongoing assistance for the secondary market for residential mortgages and to promote access to mortgage credit by increasing liquidity of mortgage investments." Today

© 2007 Vault, Inc.

Freddie Mac and his big sister hold more than $1.4 billion in mortgage portfolios.

The firm purchases single-family and multifamily residential mortgages and mortgage-related securities, which it finances primarily through the issuance of mortgage pass-through securities and debt instruments in the capital markets. By buying mortgages, Fannie Mae and Freddie Mac increase the amount of capital in the housing market.

At the same time, the two institutions purchase a share of mortgages from low- and moderate-income and central-city homebuyers. By purchasing these higher risk mortgages, lenders are encouraged to make loans to lower-income consumers, thus expanding homeownership. Together, Fannie and Freddie provide approximately half of the mortgage market's cash.

Congress steps in, sort of

In 1992, Congress, concerned about the dramatic growth of Fannie Mae and Freddie Mac and the massive effect the firms could have on the housing market, created the Office of Federal Housing Enterprise Oversight (OFHEO) to regulate the two companies' safety and soundness; the Department of Housing and Urban Development regulates their housing mission activities. Although Freddie Mac's charter exempts it from SEC registration, the company has voluntarily committed to register once it becomes timely in its financial reporting. Freddie Mac is not exempt from the investor protections provided under the antifraud provisions of the federal securities laws (that is, investors in Freddie Mac securities have the same stringent protections under federal law that investors in all other companies have).

Insiders say that Democrats, who took control of Congress in the 2006 mid-term elections, are not as inclined as Republicans to crack down on Fannie and Freddie. OFHEO chief James B. Lockhart III wants Congress to give his office the power it has given federal bank regulators and to free OFHEO from the congressional appropriations process. Lockhart claims that the powerful siblings could use their clout in Congress to trim OFHEO's budget, making it less effective. He also wants OFHEO to be able to sell either company should one of them tank, which could make the markets more aware of the companies' subordinated debt.

Another family scandal

Like its sister, Freddie Mac has also been involved in creative accounting. In early 2003, Freddie Mac announced that it would have to restate its past three years' financial statements as a result of past understatement of its earnings to reduce volatility. In short, Freddie Mac's executives managed gains on derivatives trades, deferring profits to future years. The results of the firm's restatement were announced on November 21, 2003. Freddie Mac had to pay a $125 million penalty in a settlement with regulators.

The net cumulative effect of the restatement through December 31, 2002 was an understatement of the company's net income of about $5 billion, which included $4.4 billion for 2000, 2001 and 2002 combined, plus $600 million related to periods prior to 2000. The scandal subsequently led to Freddie Mac becoming the subject of an SEC investigation. In September 2006, the company announced that the criminal probe was over, adding that the U.S. Attorney's office hadn't contacted the company in more than two years. No charges were filed by the attorney's office against Freddie Mac, however, OFHEO said it was "pursuing enforcement actions against former Freddie Mac executives." The company is trying to get back on track with regular financial reporting and in March 2007, announced full-year results for 2006.

The accounting scandal also led to Freddie Mac being slapped with a shareholder lawsuit led by the Ohio Public Employees Retirement System. Freddie agreed to a $410 million settlement in April 2006.

In August 2006, Freddie Mac agreed to pay $4.65 million to settle a class-action lawsuit relating to its 401(k) and the accounting scandal filed by the Department of Labor. The lawsuit claimed that the company violated the Employee Retirement Income Security Act because the heads of the plan provided false information to participants and poorly managed the fund. Freddie Mac didn't admit it did anything wrong, and the settlement was covered by insurance.

Management shakeout

The scandal also led to management changes. In June 2003, CEO Leland Brendsel, along with Freddie's president and CFO, was forced out. Brendsel was replaced by Gregory Parseghian, who a couple months later was forced to resign when OFHEO directed Freddie Mac's board to replace him. In December 2003, the company named Parseghian's successor, Richard F. Styron, who remains chairman and CEO today. In September 2005, Freddie Mac entered into a stipulated consent order with OFHEO to settle action

© 2007 Vault, Inc.

against the company. Under the terms of the order, Freddie agreed to produce certain documents and make available any current employees that OFHEO requests to interview in connection with its ongoing administration actions against ex-CEO Brendsel and ex-CFO Vaughn Clarke. The company also agreed to seek recovery of $24.4 million in severance benefits and stock awards received by Brendsel, as well as $750,000 in departure benefits from Clarke.

CFO Martin F. Baumann, who joined the company in March 2003 after the accounting scandal, resigned three years later. The company replaced him with Anthony "Buddy" Piszel, who was tapped to take the reins as vice president and CFO on Nov. 15, 2006.

Public service

Following the hurricane disasters in late 2005, Freddie Mac granted a three-month suspension of mortgage payments for those affected by Katrina, and a two-month suspension for those affected by Rita. The suspension was then extended to March 2006. The temporary suspension applies to every borrower with a Freddie Mac-owned single-family mortgage within FEMA-designated zones, regardless of the condition of their home. Following the suspension period, servicers had the discretion to continue suspending or reducing payments on the mortgages for an additional nine months on a case-by-case basis, depending upon each borrower's specific circumstances. In addition, Freddie Mac servicers were instructed not to report to credit bureaus any reversed and suspended payments on Freddie Mac-owned loans as a result of the hurricanes. They were also told to suspend all late fees, collection and foreclosure activities in the storm-affected areas during the suspension period, and that they have the option not to advance interest on any Freddie Mac mortgage granted forbearance under the company's special hurricane policies.

As far as full-year results for 2006, Freddie Mac saw an increase in net income to $2.2 billion, up from $2.1 billion in the previous year. Revenue dropped, however—to $5.2 billion in 2006 from 2005's $5.6 billion. Syron said in a statement that "deteriorating house prices, regional job losses and increasing mortgage payments" are making it difficult for families to stay in their homes.

Visit the Vault Finance Career Channel at www.vault.com/finance – with
insider firm profiles, message boards, the Vault Finance Job Board and more

VAULT CAREER LIBRARY   169

GETTING HIRED

Meet the Mac

Learn about the firm's career development plan, read employee testimonials and learn about benefits the firm offers on the career section of its web site at www.freddiemac.com/careers/. Candidates can also search for positions by location and job category. The firm also lists its extensive benefit offerings, career development programs and upcoming events for prospective employees at various colleges.

Freddie Mac runs a summer internship program for college students pursuing careers in finance, economics, accounting and IT. To recruit for its internship program, Freddie Mac visits several universities, including Duke, Carnegie Mellon, Hampton, James Madison, Maryland, Virginia, Virginia Tech and the University of Puerto Rico. Additionally, the firm advertises its internships at numerous other schools.

For full-time seekers, "there could be different numbers of interviews for different people going for the same job," says one insider. Another source went through "one round of interviews with staff, a manager, and a VP who I would be working with." He says, "the interviews were pretty standard and behavioral-based, looking for information on my experience, ethics and how I approach problem solving." An analyst agrees, adding, "If you use common sense, they're easy."

OUR SURVEY SAYS

To serve man

Freddie Mac's culture is "very friendly, intelligent and easygoing," comments one contact, adding that it's a "great place for serving both the communities and Wall Street." But insiders have varying opinions on Freddie Mac's corporate culture. Some say it's "very academic and not strategic at all," while others think it's "pretty open and very intellectual." At least one insider calls it "family-friendly," and another ays, "Morale is very low, especially in the HR, single family and multifamily divisions, and it's become worse since several senior executives were ousted." The one thing most sources agree on

© 2007 Vault, Inc.

is Freddie Mac's at least somewhat "political" nature. One insider even goes as far as saying, "For someone seeking employment there, I would advise that he or she is aware that the environment is highly political, and to keep any new ideas under wraps until very strong relationships have been secured with key players." A few other sources echo this opinion. One observes, "Opportunity depends on [how tenaciously you] network and how visible your work is, as well as who you work for." Another says that while "the mainstream employees are great, mostly kind and educated," management "treats everyone like babies—so all the hard work done by others only results in photo ops for the upper management." Another insider adds, "Accountability is rare, so if you want to get tenured, this is a great place to work. But if you are looking to make a difference, look elsewhere."

Just OK on comp

Sources have mixed reactions when it comes to salaries at Freddie. "My salary was fair," says one director. "It was a base of $108,000 plus 12 percent bonus. I did not get any special perks, but they do have an excellent relocation plan." Another respondent says, "Salaries vary widely even by position. For the highest levels, don't expect much over $100,000 a year. But the total package is good." One insider says, "Pay raises are lousy, except for those in management, who rate each other highly and then tell support staff that their salaries have to be compared against others in similar positions." The source adds, "So while one person works their butt off and the other does nothing, you can't get a decent raise or promotion because you 'have to compare your salary to others in your position.'" Hours seem standard, with not much overtime. Even so, depending on position, there will be some weekend visits to the office. Some insiders report making "frequent" weekend trips, "at least once a month."

As far as perks, "Vacation is the standard two weeks at first," says an insider. "Later, additional weeks are granted based on experience and tenure." Dress is "business casual" except for client contact, and the firm does offer flex working schedules. Though one source warns, "Only select people are allowed to participate." According to the firm, other benefits include "a free on-site wellness center, free on-site fitness center, near-site child care and back-up care, elder care benefit, home benefit program, sundry shop and dry cleaners to name a few." Additionally, Freddie Mac says employees "can also take advantage of an easily accessible online concierge service to locate a variety of services including travel, tourist and city information, dining, entertainment, maid service and even grocery delivery services." Other benefits include educational tuition reimbursement, employer-paid

Visit the Vault Finance Career Channel at **www.vault.com/finance** – with
insider firm profiles, message boards, the Vault Finance Job Board and more

VAULT CAREER LIBRARY   **171**

professional or trade association membership, computer purchase loan program and an on-site employee assistance counselor. One insider says, "The employees, the nice cafeteria, the free gym, the attractive work spaces and a great philanthropic spirit amongst the staff" are all perks.

Aiming for the goal

Although insiders give the firm mixed reviews on diversity, the firm's numbers are quite impressive. "The diversity program is a show piece only," offers one source. "It's not really active." Another says, "A program was generated to create criteria for promotions and becoming an officer, but it was never used effectively." Even so, the firm has been ranked No. 9 on *Fortune*'s list of the Best Places to Work for Minorities. And according to Freddie Mac, "Minorities make up approximately 45 percent of the company's workforce, and over 50 percent of this workforce is women." The firm also notes that in 2006, "approximately 60 percent of new hires were minorities," and that it has in place several internal employee network groups for African-Americans, Hispanic/Latino Americans, Asian Americans, women, the disabled, individuals dealing with elder care issues, and GLBT employees.

© 2007 Vault, Inc.

Genworth Financial Inc.

6620 W. Broad Street
Richmond, VA 23230
Phone: (804) 281-6000
Fax: (804) 662-2414
www.genworth.com

DEPARTMENTS

Mortgage Insurance
Protection Insurance
Retirement Income & Investments

THE STATS

Employer Type: Public Company
Ticker Symbol: GNW (NYSE)
Chairman: Michael D. Fraizer
SVP, Operations & Quality, & CIO:
Scott J. McKay
Revenue: $11 billion (FYE 12/06)
Net Income: $1.33 billion
No. of Employees: 6,900

KEY COMPETITORS

AIG
MetLife
Prudential

UPPERS

• "Great training program for recent grads"
• "Plenty of opportunities to grow"

DOWNERS

• Long hours
• Management gets mixed reviews

EMPLOYMENT CONTACT

www.genworth.com/employment

Visit the Vault Finance Career Channel at **www.vault.com/finance** — with
insider firm profiles, message boards, the Vault Finance Job Board and more

VAULT CAREER LIBRARY   173

THE SCOOP

A splashy IPO

Genworth Financial, ranked No. 223 on the Fortune 500, is among the leading insurance holding companies in the U.S., and has operations in 24 countries. The company was formerly part of General Electric Corp. Genworth offers primarily consumer-focused products. The company has three business segments: protection insurance, mortgage insurance, and retirement income and investments (RI&I). The company's initial public offering on the New York Stock Exchange was the biggest of the year, and the 11th-largest IPO in history, raising $2.8 billion in May 2004.

Genworth's Protection insurance group includes term life insurance and universal life insurance, long-term care insurance, and group and individual life and health insurance, as well as payment protection insurance, which is offered in 18 countries and helps consumers meet financial obligations should their incomes be interrupted. The company's mortgage insurance group helps users buy homes and offers loan payment counseling and household protection discounts. Genworth's retirement income and investments division offers annuities to provide income in retirement. Also, a money management business offers asset management services.

Free from GE

Genworth Financial was formerly GE Financial Assurance. The company was formed in 2003 to acquire General Electric's life insurance, long-term care insurance, group life and health benefits, retirement planning and mortgage insurance business in the U.S., Australia, Canada and Europe. After the IPO, GE's ownership of Genworth dropped below 50 percent, which allowed Genworth to be considered fully independent of GE.

In March 2006, Genworth announced GE's secondary public offerings were priced at $32.75 each. Genworth was not to receive any proceeds from the sale. The company also said that it will buy back 15 million shares of Class B stock from GE for $479 million. Following the completion of the transaction, GE no longer owns any shares of Genworth's common stock. GE said it would receive net proceeds of $2.8 billion from these transactions. GE sold its remaining stake in Genworth Financial to focus on faster growing markets.

   © 2007 Vault, Inc.

Chairman, President and CEO Michael Fraizer has held his position since the IPO. Prior to that, he was vice president of GE and served various in capacities after joining the company in June 1980 in its financial management program.

Centering on centenarians

In 2006, Genworth mounted a print and television ad campaign featuring six centenarians. The commercials run on cable networks, including ESPN, CNN, Fox News and Discovery, and aim to raise the profile of its insurance products, all of which are tied to security later in life. However, the primary targets of the ads are the brokers, bankers and insurance agents for the company. Genworth is looking to grow and is actively seeking new employees. But if the ads attract attention from consumers, that is an added benefit for Genworth. The company has also boosted its profile by being one of the principal sponsors of Donald Trump's now-defunct television show *The Apprentice*.

The Genworth Foundation invests in community programs around the world through charitable gifts and matching gifts. Genworth supports groups that work towards battling Alzheimer's, offer affordable housing program, and provide mentoring and after-school programs. Also, the Genworth Volunteers work with programs such as Junior Achievement and Rebuilding Together, an organization that teams volunteers with elderly homeowners in at-risk neighborhoods to help them their fix their homes.

A date with the DOJ

In November 2006, Genworth was subpoenaed by the U.S. Securities and Exchange Commission and the Department of Justice in an investigation of bid-rigging and guaranteed investment contracts sold to municipalities. The company agreed to cooperate with the investigation. More than 20 companies were subpoenaed as part of the investigation, including rival AIG.

For full-year 2006, revenue rose to $11.03 billion from $10.5 billion in 2005. Net income also rose, coming in at $1.328 billion from $1.221 billion in the previous year. Chairman and CEO Fraizer said the firm achieved the results by "funding higher return growth, making selective acquisitions, executing on strategic business exits and completing share repurchases."

Visit the Vault Finance Career Channel at **www.vault.com/finance** – with insider firm profiles, message boards, the Vault Finance Job Board and more

VAULT CAREER LIBRARY   175

GETTING HIRED

Point of contact

Get online and join what the firm terms on its web site as the "The Genworth Employment Experience." Submit your resume or apply for open positions online (in departments such as investments, mortgage insurance, protection, and retirement income and investments). "If your resume is selected," according to the firm, "your first point of contact should be with a Genworth recruiter in the staffing center or in a local office." Expect an "initial assessment either via phone or in person," and then anticipate more on-site interviews if your recruiter decides that there's a "possible fit."

OUR SURVEY SAYS

Relaxed, but a little stressed

Genworth is a "great company, especially if you are interested in the insurance industry," says one insider. It has a "great training program for recent grads from college." Although one Virginia insider calls the corporate culture "pretty relaxed," she adds that it's also a "high-stress environment that you experience in places like NYC."

Hours of work "vary by department," and the "official hours" "are 8 a.m. to 5 p.m., but the reality is 8 a.m. to 6 p.m. under two to three multiple projects." And "about a third of the time, hours are 7:30 a.m. to 7 p.m." Make sure you're on time. "Your manager will talk with you each time you are more than five minutes late." One insider notes, "During holidays and vacations, they will try to get you to stay a few extra days to help cover for other employees who are out on vacation." Another contact says that "everyone one to two levels above entry level are expected to work a little overtime," and "senior management is expected to work 10-plus hours of overtime a week." Yet another insider paints a worse picture when it comes to hours, commenting, "They expect us to work 70 to 80 hours or more a week every week for their advancement, and we get a $500 bonus each year in return."

The firm's business casual dress code, which falls along the lines of a "nice long-sleeve shirt" and "pressed Dockers with nice shoes" is a little more

© 2007 Vault, Inc.

flexible, but one source says, "The better you dress, the better you'll be treated by management."

Be bold

As far as advancement opportunities within the firm go, you may have to blaze your own path. Insiders say there are "plenty of opportunities to grow," but Genworth's a firm "for the assertive," and you should not expect "others to look out for you or help you to get promoted." There are good opportunities to advance "since there is high turnover here," and while "some employees leave during the first 90 days, some stay for years. It depends on which group you are assigned to, and how much pressure senior management is putting on that group." Genworth "is very concerned about 'project execution,'" and one source warns, "Do not screw up any part of your project, no matter how difficult the project, because they'll never forget even the smallest mistake." Managers get mixed marks. One contact says that "managers are dishonest, and have only a very limited understanding of their own business."

On the diversity front, however, the firm shines a little brighter. An insider working in the Richmond, Va., office says that "diversity is good," adding that "there are blacks, whites and Asians in equal proportions, and most employees are from India." Another source says that "diversity is talked about and also employed."

Visit the Vault Finance Career Channel at **www.vault.com/finance** – with
insider firm profiles, message boards, the Vault Finance Job Board and more

VAULT CAREER LIBRARY   **177**

GMAC LLC

200 Renaissance Center
Detroit, MI 48265
Phone: (313) 556-5000
Fax: (313) 556-5108
www.gmacfs.com

DEPARTMENTS

Automotive Financing
Automotive Insurance
Commercial Finance
Mortgage Services
Personal Insurance

THE STATS

Employer Type: Private Company
CEO: Eric A. Feldstein
Revenue: $18.16 billion (FYE 12/06)
Net Income: $2.1 billion
No. of Employees: 33,900

KEY COMPETITORS

Bank of America
Ford Motor Credit
Toyota Motor Credit

EMPLOYMENT CONTACT

www.gm.com/careers

© 2007 Vault, Inc.

THE SCOOP

More than just cars

The General Motors Acceptance Corporation (GMAC) was the financial services arm of General Motors until GM sold 51 percent of the company to a private investor group. GMAC started out offering financing to GM dealerships and their customers. However, the company has moved beyond simply providing automotive financing, and has matured into diversified financial services company, selling insurance and mortgage products and real estate services in over 40 countries. GMAC is divided into three main units: financing, insurance and mortgage. While GMAC finances new and certified used GM vehicles, within the company's automotive financing division is Nuvell Financing Services. Nuvell finances rival auto companies that do not have a financial arm, as well as used cars from dealerships that use bank financing. Kia Motors America is among the auto companies that use Nuvell for their new vehicle sales.

The company's mortgage subsidiary, ResCap Holding, is the umbrella for GMAC's residential mortgage business, which offers residential real estate loans, invests in mortgage-backed securities and packages single-family home loans for sale to investors. GMAC insurance offers commercial and personal auto insurance. GMAC also owns ditech.com, an online mortgage lender, known for its humorous television ads with their catchphrase "Lost another one to Ditech." GMAC Home Services is the parent for GMAC Real Estate, which was formed by the purchase of Better Homes and Garden's Real Estate in 1998, GMAC Global Relocation Services and GHS Mortgage.

Made in Detroit

GMAC was formed in 1919 to provide GM auto dealers with the necessary financing to maintain large vehicle inventories. At the time, most dealerships carried only a few cars, as they were required to buy their stock in cash. The invention of the assembly line allowed for the rapid production of large quantities of cars. Thus, the factories wanted dealers to buy larger quantities of cars to keep factory operations running smoothly. So, the General Motors Acceptance Corp. was formed to provide dealers with the financing necessary to keep these large inventories. GMAC initially operated in Detroit, New York, Chicago, San Francisco and Toronto. By 1920, GMAC expanded to the U.K. and by 1928 had sold about four million retail contracts.

Visit the Vault Finance Career Channel at www.vault.com/finance – with
insider firm profiles, message boards, the Vault Finance Job Board and more

VAULT CAREER LIBRARY   179

In 1999, GMAC bought Bank of New York's asset-based lending and factory business to create its commercial finance group. In 2000, the company launched SmartAuction, an online auction site for used GM vehicles. GMAC expanded to China in 2004, becoming the first foreign-based financial services company to offer vehicle financing. Also in 2004, the company opened the GMAC Automotive Bank, which raises money from FDIC-insured certificates of deposit. The bank allows the company to diversify funding sources and gives GMAC access to lower-cost sources of funding.

Enter BOA

In order to raise money for a reorganization, General Motors has been divesting many assets, including GMAC. This divestiture was prompted by investor Kirk Kerkorian and Jerome York, his former representative on GM's board. In July 2005, GMAC announced that Bank of America agreed to purchase up to $55 billion worth of GMAC retail automotive contracts for a five-year period. BoA made an initial purchase of $5 billion and agreed to purchase up to $10 billion of GMAC's U.S. retail auto finance contracts every fiscal year.

In August 2005, the company sold a 78 percent stake in its commercial mortgage operations, GMAC Commercial Holding, for $1.5 billion cash, to an equity group that included Kohlberg Kravis Roberts & Co, Five Mile Capital Partners and Goldman Sachs Capital Partners. Its mortgage operations unit is one of the company's most profitable, and this subsidiary seeks to obtain a stand-alone credit rating to enhance its ability to fund operations.

Also in 2005, GMAC restructured its residential mortgage operations, creating a new wholly owned subsidiary named Residential Capital Corporation. This allowed GMAC to up its credit rating, apart from GM.

Credit where credit is due

GMAC's credit rating has been downgraded in recent years, mostly due to its beleaguered parent GM. On November 30, 2006, a group of investors led by Cerebus Capital Management, and including Citigroup Inc., Aozora Bank Ltd. of Japan and a subsidiary of PNC Financial Services Group Inc., agreed to purchase 51 percent of GMAC from GM. The sale raised nearly $14 billion for the cash-strapped parent company. GM continues to own the remaining 49 percent of GMAC and collects a dividend from its holdings. The deal has served to lift GMAC's rating to the top speculative grade rung,

 © 2007 Vault, Inc.

after nearly a year on the S&P'S CreditWatch list. The rating is expected to rise to investment grade within the next year. Also, Moody's raised GMAC's rating to Baa3, up one notch from Ba1.

GETTING HIRED

All levels welcome

Whether you're an experienced pro or fresh out of college (a/k/a. a "salaried employee-in-training," according to the firm), GMAC has a niche waiting for you. At www.gm.com/careers, candidates can read about the various career paths available at GMAC, the firm's corporate culture, benefits, training, what life in Michigan is like and where else the firm operates throughout the world. GMAC also posts a recruiting calendar, showing the various events it will be holding on campuses. In addition, candidates can search for openings and apply online. GMAC offers undergraduate internships, which the firm says give "full-time college students on-the-job experience where they get exposed to real-world work situations and polish their business skills."

Expect going through several rounds once you've been called in for an interview. One insider says the hiring process as includes "interviews with five people" along with fielding some "pretty technical questions."

OUR SURVEY SAYS

Shape shifting

The firm is going through changes lately, some sources say. "The company is growing and detaching itself from GM," an insider resorts. But unfortunately, those changes don't exactly extend to diversity efforts, which could be taken more seriously, others add. One says that "the diversity is okay in the collections department," but that "the opportunities for advancement for people of color is nonexistent."

Guardian Life Insurance Company of America

7 Hanover Square
New York, NY 10004-2616
Phone: (212) 598-8000
Fax: (212) 919-2170
www.guardianlife.com

DEPARTMENTS

Disability Income Insurance &
   Specialty Life Products
Employee Benefits
Guardian Trust Company, FSB
Individual Life Insurance & Business
   Protection

THE STATS

Employer Type: Private Company
President & CEO: Dennis J. Manning
Revenue: $9.7 billion (FYE 12/06)
No. of Employees: 5,000
No. of Offices (not including sales offices): 6

KEY COMPETITORS

MassMutual
Nationwide
New York Life

UPPERS

- "Unlimited earning potential"
- "The firm encourages entrepreneurship"

DOWNERS

- "Our new building is too small to accommodate our growth"
- "We need more assistance with marketing or prospecting"

EMPLOYMENT CONTACT

See "careers" section of
www.guardianlife.com

© 2007 Vault, Inc.

THE SCOOP

Insuring America is no simple task

The New York-based Guardian Life Insurance Company of Americans is a Fortune 300 mutual company wholly owned by its policyholders, and the fourth largest mutual life insurance company in the U.S. Guardian has over a century of experience in the insurance industry, employing more than 5,000 staffers and 2,900 financial representatives nationwide, and providing mutual life insurance, disability, health and dental insurance products to individuals and businesses. The company also offers 401(k)s, trusts and other financial products. Most recently, Guardian acquired a majority stake in RS Investments, a San Francisco-based investment management firm specializing in mutual funds and institutional accounts.

Strength in the field

Guardian offers a full display of risk protection, investment, and wealth management products and services, sold through its subsidiaries and affiliates. These include the Berkshire Life Insurance Company of America; First Commonwealth; Guardian Baillie Gifford Limited; The Guardian Insurance & Annuity Company, Inc. (GIAC); Guardian Investor Services LLC (GIS); Guardian Trust Company; Innovative Underwriters, Inc.; Park Avenue Life Insurance Company; and Park Avenue Securities LLC. To sell its insurance and financial products, Guardian has built a commanding field force of experts in areas ranging from financial products to employee benefits. These professionals use a relationship-driven approach with clients, utilizing tools such as the Living Balance Sheet, a recently implemented technology that provides customers with an integrated view of their financial picture. The online tool provides Guardian field representatives with automatic notifications of financial events or changes, and stores copies of important personal documents.

"Guarding" life since 1860

It's no wonder Guardian founder Hugo Wesendonck had such a keen eye for safety and stability. Fleeing post-revolution Germany, he landed in the U.S. in 1848. After pooling start-up funds from fellow German refugees, he opened Germania Life Insurance Company in 1860 in New York to cover the growing number of German immigrants arriving on American shores. Two

Visit the Vault Finance Career Channel at **www.vault.com/finance** – with insider firm profiles, message boards, the Vault Finance Job Board and more

VAULT CAREER LIBRARY   183

years later, he opened a branch in San Francisco, and business spread quickly across the country, reaching territories like Colorado, New Mexico and the Dakotas.

After steady growth, the company set up headquarters in New York City's Union Square in 1911. In 1917, the company changed its name to Guardian, in response to a break with the fatherland-and some anti-German sentiment in the U.S.—after WWI. It became a mutual company owned by policyholders in 1925, eliminating stockholders and private owners. Guardian relocated in 1999, when, after branching out into financial services, it sent its headquarters downtown to Wall Street. In addition to its Manhattan office, the company has primary locations and regional offices in Appleton, Wis.; Bethlehem, Pa.; Spokane, Wash.; Pittsfield, Mass.; and Bridgewater, Mass.

A strong balance sheet

Guardian maintains a highly qualified team of investment professionals, which has paid off in strong financial performance. The firm and its subsidiaries reported $39.5 billion in assets as of December 31, 2006.

Guardian has received strong ratings all around from the major rating agencies: Moody's gave Guardian an "Excellent," Fitch gave it a "Very Strong," and A.M. Best rated Guardian a "Superior."

In 2006, Guardian's total revenue, including premium and investment income, was a reported $9.7 billion, an increase from $7.4 billion from the previous year.

Giving back to policyholders

Guardian consistently places policyholders first, choosing to pay out dividends rather than funnel profits back into the company. In November of 2006, Guardian Life released news of a record dividend payout for 2007 of $618 million to eligible life policyholders. The dividend amounts to a 7 percent increase over the previous year's dividend, and is the largest in Guardian's history. President and CEO Dennis Manning announced the dividend, noting the company's policy to "provide the greatest amount of life insurance protection for the lowest possible net cost ... for the benefits of our clients and policyholders."

© 2007 Vault, Inc.

Raising awareness among football fans

Guardian Life has carried out several public awareness campaigns in the past, conducting research on public safety and urging Americans to live healthier, safer lives. Most recently, the company targeted the younger generation's lack of life insurance, launching a public awareness campaign featuring NFL running back Warrick Dunn of the Atlanta Falcons. Dunn completed a radio media tour to promote Life Insurance Awareness Month in September of 2006.

GETTING HIRED

What's open

Applicants can check out Guardian's job listings under "list of open jobs" under "careers" on its firm's web site, or they can just submit a resume (it's "not required" that you submit a cover letter, the firm notes) and a member of the firm will contact you "if your skills and qualifications match what we are looking for." Candidates can peruse corporate openings by job title, location and business organization. Job titles can include accounting, actuarial, administration, communications, equities, finance, group insurance products, human resources, information systems, marketing, Park Avenue securities, retirement services, training, trust company, underwriter and warehouse. Those interested in a field sales position are also encouraged to apply online.

Get animated

Once you're asked in for an interview, be prepared for anything. "The questions you're asked and the personality tests you take are geared toward finding out if you are self-motivated or not," reports one insider. Others report fielding everything from typing tests to "interview questions such as 'Who's your favorite cartoon character and why?'" Another insider says that the hiring process "requires five interviews and two tests."

And if you do successfully weather the interviews and the firm decides it wants you to join the team, be prepared—the firm will do a background check to ensure that you have "no felony arrests" and a "good credit history," insiders report.

Visit the Vault Finance Career Channel at www.vault.com/finance – with
insider firm profiles, message boards, the Vault Finance Job Board and more

VAULT CAREER LIBRARY   185

Down to business

Guardian's company culture is "very friendly and professional," "businesslike" and "offers training and moral support." One insider also lauds the "detailed" training, adding that the firm's "progress monitoring" also gets a stamp of approval. But company perks, says another, aren't given in the traditional sense of the word. Instead, "all of our expenses are tax-deductible as business related expenses, so the company doesn't need to provide 'perks.'"

One insider who has "worked at Guardian for many years" has "seen many changes" recently, adding that "older employees do not get treated well and have to work three times harder because more is expected of them." The contact goes on to note that the firm "used to be a great place to work and used to be very understandable and flexible when it came to family," but now requires many staffers to "to fill out Family and Medical Leave Act papers to protect their jobs." Another contact says, "The atmosphere is pretty charged up, but it is enjoyable simply because they are waiting on you to pull in a big account and for them to get paid." One field representative says, "You're your own boss, and that's either a good thing or a bad thing depending on your work ethic." Another contact says, "Managers monitor sales and conduct training to increase sales, but they don't have to do 'motivational' activities," and adds that "they are very supportive." As far as moving up the ladder, an insider says, "Opportunities for advancement are limited to who you know," and "unless you are really liked, you can forget getting promoted unless it's a job no one else wants or they can't fill the position." Although several sources enthuse about the firm's casual Fridays, one in the Baton Rouge, La., office says, "High-quality business suits are the daily work attire."

Paving the way

Diversity with respect to women gets good marks. One insider says, "From the top down, our firm encourages hiring women," and there are "special programs within the firm" for female staffers. Guardian also "helps pay female employees' membership in national women's organizations." In regards to the hiring of minorities, one contact is "unsure of the percentage of minorities," "the encouragement and support is the same as for women." Treatment of gays and lesbians within the firm also receive high marks. One insider says, "I have never heard of a policy either way on this issue," and "believe it is left up to each local agency who they hire and they are probably unaware of sexual preference."

© 2007 Vault, Inc.

Hartford Financial Services

Hartford Plaza
690 Asylum Avenue
Hartford, CT 06115-1900
Phone: (860) 547-5000
Fax: (860) 547-2680
www.thehartford.com

DEPARTMENTS

Business Insurance
Group Benefits
Individual Life Insurance
Institutional Financial Solutions
International
Personal Lines Insurance
Retail Investment Products
Retirement Plans
Specialty Commercial Insurance

THE STATS

Employer Type: Public Company
Ticker Symbol: HIG (NYSE)
Chairman, President & CEO: Ramani Ayer
Revenue: $26.5 billion (FYE 12/06)
Net Income: $2.75 billion
No. of Employees: 31,000

KEY COMPETITORS

AIG
Allstate
Berkshire Hathaway
Chubb
CNA
ING
Liberty Mutual
Progressive
Prudential

UPPERS

- "Great home and work balance," "some managers allow flex-time"
- "Many opportunities for advancement

DOWNERS

- "Political and bureaucratic"
- "Senior leadership is largely white male"

EMPLOYMENT CONTACT

See "careers" section of
www.thehartford.com

Visit the Vault Finance Career Channel at **www.vault.com/finance** — with insider firm profiles, message boards, the Vault Finance Job Board and more

VAULT CAREER LIBRARY   187

THE SCOOP

Pledge allegiance to the stag

Founded in 1810, The Hartford Financial Services Group, Inc., or The Hartford, is currently one of the largest investment and insurance companies based in the U.S. Under its prominent red stag logo, The Hartford sells products to individuals, institutions and businesses through nearly 11,000 independent agencies and more than 100,000 registered broker-dealers in countries around the world, including Japan, Brazil and England. The company has traded on the New York Stock Exchange for 11 years, listed under the "HIG" symbol. In 2006, The Hartford ranked 78th on the Fortune 100 list.

Under its Hartford Life division, the company sells retail investment products, particularly fixed and variable annuities, mutual funds and 529 college saving plans; retirement plans, including 401(k)s and 403(b)s; products for institutions, such as institutional mutual funds, structured settlement annuities, and private placement life insurance; individual life insurance; and group benefits. International clients are managed by a separate international division, which provides wealth management, retirement and financial protection products to individual investors outside the U.S., in Japan, Brazil and the U.K. The Hartford's property/casualty business offers a variety of personal and commercial property/casualty insurance products, including homeowners, auto, general liability insurance, marine insurance and workers' compensation.

Not the textbook version

The Hartford has a celebrated history, with a client list including not one, but two U.S. presidents, and American legends such as Babe Ruth and Buffalo Bill. The company has survived national disasters such as the Great Chicago Fire, the San Francisco Earthquake and the September 11 attacks, paying out hundreds of millions in losses. With nearly 200 years of experience under its belt, The Hartford gives the impression that it can truly handle anything thrown its way. The company has its roots in the Hartford Fire Insurance Company, which was incorporated by the Connecticut General Assembly in 1810. Yale University was among its first customers, as was 16th president of the U.S., Abraham Lincoln, who purchased fire insurance from the company for his home and property in Springfield, Ill. Babe Ruth purchased a "sickness policy" to protect his earnings in case of illness, and Dwight D. Eisenhower, the 34th President of

© 2007 Vault, Inc.

the U.S., bought a policy to insure the family farm in Pennsylvania. The Hartford became a transnational company in 1910, with the opening of its first office in San Francisco. It began offering mutual funds in 1996, becoming the nation's fastest growing retail-oriented mutual fund family to reach $10 billion in assets, which it did in 2000. The firm became a Fortune 500 company in 2005, five years away from its 200th birthday.

Ranking high in every category

The Hartford was one of *BusinessWeek*'s top 50 performers in 2006 based on its sales and earnings growth, and holds numerous distinctions in nearly all of its business segments. It is the fourth-largest life insurance group based on statutory assets, the No. 1 seller of annuities in Japan, the No. 1 in fully insured group disability sales, the 11th-largest property and casualty insurer based on direct written premium, the fifth-largest commercial insurance carrier, and the No. 5 workers' compensation insurer based on net premium. Recently the National Association of Wholesaler-Distributors, an association of 40,000 wholesale distribution companies across the country, selected The Hartford Financial Services Group, Inc. as the preferred insurance provider for the marine and management liability coverage.

Leading the way

Ramani Ayer has been chairman, president and CEO of The Hartford Group since 1997. Ayer joined the company in 1973 as a member of the operations research department, and formerly served as president and chief operating officer of The Hartford's property-casualty operations, a post to which he was elected in 1991. Ayer has been a strong leader both at The Hartford and in the industry as a whole, recently speaking on behalf of insurance companies in front of the House of Representatives. In September 2006, Ayer testified to Congress describing the difficulties facing insurance companies in managing terrorism risk, and the need for the federal government to partner with private companies to insure against terrorism. "Right now it [terrorism] presents an insurmountable challenge for the private markets alone to understand or manage. Hence, terrorism risk can only be managed effectively and fairly in partnership with the federal government," said Ayer.

Living well (and green) at The Hartford

The Hartford's Simsbury, Conn.-based life insurance subsidiary has been expanding its operations, increasing its Connecticut employee base by more than 50 percent over the past 15 years. To accommodate these additions, Hartford Life has revealed plans for a new 450,000 square feet campus in Windsor, Conn., as part of a $146-million expansion of The Hartford Financial Services Group. The new facility is expected to be completed by mid-2008, and will incorporate green technology, including sun control architectural elements, recycled construction materials, and energy-efficient heating and cooling systems. It will house approximately 2,000 Hartford Life employees.

GETTING HIRED

Simply the best

"The best people can choose where they want to work," according to the firm. "And we want the best people." If you think you fall within that lofty target demographic, log on to the careers section of Hartford's web site (www.hartford.com), which provides a searchable database of job opportunities, sortable by category and geographic location. The available job categories can include accounting, actuarial, administration, business analysis, claim, contracts and compliance, facilities management, finance, human resources, information technology, insurance, investment management, legal and government affairs, loss control, medical, marketing and communications, quality and process improvement, sales, service/operations, special risk services, training and underwriting. Special information for recent college graduates and current college students is also listed on the site, as well as information about varying career development and benefits.

OUR SURVEY SAYS

Good balance, but bureaucratic

Sources give different takes regarding the firm's culture. One insider says, "The company offers a great home and work balance." However, another notes,"The culture in the P&C part of the company is very political and bureaucratic." Although the company is "well run," reports one contact, "as an employer, the company is very average." Another believes, "The corporate culture is one of complex office politics—even for an insurance company, where this is the norm—and there's posturing and bureaucracy." The source adds, "Decisions are made only by overcoming these obstacles—and the company seems to succeed in spite of its own culture."

Policies seem to be determined largely by department. One insider says, "Hours vary by position—some managers allow flex-time, while some do not." But another says, "The bond department is flexible with hours since the position does require some travel and extended hours for marketing purposes." And although "core hours run from 8 a.m. to 4:30 p.m.," "there is flex-time available, which can be discussed with the office manager on an individual basis." "Hours of operation are usually 8 a.m. to 4:45 p.m., but in the call center arena you can have a shift that goes from 2:30 to 11 p.m."

Not too fussy

Most of the time, staffers don't have to get too formal, insiders report. The dress code is "business casual," but "marketing calls and account meetings are normally suit and tie." The dress code "really depends on location and manager." An insider says, "I've seen everything from mini skirts and pajama shoes to suits and ties." But the "home office is more structured, and you see a lot of sweater vests and suits."

Advancement also seem to hinge on the department you're in. "Opportunities for advancement vary by position," and "in the senior management ranks, many position openings are not posted because favored employees are already chosen well in advance." An insider adds, "This is succession planning at its worst—candidates do not seem to be chosen by skills or ability but rather by political positioning." Another contact says, "Depending on the territory handled, internal competition for managerial positions can vary." And it may pay to schmooze. "People with political/network connections and those who fall within diversity groups move up faster," one respondent says, "but sometimes high-performing employees who don't fall into these two groups tend to have a harder time getting promoted and compensated." Another notes, "There are many opportunities for advancement, but you have to put the time in and have to go way beyond the call of duty."

Visit the Vault Finance Career Channel at www.vault.com/finance – with insider firm profiles, message boards, the Vault Finance Job Board and more

V∧ULT CAREER LIBRARY   **191**

Program in place, but not promoted

The firm has "an extensive diversity and inclusion program, but senior leadership is largely white male," says an insider, and "nothing is done to identify and promote high-performing minority employees." Another agrees, saying, "You will find that most in upper management are white males, which I believe sends a message to others trying to move up." The insider adds, "Women asking for raises is a definite 'no-no' from my experience—for some reason it is seen by the firm as being greedy and not thinking about 'the business need.'"

© 2007 Vault, Inc.

Leucadia National Corporation

315 Park Avenue South
New York, NY 10010-3607
Phone: (212) 460-1900
Fax: (212) 598-4869
www.leucadia.com

DEPARTMENTS

Banking
Manufacturing
Mining

THE STATS

Employer Type: Public Company
Ticker Symbol: LUK (NYSE)
Chairman: Ian M. Cumming
President & Director: Joseph S. Steinberg
Revenue: $862 million (FYE 12/06)
Net Income: $189.4 million
No. of Employees: 3,969

KEY COMPETITORS

Berkshire Hathaway
Blackstone Group
Enstar Group

EMPLOYMENT CONTACT

Leucadia National
315 Park Avenue South
New York, NY 10010-3607
Phone: (212) 460-1900

Visit the Vault Finance Career Channel at **www.vault.com/finance** — with
insider firm profiles, message boards, the Vault Finance Job Board and more

VAULT CAREER LIBRARY   193

THE SCOOP

Know when to hold 'em

New York-based Leucadia National is a diversified holding company whose strategy is to buy undervalued or troubled companies and increase their value, while taking advantage of any tax breaks. Leucadia owns companies in numerous industries, including manufacturing, medical product development, real estate, gaming entertainment, banking, mining and even winery operations. The company is also involved in telecommunications, including local and long-distance telephone services, Internet services, web development and collection services. And Leucadia develops commercial and residential real estate, and provides consumer and specialty insurance as well as reinsurance services. Leucadia, founded in 1854, has been ranked No. 53 on *BusinessWeek*'s list of Hot Growth Companies and was No. 20 on *Fortune*'s list of Fastest Growing Companies in 2006, up from No. 59 in 2005.

The company's folksy style and practical strategy of fixing troubled undervalued companies that make common products has led to comparisons with another somewhat famous holding company, Berkshire Hathaway. Chairman Ian Cumming and President and Director Joseph Steinberg met at Harvard Business School, both graduating in 1970. Both hold about 13 percent of the company's shares. Cumming also serves as the chairman of the board of Barbados Light & Power; director and chairman of the Finova Group; director of subsidiary Allcity Insurance; and a director of Skywest, a Utah-based regional carrier. Cumming is also a director of HomeFed and Carmike Cinemas.

Brisk business

Leucadia has kept business sales coming at a fairly vigorous pace during the past few years. In 2005, the company beefed up its manufacturing holdings with the acquisition of NSW, which makes packaging nets, case liners and other types of industrial netting. Another 2005 success was its $133 million bid to buy Idaho Timber Corporation, which remanufactures dimension lumber and specialized wood products. In July 2006, the firm sold Symphony Healthcare Services to RehabCare Group for $107 million, and in September 2006, Leucadia sold ATX Communications to Broadview Networks Holdings, receiving about $85.7 million in aggregate cash consideration. At the end of 2006, the firm ended up

© 2007 Vault, Inc.

with net security gains totaling around $117.2 million, which was mostly derived from selling publicly traded debt and equity securities.

For its fiscal year 2006, the company reported revenue of $862.67 million, up from $689 million from in 2005. Net income was $189.4 million, down from $1.64 billion in 2005, due to the sale of Tulsa, Okla.-based WilTel Communications Group.

In late 2003, the firm bought WilTel (the bankrupt Williams Communications) and its nationwide fiber network for $780 million. WilTel became Leucadia's biggest revenue generator, making up about 70 percent of its sales. But the catch was that SBC Communications accounted for most of WilTel's income, and in 2005, SBC announced that it would buy AT&T and naturally use AT&T's network instead. In late 2005, Leucadia sold WilTel to Level 3 Communications for about $680 million in cash and stock.

Katrina hits the Hard Rock

The firm was dealt a difficult hand when Hurricane Katrina struck in 2005. Leucadia holds a controlling interest in Premier Entertainment Biloxi, which owns Hard Rock Hotel & Casino Biloxi in Mississippi. With just days to go before it was scheduled to officially open, the resort was destroyed in the hurricane, leading Premier to declare Chapter 11 bankruptcy in an attempt to rebuild the casino. And after nearly two years of negotiation with insurers, Premier finally reached a settlement. The Biloxi hotel's grand opening— hopefully undeterred by nature this time around—is scheduled for July 2007.

GETTING HIRED

Variety's the spice of life

Sure, Leucadia National does diversified financials, but it has a little bit of everything else on its plate too—from real estate to wineries. But if you're looking to work for Leucadia, you may have to get creative—its web site is fairly sparse, including only a few links and no information on open positions. If you want to give it a shot anyway, try sending your resume to the firm's corporate office headquarters at 315 Park Avenue South, New York, NY 10010.

Visit the Vault Finance Career Channel at www.vault.com/finance – with
insider firm profiles, message boards, the Vault Finance Job Board and more

VAULT CAREER LIBRARY   195

Liberty Mutual

175 Berkeley Street
Boston, MA 02116
Phone: (617) 357-9500
Fax: (617) 350-7648
www.libertymutual.com

DEPARTMENTS

Agency Markets
Commercial Markets
International Operations
Personal Markets

THE STATS

Employer Type: Private Company
Chairman, President & CEO: Edmund
F. Kelly
Revenue: $23.5 billion (FYE 12/06)
No. of Employees: 39,000
No. of Offices: More than 900

KEY COMPETITORS

Allstate
Hartford
State Farm

UPPERS

• "Prefers to promote from within"

DOWNERS

• "Hierarchal and relatively slow-paced" culture

EMPLOYMENT CONTACT

See "careers" section of
www.libertymutual.com

© 2007 Vault, Inc.

THE SCOOP

Insurance from the hub of the universe

A Fortune 500 company with nearly a century of experience, Liberty Mutual is a powerful name in the global insurance industry. The Boston-based company has grown and reorganized since its inception in 1912 to become the Liberty Mutual Holding Company, Inc., a holding company for three principals companies: Liberty Mutual Insurance Company, Liberty Mutual Fire Insurance Company and Employers Insurance Company of Wausau. The group is operated as a mutual holding structure owned by its policyholders. The company in its entirety provides a wide range of insurance products and services, including private passenger automobile, homeowners, workers compensation, commercial multiple peril, commercial automobile, general liability, global specialty, group disability, assumed reinsurance, fire and surety. The company has four business units: personal markets, commercial markets, agency markets and Liberty International, with no single business unit contributing more than 30 percent of net written premium. Its personal markets affinity program currently has more than 9,800 sponsored affinity group relationships with employers, credit unions, professional and alumni associations.

Stellar reputation

Liberty Mutual holds numerous distinctions as an insurance company: it is the eighth-largest personal lines writer and the fourth-largest commercial lines writer in the U.S. The company also holds a high-ranking spot among corporations in general. In 2006, Liberty Mutual ranked No. 95 on the Fortune 500 list of the largest U.S. corporations based on revenue. In 2006, the firm's revenue was $23.52 billion, up from $21.16 billion in 2005. Net income rose for the year as well, increasing to $1.63 billion from $1.03 billion the year before. As an employer for more than 39,000 people, Liberty Mutual has been recognized as a Top 50 Employer by *Equal Opportunity Magazine*. Most recently, the company was the first corporate sponsor to be awarded by PBS with the 2006 Public Television Leadership Award, for its commitment to funding public television.

Visit the Vault Finance Career Channel at **www.vault.com/finance** – with
insider firm profiles, message boards, the Vault Finance Job Board and more

VAULT CAREER LIBRARY   **197**

Made in Massachusetts

Liberty Mutual was founded in 1912 as the Massachusetts Employees' Insurance Association (MEIA), in response to a Massachusetts law requiring employers to protect employees with workers' compensation insurance. The first branch was opened in Springfield, Mass., in 1914, and was renamed the Liberty Mutual Insurance Company three years later. In the 1930s, the company expanded to other states, opening offices across the U.S. It surpassed the $2 billion mark in written premiums in 1972, expanding internationally with the opening of its London office. Finally in 2002, the company converted to the mutual holding company structure that it operates today.

Luck o' the Irish

Ireland-born Edmund (Ted) F. Kelly became president and chief operating officer of Liberty Mutual in 1992, chief executive officer in 1998, and Chairman in 2000. With a PhD from the Massachusetts Institute of Technology, Kelly has a strong talent for mathematics, teaching at the University of New Brunswick and at the University of Missouri. He proved his leadership capabilities early on at Liberty Mutual, cutting 1,500 employees during his first few years as COO. Following this decisive act, the company's profits, which had been stagnant for several years, increased by 67 percent. As chairman, Kelly expanded the international market for Liberty Mutual, opening offices in Argentina, Australia, Brazil, Canada, France, Hong Kong, Japan, England and China. Most recently Liberty Mutual pushed into Vietnam, obtaining a full license to operate independent insurance offices in November of 2006. The company has had a presence in Vietnam since 2003, but now has permission to open a general fully owned insurance office.

Kelly was also a key force in reorganizing Liberty Mutual Group into a mutual holding company. The firm converted to a mutual holding company in 2002, whereby the three principal mutual insurance companies-LMIC, Liberty Mutual Fire Insurance Company and Employers Insurance Company of Wausau—each became separate stock insurance companies. Kelly defended the decision before the Massachusetts Division of Insurance headquarters in Boston, arguing that the move would make Liberty Mutual more competitive, allowing each company access to more capital. The three companies operate completely independently, setting their own separate business strategies, including acquisitions.

© 2007 Vault, Inc.

Weathering hurricanes and terrorist attacks

Liberty Mutual was hit big-time by Katrina and other hurricanes in 2004, suffering a whopping $1.5 billion in losses in 2005. However, revenue was up, due to the company's investment operations, as net investment income increased from $78 million to $2 billion. Following the September 11th terrorist attacks, Liberty Mutual became a strong advocate for Terrorism Risk Insurance Act, in which the government provides a limited federal backstop to insurance companies in the case of a terrorist attack. This program, which was developed by the Bush administration in the aftermath of the attacks, is currently being phased out. Liberty Mutual CEO Kelly spoke before the National Association of Insurance Commissioners in March of 2006, urging them to be a strong voice for terrorism risk legislation, "the threat of terrorism is a security issue for the entire economy, not just the insurance sector."

GETTING HIRED

Pay to play

Employees who achieve results for the firm will be rewarded with a "strong pay-for-performance and promote-from-within culture," the firm says. So if you're ready to kick out the results, get online—the firm's career site details open positions available for experienced hires, students and recent graduates. Liberty Mutual's site allows prospective applicants to review job descriptions and openings by type, including actuarial, claims (commercial and personal), finance and accounting, human resources, information systems, loss prevention, sales and underwriting. Recent college graduates can also specifically search for entry-level jobs. The web site also lists the career fairs Liberty will be attending, primarily in the summer and fall.Liberty recruits from over 100 universities across the U.S..

Visit the Vault Finance Career Channel at www.vault.com/finance – with
insider firm profiles, message boards, the Vault Finance Job Board and more

VAULT CAREER LIBRARY   199

OUR SURVEY SAYS

Conservative culture

Several sources point to the "conservative," "stuffy" corporate culture, which one notes is "hierarchal and relatively slow-paced," though "employees are generally nice and have strong values and integrity."

But management could still use a refresher course in communicating, insiders say. One notes, "I have consistently experienced a lack of communications within the leadership of the company," and "it is often put upon the shoulders of the supervisors to communicate to their employees what upcoming changes may be taking place or may affect them." The contact goes on to say, "If an employee speaks out or discloses their opinions or ideas, it is often shot down by another employee due to an unhealthy competition that has been created between employees."

One insider notes that staffers "are left to write their own appraisals in third-person style," and wonders, "Is this so the supervisors can receive the credit of writing the employee appraisals?" The contact adds, "Employees are not slotted an amount of time to do this—they need to figure it all out and balance it with between their own workload."

Cost of living up, but not salaries

"The workload required and the mandatory overtime hours make it impossible for employees to reasonably balance their work and personal lives," says one insider, "and this tends to leave employees frustrated and wanting to leave the department." The firm "prefers to promote from within," though, so if you can stick around your department, you may have a good chance of moving up.

Decent hours, formal dress

There's a "good work/life balance" at the firm, says one insider, noting that the "standard workday is seven-and-a-half hours." Another calls the hours "standard," adding that "most employees arrive precisely at 8 a.m. and leave at 5 p.m. on the dot." But the dress requirements aren't quite as casual as the hours. One source says that "'suit-and-tie business attire' is required in most offices, including Fridays," although "business casual" dress is allowed in "some offices."

© 2007 Vault, Inc.

Not great marks

Despite the fact that the company sponsors "many diversity programs during the summer to attract a wide range of college summer interns that represent a variety of races and ethnicities," actual diversity within the firm is "minimal," one insider says. Another says the firm is "extremely poor on employee diversity," and "even worse as one gets higher on the corporate ladder." The contact goes on to say that "almost all executives are white males, and the females are stuck in 'traditional' departments, such as human resources. The only 'diversity' in the company consists of white females stuck in middle management positions."

Visit the Vault Finance Career Channel at **www.vault.com/finance** – with
insider firm profiles, message boards, the Vault Finance Job Board and more

VAULT CAREER LIBRARY   **201**

Loews Corporation

667 Madison Avenue
New York, NY 10021-8087
Phone: (212) 521-2000
Fax: (212) 521-2525
www.loews.com

DEPARTMENTS

Boardwalk Pipeline Partners
Bulova Corporation
CNA Financial Corporation
Diamond Offshore Drilling, Inc.
Loews Hotels
Lorillard, Inc.

THE STATS

Employer Type: Public Company
Ticker Symbol: LTR (NYSE)
President & CEO: James S. Tisch
Revenue: $17.9 billion (FYE 12/31/06)
No. of Employees: 21,600
No. of Offices: 1 (not including subsidiaries)

KEY COMPETITORS

AIG
Altria
American Financial

EMPLOYMENT CONTACT

See "careers" section of
www.loews.com

© 2007 Vault, Inc.

THE SCOOP

The Tisch family knows a bargain when it sees one

What began as a small family-owned hotel business has since expanded to become one of the largest diversified holding companies, run by descendants of founders Preston Robert and Lawrence Tisch. The Manhattan-based company's investment strategy is based on the purchase of temporarily undervalued companies from virtually any industry. Today Loews Corporation has interests in insurance and financial services, including the publicly traded subsidiary CNA Financial; tobacco through it's Lorillard subsidiary, owning brands such Kent, Newport and True; luxury hotels, through its Loews Hotels subsidiary; watch distribution and manufacturer through its subsidiary Bulova; and oil and gas, through contract oil-drilling subsidiary Diamond Offshore Drilling, which owns about 44 oil rigs; and natural gas transmission pipeline systems operation through Boardwalk Pipeline Partners.

As a holding company, Loews monitors its holdings but does not interfere with their operations. It advises subsidiaries on important strategic, financial and capital allocation issues, but its primary motive is to generate wealth through careful acquiring companies with strong preexisting management teams. Historically the company has capitalized on dips in the economy, acquiring CNA in 1974 at a fraction of its value. The company's oil tankers were also purchased at essentially scrap value during the oil crisis of the early 1980s. Most recently, the company expanded its model to include natural gas, announcing a $4.025 billion agreement to purchase natural gas exploration and production assets in Texas, Michigan and Alabama from Dominion Resources.

Billionaires born in Brooklyn

Brooklyn-born brothers Bob and Larry Tisch used their "buy low, sell high" strategy to turn a small family hotel in New Jersey into the modern investment behemoth that is the Loews Corporation today. Prior to his death in 2005, Bob Tisch was co-owner of the New York Giants football team and had a personal fortune valued by *Forbes* magazine at $3.9 billion. He held both CEO and co-chairman positions at Loews Corporation before passing away, after which his nephew James Tisch took the reins as CEO and his son and nephew, Jonathan and Andrew Tisch, became co-chairmen of the company.

Insurance is risky business

Chicago-based CNA Financial is 89 percent-owned by Loews Corp. Insurance produces include primarily property and casualty coverages. CNA serves a wide variety of customers, including small, medium and large businesses, associations, professionals and groups and individuals with a broad range of insurance and risk management products and services. Both Loews and subsidiary CNA suffered losses in 2005 due to the hurricane-related losses and various reserve-related charges at CNA. In 2006, CNA improved its position in the commercial property -casualty insurance market and posted record earnings due to disc implied underwriting, stringent expense controls and solid investment results.

Ethical accommodations

Loews's travel subsidiary Loews Hotels is one of the top hotel and resort chains in the U.S. and Canada. The brand has19 hotels -- 11 U.S. locations incites and 2 in Canada , including Annapolis, Denver, Las Vegas, Miami Beach, Montreal, Quebec City, Nashville, New Orleans, New York, Philadelphia, San Diego, St. Pete Beach, Tucson, Washington, D.C., and Orlando—where it operates three different vacation spots: Portofino Bay, Royal Pacific and Hard Rock Hotel. Loews Hotels was voted the No. 1 "Upper-Upscale" hotel chain two years running by *Business Travel News*. Under its "Good Neighbor Policy" initiated in 1990 by Jonathon Tisch, Loews hotels actively seek to improve their neighboring communities through food donations, by providing spaces and volunteers for adult literacy, and by donating used linens, towels and furniture to local organizations. The Good Neighbor Policy was awarded the President's Service Award for community service directed at solving critical social problems.

Not quite cold-turkey

Loews recently made a move to sell shares in the tobacco company Lorillard Tobacco Company, selling 15 million shares of Lorillard's parent company, Carolina Group, in a public offering announced in August of 2006. The sale had an estimated value of $740 million. Loews had previously held a controlling 53.7 percent stake in Carolina Group, which was reduced to 37.7 percent with the sale. Lorillard is one of America's oldest tobacco

© 2007 Vault, Inc.

companies, having manufactured tobacco products for almost two and a half centuries. The company is infamous for racking up $16.25 billion in punitive damages in Engle v. R.J. Reynolds Tobacco Co., et al., the 1997 class-action lawsuit against Lorillard and three other tobacco companies.

Beyond the smoke

While a large proportion of Loews cash flow has historically come from Lorillard, the corporation has diversified its cash flow in recent years. Recently, Loews announced its purchase of gas exploration and production assets from Dominion Resources. The properties being acquired are located in the Permian Basin in Texas, the Black Warrior Basin in Alabama and the Antrim Shale in Michigan, with estimated reserves of about 2.5 trillion cubic feet of gas. The price equates to about $1.61 per thousand cubic feet. Prior to that, Loews purchased two interstate natural gas pipelines (Texas Gas in 2003 and Gulf South Pipelinein in 2004), creating a parent company, Boardwalk Pipeline Partners (NYSE: BWP) in 2005.

Moving into media

In November of 2006, Loews Corp. disclosed ownership of 2.61 million shares of media company the New York Times Co., amounting to $63 million, or about 1.8 percent of the company's Class A stock outstanding. The purchase comes at an uncertain time for the Times, which has been under pressure to disband its voting structure that allows the controlling Ochs-Sulzberger family to maintain control. The Sulzberger family owns about 20 percent of the total equity of the company.

GETTING HIRED

Under the Loews umbrella

Positions at Loews Corporation may be available in its corporate office or at the subsidiary level. CNA, Loews Hotels and Diamond Offshore invites those interested in applying for positions to go to the "careers" section of their respective web sites. Those interested in other Loews companies can contact their human resources companies directly.

Visit the Vault Finance Career Channel at **www.vault.com/finance** – with insider firm profiles, message boards, the Vault Finance Job Board and more

VAULT CAREER LIBRARY   **205**

The recruiting process at Loews is "very efficient and transparent," one insider says. "A recruiter first calls to ask if you are interested in the interview, then schedules an interview, which is typically three to four hours long." The interview is also "broken into half-hour segments, each of which is an interview with one or more people, and the interview questions are situational." And they don't keep you hanging, reports the contact. "Before I left that day, I knew the initial feelings of the first six interviewers and the timing of our next steps."

© 2007 Vault, Inc.

Marsh & McLennan Companies, Inc.

1166 Ave. of the Americas
New York, NY 10036-2774
Phone: (212) 345-5000
Fax: (212) 345-4838
www.mmc.com

DEPARTMENTS

Consulting Services
Investment Management
Risk & Insurance Services
Risk Consulting & Technology

THE STATS

Employer Type: Public Company
Ticker Symbol: MMC (NYSE)
President, CEO & Director: Michael G. Cherkasky
Revenue: $11.9 billion (FYE 12/06)
No. of Employees: 55,000

KEY COMPETITORS

AJ Gallagher
Aon
Willis

UPPERS

- "Excellent professional development program"

DOWNERS

- "Politics"

EMPLOYMENT CONTACT

See "careers" section of
www.mmac.com

Visit the Vault Finance Career Channel at **www.vault.com/finance** — with insider firm profiles, message boards, the Vault Finance Job Board and more

VAULT CAREER LIBRARY   207

THE SCOOP

Not a newcomer to New York

For more than 135 years, Marsh & McLennan Companies, Inc. has served clients in a diverse range of financial services. The firm today is a multibillion dollar public holding company for several professional services subsidiaries, holding market leading positions in all of the areas in which it operates. Subsidiaries include Marsh, a leader in risk consulting, insurance broking and insurance program management, Guy Carpenter, a risk and reinsurance specialist, Kroll, a risk consulting and technology company, Mercer Consulting Group, a global human resources and management consulting company, and Putnam, one of the largest investment companies in the U.S. The MMC group holds its headquarters in New York, but has offices all over the world, with subsidiaries employing some 55,000 staff, in over 100 countries. MMC reported revenue for 2006 of $11.9 billion, slightly up from the $11.6 billion reported in 2005.

An acquisitive history

Marsh & McLennan has its beginnings in an insurance company dating back to 1871. The company expanded to reinsurance broking in 1923, with the acquisition of Guy Carpenter & Company. MMC entered human resource consulting in 1959, upon acquiring William M. Mercer Limited in Canada. In the 1980s, MMC first introduced specialty consulting. Today the specialty consulting businesses under Mercer Specialty Consulting include strategy and operations consulting (Mercer Management Consulting), financial services strategy and risk management consulting (Mercer Oliver Wyman), organizational change consulting (Mercer Delta), economic consulting (NERA), and design and brand strategy consulting (Lippincott Mercer). In 1970, MMC acquired one of the largest mutual fund companies in the U.S., Putnam Investments, which established the company's presence in the business of investment management. The most recent addition to MMC's businesses came in 2004, with the acquisition of Kroll, a risk consulting services company providing investigative, intelligence, financial, security and technology services.

© 2007 Vault, Inc.

Changes at Marsh

In 2004 and 2005, MMC made several important changes to its business model, particularly to Marsh, which will implement higher commissions and fees with more transparency. Marsh, MMC's risk and insurance services subsidiary, has 26,000 employees and an annual revenue approaching $5 billion. The firm began rolling out compliance initiatives due to a settlement with the Office of the New York State Attorney General and the New York State Insurance Department. The compliance agreement involved the development of transparency standards, related policies, procedures, employee training and compliance monitoring groups.

Cleaning up with a new CFO

In 2005, MMC company divested its interest in private equity subsidiary MMC Capital, selling to former managers of MMC Capital operating under the Stone Point LLC entity. It also sold Marsh's Crump wholesale broking operations and Sedwick Claims Management Services. The company as a whole eliminated approximately 2,600 employee positions in 2005. In 2006, MMC appointed a new CFO, former Vice President and Treasurer Matthew B. Bartley. Prior to coming to MMC in 2001, Bartley spent nearly 10 years in international treasury and tax positions at PepsiCo, and as vice president of taxes at specialty chemicals and precious metals company Engelhard Corporation. Despite the changes, the company announced in its annual report that it expects 2006's revenue to be "significantly lower."

A climate leader

In September of 2006, MMC was recognized by the Carbon Disclosure Project (CDP) as Best in Class on the project's Climate Leadership Index for 2006. Every year, the CDP surveys the world's largest companies on investment-relevant information on climate change risks and opportunities, publishing results in its annual Index. Earlier in 2006, MMC CEO Michael Cherkasky spoke at the World Economic Forum, identifying climate change as one of the most significant long-term issues facing world businesses. MMC has initiated a goal of promoting dialogue, research and new alliances around the issue of climate change.

Visit the Vault Finance Career Channel at www.vault.com/finance – with insider firm profiles, message boards, the Vault Finance Job Board and more

VAULT CAREER LIBRARY   209

Putting pressure on Putnam

MMC's investment management arm Putnam offers a full range of both domestic and international equity and fixed income products in institutional portfolios, 401(k)s, IRAs and other retirement plans, mutual funds, variable annuities and alternative investments. Today Putnam has 3,000 employees serving roughly 204 institutional clients and over nine million shareholders. The firm distributes its funds through financial advisors, brokers, banks and financial planners to provide financial advice in conjunction with its products. The firm has a total of $187 billion (as of February 2007) in assets under management, of which $120 billion is for mutual fund investors and $67 billion for institutional accounts. In response to "repeated inquiries" about either acquiring or partnering with Putnam, in September of 2006, MMC Chief Executive Office Michael Cherkasky stated that MMC would perform a "check" of the market value of Putnam.

47 execs named tops in their field

In February 2007, *Risk & Insurance* magazine published a list of 150 of its Power Brokers, the country's top insurance brokerage executives within 27 different industry categories. Of the 150 on the list, 47 were Marsh insurance brokerage and risk advisory executives, by far the largest number of executives from any one firm. The list is based on feedback from 300 risk managers, who make their selections based on brokers' creativity in solving risk-related problems, industry knowledge and level of client service.

Going to Qatar, going global

In March 2007, the firm announced that it planned to apply for a license from the Qatar Financial Centre Regulatory Authority. Commenting on the application, Robert Makhoul, head of Marsh's Middle East operations, said, "Our plans to set up an office in the Qatar Financial Centre reflect the exciting opportunities available there. We have had solid growth in the region and believe that there will be strong demand for the kind of broking and risk advisory services we can offer companies in Qatar."

In April 2007, Marsh announced it had established a global real estate practice, naming Jeffrey S. Alpaugh to lead it. Alpaugh, who had been with Marsh throughout his 18-year career in insurance and risk management, held positions of increasing responsibility in the firm's New York, Los Angeles and Boston offices, serving as a broker, global client executive, regional real

© 2007 Vault, Inc.

estate industry practice leader and, most recently, regional client executive practice leader.

GETTING HIRED

Submit or create

On its career web site (global.marsh.com/careers), Marsh & McLennan lists openings in all cities and categories for all levels of applicants, but if you don't find the specific gig you had in mind, never fear. If you don't happen to find an opportunity that interests you, the company encourages applicants to create a candidate profile to keep on file and "may notify you by e-mail when an opportunity becomes available in your area of interest and/or expertise."

OUR SURVEY SAYS

Politics rule the roost

The company culture is "fragmented, and varies tremendously by office and department/practice." One insider says, "Politics rule the company in all locations." Another notes that "a lot of your satisfaction and success will depend upon which division you work in—some are good and some are bad." Others say that while the firm has "great potential and some really nice folks," it also includes "favoritism," and is a "strange company to work for— everything is done by consensus and committee. These people can't make a quick decision on anything."

Manage it

As far as management, insiders say that "senior leadership is weak," and "Marsh regularly begins initiatives that are started without much input from employees," and "dropped as fast as they are dictated to the troops."

The hours "can be long, but are nothing like consulting or investment banking," says one source, adding that "the average workweek, even for most senior vice presidents, is 45 hours." But the firm does provide decent programs for staff. An insider says, "One great strength of Marsh is its excellent professional development program for employees."

Another source says the firm is "not in a very diverse industry," adding that "white males run the show, and minorities are almost excluded from management ranks." Another comments that "two CIOs from Marsh are no longer here, both of them women, which makes you wonder about the culture."

© 2007 Vault, Inc.

MassMutual Financial Group

1295 State Street
Springfield, MA 01111-0001
Phone: (413) 744-1000
Fax: (413) 744-6005
www.massmutual.com

DEPARTMENT

Insurance Services
Investment Services
Retirement Services

THE STATS

Employer Type: Private Company
President & CEO: Stuart H. Reese
Revenue: $18 billion (FYE 12/06)
No. of Employees: 27,000
No. of Offices: 1,800 (worldwide)

UPPERS

- "Good income"
- Great perks: "ample vacation time," "good pension plan and 401(k) plans"

DOWNERS

- "Reorganizations that turn everything upside down"
- Doesn't promote enough from within

EMPLOYMENT CONTACT

www.massmutual.com/careers

Visit the Vault Finance Career Channel at **www.vault.com/finance** — with insider firm profiles, message boards, the Vault Finance Job Board and more

VAULT CAREER LIBRARY   213

THE SCOOP

Be prepared

Founded in 1851, the Springfield-based MassMutual divides its business into investment, insurance and retirement services. Its investment division includes life, disability income, long-term care, annuities, a private client group, structured settlements and trust services. MassMutual's investment products include annuities, structured settlements, income management services, mutual funds, education savings plans, wealth management and trust services. Finally, it offers annuities, income management, contribution protection, trust services and retirement plan services through its retirement services practice. MassMutual's clients include individuals, business owners, and corporate and institutional markets.

MassMutual likes to remind clients of its corporate motto: "You can't predict. You can prepare." With more than 155 years of growth, mergers and acquisitions under its belt, MassMutual is prepared for business, with subsidiaries and affiliates that include OppenheimerFunds, Babson Capital Management, Baring Asset Management, Cornerstone Real Estate Advisers, MML Investors Services, the MassMutual Trust Company, MML Bay State Life Insurance, C.M. Life Insurance and MassMutual International, the firm's global arm. The 2006 Fortune 500 listed MassMutual at No. 92; it was the highest ranked Massachusetts firm on the list.

Clearing the air

Robert J. O'Connell, who had served as MassMutual's chairman, president and CEO since 2000, was dismissed from his posts on June 23, 2005, following an internal investigation into his actions. The company's board of directors made the decision, saying that investigators (tipped off by O'Connell's suspicious wife) had turned up a laundry list of abuses and misdeeds, including the theft of over $30 million, personal use of company aircraft for his family and friends, bribery and other crimes. Stuart H. Reese, a 12-year veteran and CIO of MassMutual, was named president and CEO. A separate, non-executive chairman of the board was selected: James R. Birle, who had spent 13 years on MassMutual's board of directors. The O'Connell scandal brought a run of bad PR, but Reese and Birle were able to reassure clients and keep MassMutual's performance on track. At the close of fiscal 2006 the company reported $450 billion in assets under management.

© 2007 Vault, Inc.

Radio free MassMutual

What's the best way to keep field agents, sales managers, trainers and recruiters—many of whom spend a significant amount time on the road and away from the office—up-to-date on company news? For MassMutual, the answer is podcasting. Begun in February 2006 and expanded in May 2006, the company's podcast program is provided by the MassMutual National Center for Professional Development (NCPD). "Radio NCPD" creates weekly podcasts, available by free subscription to any member of the MassMutual field force. Topics include information about new MassMutual products, underwriting policies and procedures, plus interviews with top sales representatives and tips for success in niche markets.

Selling to women

In August 2006 MassMutual launched a new Selling to Women series, designed to help its agents provide better financial services to women. The exclusive four-part course was designed by MassMutual's National Center for Professional Development and its women's markets department. MassMutual said it was prompted to develop the course after industry research reported that the majority of women, despite being involved in 80 percent of all financial decisions, feel misunderstood by the financial services industry. "Selling to Women" teaches MassMutual agents about women's market power, buying preferences, business concerns and other needs; the firm also created a special section of its web site to educate women about financial planning, products and services.

Mass power

Fall 2006 brought several awards for MassMutual. In September it was named a Working Mother 100 Best Company by *Working Mother* magazine for the eighth year. That same month MassMutual's retirement services division was ranked No. 1 in the InformationWeek 500 Wireless Innovation category. This award recognized MassMutual's patent-pending electronic enhanced enrollment experience (e4) technology, designed to help simplify employees' interactions with their company-sponsored 401(k) plans. MassMutual's online presence won kudos, too, as its web site picked up top rankings from the DALBAR WebMonitor 3Q06 survey of life insurance and annuity web sites.

Visit the Vault Finance Career Channel at **www.vault.com/finance** – with
insider firm profiles, message boards, the Vault Finance Job Board and more
VAULT CAREER LIBRARY   215

Hitting payout dirt

In November 2006 MassMutual announced the distribution of approximately $1.25 billion to participating mutual life policyholders under the estimated dividend payout for 2007. This marked the highest payout ever in the firm's history and represented a 5.6 percent increase above the estimated payout for 2006. CEO Reese attributed the payout prediction to MassMutual's financial strength; as of the date of the announcement MassMutual and its subsidiaries were ranked Aa1 by Moody's, AAA by Fitch Ratings and Standard & Poor's, and A++ by A.M. Best Company.

GETTING HIRED

Mass appeal

Create a profile to keep on file with the firm for up to a year, or just browse for open positions at MassMutual's career site, which offers separate menus depending on whether prospective employees are searching corporate careers or national sales and management careers. Those interested in corporate careers can search by geographic location or job type, which can include accounting, actuarial, audit, claims, data management, finance, government relations, investments, legal, quality assurance, systems architecture and underwriting.

For candidates interested in national sales/management careers, many options are available. Again, separate menus can be found for those looking to submit resumes for jobs such as financial professionals, sales managers, business professionals (CPAs, JDs, MBAs), experienced producers and internships (for college students).

MassMutual's site also includes detailed information about its campus recruiting practices for undergraduates, graduate students and law students.

© 2007 Vault, Inc.

OUR SURVEY SAYS

Life at the top

Insiders enjoy the "gym," "cafeteria" and "travel services" provided to staff. Contacts also cite the company's "4 percent match for the thrift savings plan" and "no-load mutual funds" as draws. One source notes that perks seem to be based on level of employment. "If you get in as an officer or attorney, the salaries, bonuses, perks, training and upward advancement are great," says the contact, "but if you don't, good luck." Other benefits available to all staff include "flex-time and flexible work arrangements," "child care," "dry cleaning" and even "film processing."

The dress code is "casual except for client contact," and hours can be "very flexible" if you do a lot of business traveling, though "sometimes you have to travel on Sunday in order to be at a meeting on Monday." Office space could stand to be improved, as the cubicle setup offers "very little privacy." Although one insider reports having had "both bad and good managers," management issues may be external. One source comments that the firm "puts too much stock in listening to consulting firms who really don't know our way of business, and then they implement these suggested policies." As far as advancement within the firm, one insider puts it succinctly: "They do not promote from within."

Diversity seems to be improving in some areas. Although diversity with respect to minorities, and gays and lesbians generally receives good marks, one erespondent notes that while "the company does a fair job in recruiting women and minorities," "some male managers can still be rude to women without even realizing that they have an attitude."

Visit the Vault Finance Career Channel at www.vault.com/finance – with
insider firm profiles, message boards, the Vault Finance Job Board and more

VAULT CAREER LIBRARY   217

MasterCard

2000 Purchase Street
Purchase, NY 10577
Phone: (914) 249-2000
Fax: (914) 249-4206
www.mastercardintl.com

DEPARTMENTS

Corporations
Mid-size Companies
Public Sector
Small Business

THE STATS

Employer Type: Public Company
Ticker Symbol: MA (NYSE)
President & CEO: Robert Selander
Revenue: $3.33 billion (FYE 12/06)
Net Income: $50.2 million
No. of Employees: 4,300
No. of Offices: 37

KEY COMPETITIORS

American Express
Discover
Visa

UPPERS

• "Considers cultural diversity very important"

DOWNERS

• "We work very hard and long hours"

EMPLOYMENT CONTACT

See
www.mastercard.com/us/company/en/careers/index.html

© 2007 Vault, Inc.

THE SCOOP

Master in the field

MasterCard Inc., based in Purchase, New York, was founded in 1966 as the Interbank Card Association. It is a leading international payments solutions company that offers a range of innovative credit, deposit access, electronic cash, business-to-business and related payment programs. It was renamed Master Charge three years later and purchased by the California Bank Association, and a decade later changed its name again, from Master Charge to MasterCard. By 2003, the company had at last succeeded in overtaking rival Visa to become the largest credit card brand in the world, but it has since fallen back to the No. 2 spot. MasterCard, through its principal operating subsidiary, MasterCard International Incorporated, manages a family of widely recognized and accepted payment cards, including MasterCard®, Maestro® and Cirrus® and serves financial institutions, consumers and businesses in over 210 countries and territories. The company's award-winning Priceless® advertising campaign is now seen in 106 countries and in 50 languages, giving the MasterCard brand a truly global reach and scope. And 2006 was a historic turning point for the organization when it was listed on the New York Stock Exchange and pledged its commitment to an open governance structure, seamless organization and a new name, MasterCard Worldwide.

MasterCard ranked third in the financial data services category of *Fortune*'s Most Admired Companies in America list for 2007.

New benchmark

On May 25, 2006, MasterCard went public, and began trading on the New York Stock Exchange under the ticker MA. "Listing on the NYSE marks a major milestone for MasterCard and reinforces our commitment to continued growth and building value for our customers and stockholders," Robert Selander, the company's president and chief executive officer, told Associated Press. The market had expected the issue to open in the $40 to $43 range, but MasterCard was at $39 after a series of setbacks delayed the process.

The IPO was supposed to have gone ahead earlier in the year, when market conditions were better, but was pushed back after Selander discovered he had prostate cancer. The CEO is now back on his feet, but the underwriters were also worried by MasterCard's legal and regulatory problems; the company

Visit the Vault Finance Career Channel at www.vault.com/finance – with insider firm profiles, message boards, the Vault Finance Job Board and more

VAULT CAREER LIBRARY   219

had been embroiled in a legal wrangle as antitrust regulators investigated the credit card industry, and retailers threatened court action to lower the fees they pay on transactions. Merchant groups have already filed a class-action suit alleging unlawful price fixing of fees that hurt both merchants and consumers, but the opportunity to buy shares of one of the world's top financial services brands at a relatively reasonable price was expected to attract investors nonetheless.

And investors in MasterCard have been rewarded. Since the firm went public in May 2006, the stock has zoomed to over $140 per share as of May 2007, making MasterCard one of the most successful IPOs of 2006.

Leadership award

MasterCard Worldwide received the 2006 Frost & Sullivan Market Penetration Leadership Award for its successful leadership in the contactless payment market with its innovative MasterCard® PayPass™ program. The company has been the market leader and main innovator in contactless payments since introducing contactless card solutions in 2002 and, following initial end-user research and extensive R&D, implemented numerous contactless card solutions throughout the world, using its MasterCard® PayPass™ technology. The technology is already providing a higher level of control and convenience for customers and driving faster throughput and greater spend for retailers. Accepting the award on behalf of MasterCard, Toni Merschen, group head, Chip, MasterCard Worldwide, said: "Contactless payments have a major role to play in the replacement of cash in global commerce. We are delighted to accept the Frost & Sullivan Company of the Year Award as recognition of our market leadership and innovative approach in this area, through our MasterCard PayPass solution. Following the successful rollout of MasterCard PayPass in the U.S., we are delighted to have launched contactless payment initiatives in 2006 with The Royal Bank of Scotland in the U.K. and Garanti Bank in Turkey." Just the day before, the firm had announced its part in an m-commerce pilot in France, driven by the EMV OneSmart PayPass contactless application.

Best place to work in IT

MasterCard was named one of the top workplaces for information technology professionals on *Computerworld*'s annual Best Places to Work in IT list in 2006, marking the fourth year MasterCard had been recognized by the flagship publication.

 © 2007 Vault, Inc.

GETTING HIRED

If you don't schmooze, you might lose

While it's true that there are a few ways to break into the MasterCard biz, combing your phone book and leveraging your contacts is by far the easiest, sources say. "MasterCard is very selective when it comes to hiring," says an insider. "They get thousands of resumes per week. The best bet for getting a job is through a referral." If you don't know someone at the firm, the next best way to apply for work with MasterCard is through the career section of its web site, which is simple yet thorough. Applicants can either search for jobs individually, or let the company come to them by submitting their resumes for future openings. The job search engine allows for specific searches to be chosen among dozens of job titles and the firm's many offices worldwide. The site also features a "job cart" that allows prospective employees to apply for multiple positions simultaneously, and it won't tick anyone off. In case a job hunter doesn't see any suitable openings, he or she can also post a resume on the site, which is forwarded to a central database for review against any openings at MasterCard. Once the resume is submitted, the company will send an e-mail immediately confirming the submission. And because all material remains in the database for 12 months, applicants can update their resumes.

Says one source, "You need the right expertise and cultural attitude, as well as openness to work in an international environment." Additionally, it helps if you have some financial services experience. The firm also prefers candidates who can excel in a "team setting" and who are "not too confrontational or aggressive." The company reportedly does "very little campus recruiting." An insider in St. Louis says, "I had three interviews with levels from team leaders to directors and VPs. Questions were team-oriented, project-oriented and technical in nature." One European contact in technology says he went through "only two interviews, because I had the right background for the job that they were looking for.

Visit the Vault Finance Career Channel at **www.vault.com/finance** – with
insider firm profiles, message boards, the Vault Finance Job Board and more

VAULT CAREER LIBRARY   **221**

OUR SURVEY SAYS

No average employee

"Who is the typical MasterCard employee?" the firm asks on its web site. "There isn't one." The firm adds that it defines "diversity from a multidimensional perspective that encompasses our diverse skills, knowledge, viewpoints, culture and national origins." Insiders give MasterCard high marks when it comes to diversity. "We have in place formal diversity and sensitivity training," says a source. Another contact notes, "MasterCard is very dedicated to ensuring all employees receive training to ensure discrimination doesn't happen here. MasterCard is an international company and considers cultural diversity very important."

MasterCard sources enjoy working for an "easily recognizable name" in a "fairly relaxed environment." It's a "multicultural and open" firm, and "very team-oriented," with a "Midwest work ethic—everyone knows what's expected of them and performs at 110 percent." Insiders also say that middle management makes a "concerted effort to orient new employees." Information systems staffers like the fact that "technologically-speaking, we are on the cutting edge.

Hard work

"We work very hard and long hours," says an insider. "It's a fast-moving, stressful culture," reports another. A contact at the company's headquarters notes, "Official work hours are 35 hours, with flex-time in the summer and no telecommuting. The reality is 50 to 60 hours for the ambitious, but telecommuting is common." Sources in networking and information systems comment that they often work "irregular hours," because "the credit business never shuts down for a holiday." A respondent in Europe adds that he "frequently, about once a month," makes a weekend office visit. However, another reports that "all in all, work hours are not tremendous unless you make them that way." And staffers don't have to get all dressed up, either. At MasterCard, dress is "business casual," "basically no jeans or sneakers or T-shirts," and "no suits, except for outside meetings."

© 2007 Vault, Inc.

MetLife

200 Park Avenue
New York, NY 10166-0188
Phone: (212) 578-2211
Fax: (212) 578-3320
www.metlife.com

DEPARTMENTS

Annuities
Auto Insurance
Disability Income
Financial Planning
Home Insurance
Life Insurance
Long-Term Care

THE STATS

Employer Type: Public Company
President & CEO: C. Robert Henrikson
Revenue: $48.4 billion (FYE 12/06)
Net Income: $6.3 billion
No. of Employees: 65,500
No. of Offices: 400

KEY COMPETITIORS

AIG
Prudential
State Farm

UPPERS

- "Unlimited income potential" in sales
- "Many good opportunities for women"

DOWNERS

- Sales isn't for everyone: "If you choose a career in insurance, be ready for rejection"
- "Too much busy work"

EMPLOYMENT CONTACT

See "careers" link at www.metlife.com

Visit the Vault Finance Career Channel at **www.vault.com/finance** — with
insider firm profiles, message boards, the Vault Finance Job Board and more

VAULT CAREER LIBRARY   223

THE SCOOP

Life with the Met

MetLife, ranked No. 37 on the 2007 Fortune 100, is the largest public life and health insurer in the U.S. The company works through three principal segments: an institutional division that provides group benefits products to large and small businesses; a suite of insurance products for individuals; and banking and investment services. The company's international segment offers similar products to companies and individuals overseas, primarily in Latin America and the Asia/Pacific region.

Its flagship insurance firm is Metropolitan Life Insurance Company, in addition to subsidiaries that include MetLife Investors (variable and fixed annuities, life insurance), General American (underwrites life insurance), and Metropolitan Property and Casualty (auto, home and related coverage). MetLife made some major acquisitions in the early 2000s, such as Mexico's largest life insurer Hidalgo in 2002 and John Hancock's life insurance operations in 2003, and divestitures like the sale of the iconic Sears Tower in Chicago for $800 million in 2004. The 2005 acquisition of Travelers Life and Annuity from Citigroup for $11.8 billion vaulted MetLife to the top spot as America's largest life insurance company, and in 2006, the historic sale of its 80-acre, 11,000-unit Stuyvesant Town-Peter Cooper Village housing complex in Manhattan—originally built for returning World War II veterans in 1947, and the largest such development in New York City—added $5.4 billion to the company's coffers.

Get Met

MetLife started out in 1868 as Metropolitan Life Insurance, sustained in its early years from mutual assistance societies for German immigrants. By the 1870s, MetLife could barely survive, though it managed by importing agents from Britain to train native agents about successful English policies in the U.S. Focusing on a personal touch, MetLife agents were taught to visit homes at the same time each week to build familiarity and maintain contact. By 1909, MetLife was the nation's largest life insurer in terms of insurance in force. Metropolitan became a mutual company (owned by policyholders) in 1915 and began offering group insurance two years later. In 1974, it began offering automobile and homeowners' insurance. Diversification efforts in the 1980s included the acquisition of Century 21 Real Estate (which was sold in 1995) and State Street Research & Management Company. In 1996, the

© 2007 Vault, Inc.

company merged with Boston-based New England Mutual Life Insurance, expanding its clientele to include the more-profitable realm of upper-income customers. In January 2000, MetLife bought GenAmerica Corp. for $1.2 billion in cash. But more growth was in store: In November 2003, it announced that it had completed its acquisition of John Hancock Life Insurance Company's group life insurance business, following regulatory approval, a move that strengthened MetLife's position in the group life area.

New CEO tapped

On March 1, 2006, MetLife appointed C. Robert (Rob) Henrikson chairman of the board of directors, president and chief executive officer of MetLife, Inc. Henrikson has been the architect of an aggressive growth strategy that included double-digit organic growth, the divestiture of non-core businesses, and an M&A strategy that resulted in market leadership in all of MetLife's core product lines. Before it was commonly talked about, Henrikson recognized the opportunities presented by the changing demographics of the international marketplace, setting the company on a course for continued success by developing innovative products and services, and strengthening the company's distribution power in the U.S. and 16 markets in Asia Pacific, Latin America and Europe.

Historic real estate divestiture

In November 2006, MetLife completed the sale of its Peter Cooper Village and Stuyvesant Town properties to a group led by Tishman Speyer and BlackRock Realty, the real estate arm of BlackRock, Inc. for $5.4 billion. The properties were owned by the MetLife affiliate Metropolitan Tower Life Insurance Company, and their sale resulted in a gain of approximately $3 billion, net of income taxes, that was reflected in the company's fourth quarter and annual 2006 financial results.

Diversity goals being met

MetLife has received many accolades for its commitment to diversity in the workplace. For the third consecutive year, the company scored a perfect 100 in the Human Rights Campaign Foundation's (HRC) 2005 Corporate Equality Index, a rating system measuring how major American corporations treat their gay, lesbian, bisexual and transgender (GLBT) employees, customers and investors. HRC rates companies from 0 to 100 percent based on seven criteria such as company policies, employee benefits, training and

Visit the Vault Finance Career Channel at www.vault.com/finance – with
insider firm profiles, message boards, the Vault Finance Job Board and more

VAULT CAREER LIBRARY   225

support networks. Not surprisingly, HRC named MetLife to its Best Places to Work for GLBT Equality list released in January 2006. The company is also on *DiversityInc*'s Top 50 Companies for Diversity.

Great for moms

In 2006, for the eighth consecutive year, MetLife was named to *Working Mother* magazine's list of the top 100 companies for working mothers. "MetLife is exceptional for its continuing commitment to working mothers, and we salute them for making the 100 Best for the eighth time," said Carol Evans, CEO of Working Mother Media, in a press release. "Every year, we see companies upping the ante, establishing new paradigms for quality of life among their employees and redefining the status quo for workplaces across the country. Among the many worthy entrants, the winners really set the gold standard." Suzanne Riss, editor-in-chief of *Working Mother* magazine, congratulated the firm "for helping its working mother employees balance the demands of their work and home lives. MetLife recognizes that outstanding family-friendly programs not only improve employees' lives but also give the company leverage in its ability to attract and retain top talent."

Record earnings

For fiscal 2006, MetLife booked record net income $6.2 billion, a significant increase versus the $4.7 billion it booked in 2005. Meanwhile, revenue rose to $48.4 billion in 2006 from $44.7 billion 2005, and total assets increased by 10 percent during the year to $527.7 billion at the end of 2006.

GETTING HIRED

Long and winding road

Under "careers" at www.metlife.com, applicants can search opportunities and learn about MetLife's "flexible career paths." The firm also notes that it's "not uncommon for individuals to cross job functions, lines of business and even geographic regions as their careers progress with MetLife." In addition, the web site offers in-depth descriptions of working life at Met in a number of different job categories, including administration, actuarial, auditing, claims, eBusiness, finance, IT, investments, marketing, sales, underwriting, and wellness and fitness. The firm provides a searchable database of job openings and encourages interested candidates to apply online or submit a resume for future consideration.

OUR SURVEY SAYS

Better than others

MetLife has a "very laid-back corporate culture" that's "conservative, but much less so than other insurance companies." Another notes, perhaps wryly, that "we're the No. 1 life insurer, and with the backing of Snoopy, I believe I have more support for success than with any other commission-based financial or insurance company in the U.S." The culture may ultimately depend on your office. One contact says that "each field office is relatively unique and reflective of the both the managing partner/managing director and management team at the helm." A different informant believes "working at MetLife is great and there is great opportunity in it if you like to work." Are there any downsides to the culture? "Some managers are tough," grumbles a respondent.

A former insider notes that it "felt like upper management didn't care too much about employees," adding that there was "very low morale and nothing done about it." A contact enigmatically comments that "managers seem to go on mental health leaves on a regular basis." But another notes that "management recognizes talent," and "does a fairly good job when it comes to performance reviews and promotions." The firm also "does a good job of providing opportunities to transfer internally." One source says that "most managers allow telecommuting as needed for bad weather, sick kids, etc." Another suggests that management take on more responsibilities, noting, "I would like a better field management relationship where sales is less responsible for business processing and management is more responsible for generating leads."

MetLife also holds "monthly 'town hall' meetings where the company goes over the numbers, tells you what to expect and how things are going" but tends "not to listen to employee input" and "are very guarded if anyone has any complaints about the way things are working." And the firm seems to really take pleasure in its get-togethers—one insider notes that "MetLife's

Visit the Vault Finance Career Channel at **www.vault.com/finance** – with
insider firm profiles, message boards, the Vault Finance Job Board and more

VAULT CAREER LIBRARY   **227**

common nickname is "MeetLife," due to the culture's proclivity for holding meetings."

What's your goal?

The sales force receives "no perks except for discounted shopping for cars, cell phone and various other items," comments an insider. But another says, "If earning large amounts of money is your object, then a career in sales might be the way to go." A source agrees, revealing that "the sales organization has allowed me to build my business from the ground up. The compensation is great and I set my own hours and dress to satisfy my clients." One insider puts hours at approximately "40 to 55 hours per week" but with a "heavy workload." Another says, "Those who don't put in the long hours will not last here." It may also depend on how long you've been with the firm. A respondent says that "hours will vary according to function," and "old-school MetLifers keep early hours (i.e. a 6:30 to 7 a.m. start), but most workdays begin between 7:30 and 8:00 a.m., with few staying past 8 p.m." Another insider working in Brooklyn notes that "as a new representative, you are required to attend Saturday morning phone sessions in order to make appointments."

But not all sources are singing the same tune when it comes to hours. Another sales source raves, "I enjoy the flexibility. I control my own destiny, set up my own schedule, and do what I want to do when I want to do it." The same contact, however, cautions that "it took me a few years of frustration and rejection to get to a point where people began to trust what I said and believe that I had their best interests at heart. If you choose a career in insurance, be ready for rejection."

Pajama party

One Texas insider says that the dress code is flexible, noting, "I can wear a tie or go business casual when I have client meetings, but I can stay in my pajamas if there aren't any meetings scheduled." On the whole, MetLifers generally indicate that the company is moving towards casual, although one contact explains, "I try to be casual, but the company takes a very dim view on too casual."

© 2007 Vault, Inc.

Getting there

Compensation at MetLife is "getting more competitive," notes an insider, adding that it's "to be expected when working on buy-side and for insurance." But "on the flip side, the hours are not nearly as grueling." "From what I have seen," one MetLifer says, "the pay is competitive and the perks are pretty good." Another insider notes there are "many vacation days, but not many perks." The one thing that all MetLife insiders can agree on is benefits. A former MetLife employee says, "The benefits were wonderful: 401(k), good health plan, dental, all the rest." Another benefit that draws praise is tuition reimbursement.

Sea of faces

"We are an ethnically diverse firm," says an insider simply. Indeed, Most respondents give positive reviews on MetLife's diversity. "The company absolutely practices EEO," says one. Another source testifies, "I would have to say that the top officers in the company are mostly men, but there are many good opportunities for women all over the company." One respondent agrees, saying, "Women are welcome and often excel."

Visit the Vault Finance Career Channel at **www.vault.com/finance** – with
insider firm profiles, message boards, the Vault Finance Job Board and more

VAULT CAREER LIBRARY   229

Moody's Corp.

99 Church Street
New York, NY 10007
Phone: (212) 553-0300
Fax: (212) 553-4820
www.moodys.com

DEPARTMENTS

Corporate Finance
Financial Institutions & Sovereign
 Risk
Public Finance
Structured Finance

THE STATS

Employer Type: Public Company
Ticker Symbol: MCO (NYSE)
**Chairman & CEO; President, Moody's
Investors Service:** Raymond. W.
McDaniel Jr.
Revenue: $2.04 billion (FY 12/06)
Net Income: $753.9 million
No. of Employees: 2,900
No. of Offices: 33 (worldwide)

KEY COMPETITORS

DBRS
Fitch
S&P

UPPERS

• "A very diverse and relaxed
  atmosphere"
• "Control of own work"

DOWNERS

• "Lack of clear career path"
• "Not enough diversity in type of
  work"

EMPLOYMENT CONTACT

See "careers" at www.moodys.com

© 2007 Vault, Inc.

THE SCOOP

Rating the world

Founded in 1900, Moody's Corporation is one of the most prominent and widely utilized sources for credit ratings, research and risk analysis on debt instruments and securities. In addition, Moody's provides corporate and government credit assessment and training services, credit training services and credit software to financial institutions, with 9,000 accounts at 2,400 institutions worldwide. The firm's ratings and analyses track 100 sovereign nations, 11,000 company insurers, 25,000 public finance issuers and 70,000 structured finance obligations. The firm employs more than 1,000 analysts. Moody's was born out of The Dun & Bradstreet Corporation, under which it operated until September 2000. At that point, Dun & Bradstreet split into two publicly traded companies: Moody's Corporation and D&B Corporation. The newly formed D&B comprised Dun & Bradstreet's business information services, and Moody's contained the remaining ratings, and related research and credit risk management services.

Moody's ratings business consists of four groups: structured finance, corporate finance, financial institutions, and sovereign risk and public finance. The firm's primary clients include corporate and government issuers as well as institutional investors, banks, creditors and commercial banks. While print was traditionally the firm's primary medium, Moody's research web site continues to grow in popularity. In addition to research, current ratings and supplemental information are available online at no charge.

The power of two

The firm operates in two business segments: Moody's Investors Service and Moody's KMV. Moody's Investors Service publishes the ratings on credit obligations. The unit also publishes the credit research, which includes research on equity and debt issuers, industry studies and credit opinion handbooks.

Moody's KMV consists of the combined businesses of KMV LLC and KMV Corporation, acquired by Moody's in April 2002; and Moody's Risk Management Services, which provides credit risk management products for banks and investors in credit-sensitive assets and serves more than 1,600 clients in over 80 countries, including most of the world's largest financial institutions. Moody's KMV's credit analysis tools include models that

Visit the Vault Finance Career Channel at www.vault.com/finance – with
insider firm profiles, message boards, the Vault Finance Job Board and more

VAULT CAREER LIBRARY   231

estimate the probability of default for many public firms globally; the unit's RiskCalc models serve the same function but cover privately held firms. In addition, Moody's KMV offers quantitative portfolio credit optimization services.

A good year

2006 was a banner year for Moody's. Revenue was $2.04 billion, up from $1.73 billion in 2005. "In the U.S., the continuation of low long-term interest rates and a growing economy encouraged corporate borrowers to pursue business spending and investment, including aggressive merger and acquisition activity and borrowing to repurchase equity," CEO Ray McDaniel said in a statement.

Promoting competition

Due to the accounting scandals at WorldCom and Enron (which received high ratings from Moody's and S&P), corporate CFOs, as well as lawmakers, began pressuring the SEC to regulate ratings companies. Only five firms are acknowledged by the SEC as "nationally recognized" credit raters, with Moody's and archrival S&P controlling 80 percent of the market and seeing profit margins of more than 50 percent. The other three are Fitch Ratings, Dominion Bond Rating Services and A.M. Best Co. The Credit Rating Agency Reform Act was signed into law in fall 2006, designed to make the credit rating business more competitive and ensure transparency. The new rules will make it easier for new competitors to enter the market and give the SEC oversight power. The new regs also require ratings firms to provide more disclosure of ratings methods and implement policies to avoid conflicts of interest. The jury is still out on if the new rules will ease the stranglehold Moody's and S&P has on the ratings business, but analysts expect that new competitors will take the tack of offering ratings paid for by investors instead of debt issuers and focusing on specific types of debt.

© 2007 Vault, Inc.

GETTING HIRED

Pretty particular

While Moody's uses everything from "internal recommendations" to "recruiting firms" to discover potential candidates, the firm is "very particular on both education and experience." Still, job seekers can check out the "careers" section of www.moodys.com and search for jobs by title, department and location, including international outposts. According to the firm, "If you thrive in a collegial, think-tank atmosphere, you should consider Moody's." The firm says it typically gives junior employees "direct access to senior staff from the start," adding, "The door is open, giving you an unusual opportunity to hone your skills in an informal setting." Moody's offers "opportunity for professional growth in analytics, information technology, marketing and administration.

Candidates can expect to meet "up to 12 different people in various positions" during the hiring process. "Some interviews are in person, some are over the phone." One contact says his interview consisted of meeting with "a recruitment specialist, then two managing directors, the team leader of the team I was being considered for, another team leader and three analysts." Insiders say the firm is looking for someone who "won't embarrass the firm in front of a client," "can deliver bad news and be responsive to inquiries," can think in a logical way and arrive at a logical conclusion," "is trustworthy and ethical," and "is interested in getting the rating right." Interview questions "typically center on past experiences." One source reports being asked "a range of things, from my motivation and experience through very specific and detailed questions about structured finance." Although not a hard and fast rule, students at top-25 schools are given preference. Interviewing can last several months; the key is to be persistent until you get an answer.

OUR SURVEY SAYS

Cooperative community

The atmosphere at Moody's is "generally collegial and cooperative," says one insider, adding that "there are surprisingly few political tensions and very

Visit the Vault Finance Career Channel at www.vault.com/finance – with
insider firm profiles, message boards, the Vault Finance Job Board and more

VAULT CAREER LIBRARY   233

little hierarchy." But newbies to the firm should take note: "Since most people are highly educated and pretty smart, a new joiner can be a bit intimidated." Another says, "The corporate culture at Moody's is not as conservative as the big banks, meaning there is a very diverse and relaxed atmosphere." And while "analysts work hard," "they all have a life outside work."

Insiders say life at Moody's, while no day at the beach, can be very rewarding. The firm has a "very respected name" and a "team of very smart and savvy analysts." Beware that the firm has a "high turnover rate," and that it "takes six months to get up to speed as to what is expected." It also "takes one to two years to get comfortable and be trusted with tougher assignments, but if you prove yourself, things ease off a bit." "If you can put up with a gossipy environment, and crazy deadlines, there is a degree of satisfaction in the work done, and it certainly won't be repetitive." But while there's "no pressure to bill or record time," "sometimes there's a high volume of work and high expectations of what can be done," says an insider. Also, "there is room for advancement, even rapidly, but up to a certain point." Another contact notes, "Opportunities for advancement are hierarchical, so don't count on being promoted until you've put your years." But don't worry too much about the pecking order. One respondent says, "Moody's values all levels of employees, so don't expect snobbery here," and "employees are very respectful of each other and focus much on team-building."

Perks are decent. There are "stock options and shares that form part of the bonus," and "a stock purchase plan with stock sold to employees at a discount." The firm also offers "a car service after 8:30 p.m." and "business class travel." Sources report that although "management can be a bit distant," "there are "generally good relations" between the levels. Training also seems to be improving. One contact notes that although "many people used to feel it was sink-or-swim" when it came to training, "this is changing slowly." Dress code is "business casual unless you have a meeting, then it's business formal." And the hours are "generally reasonable: 40 to 50 per week." One employee says, "Hours are usually 8 or 9 in the morning 'til 6 or 7 at night," but "hardly anyone stays past 8 p.m." Travel is "restricted to three to four days per month, sometimes more, sometimes less." "Most are day trips." Although pay doesn't win any awards, "health benefits and vacation time are pretty generous." And get ready to get down. "Moody's throws great parties," reports an insider.

Diversity also gets a pretty good rep at the firm. One source notes that women receive "good representation at all levels," and "there are no real

© 2007 Vault, Inc.

issues" with the representation of minorities. Diversity with respect to gays and lesbians also receive high marks from employees.

Visit the Vault Finance Career Channel at **www.vault.com/finance** – with
insider firm profiles, message boards, the Vault Finance Job Board and more

VAULT CAREER
LIBRARY

235

Nationwide Financial Services

1 Nationwide Plaza
Columbus, OH 43215-2220
Phone: (614) 249-7111
Fax: (614) 854-5036
www.nationwidefinancial.com

DEPARTMENTS

Financial Services
Property & Casualty Insurance

THE STATS

Employer Type: Public Company
Ticker Symbol: NFS (NYSE)
Chairman: Arden L. Shisler
CEO & Director: William G. Jurgensen
President and COO: Mark R. Thresher
Revenue: $4.42 billion (FYE 02/07)
Net Income: $713.8 million
No. of Employees: 35,000

KEY COMPETITORS

John Hancock Financial Services
MassMutual
Prudential

UPPERS

- Good managers
- Great advancement opportunities

DOWNERS

- "Bureaucratic," "dealing with headquarters"
- "Slow to make decisions"

EMPLOYMENT CONTACT

nationwide.com/nw/careers

© 2007 Vault, Inc.

THE SCOOP

On your side

Many people know Nationwide from its "Life Comes at You Fast" ad campaign featuring a rapidly aging Fabio, and sports fans may recognize the company from the Nationwide Arena, home of the NHL's Columbus Blue Jackets. From its humble beginnings insuring farmers in the Buckeye State, Columbus, Ohio-based Nationwide Financial Services, the holding company for Nationwide Life Insurance and other divisions of the insurance giant, is one of the world's largest diversified insurance and financial services firms with over $157 billion in statutory assets with more than 16 million policies in force. Nationwide provides a range of financial and insurance services, including auto, homeowners, life, health, commercial insurance, administrative services, annuities, mutual funds, pensions and long-term savings plans. The firm is ranked 99 on the Fortune 500 list.

The Nationwide Mutual Insurance Company has about 16 subsidiaries, including Allied Property and Casualty Insurance, Farmland Mutual Insurance, Scottsdale Indemnity Company and Nationwide Agribusiness. Nationwide ranks fourth in homeowner insurance, sixth in auto insurance and is the sixth-largest total property and casualty insurer. Nationwide is also the No. 1 provider of qualified retirement plans, eighth in variable life insurance and thirteenth largest U.S. life insurer based on assets. Nationwide owns a 60 percent stake in Nationwide Financial Services.

Buckeye nation

In 1919 members of a farmers' collective established their own auto insurance company, the Ohio Farm Bureau Federation, mainly to avoid having to pay city rates. The firm operated in 12 states and Washington, D.C., by 1943 and began to add regional offices in the early 1950s. With westward expansion and the addition of 20 more states, the company changed its name to Nationwide Insurance in 1955. Nationwide continued to grow in the 1960s and 1970s, and in 1978, moved into its international headquarters, One Nationwide Plaza, a 40-story structure that became Central Ohio's largest office building. The 1980s showed further expansion, as the company added Colonial Insurance of California (1980), Financial Horizons Life (1981), Scottsdale (1982), and the largest, Employers Insurance of Wausau (1985). Earnings fluctuated in the 1990s while the company added Wausau and consolidated offices.

Nationwide Financial went public in 1996, and the company initiated a reorganization in 2004, splitting the business into segments-individual protection, individual and corporate-owned life insurance; retirement plans, which includes both public and private retirement plan business; individual investments, which includes annuities and advisory services; and in-retirement, made up of other retirement products for individuals.

On your side

The Nationwide Foundation announced in September 2005 that it would donate $500,000 to the Red Cross Disaster Relief Fund. The Foundation also offered to match all personal contributions of Nationwide employees to the United Way Hurricane Katrina Response Fund. Nationwide also dispatched catastrophe response teams of agents, claims representatives and associates from across the country to serve its customers; Nationwide Financial Services helped customers access retirement plan and life insurance assets to cover emergency expenses; and suspended policyholder obligations for at least two months for customers involved in the disaster.

The Nationwide Foundation is an independent corporation that awards grants to nonprofit organizations focused on health and human services, higher education, culture and the arts and civic programs. In 2005, the Foundation announced a commitment to give out grants totaling more than $14 million to assist more than 1,000 nonprofit organizations, including some 700 United Way chapters across the U.S. Combined with donations from Nationwide employees, the company's total charitable contributions for 2005 came to almost $22 million. The company is also a sponsor of all 36 varsity sports at Ohio State University. Nationwide Insurance was named one of the best places to work in Pennsylvania in 2005.

Taking a leap

Nationwide saw an upsurge in its returns for 2006. Total revenue came in at $4.42 billion, up from $4.31 billion the previous year. Net income for 2006 increased to $713.8 million, up from $598.7 million the previous year. Total assets were up as well in 2006, jumping to $119.4 billion from $116.16 billion the previous year. CEO Jurgensen noted the firm "made great progress during 2006" and met objectives such as "restoring variable annuity sales momentum, building new capabilities and improving capital efficiency."

© 2007 Vault, Inc.

Planned purchase

In February 2007, the firm announced that it planned to buy NWD Investment Management (formerly known as Gartmore Global Investments). Since, the deal has already received approval by special committees of the board of directors of both Nationwide and NWD Investment Management. The transaction is expected to be valued at around $225 million in cash, Nationwide reported. Jurgensen said in a statement that the combination of NWD Investment Management's retail mutual fund business with Nationwide Financial's distribution and core investment and packaging capabilities "makes tremendous sense for our customers and shareholders by strengthening our ability to help consumers prepare for and live in retirement."

GETTING HIRED

Bring your own flair

The careers section of the firm's web site (www.nationwide.com/nw/careers) offers a wealth of information for job seekers, who are encouraged to upload their resumes and apply for positions online. The company holds resumes in its database for three months, accessing them to match them to newly available posts. Since Nationwide receives over 50,000 resumes annually, its HR department only contacts those whose qualifications best match the needs of the job description. Various career paths at the company include marketing and sales strategy, customer service, financial accounting, insurance, customer solutions center, office service and property management, information systems and technology, and human resources. Paid internships are also available. One insider notes that internships are a good opportunity to get your foot in the door, adding that "the goal of the internship program is to hire the interns that are solid performers."

OUR SURVEY SAYS

Love it or loathe it

Reports regarding the firm's culture range from positive ("a strong values-based organization" that's "family-oriented") to not-so-positive ("very corporate," "extremely conservative"). One source gives the culture a ringing endorsement, commenting that the firm is "doing a great job asking associates what they want, and making applicable and wise decisions for the benefit of our associates." Another says that the firm "supports developmental opportunities" and "has a huge commitment to community service."

Company perks mostly get thumbs-up. The firm offers an "on-site gym," a "comprehensive health and wellness program for associates and families" and the Columbus, Ohio, office gives "discounted tickets to various events within Columbus." An insider notes that "once you have worked there for a year, the company has a decent education reimbursement program."

Sources also laud the "support of management," "opportunities for advancement" and "leadership development." However, one notes that "opportunities for advancement are somewhat limited," as the firm "appears to hire from the outside more than from within for management and other higher positions." Although "all jobs are posted on the intranet with the company, there are ads in the local newspaper for management or leadership opportunities that are never offered to internal employees."

No fancy pants

Insiders describe the dress code as "not fancy, but very conservative." Capri pants are banned in the workplace, causing one respondent in Florida to remark that the rule may have been passed down from headquarters in Columbus, Ohio. "It's cold in Ohio all the time, so I guess that they don't consider capris the wardrobe staple that it is in the South," comments the insider, adding that although the dress code requires women to wear pantyhose, "this requirement was officially waived in Florida last year due to the ridiculous idea of wearing pantyhose in Florida. Do they even sell pantyhose in Florida?" Others say the dress code is "loosening up" overall, recently offering casual Fridays.

One insider says the firm is "very active in promoting diversity" and "appear to be very interested in hiring bilingual candidates, and promoting minorities." But another contact notes that ethnic diversity within the firm is

© 2007 Vault, Inc.

"minimal," adding that "lip service is paid to diversity." But diversity with respect to women gets good marks, though one insider suggests that the company create "specific programs designed for females interested in financial services."

Visit the Vault Finance Career Channel at **www.vault.com/finance** – with
insider firm profiles, message boards, the Vault Finance Job Board and more

VAULT CAREER LIBRARY   241

New Century Financial Corp.

18400 Von Karman Avenue
Suite. 1000
Irvine, CA 92612
Phone: (949) 440-7030
Fax: (949) 440-7033
www.ncen.com

DEPARTMENTS

Retail Sub-prime Mortgage Loans
Wholesale Sub-prime Mortgage
   Loans

THE STATS

Employer Type: Public Company
Ticker Symbol: NEW*
**Chairman, Director, New Century
Mortgage:** Robert K. Cole
**Vice Chairman, President & CEO;
Chairman & CEO New Century
Mortgage; Chairman NC Capital:** Brad
A. Morrice
Revenue: $2.44 billion (FYE 12/05)
Net Income: $416.5 million
No. of Employees: 7,200
No. of Offices: 222

*Suspended from NYSE in March
2007; currently trades under NEWC on
Pink Sheets*

KEY COMPETITORS

Advanta
Countrywide Financial
Pacific Premier

EMPLOYMENT CONTACT

www.ncen.com/career_opportunities/
index.html

© 2007 Vault, Inc.

THE SCOOP

Making good on bad credit

Bad credit? No problem! It's a New Century! Founded in 1994 with about 40 percent of its loan volume generated in California, New Century Financial provides sub-prime mortgage loans mainly for single-family residences, with its wholesale division generating and buying loans through a network of 35,000 independent mortgage brokers and making up 88 percent of sales. The retail division, which accounts for 12 percent of sales, targets individual customers through 216 offices in 35 states. The company sells many of its mortgages in pools of loans to institutional buyers such as Morgan Stanley Dean Witter. New Century began trading in 1997 on NASDAQ and in 2004 converted to a real estate investment trust (REIT), a company that generates the majority of its income from real estate mortgages, giving it tax advantages. The company began trading on the New York Stock Exchange (NYSE) under the symbol "NEW" in October 2004.

New Century had loan production volume of $56.1 million in 2005. Through the first half of 2006, New Century was the third largest sub-prime mortgage player in the U.S., behind Wells Fargo Home Mortgage and HSBC Finance. New Century had $25.60 billion in loans and a 7.70 percent market share, up from $23.7 billion in the first half of 2005.

Dawn of a New Century

New Century's founders, Bob Cole, Brad Morrice and Ed Gotschall, worked at Plaza Home Mortgage, a large prime mortgage lender, and launched Option One Mortgage. Plaza and Option One were sold in 1995, and the three formed New Century. After securing venture capital funding, New Century went public in 1997. The firm won the Ernst & Young Entrepreneur of the Year Award in 1998 for financial services for Orange County California. *Fortune* named New Century to its 100 Fastest Growing Companies—ranking 12th in 2003 and third in 2004. The firm ranked third on *The Wall Street Journal*'s Top Guns list of the best performing companies in 2005 and the same year moved from the Russell 2000 Index to the Russell 1000.

New Century works with a variety of nonprofits, including Habitat for Humanity, sponsoring several local and national homebuilding projects; the Camino Health Center, building a new facility that provides affordable care to the underserved; Junior Achievement; Opportunity Schools, sponsoring a program for children with learning challenges; and the Volunteer Center of Orange County, supporting nationwide volunteer programs. Subsidiary Home 123 inked a marketing deal with NASCAR in 2005 to become the "Official Mortgage Company of NASCAR."

Branching out

New Century acquired online direct mortgage provider Home123 in 2004 and a year later bought U.S.-based RBC Mortgage Company, a division of Royal Bank of Canada, complementing Home 123's existing non-prime mortgage business and growing its number of branches to 135. In July 2006, Brad Morrice took over as CEO, retaining his roles as vice chairman and president, succeeding Robert K. Cole, who continues to serve as chairman of the board. Taj Binda took over as CFO in November 2006, replacing Patti M. Dodge, who became executive VP, investor relations.

In November 2006, the company announced it inked a deal to acquire some assets and liabilities of Fishers, Ind.-based Irwin Mortgage Corp.'s servicing operations, an indirect subsidiary of Irwin Financial Corp., for an undisclosed amount. New Century expects the deal to close in January 2007. Ameriquest, one of New Century's main rivals, announced plans to cut almost 4,000 jobs in May 2006, closing 229 branches due to a slowing real estate market.

A rocky start to 2007

In February 2007, the firm announced that it would not be filing its fourth-quarter earnings for 2006. Accounting errors were to blame, said the firm, who added that 2006's previous quarters would be restated for the same reason.

In March of the same year, things weren't looking much rosier. That's when the Securities and Exchange Commission announced that it would be conducting a preliminary investigation into the firm based on the accounting errors that boosted the numbers in the firm's loan portfolio. And in the same month, the New York Stock Exchange announced that the New Century's stock listing will be suspended. In the meantime, the company's shares traded on Pink Sheets (a system that shows prices for securities, but isn't a stock exchange) under the NEWC symbol. And in April 2007, the company filed for Chapter 11 bankruptcy—and said in a filing with the SEC that it had disposed of all the loans it initiated but had not yet funded.

© 2007 Vault, Inc.

GETTING HIRED

Procure an invitation

The firm is somewhat selective, recruiting through its "invitation only" open houses (the open houses are "not job fairs," the firm specifically notes, but "if invited, you'll be interviewing 'face to face with New Century Mortgage/Home123 representatives only'") as well as resumes submitted by applicants via its web site. Applicants can browse open positions on its web site (www.ncen.com/career_opportunities) or submit a resume to careers@ncen.com. Under "open positions" on the web site, the firm also offers "two- to eight-week" internships for students who are 16 or older.

OUR SURVEY SAYS

Room for growth

Though the firm's office culture gets good marks from some insiders, one source calls the atmosphere "serious," with "humorless managers." But it may be turning around. An insider calls the business outlook "very good," adding simply, "it's growing." Dress is casual except for client contact, and diversity with respect to women, minorities, and gays and lesbians all receive high marks from insiders.

Visit the Vault Finance Career Channel at **www.vault.com/finance** – with
insider firm profiles, message boards, the Vault Finance Job Board and more

VAULT CAREER LIBRARY   245

New York Life Insurance Company

51 Madison Avenue
New York, NY 10010
Phone: (212) 576-7000
Fax: (212) 576-8145
www.newyorklife.com

DEPARTMENTS

Group Health Disability Income
Impaired Risk Life & Annuity
Institutional Asset Management
Investments
Life Insurance
Lifetime Income
Long-Term Care Insurance
Sponsored Marketing Relationships
Retail Mutual Funds
Retirement Income
Retirement Plan Services
Securities Products & Services

THE STATS

Employer Type: Private Mutual
Chairman & CEO: Seymour Sternberg
Operating Revenue: $12.3 billion (FYE 12/06)
Net Income: $2.3 billion
No. of Employees: 8,380 in the U.S. and 5,200 abroad
No. of Offices: Hundreds of U.S. offices (and thousands of career agents)

KEY COMPETITORS

MetLife
Prudential
TIAA-CREF

UPPERS

- "Great people in management"
- "People care about each other and work together"
- "Corporate structure is stellar"

DOWNERS

- "Long hours"
- "Poor support of products"
- "Bureaucracy central"

EMPLOYMENT CONTACT

See "sales careers and employment" link at www.newyorklife.com

© 2007 Vault, Inc.

THE SCOOP

Nothing like New York

A Fortune 100 company founded in 1845, New York Life Insurance Company is the largest mutual life insurer in the U.S. and one of the largest in the world. Headquartered in New York City, New York Life's family of companies offers life insurance, retirement income, investments and long-term care insurance. New York Life Investment Management LLC provides institutional asset management and retirement plan services. Other New York Life affiliates provide a variety of securities products and services, as well as institutional and retail mutual funds.

On the investment side, New York Life's affiliates provide institutional asset management and trust services and, through subsidiary NYLIFE Distributors Inc., offer securities products and services such as institutional and retail mutual funds, including 401(k) products. As a mutual insurance company, New York Life works for the benefit of its policyholders, or members. New York Life's subsidiaries have more than $265 billion in assets under management and more than $12 billion in operating revenue as of April 2007. The company has offices across America, as well as in Argentina, China, Hong Kong, India, Mexico, Philippines, Taiwan, Thailand and South Korea, and has earned some of the highest marks for financial strength in the biz; it ranked 78th in the 2007 Fortune 500 list of the largest American corporations.

Perhaps its success is best articulated by New York Life Chairman and CEO Sy Sternberg: "The primary responsibility of a mutual insurance company is to ensure that the long-term benefits promised to its policyholders are secure and protected. By remaining a mutual, New York Life can continue to manage for the long term, instead of the quarter-to-quarter orientation of the investment community."

History of innovation

New York Life traces its history to 1845, when it opened in New York City as the Nautilus Insurance Company. The insurer changed its moniker to the present-day New York Life Insurance Company just a few years later, in 1849. The company started with assets of just about $17,000, but it wasn't long before its coffers began to swell. Soon, New York Life was making a name for itself through a series of innovative business practices. In 1860, before any state law required it, the company developed the non-forfeiture option, which became the foundation of guaranteed cash values found in policies today. This enables a policy to remain in force even when a premium payment is inadvertently missed. By the latter-1800s, New York Life became the first American life insurance company to pay a cash dividend to policyholders, and in 1892 it became the first major company to issue policies with an incontestable clause, setting a time limit on the insurer's right to dispute a policy's validity based on material misstatements made in the application.

The company took a big step in 1894 when it became the first insurer in the U.S. to issue life insurance to women at the same rates as men. In fact, Susan B. Anthony, the 19th-century American social reformer, was one of the first women to get an insurance policy, and her insurer was New York Life. Then, in 1896, New York Life became the first company to insure people with physical impairments or hazardous occupations. In another industry first, the company issued a policy in 1920 with a disability benefit that presumes total disability to be permanent after a predetermined number of months.

Going to the customer

The company wasn't just forward thinking in terms of how it issued its policies, but also in how it conducted other business-related matters. In 1892, it became the first insurer to organize a branch office system, establishing an integrated network of general offices across the country. Today, these "GOs" serve the company's 10,500 licensed agents in the U.S. and 29,600 agents internationally. In May 1998, New York Life launched the Virtual Service Center on its web site, becoming the first major life insurer to provide a full range of customer service capabilities on the Web. At the Virtual Service Center, customers can request policy cash, loan and dividend values; download change-of-address and beneficiary forms; report the death of an insured person; and more.

A healthy year

New York Life set many company records in 2006. That year, the firm's net income increased to $2.3 billion, up considerably from $855 million the previous year. Operating earnings and operating revenue established new records as well, coming in at $1.1 billion and $12.3 billion respectively. Assets under management saw a jump too—to $265 billion in 2006, up $39 billion from 2005. New York Life also set records for insurance and

© 2007 Vault, Inc.

investment sales—insurance came in at $2.8 billion for 2006, and investment sales came in at $34.9 billion.

GETTING HIRED

To live and work in New York

Whether you're angling for a long-term position or an internship, your first stop should be the careers section of New York Life's web site, where you can get the skinny on becoming a sales agent with the firm or just find tips on "living and working in New York City." The site also offers links to available opportunities both as an agent and in the corporate office. Potential agents can read about New York Life's training program, benefits package and information about potential income. The site also offers a database of job opportunities at New York Life's office locations as well as field positions. Offices are located in Tampa, Fla.; Alpharetta, Ga.; Kansas City, Mo.; Westwood, Mass.; Clinton, N.J.; Parsippany, N.J.; Sleepy Hollow, N.Y.; New York City; and Austin, Tex.

The firm is "extremely selective," notes one source, adding that the firm tends to "interview 25 people in order to hire one." Interview experiences tend to vary depending on department, but one contact says that candidates are normally given a test, then "at least two interviews to determine suitability, then they go over compensation and target marketing." There are also "follow-ups on compliance and regulation issues due to the nature of the job." One respondent reports having gone through "a screening interview, a selection interview, a training interview and a compensation interview. Then the company took me and my wife out for dinner." The contact calls the process "very impressive," adding, "They knew—and I knew—that this was the right thing for me to do when the process was completed."

Visit the Vault Finance Career Channel at **www.vault.com/finance** – with insider firm profiles, message boards, the Vault Finance Job Board and more

VAULT CAREER LIBRARY   249

OUR SURVEY SAYS

Express success

"There is very much a feeling of family here," notes an insider. "The highest level of management is accessible and visible," and "for a company this size, we are a close-knit group." Another says the firm "is stable and keeps its promises to employees," adding, "Since they are not publicly traded, they think long term." Indeed, loyalty seems to run deep as well. One insider "wouldn't consider leaving, even for a $25,000 raise in pay." Management is "fair, willing to give credit where credit is due," "goes to bat for you" and "stands up for you."

Advancing within New York Life seems to be a matter of sticking around. The firm is a very "promote-from-within organization," says one insider, adding that the "best way to get your foot in the door is join the sales force, demonstrate success in sales for at least two years, and then look around the company at other options." Another says, "There is a very clearly defined path into management through the sales area, which is great for someone that would like to recruit, train and coach new hires." The firm also offers a "formalized training program for [the] new salesperson that's highly ranked across all industries." Yet another contact adds," There are tremendous opportunities for career-minded people who want to work hard." Though when first starting with the firm, one insider says to expect "long hours along with evenings and weekend appointments occasionally at first."

Good marks all around

The dress code is "business attire," and one insider notes that "in the summer we were allowed to wear business casual, but it was frowned upon." Work hours meet with approval. One insider comments that "the hours are more than reasonable" and "generally we'd be in by 8 a.m. and out by 5 p.m. Sometimes we'll be there until maybe 7 p.m., but there's a lot of downtime."

Company perks get high marks. There's a "state-of-the-art gym on site," "a company-subsidized cafeteria in the building," "car service and dinner provided if you work late," and "comp days given if you have to work on a weekend." In addition, "continuing education is encouraged"—the firm offers a tuition reimbursement program. New York Life also offers on-site back-up child care and an on-site employees' health department.

© 2007 Vault, Inc.

Welcoming diversity

The firm's diversity with respect to women is "getting better," comments an insider. Another says that workplace diversity is "well appreciated and well welcomed," adding that the firm has "specific programs for women, along with those of Indian, Asian, Hispanic and African-American descent." In addition to these areas, the firm has employee network groups for GLBT employees.

Visit the Vault Finance Career Channel at **www.vault.com/finance** – with
insider firm profiles, message boards, the Vault Finance Job Board and more

VAULT CAREER LIBRARY   251

Northwestern Mutual

720 E. Wisconsin Avenue
Milwaukee, WI 53202-4797
Phone: (414) 271-1444
Fax: (414) 665-9702
www.nmfn.com

DEPARTMENTS

Asset & Income Protection
Business Needs Analysis
Comprehensive Financial Planning
Education Funding
Employee & Executive Benefits
Estate Analysis
Investment & Advisory Services
Personal Needs Analysis
Retirement Solutions
Trust Services

THE STATS

Employer Type: Private Company
President & CEO: Edward J. Zore
Net Revenue: $19.7 billion (FYE 12/06)
Net Income: $829 million
No. of Employees: 4,800 (corporate home office)
No. of Offices: 350+

KEY COMPETITORS

AIG
New York Life
Prudential

UPPERS

- "Very family-oriented"
- "Excellent" relationships with their managers

DOWNERS

- Improving, but still "room for improvement" with regards to diversity hiring
- Some offices maintain a formal dress code

EMPLOYMENT CONTACT

See "careers" section of
www.nmfm.com

© 2007 Vault, Inc.

THE SCOOP

There's more to life than insurance

Best known as one of the oldest insurance companies in the U.S., Northwestern Mutual is the largest direct provider of individual life insurance in the country. In the business since 1857, 2007 marked the 24th time that the company was recognized by *Fortune* as America's Most Admired Company in the insurance category. But today, Northwestern also provides a variety of investment products and services. The company, which ranked No. 116 by revenue in the 2006 Fortune 500, offers individual and institutional investment management through its Northwestern Mutual Investment Services (NMIS) subsidiary. In addition, the Russell Investment Group provides investment management and advisory services, and Northwestern Mutual Wealth Management Company provides financial planning, investment management and trust services. Long-term care insurance is offered through another subsidiary, Northwestern Long Term Care Insurance Company.

In 2006, the company's revenue rose to $19.7 billion from $18.4 billion in 2005. Total assets also rose to $145.1 billion in 2006 from $133.06 billion in 2005. Net income dipped in 2006, however, to $829 million from $924 million the year before. In a statement, President and CEO Edward Zore said that the "economic and competitive environments" in 2006 were "challenging" for the company.

In a good mood

In 2006, Northwestern Mutual garnered impressive support from three top ratings agencies. Moody's gave the company an "Exceptional," or Aaa, rating in March 2006, noting, "Northwestern Mutual has regularly ranked among the highest in the industry when comparing dividend payout histories, helping to solidify the company's strong competitive position with clients." A.M. Best said of Northwestern Mutual in May 2006, "The growth and stability of the inforce business, combined with Northwestern Mutual's focus on operating fundamentals, has enabled it to consistently generate favorable earnings from its traditional individual life insurance segment." A.M. Best gave the firm a "Superior," A++ rating. Also in May 2006, Standard & Poor's said Northwestern Mutual was "Extremely Strong," giving it an AAA rating, noting, "The rating reflects the company's position among market leaders in individual life insurance business, its extremely strong capitalization and very

Visit the Vault Finance Career Channel at www.vault.com/finance – with
insider firm profiles, message boards, the Vault Finance Job Board and more

VAULT CAREER LIBRARY   253

strong operating performance. Other factors include the company's very strong and unique investment strategy and strong liquidity." In February 2007, the University of Michigan revealed that Northwestern also won the highest customer satisfaction score for life insurers in the college's American Customer Satisfaction Index for 2006.

So long, Mason Street

In March 2006, Northwestern announced the completed sale of its nearly nine-year-old Mason Street mutual funds unit. Assets in 10 of the 11 funds in Mason Street went to American Century Investments, with the remaining fund going to Federated Investors, Inc. The president of Mason Street Advisors said the group had never grown as anticipated due to a combination of factors that included the stock market collapse of the early 2000s and the cost of regulatory compliance after the mutual fund industry scandal. In March 2006, Mason Street Funds held assets of $1.3 billion—certainly nothing to scoff at but dwarfed by many others in the industry, such as American Century ($80 billion) and Federated ($40 billion). Mason Street Advisors continues to provide investment management services and manages over $69 billion in assets.

Career power

In November 2006, for the fourth consecutive year, Northwestern Mutual was named one of The 50 Best Companies to Sell For by *Selling Power* magazine. The company was selected for the second year in a row as the second-best service company to sell for. *Selling Power*'s list—based on data gathered through extensive surveys of each corporate candidate—focused on three key categories: compensation, training and career mobility. Using these categories, the selection committee took into account such metrics as average starting salaries, benefit packages, company-sponsored sales training, turnover and advancement opportunities. The ranking primarily took place among companies with sales forces larger than 500. "To be named one of the best companies to sell for over the last four years is a testament to the career opportunities available to potential representatives in the Northwestern Mutual system," said Bill Beckley, executive vice president at Northwestern Mutual, in a company press release.

The *Selling Power* honor came just two months after another renowned publication, *BusinessWeek*, named Northwestern Mutual Financial Network as one of the top 50 Best Places to Launch a Career. The rankings—on which

© 2007 Vault, Inc.

Northwestern Mutual joined such well-known organizations as General Electric, Goldman Sachs, Google, MTV Networks, NASA and Walt Disney—is based on responses from career services directors, employers and 37,000 undergraduates. It examined information on hiring, pay, benefits and retention, and also asked respondents for whom they would most like to work.

Long-term profits

Northwestern Mutual's Long Term Care Insurance Company subsidiary may see a spike in profits in the coming years, as the federal government encourages consumers to purchase long-term care insurance. According to a November 2006 article in *The Wall Street Journal*, "In the pension-overhaul bill signed in August, Congress included a measure that will allow consumers beginning in 2010 to pull money out [of] any annuity they already own, and use that cash on a tax-free basis to buy a long-term care contract." What's more, says the *Journal*, "The new law allows consumers to completely exchange an annuity for a long-term-care policy without triggering a taxable event, a potentially good strategy for retirees buying LTC in their 70s, when policies can be exceedingly expensive."

GETTING HIRED

Log on

The careers section of Northwestern's site is split into three pages: financial representative careers, corporate careers and financial representative intern opportunities. The financial representative site walks prospective applicants through life as a Northwestern agent, from the application procedure and hiring process to lifestyle and benefits. Job seekers can apply at www.careers.nmfn.com, which offers a searchable database of job openings in a number of different categories, including accounting/finance, actuarial, audit/tax, broker/dealer, customer service, investment /securities, legal/compliance, medical services, public relations/communications, telecommunications and underwriting/claims.

Visit the Vault Finance Career Channel at **www.vault.com/finance** – with
insider firm profiles, message boards, the Vault Finance Job Board and more

VAULT CAREER LIBRARY   255

Mutual decision

The interviewing process at Northwestern Mutual is "in-depth" and "very selective." On average, a network office might conduct "800 to 1,000 interviews per year" from which only "18 to 20" are offered a contract. The multistep interviewing process could involve several interviews; the number varies according to position and office. One financial representative reports first interviewing with "a recruiter," then going through some "testing," then interviewing with "the managing partner, the assistant managing partner, three financial representatives and, finally, the managing partner again." Another rep, though, had four interviews, all with the managing partner. Sometimes, following their in-person interview, candidates are given a "homework assignment" in which they have to write "their 10-year vision" of their career as a financial professional.

"We come to a mutual agreement if this career and culture is the right fit for a candidate," says one manager. To attract candidates, Northwestern Mutual recruiters use various methods, including online job postings, on-campus recruiting, career fairs and referrals, "mainly from other financial representatives" within the company.

A summer well spent

The firm also has a summer internship program, which "certainly helps in getting a position fulltime after graduation." Northwestern's program, rated one of Princeton Review's top-10 internships in the country, is "a great opportunity to test drive the career." One rep who sold insurance products as part of his summer internship says the program gave him "a big head start." In fact, "I had already established a small client base when I went full time into my career."

OUR SURVEY SAYS

To each its own

While "the climate of each office is different" and "each has its own feel to it," Northwestern Mutual is your quintessential financial institution, where the culture is described as "very professional." The firm fosters a "values-based" culture of "growth" and personal accountability where managers give

© 2007 Vault, Inc.

financial representatives the freedom to make a lot of their own decisions. The environment is one of professional independence, allowing individuals to "build the income and lifestyle you wish." And "since most people in the office are agents and earn their income from commissions, they have flexibility in how they dress, the hours they work, and the culture they develop with their own individual assistants."

Overall, work is "fun," and this mentality is reflected in the kind of hours people put in. Generally speaking, financial reps work reasonable hours, "rarely" or "never" putting in time on the weekends. "Our families hold our calendars after 6 p.m. and on weekends." The company is "very pro-Northwestern Mutual on the one hand, but very family-oriented" on the other. Some reps choose to "frequently" work weekends, but "the pressure [to do so] comes from themselves." Of course, "the more you work the more you can make."

Financial representatives at Northwestern Mutual consider "what they make" to be on par with or above the industry average. Along with generous salary and commission packages (when applicable), insiders enjoy "great," "fully-funded" benefit and contribution plans, as well as pension, renewal income and other bonuses. Although benefits and performance-based perks vary from office to office, many financial representatives are eligible to receive stipends that can be applied toward continuing education and training.

Smokers want Northwestern to butt out

Yet there are a few drawbacks for Northwestern corporate staff, at least for those who smoke. In January 2006, a new policy went into effect charging smokers (whether they smoke at home or outside the office on the job) an extra $25 a month for health insurance coverage. With American companies scuttling to find ways to curtail escalating health costs, an increasing number of employers are looking into controllable behaviors or conditions—smoking, obesity, high cholesterol, lack of exercise. Companies like Northwestern say that not only is it unfair to charge workers with healthy lifestyles extra to subsidize their unfit co-workers, but that an extra $25 a month might be incentive enough for their staff to stamp out their bad habits (and enjoy a longer career). At Northwestern, the $25-per-family monthly surcharge applies if any family member smokes, even if the employees themselves do not. There's an interesting loophole, however. A spokesman for Northwestern Mutual told *Cigar Aficionado* magazine that the firm makes "an exception for cigar smokers," adding that "those that smoke 12 or fewer

Visit the Vault Finance Career Channel at **www.vault.com/finance** – with insider firm profiles, message boards, the Vault Finance Job Board and more

VAULT CAREER LIBRARY   257

cigars per year are still eligible to get nonsmoker policy rates; 13 or more get smoker rates."

Excellent relationships

In addition to monetary benefits, reps enjoy "excellent" relationships with their managers, who get high marks across the board. Most managers try to share with their offices "the good and the bad, so they know where I stand personally and professionally," says one manager. Advancement is "very easy" at Northwestern from "management and production" perspectives. "In terms of production, if you utilize the sales strategies, you can have enormous production over the years. If managerial work is of greater interest to you, you can go through the management path, which starts with being a college unit director [who is] in charge of college interns, field director who is in charge of new representatives, and ultimately managing director or managing partner."

The look inside

Northwestern also scores well for the training programs it offers to its field force. Attire is "formal always"—men in jackets and ties, women in suits— and sources enjoy it. "We do not do 'dress-down days,'" says one, "and I hope we never will." But again, it may depend on the office, because "while some offices are incredibly strict about wearing a suit and tie daily, others do not mind if interns neglect to wear a jacket." One insider says that "most dress in business casual or in suits," but another calls the dress code "harsh," adding that "the office manager walked around making sure everyone was within the dress code."

Progress report

Though Northwestern Mutual has been actively improving in the area of diversity, especially "in the past five years," there are still those "old-school veterans who do not have any willingness to change." Still, one source says, "I no longer feel like the token female in my firm." Northwestern Mutual, according to an insider, has "learned so much" about integrating women into the culture, "and continues to be coachable." Similarly, the company, "primarily straight" and "male-dominated," has made strides in its receptivity to gay employees. "I am impressed with how much Northwestern Mutual has learned about the gay and lesbian community," says one contact. "They continue to be open to suggestions and seem genuine in their willingness to

© 2007 Vault, Inc.

learn about how they can be more aware than in the recent past." The firm also "continues to research" ethnically diversifying the firm, but there is still "room for improvement."

Visit the Vault Finance Career Channel at **www.vault.com/finance** – with
insider firm profiles, message boards, the Vault Finance Job Board and more

VAULT CAREER LIBRARY

259

The Progressive Corporation

6300 Wilson Mills Road
Mayfield Village, OH 44143
Phone: (800) 766-4737
www.progressive.com

DEPARTMENTS

Commercial Auto
Personal Lines
Other-Indemnity

THE STATS

Employer Type: Public Company
President & CEO: Glenn M. Renwick
Revenue: $14.79 billion (FYE 12/06)
Net Income: $1.65 billion
No. of Employees: 27,778
No. of Offices: 460+

KEY COMPETITORS

Allstate
GEICO
State Farm

UPPERS

- "Great opportunities for advancement"

DOWNERS

- "Workload is large"

EMPLOYMENT CONTACT

See jobs.progressive.com

© 2007 Vault, Inc.

THE SCOOP

That's progress

The Progressive Corporation provides automobile insurance and other specialty property-casualty insurance and related services, and operates in three segments: personal lines, commercial auto, and other-indemnity. The personal lines segment writes insurance for private passenger automobiles and recreational vehicles through both an independent insurance agency channel and a direct channel. The commercial auto segment writes primary liability and physical damage insurance for automobiles and trucks owned by small businesses primarily through the independent agency channel. The other-indemnity segment provides professional liability insurance to community banks, principally directors, and officer's liability insurance. It also provides insurance-related services, primarily providing policy issuance and claims adjusting services in 25 states for Commercial Auto Insurance Procedures/Plans. The company is headquartered in Mayfield Village, Ohio, and placed at No. 159 in the 2007 Fortune 500 rankings of America's largest companies (based on 2006 revenue).

Joe and Jack

On March 10, 1937, two young lawyers, Joseph Lewis and Jack Green, started Progressive Mutual Insurance Company to provide vehicle owners with security and protection. And ever since its earliest days, Progressive has taken an innovative approach to auto insurance. Case in point: It was the first auto insurance company to offer drive-in claims service, as well as the first to accept installment payments in addition to traditional annual payments, an early hint that the company is all about making auto insurance more accessible to more people.

The firm grew through the 1960s, and went public in 1971. Three years later, it relocated its headquarters to the Cleveland suburb of Mayfield Village, and kept growing steadily for the next 20 years. In 1987, it surpassed $1 billion in premiums and was listed by the New York Stock Exchange as PGR. In 1992, it was recognized as the largest seller of auto insurance through independent insurance agents. In 1994, the firm surpassed $2 billion in written premium and introduced 1-800-AUTO-PRO, a cutting-edge auto insurance rate comparison shopping service. Consumers no longer had to compare different insurers' rates; with one phone call, they could get a quote from Progressive and comparison rates for up to three competitors. If they

Visit the Vault Finance Career Channel at www.vault.com/finance – with insider firm profiles, message boards, the Vault Finance Job Board and more

VAULT CAREER LIBRARY   261

chose to buy from Progressive, they could purchase a policy right over the phone.

In 1995, when the Web was just gaining popularity, Progressive stepped ahead of the competition and became the first major auto insurer in the world to launch a web site. It was primarily informational, but soon became more interactive. By 1996, consumers could obtain comparison rates online, and by 1997, they could buy auto insurance policies online in real time.

Today, Progressive is the third-largest auto insurance group in the U.S., thanks to such innovations as comparison rates and 24/7 customer and claims service. And growth has remained steady. Progressive increased annual sales from $3.5 billion in 1996 to $14.8 billion in 2006.

Recognized

In September 2006, the firm was been named to *Business Week*'s inaugural list of the best places for new college graduates to begin their careers. "Our goal is an environment where our people enjoy working hard, are motivated to do their best and where they can grow constantly. Making *Business Week*'s ranking helps to signal to new graduates that we want the nation's best and brightest," said Matt Thornton, Progressive's national recruiting director.

How low can you go?

In March 2007, Progressive decided to lower its prices by about 8 percent for certain auto policies. The cuts, Renwick reported, will be effective within 27 states. In April of the same year, the firm announced that it would also be cutting its insurance rates for motorcycles, boats and RVs.

Some insiders say the cuts were spurred by ongoing competition between Progressive and its major rival, GEICO. Indeed, even Renwick conceded the contention, commenting that "Progressive is always at its best when it's getting challenged," adding, "I think you're going to find it's a GEICO/Progressive fight for a good number of years to come."

© 2007 Vault, Inc.

GETTING HIRED

Just their type

On its career site, the company says its "type" of employee is the "curious, reliable and driven" sort. If you happen to be one of those (or, says one insider, if you're "very young," which is what the firm "tends to hire"), check out the careers section of Progressive's web site (jobs.progressive.com), where job seekers have the ability to create an account and upload their resumes to apply for positions online. The various career paths available at the company include claims, IT, customer service, inside sales and professional positions that assist customers by offering "superior buying, ownership and claims experiences." Progressive staffers work out of six major locations across the country: Austin, Cleveland, Colorado Springs, Phoenix, Sacramento and Tampa. Additionally, there are links for students and recent graduates to find information of recruiting events where they can speak with Progressive representatives, as well as information on the internships offered.

Time to talk

Be prepared to have a lot of tales to tell once you're called in for an interview. Says one insider, "The entire interview involves you telling stories about how you handle or would handle various scenarios put forth by the interviewer." Another says she went through her first interview with a recruiter via phone, "had to go in and take a logic test by computer," and then had a "second interview with two branch managers." And since the second interview went well, "they waived the third interview with two branch managers." One soufce confirms, "It was a lot of interviewing," but adds that "the process moved very quickly."

OUR SURVEY SAYS

Get organized

Some employees call the culture "stressful," but others say, "Many of those who complain about having too much to do are unorganized or inefficient." One insider says that Progressive "is probably the best company I have ever worked for," and "the work environment is great." Others add that "advancement can be quick if you are good." Indeed, there's "great opportunity for advancement." Although "turnover can be high," "the possibilities are great if you stick it out."

Still, sourcereport, "the hours are long," and "even though you only work 40 hours on paper, it takes about a year-and-a-half to actually become proficient enough to leave within an hour of your quitting time." However, there are reports on the other side of the hour coin. One respondent says, "The workload is large, but not impossible. I have not needed to put in any extra time." The contact adds, "There are bonuses available if you work a weekend day, and there is another bonus on top of that if you work from 10 a.m. to 7 p.m. instead of 8 a.m. to 5 p.m." The dress code, however, follows a clearer structure. One insider calls it "simple, never any suits or ties," but the firm doesn't allow "jeans or shirts with other company logos on them."

The company could give more weight to expanding diversity efforts, sources say. One insider adds, "The minorities at the office pretty much resemble the areas where the offices are located," but another notes, "There is no diversity in management."

© 2007 Vault, Inc.

Prudential Financial

751 Broad Street
Newark, NJ 07102-3777
Phone: (973) 802-6000
Fax: (73)02-4479
www.prudential.com

DEPARTMENTS

Benefits & Services
Commercial Property
Institutional Investors
Insurance
Investments
Real Estate

THE STATS

Employer Type: Public Company
Ticker Symbol: PRU (NYSE)
Chairman, CEO & President: Arthur F.
Ryan
Revenue: $38.49 billion (FYE 12/06)
Net Income: $3.43 billion
No. of Employees: 38,853
No. of Offices: 70

KEY COMPETITIORS

AXA Financial
Citigroup
MetLife

UPPERS

- "Growing and innovative business"

DOWNERS

- "Not particularly great or competitive overall compensation"

EMPLOYMENT CONTACT

See "careers" link at
www.prudential.com

Visit the Vault Finance Career Channel at **www.vault.com/finance** — with
insider firm profiles, message boards, the Vault Finance Job Board and more

VAULT CAREER LIBRARY   265

THE SCOOP

Rocking the insurance industry

Prudential's logo, the Rock of Gibraltar, is one of the most recognizable corporate symbols. For years, Prudential has tried to capitalize on its image of solidity as one of the largest and most reputable insurance companies in the U.S. It is the No. 2 U.S. life insurance company and one of the top insurers in the world, and ranked 66th among the 2007 Fortune 500. Prudential's offerings include life insurance, annuities, mutual funds, asset management, and pension- and retirement-related investments and administration. The company also provides brokerage services through a minority interest in Wachovia Securities LLC, a partnership created by the 2003 merger of Wachovia's and Prudential's retail brokerage businesses. The new corporation, 62 percent of it owned by Wachovia and 38 percent of it owned by Prudential, has total client assets of over $616 billion with approximately 3,800 brokerage locations.

The firm's business is organized into two main units: financial services businesses and closed block business. The financial services business operates through three operating divisions: insurance, investment, and international insurance and investments. The closed block business, established in December of 2001 at the time of demutualization, is managed separately from the financial services businesses. Closed block business includes the firm's participating assets and insurance and annuity products that are used for the payment of benefits and policyholder dividends on these products; it also includes other assets and equity that support these products and related liabilities. Due to the demutualization, Prudential no longer offers these participating products.

Female-friendly

The firm regularly picks up honors and awards for its workplace environment. The latest came in April 2007, when Prudential Financial was named to *Essence* magazine's list of the 25 Great Places to Work for Black Women. *Essence* asked more than 60 business insiders—headhunters, human resources representatives, research firms and nonprofit organizations—to nominate companies with solid reputations for hiring, retaining, supporting and promoting black women. According to Linda Spradley Dunn, president and CEO of Idamar Marketing and Communications, who nominated Prudential for the list, "Prudential has a strong track record of promoting

© 2007 Vault, Inc.

African-American women and placing them in key leadership positions as well as working with black-female-owned companies."

Prudential Financial was also recently named one of the Top Companies for Executive Women by the National Association for Female Executives, which selects top companies based on their representation of women overall, in senior management and on their boards of directors. In addition, for the seventh consecutive year, Prudential Financial was ranked by *DiversityInc* as one of the Top 50 Companies for Diversity. In the latest rankings, Prudential came in at No. 24. "Prudential Financial is much different from the average corporation; it is a true champion of diversity," noted Luke Visconti, partner and cofounder of *DiversityInc*.

Solid as a rock

Prudential can trace its history to the Prudential Friendly Society, founded in 1875. The next year, Prudential issued its first death claim, for $10, and adopted the familiar image of the Rock of Gibraltar as its corporate logo. In 1943, Prudential mutualized, becoming a company owned by its policyholders. By 1966, Prudential had grown significantly, outstripping Metropolitan Life as America's largest insurance firm. In 1981, it diversified into the investment business through the acquisition of the securities brokerage firm Bache Halsey Stuart Shields, which led to the creation of Prudential Securities. The 1990s were less halcyon: Several states began to investigate Prudential's sales practices, including allegations of "churning" clients. (Churning refers to excessive trading, for the purpose of generating commissions.) Despite active efforts by the company to correct any abuses, by 1996, 30 states determined that Prudential had knowingly permitted wrongdoing and by 2000, the company had paid out $2.8 billion in settlement fees.

Buying and selling

In addition to the divisional restructuring and the retail brokerage merger of 2003, Prudential has been very active in both acquiring and divesting assets and businesses. In 1998, Prudential sold much of its $6 billion worth of national real estate holdings, including the its Prudential Center in Boston and the Embarcadero Center in San Francisco to Mortimer Zuckerman's Boston Properties group for $1.74 billion.

It also sold its health care business to the Hartford-based Aetna Corp. in 1999 in a transaction worth $1 billion. Meanwhile, the company acquired two

Visit the Vault Finance Career Channel at www.vault.com/finance – with insider firm profiles, message boards, the Vault Finance Job Board and more

VAULT CAREER LIBRARY   267

insurance firms, which has had a positive effect on the its bottom line: Gibraltar Life in April 2001 and American Skandia, the U.S. division of Sweden's Skandia Insurance Company, in May 2003. More recently, the Prudential Real Estate Investors (PREI) unit acquired Berlin's ewerk office and the Videojet Technologies headquarters building in Chicago in March 2007.

Legal wrangle

In December 2006, Prudential agreed to pay $19 million to settle a New York State investigation into its group insurance business and to change its business practices. The settlement was the latest in a series won by outgoing New York Attorney General Eliot Spitzer (now governor of New York) as part of an investigation into alleged price fixing and bid rigging in the insurance industry. Prudential will pay $2.5 million in penalties to New York State and $16.5 million to certain group insurance policyholders. Spitzer had been fighting to do away with contingent commissions, which insurers offer to brokers who steer business toward their company. The commissions represent a potential conflict of interest for the brokers, who might not be getting the best price for their clients.

The volunteers

Prudential's Global Volunteer Day, formerly known as Prudential's National Volunteer Day, grew out of its local initiatives area, which coordinates volunteer efforts by Prudential employees and works to address community needs. The first company-wide Volunteer Day was held in 1995 with 5,000 employees participating in 100 projects. It now includes nearly 34,000 participants at about 900 projects in more than 15 countries. The day is organized by employees who independently identify partner organizations or issues to which they want to donate their efforts. Projects range from building homes to tutoring students, running in marathons, collecting clothes and feeding the homeless. Prudential Financial's 11th annual Global Volunteer Day was held on October 7, 2006.

Ending the year right

Prudential finished 2006 on an up note, booking $893 million in earnings for the fourth quarter, up from $377 million for the fourth quarter of 2005. The increase in earnings were larely due to the prowess of its investment division, which booked $355 million of operating income for the quarter, versus the $4

© 2007 Vault, Inc.

million loss it incurred the previous year's fourth quarter. This still wasn't enough to put the firm in the black for the year, as Prudential's earnings dropped 2 percent to $3.1 billion.

GETTING HIRED

Only the best

Get ready to dazzle 'em, because "the company is searching for the best talent in the marketplace," comments one contact. Prudential's extensive careers section of its web site allows candidates to search for jobs by department and location, and offers prospective hires the ability to create an online profile, which the firm uses to match up with open positions. The site also describes the culture at Pru and the benefits the firm offers to staff, and has a college recruiting section that gives graduates an idea of what majors typically go with what positions. Aside from college recruiting and its own web site, the firm also hires through newspaper ads and employee referrals. Insiders report going through at least two rounds of interviews. One source says, "I interviewed with a recruiter, the hiring manager and the hiring manager's superior." It's not easy to land a spot these days. "Labor is abundant and companies are a lot more fussy about looking for the exact fit," adds that contact. "You have to sell your skills in relation to the job. Money is tight all over.

Another contact reports that "the first interview was standard." The contact goes on to say that candidates "are tested on reading comprehension and mathematics" as well as "future plans and career goals." Of course, also expect to be asked about "prior experience." An analyst says he went through "two interviews, one with a director and one with an HR employee." One contact, who went through a headhunter to land a spot at Pru, says, "I interviewed with someone in human resources first, who asked me salary information on the first interview, and that shocked me. They wanted to know if they could afford me." The next interviews "with a director and a hiring manager" were less shocking. "I hit it off with the director," says that respondent. "We chatted about work scenarios for an hour-and-a-half and in the last 30 minutes went through the typical interview questions—strengths, weakness, 'why should we hire you?'" The contact adds, "The hiring manager interviewed me for 40 minutes and asked about my work

Visit the Vault Finance Career Channel at www.vault.com/finance – with insider firm profiles, message boards, the Vault Finance Job Board and more

VAULT CAREER LIBRARY 269

experience." Another insider reports going through four interviews and meeting with "a recruiting manager and department managers."

OUR SURVEY SAYS

Mixed bag

"The corporate culture is remarkably supportive from within the rank and file of workers," says one source. But largely, insiders are split on Pru's culture. Some praise it and others criticize it. "Although they are a large company and have felt their fair share of pain," explains one source, "there is a general humanity that pervades relationships at the firm. It may not be the most lucrative place on the Street, but you will like your co-workers, you will be able to have a life outside of work, and you will be treated with respect." Another says while "there are obvious advantages, like having well-defined role structures and a total lack of ambiguity around what you are expected to do," the atmosphere "can seem bureaucratic at times, specifically when you'd want to drive change of any kind. Conservatism is just expected from you." And "in terms of work pressure, let's just put it this way—you're unlikely to die of hypertension," says one wry insider. "The environment is clearly not cutting-edge nor is the momentum heart-wrenching. The only exception to this rule could be if you are on the sales side."

One source calls it a "very professional corporate culture" where "employees are treated respectfully." Others call it a "nose-to-the-grindstone" type of place, and a former insider goes so far as to call it "disorganized" and "hostile." Even so, that contact does say, "I genuinely liked two managers, who were always willing to work with you." Another contact says that "managers are not too strict or demanding, and are very welcoming of new employees and interns," adding that "managers are not too stingy with expense accounts, and often treat their teams to lunches and include them at conferences." Yet another insider says that "dialogue is encouraged" between managers and staff.

Diversity is another issue insiders are split on. "In general, Prudential has a very good record on diversity," says an insider. Another says it's "very diverse," and the firm "takes pride in its diversity practices." However, one source paints a different picture. "My first impression was that the company seemed concerned with its diversity representation. Pru wants to have

© 2007 Vault, Inc.

employees who represent the marketplace. Unfortunately, now I do not feel that diversity is valued, even if the numbers may look good." Another says the firm is "diverse with many women and some minorities," adding that it "actively recruits minorities through select programs for impressive minority job candidates." An insider says, "Management and leadership are mostly comprised of white males, leaving the heralding of diversity limited to lower paying and lower status jobs with little to no room for advancement."

Pay seems to be no different: sources have both good and bad things to say. One source says, "To its credit, Pru offers excellent benefits, although not particularly great or competitive overall compensation." Another agrees, calling comp "way below industry average" and says, "Prudential has a history of paying their employees below industry average." Another respondent, though, says of pay, "I think it's appropriate." With the economy in the state it's in, it comes as no surprise that pay "increases for 2003 were minimal based on performance." Perks include "investment options and a 401(k), but Prudential Securities no longer receives a match on 401(k)," notes one insider.

Varied but reasonable

"The hours vary according to the department and the job function," reports an insider, "but for the most part are reasonable. I worked 9 to 5, Monday through Friday." Several insiders report that their groups allow staffers to make their own hours. "Flexible hours are available for most employees," says a source. Another notes, "Flexible hours were offered to me by my director, but my manager seemed to have a problem with the fact that I worked earlier than 9 to 5. Yet he'd call me at 8 a.m. requesting that I 'look into something' before he arrived." That contact adds, "Slackers left early in my boss' opinion." Another source, who says hours are good (he "never" has to come in on the weekends), explains the overtime, or rather former overtime policy available to some staffers. "Overtime was initially available, but later rescinded. When it was available, it was so difficult to have the time approved, most employees stopped applying." If you put in the hours, you'll get the promotion, says a source. "Opportunities for advancement are really for those who can put in the long hours." Another contact disagrees. "Opportunities for advancement were there, but like most large corporations, it depended on access to a mentor more than to hard work." And another source offers yet another take: "The economy has restricted everyone's upward mobility, and at Prudential, it's no different."

Visit the Vault Finance Career Channel at **www.vault.com/finance** – with insider firm profiles, message boards, the Vault Finance Job Board and more

VAULT CAREER LIBRARY   271

Don't dress it up

With the exception of client contact, most insiders report that business casual is typically the law of the land. "The business casual dress code takes the pressure off of dressing to impress," says a former insider, who adds, "We all knew when to dress up if an executive held an important meeting. I was overdressed during the job interview, but was told then that I wouldn't need a suit." Of the casual Friday policy in his office, one source in Philadelphia reports, "The dress code was not enforced; some of the outfits were downright scary."

© 2007 Vault, Inc.

Sallie Mae

12061 Bluemont Way
Reston, VA 20190
Phone: (703) 810-3000
Fax: (703) 984-5042
www.salliemae.com

DEPARTMENTS

Education Loan Origination
Collections Services
Loan Servicing

THE STATS

Employer Type: Public Company
Ticker Symbol: SLM (NYSE)
Chairman: Albert L. Lord
Vice Chairman & CEO: Thomas J. Fitzpatrick
Revenue: $8.75 billion (FYE 12/06)
Net Income: $1.16 billion
No. of Employees: 11,000
No. of Offices: 24

KEY COMPETITORS

Bank of America
KeyCorp.
Student Loan Corp.

UPPERS

- "Stability and the benefits"
- "Problems will eventually be worked out and solved"
- "The president and CEO of this company is a genius"

DOWNERS

- "Long hours"
- "Inexperienced leadership"
- "New subsidiary going through structuring and communication problems"

EMPLOYMENT CONTACT

www.salliemae.com/about/careers_sm

Visit the Vault Finance Career Channel at www.vault.com/finance — with insider firm profiles, message boards, the Vault Finance Job Board and more

VAULT CAREER LIBRARY   273

THE SCOOP

Paying for college

You may not recognize SLM Corp., but you're probably familiar with the company's nickname, Sallie Mae, especially if you're still paying off student loans. The company manages more than $137 billion in student loans for more than 10 million borrowers. Through its Upromise affiliates, Sallie Mae also handles more than $11 billion in Section 529 college-savings plans.

Sallie Mae was originally created in 1972 as a government-sponsored entity, but terminated all ties to the federal government in 2004. Through its specialized subsidiaries and divisions, Sallie Mae also provides debt management services, as well as business and technical products to a range of business clients, including colleges, universities and loan guarantors.

Headed for a buyout

In April 2007, the 35-year-old Sallie Mae agreed to be bought out to the tune of $25 billion, or $60 a share. JC Flowers & Co. led the way (along with private equity firm Friedman Fleischer & Lowe LLC), with a plan to invest $4.4 billion and take a 50.2 percent ownership in the education lender, while Bank of America and J.P. Morgan Chase & Co. planned to put up $2.2 billion each—and thusly, will each own 24.9 percent of the company. The buyout was unanimously approved by Sallie Mae's independent board members, who in turn urged shareholders to also approve the deal.

After the closing of the deal, which is expected to take place in late 2007, Sallie Mae's existing management will continue to run the company as well as "originate student loans under its internal brands," according to the company. *The Wall Street Journal* reported "the deal represents a turning point for both the private-equity industry and the student-lending business," adding that in the past, leveraged buyout firms typically haven't made large investments in financial services companies.

In a statement, J. Christopher Flowers, managing director at J.C. Flowers, said that "both Bank of America and JPMorgan Chase have fully committed to support the company with short- and long-term financing."

© 2007 Vault, Inc.

The fund and praise

In 1992, Sallie Mae established the charitable organization The Sallie Mae Fund, which achieves its mission-to increase access to a postsecondary education for America's children—by supporting programs and initiatives that help open doors to higher education, prepare families for their investment and bridge the gap when no one else can. In November 2006, Sallie Mae received the Ron Brown Award for Corporate Leadership for three of its charitable programs to increase access to higher education: The Sallie Mae Fund: Latino College Access Campaign, Project Access: DC and The Sallie Mae Fund Scholarship Programs. *Business Ethics* magazine named the company one of America's 100 Best Corporate Citizens in April 2006.

The company has also received praise as an employer, being named to *Computerworld*'s 2006 list of the top workplaces for IT professionals and the Indiana Chamber of Commerce named it one of the Best Places to Work. *Washingtonian* magazine also recognized Sallie Mae as one of the districts Great Places to Work, citing the company's work environment, benefits program and charitable contributions. Sallie Mae launched 2Futuro, a college financing and outreach program for Hispanic students in conjunction with USA Funds, in July 2006. The program allows students and their parents to apply for loans in Spanish and offers access to scholarships, grants and financial aid information in Spanish through its web site.

Privacy issues

Founded in 1972 as a government-sponsored enterprise to address problems that arose from the federal Guaranteed Student Loan program of 1965, Sallie Mae's initial task was to convince banks to grant student loans, considered at the time to be poor risks. For the next two decades, the company remained partially subsidized by the government. But in 1994, President Clinton proposed direct government loans to students, implying the elimination of Sallie Mae. In 1995, Congress granted the company the opportunity to become completely private instead of being phased out. This led to a fierce proxy battle, which came to a head in August 1997, with the shareholders firing the company's management, putting current Chairman Albert Lord and his team in charge, and greenlighting his privatization plan. The privatization process was completed in December 2004. Sallie Mae fired its CFO in July 2005 for inflating revenue to receive a higher bonus and named Arthur Andersen vet C.E. Andrews to the post in February 2006.

Visit the Vault Finance Career Channel at **www.vault.com/finance** – with insider firm profiles, message boards, the Vault Finance Job Board and more

VAULT CAREER LIBRARY   275

Sallie Mae bulks up

Since its early days, Sallie Mae's growth in assets has been rapid, from over $1 million in 1973 to about $116 billion in 2006. Over the past few years, through the efforts of Albert Lord, the firm has moved to embrace other financial practices, such as repackaging student loans as securities (lumping together many student loans and selling them as bonds to investors), and making a number of strategic acquisitions. In September 2004, the company bought a majority stake in Arrow Financial, a collections company, and, in October 2004, completed its purchase of Southwest Student Services Corporation. In December 2004, Sallie Mae completed the purchase of Seattle-based student loan originator and secondary market, Student Loan Finance Association.

The feeding frenzy continued in 2005 with the purchase of GRP Financial Services, which buys and services distressed mortgages as well as selling single-family housing that it acquires through those services. The same year Sallie Mae went overseas, selling student loans in the U.K. and Ireland for U.S. students attending schools there and for students from those countries enrolled in U.S. colleges. Sallie Mae bought college savings plan administrator Upromise in June 2006, its first acquisition of a college savings program. Upromise has contracts to administer tax-free Section 529 college-savings plans in Arkansas, Colorado, Iowa, Missouri, Nevada, New York and North Carolina. The subsidiary has a staff of 250, manages $10 billion in assets and has 10 million borrowing customers.

Investing in the future

With college costs skyrocketing and wages remaining stagnant, Sallie Mae has seen a rise in payment defaults from students, and these "loans of forbearance" are traditionally understated in its SEC filings. But, looking to make lemonade, the company has turned bad debt into a profit center with the acquisition of Arrow Financial, which purchases and collects on defaulted loans. In 2006, Sallie Mae saw net income drop to $1.16 billion from $1.38 billion the previous year. And Reuters news agency reported that Sallie Mae shares had dropped noticeably after November 2006, "after voters effectively gave control of the Senate and House of Representatives to Democrats, whose platform included reducing student loan rates."

 © 2007 Vault, Inc.

GETTING HIRED

Choosy

The company's choosiness when selecting candidates "depends on the department," says one insider, adding that "in the accounting, finance and legal areas, the company is very selective." Starting with Sallie Mae as an intern may be a good way of getting your foot in the door, however. One former intern notes, "I only had one interview before I was hired."

As for the interviews, a financial services insider says, "There are usually two interviews, one with immediate management and one with VP-level management." According to one source, candidates can "submit a resume online, after which you'll possibly get screened by HR and maybe invited to attend a preemployment session. If that's successful, then you'll get an interview with a department supervisor and maybe hired."

If you don't see a position listed that happens to catch your fancy at the firm's careers section of its web site (go to "careers at Sallie Mae" under "about us" on the firm's homepage), consider submitting your resume anyway. "If you don't see an opportunity that matches your skills and interest," the company will keep your resume and keep you in mind for future openings.

OUR SURVEY SAYS

Play hard

The company culture promotes a "work hard, play hard" ethic, placing an emphasis on "high performance." Sources also call the culture everything from "conservative" and "really interesting" to "high-strung" and "cost-conscious." "It is a meritocracy," notes one contact. "If you are good, you will be promoted quickly."

Nice perks

Sallie Mae offers "exceptional benefits, including retirement matching, stock options and a stock purchase plan." It also offers an "in-house gym," "cafeteria," "tuition reimbursement" and "community service benefits." The

Visit the Vault Finance Career Channel at **www.vault.com/finance** – with
insider firm profiles, message boards, the Vault Finance Job Board and more

VAULT CAREER LIBRARY   277

"casual always" dress code also gets high marks. And hours aren't so bad, say insiders, though there could be some weekend work; one respondent says he visits the office on a Saturday or Sunday "at least once a month."

Thumbs up

The firm gets high marks in regards to diversity with women, minorities, and gay and lesbian hiring. Sallie Mae is "very big on diversity and does not discriminate for any reason." The firm is "known as an excellent place for women and working mothers." It also offers "adoption assistance services, and employees get many discounts at local businesses."

© 2007 Vault, Inc.

Scottrade, Inc.

12800 Corporate Hill Drive
St. Louis, MO 63131-1834
Phone: (314) 965-1555
Fax: (314) 543-6222
www.scottrade.com

THE STATS

Employer Type: Private Company
CEO: Rodger Riney
Revenue: $796 million (FYE 9/06)
No. of Employees: 1,731
No. of Offices: 300

KEY COMPETITORS

Charles Schwab
E*Trade Financial
TD Ameritrade

UPPERS

- "Open communication from the top down"
- "Friendly co-workers"

DOWNERS

- "Dry" environment
- "More guidance from supervisors"

EMPLOYMENT CONTACT

See "employment" link at
www.scottrade.com

Visit the Vault Finance Career Channel at **www.vault.com/finance** — with
insider firm profiles, message boards, the Vault Finance Job Board and more

VAULT CAREER LIBRARY   279

THE SCOOP

Scottrade in Scottsdale

It may seem hard to believe for a company with such a considerable web presence, but Scottrade started up long before online trading existed. In 1980, Rodger Riney founded Scottsdale Securities in Scottsdale, Ariz., and in 1982, he started branching out—and never looked back. By 1986, Scottsdale Securities had opened its third branch office, in Dayton, Ohio, and by 1990, it had 14 offices with locations in Springfield, Mo.; Southfield, Mich.; Pittsburgh, Penn.; Oakbrook Terrace, Ill.; Bloomington, Minn.; Irvine, Calif.; La Mesa, Calif.; Milwaukee, Wis.; Clearwater, Fla.; and Englewood, Colo.

In 1994, Scottsdale Securities made it onto *Inc.* magazine's 500 Fastest Growing Private Companies in America list and. In 1996, a year after making *Inc.* magazine's 500 Fastest Growing Private Companies in America for the second consecutive year, Scottrade offered online trading to its already substantial customer base. By 1999, the company had 100 offices, and during the year it opened 20 more—the most in any year to date. In 2000, Scottsdale Securities changed its name to Scottrade to reflect the domain name of its web site. Scottrade was born.

At the turn of the century, things really began to take off. By the end of 2001, the firm had 147 offices. It opened 24 more in 2002, including its first in Manhattan, bringing its brick-and-mortar presence to 170 offices. And fast on the heels of its next move—the 2003 launch of Scottrade Chinese, available to customers in the U.S., China, Hong Kong and Taiwan—Scottrade passed two more milestones, opening its one-millionth customer account and being named Highest in Investor Satisfaction With Online Trading Services by J.D. Power and Associates for an unprecedented fourth consecutive time. In 2004, Scottrade launched ScottradeELITE, an online trading platform for active traders, and picked up yet another Highest in Investor Satisfaction Among Online Trading Services rating by J.D. Power and Associates for the fifth consecutive time. And *Kiplinger's Personal Finance* magazine named Scottrade the Best Mutual Fund Selection for 2004 based on its first-class service and wide selection of no-load mutual funds, as well as its low fees and quick response times.

To celebrate its 25th year as a discount brokerage firm in 2005, Scottrade offered a new flat-rate commission of $7 for all online market and limit orders, and later that year received still more unprecedented kudos: its sixth consecutive J.D. Power and Associates award for investor satisfaction. In

© 2007 Vault, Inc.

2006, CEO Rodger Riney rang the NASDAQ closing bell on January 18 to commemorate the company's partnership with the exchange. It appears the sky's the limit for this online broker, which seems to mean there's nowhere to go but up.

More offices added

In December 2006, Scottrade opened a new branch office in Boynton Beach, Fla. "While most of our customers trade online, our customers appreciate the level of customer service they receive through their local branches," said Riney in a press release announcing the opening. "Our branch network is important in our mission to provide online investors with the best value in the industry." Scottrade has 27 other branch offices in Florida.

Customer satisfaction awards

In May 2006, Scottrade was named the top winner in the Online Brokerage Category of the Brandweek Customer Loyalty Awards bestowed by Brand Keys. Scottrade ranked higher than Charles Schwab, Fidelity, E*Trade, Merrill Lynch, TD Waterhouse and Ameritrade (now known as TD Ameritrade). In the survey of over 16,000 consumers, Scottrade "commanded the highest customer loyalty" in the online brokerage industry. The survey asks customers to rate their relationships with brands in 35 categories. Also in 2006, *Barron*'s magazine's annual ranking of online brokerage firms gave Scottrade four stars—in addition to awarding the firm the top spot in its usability and customer support categories. In 2007, Scottrade was again named the top winner in the Online Brokerage Category of the Brand Keys Customer Loyalty Engagement Index.

A nice jump

Scottrade reported a 72 percent increase in revenue for its fiscal year 2006 (the 12 months ending September 30, 2006). Revenue leaped to $796 million, compared to $464 million in fiscal year 2005, while customer assets increased $9.6 billion to $51.1 billion. Trade volumes and active accounts also saw significant increases versus fiscal 2005, and Scottrade's branch office network experienced the most rapid growth in the industry. The firm expanded its branch network by 16 percent in fiscal year 2006, opening 39 new branch offices. As of May 2007, it had 299 branch offices nationwide—the second-largest number of locations in the online investment industry—and was planning to open its 300th office in June.

GETTING HIRED

Selective—and fast

Scottrade is "very selective in their hiring process," and the firm works quickly when it sees someone it wants. "I sent in an application and within a week I received a call from the human resources department," one insider says. Another notes that the firm also has a short turnaround time when it comes to hiring. "It's a very quick process," he says. "I knew in less than a week after the interview if I had the job."

Regardless, expect to go through several rounds of interviews, the first of which may be conducted via phone. Contacts report varying experiences, from "a phone interview with the head office, then one in person with the branch manager," to "one phone interview with HR and one in-person interview with the branch manager."

Put your thinking cap on

Get ready to field "behavioral questions" during the interview. Insiders say candidates might be asked questions such as "How do you respond to criticism?" or "How do you feel about dealing with employee conflict?" Another possible question is "What aspects of your previous jobs did you like or dislike?" And prepare for a pop quiz or two, too. "I took some tests on a computer that included grammar, attention to detail and reading comprehension tests," notes one source. In addition, expect a few out-of-the-ordinary interview activities. One contact reports going in for a third interview that involved "making a 10-minute presentation on the subject of my choice." Just make sure you're prepared—and "be sure to have concrete dates you are available to start work," suggests an insider.

The firm looks for potential candidates in more than one spot. Scottrade recruits online and on campus at universities such as St. Louis, Washington and Southern Illinois. The firm also has an internship program where interns "assist customers and brokers as much as possible with paperwork and daily activities," but also "receive the opportunity to cross-train with most of the full-time associates in the department." And if you're looking to get hired on full time, give the internship a shot. "I do feel my internship played a huge role in my getting hired by the firm," one source says. Alternately, you can check out the employment link at www.scottrade.com for current openings.

© 2007 Vault, Inc.

OUR SURVEY SAYS

Family time

Scottrade is "very professional" but simultaneously "friendly," "relaxed," "approachable" and "like a big family." One insider refers to the culture as "much like a microcosm of a large Midwestern city." And the firm has "built its success on a foundation of doing what's right" in addition to being "very positive about helping you succeed to move up in the company." "We are all excited about our future and united in our common purpose." There's a focus on customer service, as well as "doing what's right for the employees and customers." And one pleased insider says, "The people I work with are great and willing to help me if I have a question or problem."

Benefit bonanza

On the perk front, sources practically wax lyrical about the "excellent" 401(k) plan, which provides a "very generous company match." Scottrade is serious about employee health, too, offering a "$250 annual gym reimbursement," "low-cost health coverage that includes free vision," and a wellness program that "goes above and beyond," providing contests and reimbursements for staff who wish to lose weight and quit smoking. Scottrade also provides "many corporate-sponsored employee events," "mass transit relief" and "ticket raffles for local sporting events." Offices also receive a collective thumbs-up. The area is "safe," "always has ample parking" and has "easy access to the freeway."

An honest day's work

While staffers typically work "solid eight-hour days," more than one insider comments on the absence of a lunch hour. "We often eat lunch while we are working," but there's "no pressure to work more than that without compensation." And there's not a lot of overtime, either—"the company understands the importance of a work/home life balance." Managers are good about not demanding too much from employees, too. "Everyone is great," there's "no micromanaging" and "management treats employees with respect."

Visit the Vault Finance Career Channel at **www.vault.com/finance** – with
insider firm profiles, message boards, the Vault Finance Job Board and more

VAULT CAREER LIBRARY   283

No hose in summer

While the dress code generally follows a "formal always" mandate, the last Friday of the month is a "casual day—with guidelines." But "some departments are less formal" and ties are not required in every department. There's also a "casual summer" dress code, and "women do not have to wear pantyhose from Memorial Day to Labor Day."

Learning process

Sources give high marks to the firm's training program, which involves "three weeks of dedicated training that introduces new employees to Scottrade." Scottrade provides ongoing training as well, offering staff "a 'university' that provides online courses, internally conducted courses and access to outside training." And if you don't take advantage of the programs, says one respondent, it's your own fault—"there is no reason not to get training with our company."

All-inclusive?

Diversity efforts receive mostly good feedback from insiders, who say Scottrade is "receptive" to being inclusive. Though one source notes, "I am one of the only female brokers in my region," have few complaints in this area. Another source comments, "We have many management positions allocated to both women and men." And things look pretty good on the ethnic diversity front, too. One source notes, "We have management from a wide array of racial backgrounds."

© 2007 Vault, Inc.

Standard & Poor's

55 Water Street
New York, NY 10041
Phone: (212) 438-2000
Fax: (212) 438-7375
www.standardandpoors.com

DEPARTMENTS

Credit Market Services
Investment Services

THE STATS

Employer Type: Business segment of McGraw Hill
President: Kathleen A. Corbet
Revenue: $2.75 billion (FYE 12/06)
No. of Employees: 7,500

KEY COMPETITORS

A.M. Best
Dow Jones
DBRS
Fitch
FTSE
Moody's
Morningstar
Russell
Thomson Financial

UPPERS

- Pleasant work environment
- Hours are "great"

DOWNERS

- "Employee motivation and retention are not high"
- Slow advancement

EMPLOYMENT CONTACT

www.standardandpoors.com/careers

Visit the Vault Finance Career Channel at **www.vault.com/finance** — with insider firm profiles, message boards, the Vault Finance Job Board and more

VAULT CAREER LIBRARY   285

THE SCOOP

Poor in name only

When Henry Varnum Poor published his *History of Railroads and Canals of the United States* in 1860, he probably never dreamed he would be creating what would become a global corporation with enormous influence over capital markets and the world economy. However, 81 years later, a 1941 merger of Standard Statistics and Poor's Publishing Company created one of the world's most prominent independent credit ratings, market indices, risk evaluation, investment research and data companies. A quarter-century after that combination, in 1966, the company was acquired by McGraw-Hill, the multibillion-dollar publishing company known for its elementary and high school textbooks and other media businesses.

Today, New York-based Standard & Poor's operates through six main divisions: credit ratings, data services, equity research, funds, indices and risk solutions. Over $1 trillion in investor assets is directly tied to S&P indices, more than all other indices combined. The firm has the world's largest network of credit ratings analysts, and its equity research division is the world's largest producer of independent equity research. More than 1,000 institutions—including 19 of the top-20 securities firms, 13 of the top 20-banks, and 11 of the top-20 life insurance companies—license its research for their investors and advisors. Standard & Poor's team of experienced U.S., European and Asian equity analysts assess approximately 2,000 equities across more than 120 industries worldwide. Furthermore, Standard & Poor's funds research offers in-depth mutual fund reports on over 15,000 U.S. domestic mutual funds and ratings on over 1,800 funds worldwide.

Word on the Street

Standard & Poor's has routinely garnered industry praise for its work. In 2006, eight S&P equity analysts were named winners of *The Wall Street Journal's* Best on the Street awards, an annual assessment of the stock picking performance of over 1,000 analysts commissioned by the newspaper. S&P was tied for second with J.P. Morgan Chase and Credit Suisse behind Citigroup and A.G. Edwards, both for which won nine awards. Globally, the firm has also been recognized as an industry stalwart. Standard & Poor's has been named Best Loan Rating Agency in Europe by *Euroweek*, and Best International Ratings Agency and Best Rating Agency in Asia by *International Securitization Review*. S&P was also named 2006 Index

© 2007 Vault, Inc.

Provider of the Year by London-based *Structured Products* magazine, a monthly that covers derivatives-based investments.

In the spring of 2006, the Capital IQ division, which provides integrated financial information and a public and private capital market database, was selected by the Software & Information Industry Association as a finalist in the 21st Annual Codie Awards for Best Online Professional Financial Information Service and Best Business Information Service. It was the third consecutive year that Capital IQ was selected as a finalist. In 2004, Capital IQ was a finalist for the Best Software Service category and, in 2005, for Best Online Professional Financial Information Service and Best Solution Integrating Content into an Application.

S&P has seen good returns in the past six years. Since 2000, revenue has more than doubled to $2.75 billion in 2006, and operating profits have jumped from less than $400 million to $1.2 billion.

Hitting 500

Financial news reports on radio and TV make reference to the performance of the S&P 500, one of scores of indices compiled by the company to track the latest results of stock exchanges around the world. Unlike the Fortune 500, which lists the biggest companies in the world, the S&P 500 lists large public companies that trade on U.S. stock exchanges. The companies that comprise the list are chosen to represent different industries and then their individual performance is weighted according to their overall size. Together with the Dow Jones Industrial Average, the S&P 500 is viewed as the key barometer of the U.S. stock market. Individual companies and mutual funds often measure their performance against these indices. Other S&P indices track specific contents and countries, from Russia to India to Australia.

Besides the index business, S&P also earns fees for rating bonds around the world. The credit ratings division is a profitable one: *Barron*'s reported that the unit's profit margin is 42 percent and that much of the new business is focused in foreign markets. S&P makes 37 percent of its ratings revenue abroad, and that figure should reach close to 50 percent by 2010. To protect its turf, McGraw-Hill filed a suit in November 2006 against International Securities Exchange (ISE) to prevent ISE from listing, trading and profiting from index options based on the S&P 500. The Options Clearing Corp. was also named as a defendant in the suit.

The company also publishes a wide array of reports. In the *Dividend Record*, S&P publishes the dividend reports on more than 23,000 securities, including

12,000 equity, bond, and money market funds and 450 closed-end funds. *The Outlook*, another publication, is an online and print investment advisory newsletter for individuals and financial professionals. It provides research, investment ideas and market perspective, including buy, hold and sell recommendations of the 1,500 stocks ranked according to Standard & Poor's Stock Appreciation Ranking System. The company added a daily two-minute video clip to its web site in November 2005 to give commentary on the economy, markets and industries. The free streaming media service distills S&P's weekly investment research for institutional and private investors as well as members of the financial media.

Adding Vista

S&P boosted its institutional research products and investment information platforms in April 2005 when it acquired Vista Research Inc., an independent primary research firm founded in 2001. Institutional money managers and hedge funds use Vista to access a broad network of top-quality industry practitioners who share their insights about issues and conditions affecting companies and sectors based on their experience in industries such as technology, media, telecommunications and health care. Vista is also a co-founder of Investorside, a trade organization for independent research firms with over 75 members.

Overseas expansion

S&P sold its Corporate Value Consulting business in September 2005 for an undisclosed amount to Duff & Phelps, a financial advisory and investment banking firm. Earlier in the year, S&P expanded its operations in Australia when it bought the managed fund data and research business of ASSIRT from St. George Bank for an undisclosed sum. The acquisition gave S&P Australian market coverage and funds ratings history that it previously did not have.

In February 2006, S&P formed a 50/50 joint venture with CITIC Securities Co., one of the two brokerages firms listed in China, to develop benchmark indexes for the Chinese securities market. 2006 also saw S&P launch 10 indexes to track housing prices in various regions throughout the U.S. and a composite index. The S&P/Case-Shiller Metro Area Home Price Indices track the housing markets in Boston, Chicago, Denver, Las Vegas, Los Angeles, Miami, New York, San Diego, San Francisco and Washington, D.C.

© 2007 Vault, Inc.

The company pulled the plug on its Hedge Fund Index in June 2006 due to PlusFunds Group, a hedge funds operator that gathered the data for the index, filing for bankruptcy. The index was launched in October 2002.

In the aftermath of the WorldCom and Enron scandals, pressure on the SEC grew to increase competition in the lucrative ratings business. Both companies had received high marks from S&P and its main competitor Moody's. There are only five "nationally recognized" credit raters, with S&P and Moody's controlling 80 percent of the market and seeing profit margins of more than 50 percent. Fitch Ratings, Dominion Bond Rating Services and A.M. Best Co are the other three. In fall 2006, The Credit Rating Agency Reform Act was signed into law establishing new rules to make it easier for new competitors to enter the market and give the SEC oversight power. In an effort to create more transparency, the new rules also require ratings firms to provide more disclosure of their ratings methodologies and to set up policies to avoid conflicts of interest. Analysts expect juggernauts S&P and Moody's will probably still dominate the market, but that new competitors will try to get some traction by taking different tacks, such as offering ratings paid for by investors instead of debt issuers and focusing on specific types of debt.

GETTING HIRED

Go globetrotting

Interested applicants can search for open positions worldwide within the firm, from Argentina to Venezuela, under the "careers" link under the "about us" tab at www.standardandpoors.com. The firm says it's looking for "bright and enthusiastic" candidates with "diverse educational backgrounds, work experience, and personal interests."

The firm hires entry-level employees in all six of its divisions: credit ratings, data services, equity research, funds, indices and risk solutions. Candidates can also learn more about S&P's business lines, read first-person accounts by current insiders about what it's like to work for the firm, and get detailed information on entry-level positions for undergrads and grad students.

In its credit ratings division, the firm typically hires MBA and other graduate students as credit analysts. First-round interviews for these positions are held on campus (if S&P doesn't recruit at your school, you can apply online), and second-round interviews are held at the firm's New York headquarters or a

Visit the Vault Finance Career Channel at **www.vault.com/finance** – with
insider firm profiles, message boards, the Vault Finance Job Board and more

VAULT CAREER LIBRARY   289

regional office. The second round includes a full day of interviewing, which according to S&P includes "rigorous testing of your financial acumen and, for some business units, an evaluation of your ability to create written commentary." In addition to full-time credit analyst positions, the firm offers a 10- to 12-week summer associate program for "candidates who have completed the first year of an advanced degree program." According to S&P, after a one-week training program, summer associates "work closely with a senior analyst and a junior analyst mentor on relevant work assignments that offer exposure to the ratings process."

In equity research, insiders say, "New analysts have traditionally been hired straight out of graduate school," but lately have come from industry as well. "Most applicants are chosen from resumes received from Internet postings." Those chosen are then asked back to "sit for a daylong in-house exam," during which they "write a stock report based upon information provided." Those who pass this exam are then "invited back for a two-hour round of three or four interviews." Interview questions "generally revolve around current market happenings as well as two or three stock recommendations," which the "applicant has to pitch to the interviewer."

OUR SURVEY SAYS

Pleasant pace

Standard & Poor's culture is "laid-back for the most part," but "different departments can be more demanding than others." The work environment is "a pleasant change from a finance job on Wall Street," and "a good choice for those interested in a financial services job that is toned down from investment banking."

Typically, "opportunities for advancement are pretty good." It takes "generally two years to make associate director, and if you are good, two to three years to make director after that," though "there are very few managing directors." But be aware of increasing duties, warns one insider. "Responsibilities and compensation can grow without gaining a change of title."

Salaries get mediocre marks. One insider says, "Pay is increasing, but it's nowhere near the levels you could get at an investment bank." And while "S&P may not have corrected the problem with across-the-board salary

© 2007 Vault, Inc.

increases to match the increased work," a source says, "I do have to give them some credit for making good efforts to move people along." Business travel is occasionally required, but it's "dependent on your job function—it could be 25 percent of your time if you are a ratings analyst." But all of your time won't be out on the road. "Once you've been there for a couple of years, there is opportunity to work from home one or two days a week," notes one insider.

In equity research, "which is separate from the credit ratings business," "there is very much a publishing mentality." "Management is most concerned with the quantity and timeliness of published research." One source notes that "telecommuting, job sharing and a host of other activities" are options, but "all of these things are entirely dependent on who your boss is." The insider adds, "Get the right boss and work from home three days a week, but get the wrong one, and expect to hear some potentially bogus reason about why these arrangements won't work for you."

Melt and blend

Insiders note that "diversity, work hours and dress code are positives," "McGraw-Hill has very liberal corporate policies" and "employees are much more diverse than at traditional Wall Street firms." The dress code is a casual one "unless you have a meeting with a client." One insider says that the dress code is "a fairly informal business casual code, which translates to a nice collared shirt and slacks," adding that "many people wear polo shirts, but I haven't gone that casual yet."

"Hours are increasing because of higher expectations for productivity," but still, they are "flexible." Other insiders report that "working 9 to 5 is accepted as a trade-off for the lower pay," and "hours get busier at the end of the month." In equity research, "new hires are placed into a short formal training session that gravitates more towards the quirks of writing in the 'S&P style,' the editorial process and the in-house publishing systems."

Though the firm is "not a perfect melting pot of cultures," says a contact, "we do have a good mix of people. We just don't have a perfect blend yet." But women are making strides within the company. The insider goes on to note that "while the industry still appears to be dominated by white males, I work for a female managing director, who works for a female managing director, who works for a female executive managing director, who works for a female executive vice president, who works for the female president of Standard and Poor's." Another says that S&P employs "people from all over the world"

Visit the Vault Finance Career Channel at **www.vault.com/finance** – with insider firm profiles, message boards, the Vault Finance Job Board and more

VAULT CAREER LIBRARY   291

and "lots of different races," adding that "McGraw-Hill, the parent company, really emphasizes this aspect in its recruiting."

© 2007 Vault, Inc.

State Farm

1 State Farm Plaza
Bloomington, IL 61710
Phone: (309) 766-2311
Fax: (309) 766-3621
www.statefarm.com

DEPARTMENTS

Automobile Insurance
Banking
Health Insurance
Home Insurance
Life Insurance

THE STATS

Employer Type: Private Company
Chairman & CEO: Edward B. Rust Jr.
Vice Chairman, President & COO:
Vincent J. Trosino
Revenue: $60.5 billion (FYE 12/06)
Net income: $5.32 billion
No. of Employees: 79,200
No. of Offices: 13

KEY COMPETITORS

Allstate
GEICO
Progressive Corporation

UPPERS

- "Nationally known company with a strong brand"
- "Wonderful outlook, will continue to grow"

DOWNERS

- Pay could be better
- "Stressful work environment"

EMPLOYMENT CONTACT

www.statefarm.com/about/careers/careers.asp

Visit the Vault Finance Career Channel at **www.vault.com/finance** — with insider firm profiles, message boards, the Vault Finance Job Board and more

VAULT CAREER LIBRARY   293

THE SCOOP

A huge neighbor

State Farm is a leading U.S. auto and home insurer. The company also runs State Farm Bank, a federal savings bank charter, which offers banking, annuities and mutual funds through agents, by phone, mail and Internet. However, insurance is still the primary money maker for the company, which insures nearly 20 percent of all U.S. autos, and accounts for over 50 percent of its policies and nearly 65 percent of its property and casualty premiums. Homeowners' insurance is also an important part of the company's business. State Farm insures approximately 20 percent of all single-family homes in the U.S.

Ranked No. 31 on the latest Fortune 500 list of largest companies, State Farm runs over 755 claim offices nationwide to process the 71.6 million policies currently in force. Additionally, State Farm offers life and health insurance.

Born on the Farm

In 1921, George J. Mecherle was forced to change careers when his wife became ill. A successful farmer, he left his trade and took a job as an insurance salesman. He disagreed with the current thinking that farmers were charged the same rates as others, believing that since they drove less and had fewer losses than those who lived in cities, they should get a better deal on insurance.

So, in 1922, Mecherle started his own insurance firm, State Farm Insurance, as a mutual automobile company owned by its policyholders. The company charged a one-time membership fee, and, as opposed to competitors, offered annual payment plans and determined rates by a seven-class system, not by the standard of having varied rates for each model.

In 1926, City & Village Mutual Automobile Insurance was formed to insure non-farmers, and in 1929 the company formed State Farm Life Insurance. State Farm Fire Insurance was launched six years later.

In 1937, George Mecherle became chairman, and his son, Raymond, was named president. From 1954 to 1958, State Farm was run by Adlai Rust. Under his leadership, homeowner's insurance was added to State Farm's offerings. In 1958, Edward Rust took over. Currently, his son, Edward Jr.,

© 2007 Vault, Inc.

holds the title of chairman and CEO. Since its founding, the company has been run only by the Mecherle and Rust families.

Today, State Farm Mutual Automobile Insurance Company is the parent company of several wholly owned subsidiaries, including State Farm Life Insurance Company, State Farm Fire and Casualty Company, State Farm Indemnity Company and State Farm General Insurance Company, among others.

Legal troubles

From 1974 to 1987, State Farm faced several gender discrimination suits. A class-action suit against the company stemmed from a 1975 EEOC complaint by Muriel Kraszewski, a former secretary with the company who was rejected as an agent by eight State Farm offices. In 1992, 814 women were awarded a $157 million settlement, amounting to average payments of $193,000 each. State Farm has since tried to hire more women and minorities, and has been named one of the 50 Best Companies for Latinas to Work by *Latin Style* magazine every year since the survey's inception in 1998.

In 1996, State Farm faced a discrimination suit from the Department of Housing and Urban Development, which accused the company of discriminating against potential customers in minority-populated areas. State Farm thus changed its underwriting standards by eliminating age and value restrictions for replacement cost coverage and opened several additional offices in urban neighborhoods in response to the suit.

Katrina backlash

State Farm was hard hit by the 2005 hurricane season and underwrote losses of $2.8 billion. The insurance industry faced hundreds of lawsuits for refusal to cover damage from Hurricane Katrina, and State Farm was no exception. Most notably, Mississippi Senator Trent Lott sued State Farm Fire & Casualty Co. in December 2005 to force the company to pay for damage to his house on the Gulf of Mexico, which was destroyed by Hurricane Katrina. Also, in November 2006, it was announced that State Farm's handling of Hurricane Katrina claims will face more scrutiny in Mississippi.

Although State Farm took a hard financial hit in 2005 due to the hurricane season, the company rebounded in 2006. Net income was $5.32 billion, up from $3.24 billion in 2005. Revenue also increased in 2006, to $60.5 billion from $59.2 billion in 2005. State Farm's Chief Financial Officer Michael

Visit the Vault Finance Career Channel at **www.vault.com/finance** – with insider firm profiles, message boards, the Vault Finance Job Board and more

VAULT CAREER LIBRARY 295

Tipsord said that "2006 was a profitable year, but our evaluation of financial success is defined by our accomplishments over a longer period of time than one year. Given the potential for volatility in the insurance business, we must avoid the temptation of attributing too much significance to short-term financial results."

Branching out

State Farm keeps busy with more than insurance. The company has sponsored the PBS television show *This Old House* for over 10 consecutive years. State Farm is also very involved in sporting event sponsorship, in cold weather (the U.S. Snowboard Association, the U.S. Figure Skating Championships, the Women's Basketball Tip-Off Classic) and warm (the State Farm Bayou Classic football game and the LPGA State Farm Classic).

State Farm also uses its Good Neighbor Citizenship Program to provide resources to boost achievement within the nation's schools and build strong communities. Also, the company participates in a number of partnerships, including Partners for Child Safety, Youth Service America, Kids Voting USA and the National Service Learning Partnership.

Leader in diversity

The company continues to garner awards for its commitment to diversity. In 2007, *Hispanic* magazine included the insurance company on its 2005 Corporate 100 list for creating business and job opportunities for Hispanic Americans, the 15th consecutive year of recognition. The firm was chosen as Corporation of the Year by the national African American organization 100 Black Men of America, Inc. in 2006. Also in 2006, *The Black Collegian* magazine honored State Farm for its commitment to diversity recruiting. The Korean American Coalition awarded State Farm with its 2005 Corporate Stewardship Award, and the Southeast Asian Resource Action Center bestowed its Lifeline Award on the company. Additionally, *G.I. Jobs* Magazine has put the company on its Top 25 Most Military-Friendly Employer list, and *LATINA Style Magazine* has placed State Farm on its Top 50 Best Companies for Latinas to Work For list.

© 2007 Vault, Inc.

GETTING HIRED

The site's got it

Peppered with interview tips, sample interview questions and hints on "preparing an ideal resume," the careers section of State Farm's web site offers potential job candidates a little bit of everything. In addition, the site offers links to applying for becoming an agent or joining the company in a corporate function. The site also lists a number of recruiting events across North America for college students and recent graduates. State Farm links to its job opening on the Hotjobs web site, and lists job types both at regional departments throughout the U.S. and parts of Canada, and at its corporate headquarters in Bloomington, Ill. Job opportunities can include accounting, administrative services, agency, claims, human resources, insurance support centers, marketing, mutual funds, systems/IT and underwriting.

OUR SURVEY SAYS

Plowing through

Contacts report a variety of day-to-day experiences with State Farm life. "State Farm is a great place to work," says one. Another agrees that "it's a fantastic company to work for." "Life at the Farm is just grand," beams a particularly happy insider. Another long-term State Farmer says, "I've been an agent for 18 years and have really enjoyed it." But one source says, "Employee morale is pretty low in my office. I'll be leaving shortly after I get all my licenses." Another notes, "There's a lot of talk about family and closeness within the company, but most people don't care about you as a person. State Farm is not the company that it used to be. Their focus is off." One insider believes, "There is somewhat of a culture of mediocrity at State Farm." The source adds, "Managers will tell you that it is virtually impossible to terminate poor performers, even with the best documentation, numerous follow-up meetings, etc. It can be challenging to maintain a climate of excellence amid this culture."

Visit the Vault Finance Career Channel at **www.vault.com/finance** – with insider firm profiles, message boards, the Vault Finance Job Board and more

V/\ULT CAREER LIBRARY   **297**

Move within

Job security is decent, insiders say. One notes that "when reductions need to occur, State Farm generally will handle through attrition or allowing people to transfer elsewhere within the company." Another source raves about "lots of opportunities for advancement, with a little hard work." Another says, "If you're a go-getter, you should have plenty of opportunity to advance to a fairly high level." The same contact gives some advice on advancement: "You should become involved in extracurricular activities so that you can get acquainted with as many State Farmers as possible. Some activities might be different sports organized by the activities organization. [You can also join] Toastmasters, which develops your public speaking skills, or one of the many clubs."

Making headway in some areas

The company seems to be progressing in many areas, sources say, but not all. For example, regarding dress, one respondent says, "State Farm also allows casual business dress now, something years ago I would never have dreamed they would do." On the topic of pay, sources express some uncertainty but note that "if you work hard, you should be rewarded quite well." But one claims processor notes, "Overworked and underpaid is mostly what I hear when talking to anyone that is not in a management position or has worked there for 15 years."

However, diversity seems to be changing at State Farm, with the number of women and members of minority groups "constantly increasing at the upper-management levels." One insider says that "they make a good effort to encourage diversity," adding that "many consultants are Indian nationals working on visas."

Managing your hours

"Manager discretion" tends to determine the flexibility of working hours, say insiders. "Standard hours are 8 a.m. to 4:45 p.m.," and "every three months you can choose to change your hours." One choice available is the option of working four, 10-hour days with a three-day weekend. The flexible hours correspond with State Farm's comprehensive benefits packages, detailed at www.statefarm.com.

© 2007 Vault, Inc.

SunGard Data Systems

680 East Swedesford Road
Wayne, PA 19087-1586
Phone: (800) 825-2518
www.sungard.com

DEPARTMENTS

Alternative Investments
Banking
Benefit Administration
Brokerage & Clearance
Capital Markets
Corporates & Treasury
Energy
Government
Higher Education
Insurance
Institutional Asset Management
Investment Banking
Public Sector
Trading
Wealth Management

THE STATS

Employer Type: Private Company
Chairman: Glenn H. Hutchins
CEO: Cristóbal I. Conde
Revenue: $4.32 billion (FYE 12/06)
No. of Employees: 16,000
No. of Offices: Offices in more than
30 countries

KEY COMPETITORS

Broadridge
DST
Fiserv
Misys
Thomson Financial

EMPLOYMENT CONTACT

See "jobs" link at www.sungard.com

Visit the Vault Finance Career Channel at **www.vault.com/finance** — with
insider firm profiles, message boards, the Vault Finance Job Board and more

VAULT CAREER LIBRARY   299

THE SCOOP

Rising Sun(Gard)

The largest privately held software company in the U.S., SunGard and was taken private in August 2005 in a leveraged buy out valued at $11.4 billion, which at the time was the second-largest LBO and still ranks as the largest LBO of a software company. With revenue exceeding $4 billion in 2006, SunGard is a leading provider of software solutions for financial services, higher education and the public sector. The firm boasts more than 25,000 customers in more than 50 countries—including the world's 50 largest financial services companies—and ranked No. 500 on the 2007 Fortune 500 list of America's largest corporations.

More than 10,000 businesses and institutions across North America and Europe rely on SunGard to help them keep their people connected with the information they require in order to do business. These customers include corporations and nonprofits in nearly every sector of the economy. SunGard's availability services help these organizations minimize their exposure to threats with the potential to interrupt their operations. These threats include breaches of security, network or hardware failures, data loss, power failure and extreme events ranging from natural disaster to terrorism.

SunGard provides software and IT services to institutions in virtually every segment of the financial services industry. These solutions meet a multitude of needs such as increasing efficiency, improving customer service, complying with regulations and capturing growth opportunities through innovation.

SunGard also provides colleges and universities with strategic consulting and technology management services, helping them improve constituent services, increase accountability and provide better educational experiences. In addition, the firm serves public sector customers, including municipalities, counties, police and fire departments, and public and private K-12 schools. For these clients, SunGard offers a broad range of services, such as integrated financial and administrative systems, emergency police dispatch, permitting and code enforcement, and class scheduling and report card management.

Peer recognition

In November 2006, SunGard was ranked the No. 1 technology provider in the American Banker/Financial Insights Top Ten Capital Markets Vendor listing.

© 2007 Vault, Inc.

The ranking is a new category of the annual financial services industry FinTech 100 vendor rankings developed by *American Banker* and Financial Insights, an IDC company. Based on public information and interviews with industry players, the FinTech 100 ranks the top technology and service providers to the financial services industry. *American Banker* and Financial Insights also ranked the Top 10 vendors in the capital markets industry, and SunGard came out ahead of the rest.

SunGard products regularly receive best-in-class industry awards. So far in 2007, awards have included: AIIM's Carl E. Nelson Best Practices Award (in enterprise content management); Aite Group Best-In-Class High-Net-Worth Advisor Platform; Global Finance Best Treasury Workstation and Best Receivables Solution; and IQPC Shared Services Vendor Organization of the Year.

Recent big buys

Since its founding in 1983, SunGard has completed more than 150 acquisitions. In 2006, SunGard's financial systems business completed 10 acquisitions valued at $163 million, including Integrated Business Systems, Inc. (IBSI), a Melville, N.Y.-based provider of software solutions and related services to hedge funds, and Carnot, AG. of Frankfurt, Germany, a provider of business process management software. More recently, in April 2007, SunGard acquired the tech consulting firm Finetix and fuels management company Energy Softworx.

GETTING HIRED

Inclusive and international

From Sacramento to Stockholm, SunGard offers international positions ranging from application engineer to technical writer in the careers section of its web site. Detailed job descriptions and more are also available via the site. During various points in the interviewing process, job candidates report speaking with managers, HR and, further on in the process, "all of the team." One source notes that during the interview, "most of the questions asked related to the job and teamwork."

Visit the Vault Finance Career Channel at **www.vault.com/finance** – with
insider firm profiles, message boards, the Vault Finance Job Board and more

VAULT CAREER LIBRARY   301

OUR SURVEY SAYS

Steady and ready

One insider says the company was a"steady place" with "some politics" that has progressed and its "grown up from a mom-and-pop operation," but "still stays so in some areas." The contact goes on to note that SunGard is "a good place to be for a long time," and "most people tend to stay there forever, though a few leave after less than a year." Another calls it a "good place to work." But one respondent notes that there is a "lack of communication from management so that employees never know where they stand." Salaries are "decent," but "are less than what you might earn in an IT role at a Wall Street investment bank," insiders say. Perks include "three weeks of vacation," "two personal days," "12 sick days" and "medical coverage."

© 2007 Vault, Inc.

Thornburg Mortgage

150 Washington Avenue
Suite 302
Santa Fe, NM 87501
Phone: (505) 989-1900
Fax: (505) 989-8156
www.thornburgmortgage.com

DEPARTMENTS

Residential Mortgage Lending

THE STATS

Employer Type: Public Company
Ticker Symbol: TMA (NYSE)
Chairman & CEO: Garrett Thornburg
Revenue: $2.53 billion (FYE 12/06)
Net Income: $297.7 million
No. of Employees: 187
No. of Offices: 1

KEY COMPETITORS

Wells Fargo

EMPLOYMENT CONTACT

See "career opportunities" under
"about us" on
www.thornburgmortgage.com

Visit the Vault Finance Career Channel at **www.vault.com/finance** — with
insider firm profiles, message boards, the Vault Finance Job Board and more

VAULT CAREER LIBRARY 303

THE SCOOP

Making sense of it all

Thornburg Mortgage's bread and butter is making complicated stuff seem simple. More specifically, the Santa Fe, N.M.-based mortgage lender focuses on single-family adjustable-rate mortgages (ARMs) for affluent borrowers with sophisticated financial profiles. A relative new kid on the block—Thornburg Mortgage was founded in 1993—the company started out as an investor in mortgage-backed securities. Today, it is a fully integrated mortgage lender with $55.2 billion in assets, and a clear head about its identity. It provides a specific type of mortgage product, jumbo and super-jumbo ARMs, to a specific type of client—successful, finance-savvy men and women with superior credit histories. Thornburg Mortgage admits that its strategy is "not for everyone," but contends that it's this very focus that allows it to achieve the following goals: reduce red tape by eliminating much of the paperwork and fees, provide handcrafted loan solutions to address the opportunities and challenges of clients, and apply a common sense underwriting approach with stringent credit quality guidelines and constantly seek out opportunities and innovations.

CEO Garrett Thornburg began developing his empire before he got in the business of adjustable-rate mortgages. He started in 1982 with Thornburg Investment Management, an employee-owned investment firm with $37 billion in assets as of March 31, 2007. Two years later, Thornburg, who still holds the chairman and CEO titles at all three of his companies, established Thornburg Securities Corporation, a broker-dealer member firm that distributes Thornburg Mutual Funds.

Adding Adfitech

In August 2006, Thornburg Mortgage announced that it would acquire Edmond, Okla.-based Adfitech, a provider of quality control, post-closing audit and document delivery services to the mortgage industry, from a subsidiary of homebuilding company Centex. According to a Thornburg Mortgage press release announcing the deal, all of Adfitech's services will represent a new source of revenue for Thornburg Mortgage.

"This acquisition supports our long-term goal to build a successful mortgage lending operation by expanding our operational capabilities to include an in-house capability that will support many of our back-office lending

© 2007 Vault, Inc.

operations," said Larry Goldstone, president and chief operating officer of Thornburg Mortgage.

Under the terms of the deal, Adfitech and its 323 employees will become a wholly owned subsidiary of Thornburg Mortgage Home Loans Inc., Thornburg Mortgage's wholly owned mortgage loan origination and acquisition subsidiary. Adfitech will continue to operate as a separate business unit and continue to serve its mortgage lending clients on a business-as-usual basis. It will also continue to function as Thornburg Mortgage's central document repository and provide data input, document imaging and file management to support Thornburg Mortgage's lending business. Thornburg Mortgage and Adfitech will continue to operate from their respective headquarters.

In the right place at the right time

When Merrill Lynch announced in September 2006 that it would buy the mortgage operations of National City for $1.3 billion, Thornburg Mortgage was one of several mortgage lenders whose shares rose after the deal demonstrated that institutional investors and investment banks may be interested in home loans. After the Merrill deal was announced, Keefe, Bruyette & Woods analyst Bose George told the Associated Press, "It seems like the investment banks are willing to buy these companies if they can get them at a moderate price. This deal along with a couple of previous deals does suggest there's interest in sub-prime volume." The AP explained, "Stocks of mortgage lenders have been very weak for the past year as investors factor in expectations for mortgage loan defaults amid a slumping housing market and eroding credit quality. While lenders haven't begun reporting large-scale defaults yet, most investors believe it's only a matter of time." After news of the deal broke, Thornburg Mortgage gained 66 cents, or 2.9 percent, rising to $23.21.

At the end of 2006, Thornburg Mortgage reported that full-year revenue increased to $2.53 billion for the year, up from $1.54 billion the year before. Net income increased as well, to $297.7 million from $282.8 million in 2005. Chairman and CEO Garrett Thornburg said that attributed the solid results to maintaining "a focus on only originating and/or acquiring excellent credit quality ARM assets, hedging our borrowings to offset interest rate fluctuations, and utilizing an array of asset acquisition, financing and capital strategies."

GETTING HIRED

Every job has its Thornburg

At www.thornburg.jobs, candidates can browse all job openings listed by Thornburg Companies, including specific opportunities under Thornburg Mortgage (the firm notes that unless it's specifically listed as otherwise, the positions will be located in the downtown Santa Fe, N.M., offices). Candidates can also check out a listing of benefits offered by the firm. Interested applicants are invited to send off a resume directly to humanresources@thornburg.com.

© 2007 Vault, Inc.

Toyota Financial Services

19001 S. Western Avenue
Torrance, CA 90509
Phone: (310) 468-1310
Fax: (310) 468-7829
www.toyotafinancial.com

DEPARTMENTS

Auto Lending
Commercial Lending
Credit Cards
Warranties

THE STATS

Employer Type: Subsidiary of Toyota
Financial Services Corporation (TFSC)
President, TFSC: Hideto Ozaki
**President & CEO, Toyota Financial
Services:** George E. Borst
Revenue: $5.2 billion (FYE 03/06)
Net Income: $580 million
No. of Employees: 3,000
No. of Offices: 37 (30 sales offices, 3
regional offices, 3 customer service
centers and headquarters)

KEY COMPETITORS

Capital One Auto Finance
Ford Motor Credit
GMAC

UPPERS

- Good benefits
- "Great company parties"

DOWNERS

- Frequent reorganizations
- Long interview process

EMPLOYMENT CONTACT

See "careers" under the "about TFS"
section on www.toyotafinancial.com

Visit the Vault Finance Career Channel at **www.vault.com/finance** — with
insider firm profiles, message boards, the Vault Finance Job Board and more

VAULT CAREER LIBRARY   307

THE SCOOP

Dedicated money arm

Toyota Financial Services (TFS), in name, has only existed since 1999, when a brand identity was created to serve as a financial and insurance umbrella for the popular Japanese automaker. But the company's offerings have been evolving for over two decades. In that time, TFS has grown from a small, eight-person operation to over 3,000 employees and $65 billion in managed assets. It is the third-largest captive loan operation in the U.S. after GMAC and Ford Motor Credit, and the eight-largest specialty—financing company in the country. TFS is the brand name used to market the products and services offered by two divisions: Toyota Motor Credit Corporation (TMCC) and Toyota Motor Insurance Services (TMIS). In 2006, revenue increased to $5.2 billion from $4.1 billion a year prior, but net income fell—from $762 million in 2005 to $580 in 2006.

TMCC, which commenced operations in 1983 when it approved a finance contract for a used Toyota Corolla, provides retail and wholesale financing, retail leasing and vehicle protection plans to authorized Toyota and Lexus dealers, as well as to Toyota Material Handling dealers and their customers in the U.S. TMIS offers credit insurance, extended service contracts and other vehicle protection plans. In addition to the TMCC and TMIS offerings, TFS provides wholesale financing to Toyota and Lexus dealers, as well as to Toyota's industrial equipment and marine sports dealers.

Creating new opportunities

The success of Toyota's financial arm left top brass at the automaker stewing over what else it was capable of. In August 2004, the Federal Deposit Insurance Corporation approved the opening of Toyota Financial Services Bank, headquartered in Nevada, to provide cash management services to Toyota dealers on the West Coast. Since expanding its horizons West, TFS had looked even further, toward credit card services. Through Toyota Financial Services Bank, TFS launched the Lexus Pursuits Visa® in 2005. The goal is to expand the Toyota and Lexus brands beyond just cars and to enhance customer loyalty-cardholders earn points on future Lexus car purchases and services every time they make a purchase. The move into credit card products more closely aligns TFS with one of its biggest competitors, GMAC, which in addition to auto financing, offers mortgages and other non-car related financial services.

© 2007 Vault, Inc.

Tracking down used cars

In October 2006, TFS teamed up with Manheim, an automotive remarketing company, to develop an online tool to help Toyota and Lexus dealers locate and purchase used vehicles. The tool, Toyota Financial Services Remarketing Portal, offers integrated online access to all Toyota, Lexus and Scion vehicles from a variety of sales channels. It also include the Dealer Message Center, which allows TFS to communicate with all dealers in one convenient place, a listing of all TFS sales at Manheim and ADESA auction locations, and an up-to-the-minute promotions page with information on everything from special buy fees to transportation assistance. Dealers can also access the latest price information on vehicles, and can use the site's search function to view all TFS vehicles available from any combination of inventory sources.

The power of MTV

TFS played its hand at capturing the coveted young adult age group in September 2006, when it teamed up with mtvU, MTV's 24-hour college network. The two organizations sponsored a sweepstakes through which students filled out a short survey at mtvU.com for a chance to win a 2007 Toyota Yaris. In addition to a brand new Toyota Yaris, the winner received a Toyota Auto Care Pre-paid Maintenance package, which included extra bonuses like free maintenance and roadside assistance. To entrants, TFS also offered tips on building strong credit and on how to make the dealership process smoother. This wasn't the first time TFS took advantage of the MTV "cool factor." Earlier in 2006, the company and mtvU teamed up in a "*Real World*-like" adventure, and took a college student interested in buying a car through the financing experience from start to finish. The "Reality Checks (and Balances)" video spot featured a student making his way through the credit jungle of information and into a Toyota dealership where he was helped through the process.

GETTING HIRED

Applicants wanted

On the careers site (under "about us" at www.toyotafinancial.com), candidates can search for jobs worldwide, apply online and read about career

Visit the Vault Finance Career Channel at **www.vault.com/finance** – with
insider firm profiles, message boards, the Vault Finance Job Board and more
VAULT CAREER LIBRARY   **309**

advancement opportunities and benefits. Job listings are sorted by category, country, company and keyword, and each listing provides a thorough overview of tasks, responsibilities and qualifications. Most candidates can expect to go through "a multiple part interview process, consisting of situational questions asked several different ways by two to three people." The firm also offers summer internships in several areas, including accounting, business technology solutions, commercial finance, financial planning and analysis, risk management and treasury, among others. Internships typically begin in May or June, and the firm says applicants "must have completed their sophomore year of an undergraduate program" and "majors in business administration, finance, management, marketing or other related majors." "Interns must also possess advanced computer skills with MS Word, Excel and PowerPoint."

The hiring process seems to have evolved over the years, insiders report. One respondent says that it was "extensive" once upon a time, but has undergone changes. Another contact reports going through a three-hour interview and subsequently waiting "two to three weeks" before being notified of an offer. The process still involves a "multiple-part interview process" that tends to be spread out over several days, and involves "situational questions asked several different ways by two to three people."

OUR SURVEY SAYS

Business as usual

The culture at Toyota Financial is "very business-minded" and "very conservative," note insiders. Daily work at the company "can be very challenging," says one insider, and is frequently complicated by "major reorganizations" and "countless job reshuffles." But since there are "excellent benefits," "most people are willing to put up with the constant change."

Hours are largely driven by customer needs. "We recently extended our hours to meet the demands of our customers," says one insider, who adds, "My particular department is open from 7 a.m. to 10 p.m. Our collections and customer service departments are open from 7 a.m. to 9 p.m,. and we are also open until 5 p.m. on Saturdays." But there's some flexibility, too. One insider says, "We offer different shift options that assist some associates with

© 2007 Vault, Inc.

balancing their home and work lives." Dress is slightly less flexible. One source says, "Our dress is business attire, except for our business casual Fridays."

Perks sometimes come in the form of parties. There are "several business functions throughout the year," including the "popular" annual holiday party. "Toyota does not hold anything back for the occasion, and includes great prizes, great food and great entertainment."

Visit the Vault Finance Career Channel at **www.vault.com/finance** – with
insider firm profiles, message boards, the Vault Finance Job Board and more

VAULT CAREER LIBRARY   **311**

The Travelers Companies, Inc.

385 Washington Street
St. Paul, MN 55102
www.travelers.com

DEPARTMENTS

Business Insurance
Claim Services
Corporate Services
Financial, Professional &
 International Insurance
Personal Insurance

THE STATS

Employer Type: Public Company
Chairman & CEO: Jay S. Fishman
Revenue: $25.09 billion (FYE 12/06)
Net Income: $4.21 billion
No. of Employees: 33,000

KEY COMPETITORS

AIG
Allstate
GEICO
Progressive
State Farm
The Hartford

UPPERS

- "Getting feedback"

DOWNERS

- More "job descriptions and career paths" needed

EMPLOYMENT CONTACT

www.travelers.com

© 2007 Vault, Inc.

THE SCOOP

Time to travel

A Fortune 100 firm with more than $25 billion in annual revenue, The Travelers Companies, Inc. is one of the largest property and casualty insurance companies in the U.S., providing a range of commercial, personal property and casualty insurance products and services to businesses, government units, associations and individuals. The firm draws upon the traditions of two of the oldest most respected companies in the industry.

St. Paul Companies was established in St. Paul, Minn., as the St. Paul Fire and Marine Insurance Company in 1853, back when the region still constituted the Northwestern frontier of the U.S. and local businesses had difficulty getting Eastern insurers to speed up payments on claims, which created room for a local insurer to pick up the slack. Within a few decades, the company had expanded its business across the country and was financially sound enough to pay out all the claims from two disasters: the 1871 Chicago fire and the San Francisco earthquake of 1906.

The Travelers Insurance Company was formed in 1864 to insurie travelers against loss of life or personal injury while journeying by railway or steamboat. A year later, the company expanded to offer protection against accidents of all kinds.

On April 1, 2004, The St. Paul and Travelers merged to form the St. Paul Travelers. In 2007, the company reacquired the familiar red umbrella trademark, which continues to be most closely identified with Travelers. The company also changed its name to The Travelers Companies, Inc. and began trading on the New York Stock Exchange under the new stock symbol "TRV." At last count, the firm's total assets were $113.76 billion, and the firm had approximately 33,00 employees. Travelers is headquartered in St. Paul, Minn., and has a major office complex in Hartford, Conn.

Job growth in Hartford

In January 2006, the firm announced plans to add 1,000 employees across the U.S., hinting that a substantial number would be added in Hartford. Travelers has more than 6,000 employees in Connecticut and, as of May 2007, had more than 1,700 open positions.

Visit the Vault Finance Career Channel at www.vault.com/finance – with insider firm profiles, message boards, the Vault Finance Job Board and more

VAULT CAREER LIBRARY   313

Katrina's ripple effect

In December 2006, Travelers announced it would stop renewing many commercial insurance policies in the New Orleans area in 2007, stoking fears that other insurers would follow suit and pull out of the market after Hurricane Katrina. A spokeswoman for the firm said Travelers would stop renewing property business policies for some small- and midsized businesses, mostly in Orleans Parish, starting in March of 2007. The firm was the first insurer to announce that it will stop renewing commercial policies in Louisiana in the wake of Katrina. It will, though, continue to be active in Louisiana' insurance market, continuing to renew other types of policies, including those for homeowners.

Looking good in 2006

The firm had a strong 2006, booking $4.28 billion in net income for the year, up from $1.62 billion in 2005, a 159 percent increase. Revenue was also up, reaching $25.09 billion from $24.37 billion in the previous year. Chairman and CEO Jay Fishman was "extremely pleased" with the firm's performance, and also pointed out in a press release that he was pleased the firm's revenue exceeded $25 billion for the first time, and it managed to increase "net written premiums 5 percent for the year."

GETTING HIRED

Beyond St. Paul and Hartford

Encouraging everyone from new graduates, interns and "motivated professionals" to apply, the firm has positions available across the U.S. While the firm maintains significant locations in St. Paul and Hartford, field locations account for the bulk of available positions and existing employees. The careers section of Travelers' web site (www.travelers.com) hosts a database of employment opportunities at the firm, searchable by geographic location or job category, which can include actuarial, administrative, business analyst, claims, corporate services, executive, finance and accounting, investments, legal, marketing and sales, product management, policy services, risk control and underwriting. Job seekers can apply for positions online.

    © 2007 Vault, Inc.

Accounts regarding interviews with the company vary. Candidates call it everything from a "great process" to "long and intimidating." One contact describes having to take a "placement test to see how well your data entry skills and comprehension for insurance measure up," followed by "a four-hour interview" that included "one hour in a call simulation, one hour with HR, one hour with a manager and a one-hour shadow with an employee." Other insiders say to expect at least "two rounds of interviews," mostly "behavioral interviewing," and note that "the process takes about four to six weeks."

OUR SURVEY SAYS

Fun work

Travelers "is an awesome company to work for," says one insider, adding that "the people are friendly, and it's just fun work." Another says, "The underwriting operation is the best in the business-and A++ in my book," but that "the operations side of our business is a solid C at best." Another calls the corporate culture "very organized," but adds that new hires "must be computer-savvy and ready to buy into the corporate culture of being No. 1, or survival will be difficult." One insider adds that "the company could be more receptive to new ideas."

Laid-back dress, flexible hours

For the most part, sources report satisfaction with the "business casual" dress code. One insider notes that on occasoin "Friday is 'dress down day' for $1, which goes into the employee activities committee." (Dress down days are not offered in all locations.) Hours get good marks, too. A contact says, "Standard shifts run either 8 a.m. to 5 p.m., with some flexibility," depending on business need. Another agrees, adding that there's "flexibility to start earlier or later as long as you fulfill the eight-hour requirement."

Getting to the top

"There are plenty of chances for moving up the ladder," an insider says, adding that "you start out in this position as an agency counselor, assisting agents through policies and answering general questions, and you then move

Visit the Vault Finance Career Channel at www.vault.com/finance – with
insider firm profiles, message boards, the Vault Finance Job Board and more

VAULT CAREER LIBRARY   315

up to getting licensed in the other states and deal directly with insureds."
Another notes you're "more likely to advance if you're willing to transfer to
other locations, consistently give superior performance, are sales-oriented
and toe the company line." Yet another contact says, "If you are a hard
worker, there is opportunity to advance," but adds, "Some of the local
opportunity is due to the relatively high turnover rate at the middle
management level." However, management gets generally high marks. One
insider notes, "Managers don't breathe down your neck."

Less diversity in higher levels

Although Travelers was recently named a Best Diversity Company by
Diversity/Careers in Engineering & Information Technology magazine,
diversity at the firm seems to differ according to rank. One insider says, "At
the entry-level positions, there is moderate diversity," but "above middle
management, there is little to no diversity in key positions." Indeed, "most
positions with power are occupied by white males." Another comments that
"the company doesn't seem to discriminate, but there are very few minorities
in the Boston office and other offices I have visited. The higher you go, the
fewer minorities you see." The contact goes on to say that gender balance
within the company fares better, and "there are a good ratio of females to
males on many levels. There's no glass ceiling for women in the company."
The company is making an effort, says a contact, pointing out that the firm
holds "annual to biannual diversity and sexual harassment training."

© 2007 Vault, Inc.

Unum

1 Fountain Square
Chattanooga, TN 37402
Phone: (423) 294-1011
Fax: (423) 294-3962
www.unum.com

DEPARTMENTS

Disability Insurance
Leave Management Services
Life Insurance
Long-term Care
Voluntary Benefits

THE STATS

Employer Type: Public Company
Ticker Symbol: UNM (NYSE)
President & CEO: Thomas R. Watjen
Net Revenue: $10.54 billion (FYE 12/31/06)
Net Income: $411 million
No. of Employees: 10,000
No. of Offices: Major presence in 4 U.S. cities, plus 38 field offices

KEY COMPETITORS

Aflac
Hartford Life
Metlife
Prudential

UPPERS

- Corporate culture is "turning to open communication and sharing of information"
- Flexible hours

DOWNERS

- Some offices better than others as far as diversity goes
- Compensation is "on the low side of market value"

EMPLOYMENT CONTACT

See "careers" section of
www.unum.com

Visit the Vault Finance Career Channel at **www.vault.com/finance** — with insider firm profiles, message boards, the Vault Finance Job Board and more

VAULT CAREER LIBRARY   317

THE SCOOP

"We've got your back"

Unum is the largest disability insurer in the U.S. It provides disability income protection to people who, thanks to payments from Unum, are able to keep up with their bills and put food on the table should they suffer a debilitating injury or illness and need to take time off from work. The company also offers life, long-term care and supplemental insurance to millions of clients.

Unum plans are used by almost one in every five U.S. employers that provide group disability insurance coverage—that equates to more than 11 million American workers covered by income protection disability insurance. UnumProvident boasts more than one million customers, and a total of 21 million insured policyholders worldwide.

Headquartered in Chattanooga, Tenn., the company also has offices in Portland, Maine; Worcester, Mass.; and Glendale, Calif. And it also has a subsidiary in England, Unum Limited and Colonial Life & Accident Insurance Company in South Carolina.

Coming together

After it was incorporated in 1910, Provident Life and Accident experienced several periods of growth and a few subtle name changes. In 1997, Provident Life & Accident Companies acquired Massachusetts-based Paul Revere Life Insurance Company. But a final, major change made the company what it is today. In 1999, Provident, which had a strong foothold in the individual policies market, merged with UNUM, a life insurance company that was established as a main player in group disability coverage and international operations. Thus, the new Unum was born.

The trouble with merging

When UNUM and Provident united, the top brass discovered they'd have to manage the merger through technology—but they didn't realize the extent of that task right away. The new company's managers had planned to use advanced computer and telecommunication systems, which would reduce the duplication of staffers and offices by letting product lines and specialty groups work nationally. But sorting out e-mail, internal chatter and phone systems didn't run as smoothly or as soon as they'd hoped.

© 2007 Vault, Inc.

Fortunately, the company found a way to deal with its technological challenges. It came up with a three-pronged solution: a steering committee that put senior techies in charge of strategic decisions; other business transition groups to manage customers' needs; and working groups whose main aim was to hone in on tech and infrastructure problems.

International shakeup

Unum also made changes to overseas operations. In January 2004, the company sold off Unum Japan Accident Insurance Company, its wholly owned subsidiary, to Hitachi Capital Corporation for almost $23 million. It also sold its Canadian operations, the old Provident Life and Accident Insurance Company, to the Royal Bank of Canada, for an undisclosed amount in March 2004. In the embattled country of Argentina, the company restructured, boosting operations with an infusion of capital into the new holding company it created, Unum Latin America Holdings S.A.

New captain calms the waters

In March 2003, the company put CEO Thomas Watjen in charge on an interim basis, and in September, the board voted unanimously to keep him there. By late spring 2003, the company had completed an equity and debt offering of nearly $1 billion, which, along with a conservative financial plan, helped shore up its balance sheet. For 2000, the company had posted an annual net income of $564 million. Yet in 2003, it posted a loss of $386.4 million in net income—due to the generally weak economic environment, low level of interest rates and income loss from discontinued operations— even though sales had continued to grow. By 2004, the stormy waters seemed to have calmed as Watjen settled into his first full year as CEO.

In 2006, the firm reported a slight increase in total revenue—$10.54 billion from $10.3 billion the previous year. However, net income decreased from $513.6 million in 2005 to $411 million in 2006.

Its financial report for the first quarter of 2007 was a good start to the year, with solid operating trends across all of business areas and earnings coming in ahead of Wall Street analysts' estimates. Net income for the quarter was $178.3 million compared to net income of $73.4 million in the first quarter of 2006. And operating income totaled $174.6 million, compared to $129.2 million. Since Watjen became CEO in early 2003, Unum's market value has increased from approximately $2.4 billion to more than $9.7 billion, and shareholder returns have outpaced the S&P 500 by a two-to-one margin.

Visit the Vault Finance Career Channel at www.vault.com/finance – with insider firm profiles, message boards, the Vault Finance Job Board and more

VAULT CAREER LIBRARY   319

At the company's annual meeting in May 2007, Watjen said the company will begin to focus more on top-line growth going forward while maintaining its pricing discipline and emphasis on profitability. "We have made tremendous progress since 2003, and as a result we are stronger operationally and financially than we've been in many years. While there is clearly more work to do, we're now in a position where we're building sustainable momentum," he said, adding, "Looking ahead, our areas of focus include consistently executing our business plan, better leveraging our leadership positions, successfully satisfying the requirements of our regulatory settlements and maintaining our position as employer of choice in our industry."

You win some, you lose some

In September 2006, Robert Greving was reinstated as Unum's CFO following his successful recovery from surgery earlier in the year. On June 16, the company announced that Greving had been placed on an extended leave of absence to recover from surgery and that Joseph Zubretsky, senior executive vice president of finance, investments and corporate development, had assumed the CFO role on an interim basis.

Just a day before Greving came back as CFO, Unum's chairman since 2003, William Pollard, announced that he would retire from the board at the end of 2006. The company named Jon S. Fossel, on Unum's board since 2002 and chairman of the finance committee, to take over as chairman. Fossel is a former chairman and CEO of the OppenheimerFunds, from which he retired in 1996.

Settling up

In November 2006, Unum closed the book on a two-year-long investigation into the company's broker compensation. In New York, Unum was targeted as part of then-Attorney General Eliot Spitzer's effort to eliminate contingent commissions, which are offered by insurers to brokers who steer clients toward their company—at Unum, the commissions were paid to brokers who were able to renew its policies despite rate increases. As part of its settlement Unum agreed to cease contingent commission payments, disclose insurance-broker compensation and pay $17.4 million. Under the agreement, "Unum becomes the first disability carrier to agree not to pay contingent commissions on all group insurance products and to provide full disclosure of commissions to clients," according to Reuters. On the same day that the New

© 2007 Vault, Inc.

York settlement was announced, Unum settled with California regulators on the same issue.

According to company press release announcing the settlements, "Unum will be implementing a new, simpler compensation program for its employee benefits products. Additionally, the company is expanding its disclosure of broker compensation programs, enhancing a policy that is already among the most comprehensive in the industry. Unum had previously taken a number of steps to enhance transparency by establishing, in March 2005, disclosure policies that provided customers with a means of obtaining information about the compensation paid to their brokers. The company at that time discontinued all programs that provided loans, equity investments, contests, trips or other incentive programs to brokers."

GETTING HIRED

United with Unum

Find recruiting events, get the skinny on benefits or just take your online job cart and do a little career shopping—Unum's site has a little bit of everything.

The careers section of the firm's web site (www.unumprovident.com/careers) also enables job seekers to set up an account to create and/or submit a resume and set up automated job agents, as well as search job openings. Jobs are searchable by location and job type, which can include actuarial, administrative, claims, communications, finance, human resources, information technology, legal, product development, project management, sales and underwriting.

OUR SURVEY SAYS

Sharing is caring

The corporate culture is "turning to open communication and sharing of information," one insider says. But "many cuts have been made over the past

Visit the Vault Finance Career Channel at **www.vault.com/finance** – with insider firm profiles, message boards, the Vault Finance Job Board and more

VAULT CAREER LIBRARY 321

few years," and while "at first it cut the fat, we're getting to the point where we're cutting the muscle in certain areas."

The company does offer good benefits (including benefits for same-sex partners) and "flexible hours," though one insider notes that "depending on the job and level, hours can be long. " Sources also laud the dress code ("jeans most of the time" although "no sneakers or T-shirts" are allowed). But compensation is "on the low side of market value," and there's also "marginal opportunity for advancement." One insider notes that advancement opportunities "used to be more prevalent, but now that there have been cuts, there are fewer openings to move up now." And though "opportunities are presented," "you just have to be the most motivated person in order to get there." There is also "a definite cap to the advancement potential, even for someone with an MBA." Another insider agrees with the assessment, adding that there are "limited opportunities for career advancement unless you're working at corporate headquarters."

Unumgets average marks for its diversity efforts. One insider notes that though there's "not much diversity within the Chattanooga, Tenn., area," "in our national offices, we celebrate it."

© 2007 Vault, Inc.

USAA

9800 Fredericksburg Rd.
San Antonio, TX 78288
Phone: (210) 498-2211
Fax: (210) 498-9940
www.usaa.com

DEPARTMENT

Banking
Financial Planning
Insurance
Investments

THE STATS

Chairman & CEO: Robert G. "Bob" Davis
Employer Type: Private Company
Revenues: $13.416 billion (FYE 12/06)
Net Income: $2.33 billion
No. of Employees: 21,800
No. of Offices: 6 (USA); 2 overseas (London, Germany)

UPPERS

- "Pretty decent bonus package" and good benefits

DOWNERS

- Some aspects of diversity hiring could be better

EMPLOYMENT CONTACT

www.usaa.apply2jobs.com/

Visit the Vault Finance Career Channel at **www.vault.com/finance** — with insider firm profiles, message boards, the Vault Finance Job Board and more

VAULT CAREER LIBRARY   323

THE SCOOP

Ten-hut!

One day in 1922, a group of Army officers gathered in San Antonio to discuss a problem: because their military careers meant frequent relocation, their car insurance policies were expensive and difficult to maintain. The 25 officers decided to form a mutual company to insure each other's vehicles, and to create policies tailored to the military life. The United States Army Automobile Association is now known as USAA, and has grown to over six million members. It operates from six offices around the country and two overseas offices in London and Frankfurt.

USAA products and services are available only to members: active duty officers and enlisted personnel, spouses and children of USAA members, National Guard and Selective Reserve officers and enlisted personnel, retired military personnel and officer candidates in commissioning programs. In 2006, USAA reported a net worth of $13.12 billion.

Business unusual

"We're not a household name," USAA declares on its web site, "and you won't see our logo in a Super Bowl commercial." Indeed, USAA's business is different from conventional insurance companies in many ways. It relies on direct marketing to sell its products and policies; in addition to insurance, banking and financial services it does a brisk business in mail-order catalog sales, offering computers, jewelry, furniture and other items to members wherever they may be posted.

USAA's insurance division provides annuities, Medicare solutions and automobile, home and property, life, business and long-term care insurance. Its investments business includes mutual funds, IRAs, college savings plans, annuities, asset management plans and brokerage services. Members can use USAA's banking services, which include checking and savings accounts, loans, credit cards and CD products. USAA financial advisors provide advisory and planning services tailored specifically for military concerns— how a family might budget for a deployment, for example. (All USAA financial advisors are salaried employees and not commissioned, thus their advice is not based on achieving sales goals.)

© 2007 Vault, Inc.

Log on from anywhere

USAA prides itself on keeping its technology on the cutting edge—a September 2006 report in *Computerworld* magazine named it No. 17 in the country's 100 Best Places to Work in IT. To encourage members to conduct their business online, USAA's web site lets customers file claims and access all their accounts, policies and financial management tools. The company also offers online-only rates, billing plans and special offers for those who manage their banking and investments online. USAA members can also set up billing schedules that match their military pay schedules.

Top brass

As of 2006, USAA's property and casualty insurance group and its life insurance group were rated A++ by A.M. Best and AAA by Standard & Poor's. Moody's rated the property and casualty insurance group Aaa and the life insurance group Aa1. USAA is one of just two U.S. property and casualty companies to receive the highest possible ratings from all three ratings services. Both its property and casualty and life insurance groups were named to the Ward's 50 in 2006, a list that benchmarks the country's top-performing insurance companies.

USAA was also recognized by *BusinessWeek* in March 2007 as the top customer service organization in the country. In its first ever ranking of "25 client-pleasing brands," *BusinessWeek* named USAA its No. 1 firm, saying USAA "has long been hailed for the way it treats its predominantly military customers and their families." USAA beat out other big brands in customer service such as Four Seasons Hotels and Resorts (which ranked No. 2), Starbucks (No. 10) and Apple (No. 18).

Working well for women and military

In 2006, USAA picked up several awards, including a spot on *Working Mother*'s 100 Best Companies for Working Mothers list. For the sixth year in a row it was named to the *LATINA Style* 50, an annual list that recognizes the best American businesses for Hispanic working women. USAA was ranked No. 5 in *G.I. Job*'s 2006 Top 50 Most Military Friendly Employers and No. 1 in the magazine's survey of businesses with the most Reserve- and Guard-friendly employment policies. It was the magazine's top-ranked financial services firm and the No. 3 company for the highest percentage of veterans hired.

USAA was also recognized by J.D. Power as the company with the highest customer satisfaction scores on the 2006 J.D. Power National Homeowners Insurance Study. Overall satisfaction was determined by companies' performance in policy offerings, price, ease of billing and payment, customer service and claims processes.

Oh, deer

USAA's American offices are located in Las Vegas, Phoenix, Sacramento, Tampa, Colorado Springs and Norfolk, Va. Its headquarters in San Antonio is one of the largest single-occupancy buildings in the U.S. (some say it's second only to the Pentagon). The San Antonio office sits on a 286-acre campus that's home to dozens of native trees and plants, more than 12 species of animal life and USAA's very own deer herd.

GETTING HIRED

Let the search begin

At www.usaa.apply2jobs.com, you can create a profile and apply to positions via that route—or you can paste in your resume and let the database search your skills and match your interests to open postings. Alternately, you can search jobs by area of interest or even by positions that offer relocation assistance.

Par for the course

Reports regarding the firm's interview process vary, from accounts of USAA's style being "standard" to "pretty informal" and "laid-back." "The hiring process consisted of an initial phone interview," explains a source, "then an interview with an HR rep, the management team and then a fourth interview with an executive." Be prepared to anticipate everything from "situational-type questions such as 'give me a time when …'" to "behavior-based questions asking for a situation, action and result." Other questions may include "What are your best qualities?" and "Tell me about a time you faced a problem and how you handled it."

© 2007 Vault, Inc.

But expect the process to take "a very long time." One insider says, "I interviewed in May, but was not hired until September." Another calls her series of interviews "a long but easy process."

OUR SURVEY SAYS

The core of the culture

"Emulation of the military culture" is a description that tends to crop up when insiders explain the company ethos. But most are upbeat in their accounts, commenting that "the corporate culture is great" and "USAA has excellent core values." But your experience may hinge on your department. With respect to career advancement, one source says, "Although the Phoenix office is growing quite a bit, they keep telling the representatives that there is a lot of potential for growth and advancement, but I didn't see that in the four-and-a-half years I was there."

The dress code receives higher praise, however. Dress is business casual most of the year, and if a certain percentage of staffers participate in the United Way program, then the company will extend the casual dress" beyond the summer.

Good benefits—but raises could be better

In the compensation realm, the firm touts that "benefits start on day one" with 90 percent of the premium paid." In addition, "USAA offers a pretty decent bonus package—two bonuses a year. There's one in February and a Christmas bonus." But getting that pay increase may be tough. While they execute "performance evaluations once a year in February, the average percent increase is only about three to four percent, which in my mind is not very much."

Other perks, at the San Antonio campus, include softball fields, jogging trails, intramural sports, pilates, salsa dancing, three Starbucks coffee houses and an on-site wellness clinic and pharmacy.

Visit the Vault Finance Career Channel at www.vault.com/finance – with
insider firm profiles, message boards, the Vault Finance Job Board and more

VAULT CAREER LIBRARY   327

Could try harder

Regarding the company's diversity attempts, reports are mixed. One insider says that "USAA is diversity-oriented, and therefore we have a lot of culture within the company," but that's not necessarily the collective feeling. "They do recognize ethnic diversity, but they do not recognize diversity with respect to gays and lesbians One source adds that "you would think that a company that promotes themselves as world class would recognize this."

© 2007 Vault, Inc.

Visa USA

900 Metro Center Blvd.
Foster City, CA 94404
Phone: (650) 432-3200
Fax: (650) 432-3631
www.usa.visa.com

DEPARTMENTS

Brand Marketing
Client Services (Member & Merchant)
Corporate Relations
Finance
Human Resources
Inovant - A Visa Solutions Company
Interchange Strategy & Fees
Legal
Operations & Risk Management
Product Development & Management
 Consumer Credit
 Debit & Prepaid
 Commercial, Corporate
 Government & Small Business
 Processing Products

THE STATS

Employer Type: Private Company (U.S. operations of Visa International)*
Chairman & CEO, Visa Inc.: Joseph Saunders
President & CEO, Visa USA: John Philip Coghlan
Net Revenue: $2.9 billion (FYE 12/06)
Net Income: $455 million
No. of Employees: 3,500
No. of Offices: 13

Sometime in 2007, the firm intends to form Visa Inc. through a series of mergers involving Visa Canada, Visa USA and Visa International.

KEY COMPETITORS

American Express
DiscoverMasterCard

UPPERS

- Brand recognition—known worldwide

DOWNERS

- "Work hours are hefty"

EMPLOYMENT CONTACT

See www.visa.com/jobs

Visit the Vault Finance Career Channel at **www.vault.com/finance** — with insider firm profiles, message boards, the Vault Finance Job Board and more

VAULT CAREER LIBRARY 329

THE SCOOP

Life takes Visa

As it advertises, life takes Visa. The payment card company operates the largest consumer payment system in the world, with more than one billion credit, debit and other payment cards in circulation, ahead of MasterCard and American Express. Visa International is a private, for-profit association owned by 21,000 member financial institutions worldwide. The association's cards are accepted in more than 24 million locations in 170 countries. The association has seven regions around the world: U.S., Canada, Europe, Latin America & Caribbean, Asia Pacific, Central Europe/Middle East/Africa. Visa International is headquartered in Foster City, California. As of June 2006, there were 1.46 billion Visa cards in circulation.

Visa USA launched the "Life Takes Visa" campaign, its first new branding effort in 20 years, in January 2006. The new campaign uses the theme of empowerment. "Visa is the most recognized, most accepted and most utilized payment brand in the world—not just because of where you can pay, but because of what you can do with Visa," said Susanne D. Lyons, CMO of Visa USA in a press release. "'Life Takes Visa' reinforces our brand promise to deliver innovative products and services that can be used anytime, anywhere and that empower Visa cardholders to experience life and business their way and on their terms."

Est. 1976

San Francisco-based Bank of America created Visa's predecessor in 1958, when it launched what was then called BankAmericard. In 1966, Bank of America formed BankAmericard Service Corporation, which licensed banks outside of California to issue cards to their customers. Four years later, National BankAmericard Inc. was created, and BankAmericard transferred control and ownership of the BankAmericard program to the banks issuing the cards.

In 1973, the company launched the first global electronic card authorization system, BASE I, which reduced the time consumers needed to wait for purchase authorization from more than five minutes to less than one. Wanting to shed its image as a California company for that of a world player, the card changed its name to Visa in 1976. In another first, Visa created a global ATM network in 1983 to provide access to cash around the clock, to cardholders around the world. Today, Visa claims its Visa/PLUS ATM network is the world's largest, giving customers access to local currency at more than one million ATMs in more than 170 countries. Visa also operates the world's largest consumer payments

© 2007 Vault, Inc.

processing system. It has enough communications lines to encircle the globe nearly 400 times, and can process more than 6,300 transactions each second.

Pulling in the numbers

The firm operates in the U.S. through San Francisco-based Visa USA, comprised of 13,420 member U.S. financial institutions. Visa USA's members rely on Visa's processing system, VisaNet, to facilitate over $1.3 trillion in annual transaction volume, including 51 percent of all Internet payments. U.S. consumers carry more than 488 million Visa-branded smart, credit, commercial, prepaid and check cards that offer unsurpassed acceptance at millions of merchant locations worldwide.

In 2006, operating revenue increased 11 percent from the previous year to $2.9 billion. Net income also rose 26 percent to $455 million. Visa also noted that merchant acceptance went up 7.6 percent to 6.3 million—and sales volume increased 17 percent to $1.3 trillion. But, Visa noted in its report, "our business is highly correlated with overall economic conditions and consumer spending patterns. Economic indicators suggest that the U.S. economy will grow at a slower pace in 2007, reflecting the impact of the softening housing market and slower job growth, tempered by continuing business spending and moderating energy prices."

Handling security

Visa USA's new leader certainly has his work cut out for him in the area of credit card security. Over the past few years, credit card companies—particularly big guns Visa and MasterCard-have been heavily criticized for their handling of security. In June 2005, CardSystems, a payment processor, announced that it had identified a "potential security incident" in May of the same year, and that it had contacted the Federal Bureau of Investigation, as well as Visa and MasterCard so that the companies could advise their customers of the situation—it is estimated that over 20 million Visa accounts and 14 million MasterCard accounts worldwide may have been affected. But in a statement, Visa seemed unwilling to take any of the blame: "In this case, the processor failed to comply with security rules set forth by Visa. By their own admission, CardSystems Solutions violated standards for data storage that have been in effect and mandatory since 2001 for any entity that stores, processes, or transmits Visa cardholder data. Our rules in this area are clearly spelled out in both our Cardholder Information Security Program CISP, and the industry-wide Payment Card Industry PCI Data Security Standard."

Finding the response unacceptable, two cardholders and a merchant on behalf of all Californian cardholders and merchants affected by the security breach are

Visit the Vault Finance Career Channel at **www.vault.com/finance** – with insider firm profiles, message boards, the Vault Finance Job Board and more

V/\ULT CAREER LIBRARY   **331**

suing CardSystems, Visa International, Visa USA and MasterCard International over two issues: when the defendants became aware of and disclosed the potential breach, and the adequacy of measures taken to protect cardholder data.

Speaking at the Visa Security Summit in October 2005, Coghlan announced that Visa USA, in addition to the funds it's already invested in improving security measures, would spend $200 million on antifraud measures over the next four years. In front of an audience of bankers, law enforcement officials and merchants, Coghlan called for a comprehensive, uniform data protection standard in the U.S. "Without a national standard, we're facing a patchwork of inconsistent laws that don't apply across the board," he said. "Financial services companies are already required by federal law to maintain the highest levels of security. These rules should be extended so that every entity that retains sensitive personal information is required by federal law to have in place a strong information security program."

Coghlan also announced at the summit that investments already made by Visa USA in limiting security breaches had lowered the incidence of Visa-system fraud to just six cents per $100 transacted in the U.S. He added that Visa USA's monitoring systems flag 250,000 transactions a day for possible fraud. As of October 2005, Visa had been involved in 80 fraud investigations.

A new era

After years of operating as a private entity, Visa announced in October 2006 that it would become a publicly traded company. The decision is part of a global restructuring through which a series of mergers will take place among Visa Canada, Visa USA and Visa International. The new company, called Visa Inc., will bring together the company's U.S. and Canadian operations with those in Asia Pacific, Latin America and the Caribbean, the Middle East and Africa. According to a company press release announcing the reorganization, Visa's new structure is expected to strengthen global coordination and accelerate product development and innovation, while preserving the advantages of Visa's strong local market expertise and execution. As a result, Visa anticipates that it will improve its ability to service global customers while continuing to meet the needs of local markets. The reorganization will result in a new stock corporation owned by Visa members. After the mergers are complete, sometime in 2007, the global corporation intends to begin the IPO process and list its shares on a major stock exchange.

What will it all mean?

Going public will have many advantages for Visa and the banks that own it. As the structure of the company now stands, the banks that have a stake in Visa—

© 2007 Vault, Inc.

Bank of America, Wells Fargo and JP Morgan Chase—are potentially liable if Visa loses a lawsuit; public ownership of a portion of the company will distribute that liability. The member banks can also, if need be, raise significant sums by selling part of their stake in the company. Furthermore, analysts believe that offering shares will make the company more streamlined. Not to mention, Visa employees will no longer have stock-option envy toward MasterCard's workers. The rival company raised $2.4 billion in its own IPO in May of 2005. Visa International Chairman William Campbell said MasterCard's decision to go public was not the reason for Visa's, telling MarketWatch, "It was a reference point but not a key driver." Campbell said discussions about taking the company public had been underway at Visa for over a year prior to MasterCard's announcement.

Visa brass has been pretty tight-lipped about how the IPO will affect internal structure at the company, but senior executives have told media that the company may eliminate some jobs when it consolidates, but that other positions will also be added to accommodate expected growth. At the time of its announcement to go public, Visa said it would conduct an external search for its new leader. About a month later, Visa International CEO Christopher Rodrigues, understanding he wasn't being considered for the top post, announced that he was leaving the company. He had been both president and CEO of Visa International since 2004.

In May 2007, after a six-month search, the firm named Joseph Saunders as chairman and CEO of Visa Inc. Previously, Saunders had been named the executive chairman of Visa Inc.'s board of directors, taking on the role in February 2007. Prior to that, he served as president of card services for Washington Mutual. He has also served as president and CEO of Providian Financial (which was acquired by Washington Mutual, and chairman and CEO of Fleet Credit Card Services at FleetBoston Financial Corporation.)

GETTING HIRED

Finding the best

Visa's college hire program recruits university graduates through "campuses, alumni associations, online resources, business/employee referrals and other venues." At the "careers" section of corporate.visa.com, job seekers can also search for openings with any of Visa's six regional operating units around the world (you can also go to "careers" at www.usa.visa.com for jobs in the U.S.). The link to Visa's U.S. career site offers a list of current openings with that division. However, the links to the other regional units only provide an address and fax number where applicants can send their resumes, and offer no way of e-mailing a resume. The site also contains a detailed list of the firm's benefits, as well as office locations, corporate culture and community involvement.

One insider says the firm is selective when it comes to new hires, and adds that candidates should expect a "minimum of two to three" interviews. Another candidate says to expect to "interview with at least six people." Also anticipate "questions to determine if you will fit with the team, such as why you want to work for Visa, your interests, etc." Other insiders note that "most of the time I got a sense that the interviewer did not read my resume," and "the hiring process can be brutal if you are not just being given a job because you are someone's husband, wife, boyfriend, cousin, etc."

OUR SURVEY SAYS

Intense and rewarding

Sources give the work environment varied marks. Visa's culture is called "intense, dynamic, challenging, and creative"—yet "frustrating," say insiders. Maybe that's because at Visa, "work hours are hefty," says a risk manager at the firm. "You cannot succeed without heavy dedication inside and outside the office—40 hours is looked at as almost part-time. They have unrealistic expectations with respect to time." The contact reports going into the office on the weekend "at least once a month." A director reluctantly agrees, saying, "Depending on position, you could expect to work 60 to 70 hours per week, weekends and evenings." He adds that the firm is very top heavy, crippling opportunities for advancement. "There are too many chiefs, and not enough Indians to deliver." However, according to the firm, this will most likely change after the formation of Visa Inc. is completed.

Above its peers in pay

As for compensation, one contact, who has more than 10 years of experience in the industry, says Visa pays above average as compared to its peers. Another calls the salary package "very competitive for most positions," but adds that "one mistake I think they have made is to bring employees in at high levels when they can't meet salary requirements." Sometimes this action "results in someone coming into a job they cannot perform," comments the contact. But most don't have many compensation complaints, though one notes, "I am interviewing for a position at a less stressful company that can match Visa's salary compensation." Employee benefits include "gym memberships and other athletic facilities," plus a "two-to-one matching thrift plan," which increases to a three-to-one match after 10 years of service.

As for the future, one source notes that "for Visa to be successful, they will need to modify their business direction, which will put them in direct competition with their board banks."

Visit the Vault Finance Career Channel at **www.vault.com/finance** – with
insider firm profiles, message boards, the Vault Finance Job Board and more

VAULT CAREER
LIBRARY

335

© 2007 Vault, Inc.

About the Editor

Derek Loosvelt received his BS in economics from the Wharton School at the University of Pennsylvania and MFA in creative writing from the New School. He is a writer and editor and has worked for *Brill's Content* and Inside.com. Previously, he worked in investment banking at CIBC and Duff & Phelps.

Visit the Vault Finance Career Channel at **www.vault.com/finance** – with
insider firm profiles, message boards, the Vault Finance Job Board and more

VAULT CAREER LIBRARY 337

Decrease your T/NJ Ratio
(Time to New Job)

Use the Internet's most targeted

job search tools for finance

professionals.

Vault Finance Job Board

The most comprehensive and convenient job board for finance
professionals. Target your search by area of finance, function,
and experience level, and find the job openings that you want.
No surfing required.

VaultMatch Resume Database

Vault takes match-making to the next level: post your resume
and customize your search by area of finance, experience and
more. We'll match job listings with your interests and criteria
and e-mail them directly to your inbox.

GO FOR THE GOLD!

GET VAULT GOLD MEMBERSHIP AND GET ACCESS TO ALL OF VAULT'S AWARD-WINNING FINANCE CAREER INFORMATION

◆ **Employee surveys** on 100s of top finance employers with insider info on:
  - Company culture
  - Salaries and compensation
  - Hiring process and interviews
  - Business outlook

◆ **Access to 100+ extended** insider finance employer profiles

◆ Complete access to **Vault's exclusive finance firm rankings**, including quality of life rankings

◆ Insider salary info with **Vault's Finance Salary Central**

◆ **Student and alumni surveys** for 100s of top MBA programs and law schools

◆ Receive Vault's **Finance Job Alerts** of top jobs posted on the Vault Finance Job Board

◆ Access to complete **Vault message board archives**

◆ **15% off** all Vault purchases, including Vault Guide and Finance Employer Profiles, Vault's Finance Interview Prep and Vault Resume Reviews (the WSJ's "top choice")

For more information go to
www.vault.com/finance

VAULT
> the most trusted name in career information

Educating Alex is a work of fiction. Names, characters and incidents are products of the author's imagination or are referenced to provide levity to the story and are used fictitiously. Any similarities to actual events or people are entirely by chance.

Copyright © 2013 by Katie McKinney Fox
All rights reserved.

"Goodbye, said the fox. And now here is my secret, a very simple secret. It is only with the heart that one can see rightly. What is essential is invisible to the eye."

-Antoine de Saint Exupéry, *The Little Prince*

Dedication

To twenty years of colleagues, students and their families who have taught me that strong communities foster creative minds. Most of all, thank you to my husband and wonderful family for their support of this dream.

Prelude to a Jostling

My name is Alex True and I am a mystery to most, managing to exist my entire life quite successfully hidden beneath a blanket. It's not a soft, soothing, cuddly cover that I received as a child but rather a strong, protective emotional fortress built by me that only a select few have managed to climb under. Until recently I was unsure of the treasure I have been guarding inside. But now, that's all in the midst of change.

The meeting of my lifetime, a presentation that I am about to give is a result of a serendipitous stumble- and since I don't allow myself to stumble often, this rare occurrence has given me reason to believe in the positive beauty of chance. If I think about the weight of this presentation too much more, I might puke. Instead, I gather my flash drive, my laptop, my iphone. No time for breakfast. I couldn't choke a yogurt down anyway. I check the full-length mirror on the back of my bedroom door and see that the buttons on my blazer don't match up with the holes. I'm lopsided and I don't have patience for it. My fingers aren't working. Impossible! Okay, they're fixed. Buttons aligned and I am ready as I'm ever going to be. I open the apartment door.

The vestibule is littered with discarded umbrellas. A hint of wet dog lingers in the air. I stand motionless. A bevel in the glass coupled with the drops of rain distorts my reflection in the window of the door like the funny mirror at Navy Pier. In it I am stretched out a bit and somewhat serpentine appearing even more peculiar than usual. I step out onto the sidewalk.

From under my umbrella I catch lights as they flick on in the brownstone up the street. A taxi drives by slowly hoping for a fare and pisses me off with a salute of splash across my dry cleaned pants. I should jump in but the EL stop is only another block. The rest of Lincoln Park wakes, slowly- Chicago Monday ordinary.

The tin roof of the platform echoes, low and heavy, a timpani interrupted by familiar screeches of metal on metal. Headlights approach in the gloomy distance, growing bigger and brighter. They stop. The train doors fly open and I escape the aggravating cacophony. Puddles on the seats are dripping onto the floor forcing me to stand and sway as a greasy teenager wearing headphones nudges me relentlessly with his backpack. Sloppy early spring raindrops continue to fall as we shoot deeper into The Loop. Traffic climbs below. Elevators in surrounding skyscrapers delay and I know that for most professionals, this morning will suck. Office scenes will unfold rote, expected, predictable – all except for one.

****

2

Atop The Chicago Works Tower, my colleagues assemble. The glass window walls shudder with each roll of thunder and I am eased only slightly as the attention in the boardroom is focused on the lightshow in the sky over Lake Michigan and not so much on me yet. I stride to the front of the room as a pen falls from Terry's mouth and rolls across the table. I can tell from his bulging eyes that he can't believe I am in charge of the morning festivities.

"Alex True, of all people," I hear him whisper to the out-of-place, pony-tailed man seated next to him. "Is the last person I would expect to be opening a Monday meeting at A.J. Hoyt Technologies. What a crackpot!"

I brush off his naivety and notice the lack of response to his rude mutterings by the guest at his side.

The lights dim in the already gloomy room and I take another sip of lukewarm latté, bile churning and perspiration breaking to my racing heart. Not just a caffeine rush.

I attempt to clear my throat and begin. . .

"As a child, I was intrigued by Shakespearian literature. I spent hours trying to decipher the meaning and tense of his prose. I listened to sonnets on my record player and watched British tapings of plays that my mother ordered for me from England."

The boardroom is lifeless as weary eyes try to focus on me from behind hazelnut steam rising above styrofoam soldiers around the table. I wonder about the stillness and presume, like any other rainy Monday morning, that everyone is struggling to break free from soggy brain-dampening cobwebs. So, I continue.

"For Halloween each year, I danced around in tights and velvet while my compatriots donned holey sheets and fashioned burnt cork faces. Instead of trick-or-treat, I recited quotes from Romeo and Juliet and Othello at peoples' doors. It was fun to watch them react to my whimsy. I understand how the shallow-minded might say that I was a bit of a freak both inside and out and some might agree that I still am . . ."

Still, no movement in a room full of statues. Aside from my voice, sounding a little deeper than usual and raspy from fatigue, they should all hear me. Yet, I get no reaction to my very obscure opener. To my left Terry, with his bulbous nose and beady eyes, stares at me from his pale frozen face. Across from him Jamie and Pat both propped in poses like The Thinker, elbows on arm rests, lean toward each other- rock stiff cold gazes in my direction. At the far end, Lee pumps his brain up, two forefingers braced on his temples framing his bulging frog eyes while Dannie, to his right, looks like a mummy, outstretched legs under the table, arms crossed at chest height. He just might be in a coma. The only pulse I hear in the room is my own. Even Mark, the visitor seated next to Terry, clearly out of his element but tuned into the purpose of the meeting, appears to be slightly

4

catatonic from both the fear of the magnitude of my presentation and the uniqueness of my address.

Maybe my hook is a bit off-putting for this type of setting but I don't care. I am trying to create an unforgettable introduction. So, with pellets of precipitation ravaging the wall of windows and a surrounding sky so dark and perfect for an illuminating presentation, I clear my voice and attempt to project my audience awake.

Hands shaking, I am barely able to connect the document camera to the Smartboard but I get a dose of encouragement as I catch a glimmer from the silver bracelet that my parents gave me as a college graduation gift. I am reminded of its inscription to keep calm and carry on. I wipe a bit of perspiration from my upper lip just as the light powers on and reveal a bit more of myself.

A general chuckle erupts around the table as I drop the remote to the Smartboard and I am further reminded that even the most professional of people can be rudely insensitive. I smile at Mark, who flips his pony-tail and returns to me an accepting nod, but I can't help to show a little vigor toward the rest of the group. Even though I have to win them over, the voice inside of me decides to give them all a little jolt. So, I dig into my pocket and jingle some coins pretending to jiggle a little something else.

Catching my unexpected and underhanded gesture, Jamie and Pat simultaneously snap straight up from their Thinker poses wide-eyed and cued to my presence. Equally alerted, the rest of the table concedes to the change in my pocket as I turn to the screen and reference my youthful self. In the photo, I am young, maybe eight or nine. My hair a little long in a Dorothy Hamill style, appears dark and easy to manage. The striking icy blue of my eyes draws full attention above the bone pale skin on my face. I am in full Elizabethan finery - ruffles, red and purple velvet and tights summoning a mass of typically clad ghosts, goblins and hobos up a suburban sidewalk.

"As you can see in this picture, I was happy . . . unique from the other kids in the neighborhood, but happy in my own element. I was creative and curious and very different."

"Different for sure, Alex." Dannie openly agrees with a friendly smile in an attempt to generate some emotional support in the frigid room.

I watch as glances fly from one colleague across the table to the other in startled disbelief. I see faces of

6

bewilderment wondering – "Did I miss the memo on the Monday intervention? Is this some kind of group psychotherapy session for which I didn't sign up? I always knew Alex was a misfit!"

I slip another four by six photograph under the screen of the camera in which I am marching solo with bagpipes on a football field.

"Nice kilt, Alex. Check out those stems!" Terry chokes as thunder rumbles the windows and walls. The hallway lights flicker.

"Thank you, Terry." I say with a squinty-eyed forced smile, in an attempt to squelch his heckling.

"I also enjoyed playing the pipes." I continue. "It wasn't easy to find instruction but my mother found an old Scot who worked with me every Saturday for years to help me master the wind-bag. It's what earned me a free ride to Miami of Ohio. Let me just say, every school needs a piper."

"Miami of Ohio?" Terry inquires with a raised brow. "Hardly a school for nut jobs like this!"

From the corner of my eye, I see Mark shift in annoyance of

Terry's commentary. I can tell that he is doing all that he can to refrain from losing his cool.

Dannie takes stands on my behalf pointing to Terry across the table, "Will you just let Alex get through this, this, whatever this is. You aren't helping to move things along." He sits with a thud, reaches for his cup and sucks down the rest of his less-than-steamy latté.

I pull up my iTunes and play a brief personal bagpipe recording of O, Danny Boy until I see the faces of my colleagues in early morning agony, over-stimulated by the caffeine and wailing pitch combo. Even Juan Carlos, who is the most gentle person I work with, appears to be gasping for air as he enters the room, so I hit the mute and apologize.

"Growing up in a conservative, traditional suburb of central Ohio, my parents were compelled to encourage me into more mainstream activities, soccer, volleyball a little lacrosse when I was young. These were not the activities that I craved but now, I understand why they did this. For themselves, they needed me to fit in somewhere."

My co-ed volleyball team photograph appears where I am posed in the back row inches above the team and coaches.

The searing intensity of my blue eyes is practically the only bright color in the picture.

"Thank God." Terry Blanchard sniggers from the side of his mouth, antsy and annoyed as wind whistles through the turbulent skies. "Where is this train wreck headed?"

Ignoring Terry's comments, I take a deep belly breath and continue. "I tried to fit in mainly to make my parents happy but my interests were far from mainstream. I struggled often and openly with social and academic norms that eventually drew me away from the suburban pigeonhole that I was not going to fit in to. Essentially, I became my only friend in high school, achieving success in odd places and ignoring jeers from the peanut galleries. It wasn't easy at first but I learned to manage adversity and . . . look where I am today."

And today, it is clear that I have managed to begin to find my place in the world. I am certain that everyone in the room, except maybe Mark, has insight into the six figures that I earn. I have an active professional life. I live in a desirable neighborhood. Fine clothes, fine car, my intelligence above all- proof to the party that as odd as I may physically appear, I am worth the effort of their attention, at least for a little while longer.

Jamie, usually quite patient, finishes his coffee and stands to grab a biscotti from the tray on the side table in an attempt to manage a little restlessness. I realize that I need to get to the point of my presentation.

"I am well aware that many of you are looking at me and thinking, "Hey what's the research analyst doing leading this morning's meeting?" Looking up from the projector, I scan the mixture of curious glances in the silent room, lean over, grab Terry's pen and hand it back to him with a gentle smile. Terry returns to me a dubious grin.

"Well, I am here today to share with you that we are going into business with children."

A synchronous empty sigh blows toward me from the sea of disengaged figures, dragging heels and shaking fists carrying the message "Not another charity! Not another plea for pocket change!"

I can feel the unsettled mood quake even more as the conference room door opens and for the first time in many years a petite, white-haired, bespectacled woman in a fine mustard yellow Chanel suit crosses the room silently taking a chair in the back corner that Juan Carlos has pulled aside for her. My team members straighten their spines and shimmy up the knots of their ties, the confused attention shifts from me to her. It is A.J. Hoyt in the flesh and the brains in the room finally register that in this boardroom above the city, it is definitely not a Chicago-ordinary Monday anymore.

A final loose picture that appears to have been taken more recently is presented. In it, children are dressed in oversized business shirts tied at their waists with twine posing in front of a castle painted on a shower curtain. Some children are holding cardboard swords and trash can lids. Others appear to be cheering.

In the momentary silence I watch and then feel the eyes in the room. First they look at the image of the children in the picture and then almost mischievously avert to me making the familiar penetrating brushstroke from my head to my toes dodging connection with my eyes as they often do out of fear of being labeled voyeuristic or judgmental.

Another crack of thunder and I jump, shaking off some of the stares but in the air the usual questions dangle like wisps of spider web waiting to tangle my colleagues in an awkward professional stance - unspoken, unanswered, always wondering the same type of questions, Do I shave? Is there anything hiding under my blazer? Am I wearing boxers or bikinis? It is an experience that is both strangely empowering and isolating at the same time but I am used to it.

In fact, I often play it up. I choose to dress the way I do. I wear my hair in a simple cut. There is nothing about me that screams either Ken or Barbie. My anatomy is exclusive and should not be the focus of shrewd business.

Dismissing the distraction felt from the eyes that bounce up and down like ping pong balls around the large table, I gather my thoughts and continue, "Okay, okay you might be asking yourselves . . . children? Children? What's Alex talking about? We deal with adults and technologies, new businesses and money. The truth is, though, that I am talking about adults, future adults, future technologies, future businesses and future monies. I am talking about a special school full of kids that are so bright and so creative that any one of them just might be our company's next big ticket."

I notice as Terry Blanchard and the others lean forward with slight investment.

"You might think that the kids in this picture are dressed for a school performance. When in fact, these children are actually participating in a weekly Renaissance hour that was engineered by one of their own. These children are uniquely impassioned about Renaissance life and at the ages of ten and eleven they convinced a teacher at their school to support their pursuits."

Juan Carlos freshens my cup and I take a power sip of coffee and continue. "Creative, confident, cultured, extremely bright and fortunately lucky enough to have landed in a special place where a handful of caring adults foster these attributes, these kids are a lot like me. How should I put it? Unconventional."

"You can say that again." Says Terry giving me a rueful nod as I proudly carry on.

"I spent my life battling demons that might actually have been angels. I wanted to be like everyone else but nature took me down different paths. My parents attempted to shape me into a normal child because normal was all that their neck of Columbus could handle but after time it became uninspiring and depressing to me to try to fit in. So, my parents tossed up their hands and just encouraged me to live authentically. My ability to think creatively and to challenge norms has given me a global edge as an adult."

Taking a slow breath, I realize that I still can't escape the eyes. What is it about them? Always dodging glances hoping for a clue, to know me better but never risking an openhearted effort.

Lost in reflective hesitation, memories wash over me of a childhood and now adulthood filled with eyes throwing searing stares, scanning, some more obvious than others. Up and down, from scalp to shoe, they always pause briefly at my mid-section, no doubt wishing for x-ray vision. I shake them off and forge onward tying my presentation all together.

"It amazes me that I have discovered a city school that is doing an incredible job educating children who are not mainstream, who come up with wild ideas, who spend hours on end deciphering secret codes . . . who remind me of me. Except my childhood was shadowed by the narrow-mindedness of suburbia and theirs by the shallow hopes of poverty."

The tension of the rain stops its penetrating throb and a hint of blue sky appears off in the gray-clouded distance.

Breaking free of my co-workers visual vice, I find myself regrouping and begin to feel that the attention has begun to stream from a different light in the room. A.J. Hoyt herself, the one who has commanded this unprecedented twist to the ordinary start-of-the-week meeting, the one who founded our company and the one who has the power to hire and fire on a dime, is focusing on me. Not how I appear but more importantly on what I have to say. She smiles and encouragingly nods a confident gest for me to keep the meeting rolling.

"I believe that if A.J. Hoyt Technologies partners up with this particular school we could be investing in unprecedented possibilities. Dodson Street School is one of Chicago's few magnet programs that accepts children from the south-west quadrant of the city who have scored at or above the ninetieth percentile in reading and math on the Illinois Standardized Academics Assessment and whose I.Q.

scores are above 130. These are some incredibly bright and extremely talented children. One downfall of their circumstance is that they come from some very sad situations and rough neighborhoods. Another is that these children perform so well that their general standardized test scores don't qualify them for the support and services that schools of lower performing students receive."

A warm roll of sunlight spans the boardroom. With eyes squinting in rays of sunshine, the team at A.J. Hoyt Technologies is all of a sudden showing signs of curiosity and thoughtful contemplation.

Along with the team of colleagues and A.J, siting next to Terry, is Mark. He is tieless and longhaired and unaffected by the entrance of the little old white haired woman. His eyes have joined the squinters in the breaching sunlight around the table but instead of wondering whom the revealing spirit is standing at the head of the meeting, his eyes dance at the sight of me - an intriguing human being whose soulful directive is engaging him, pulling him, dragging him deeper and deeper into my unknown abyss.

I decide to explain the circumstance that has lead to this meeting.

"By chance, I was out on the south-west side investigating a new site for IDEA, one of the start-up companies that we are backing, and I got lost. My GPS was a bust. I entered the Dodson Street School office looking for a washroom and for directions and was shocked by the poor physical state of the place and the antiquated systems that they are being forced to rely upon in the office alone." I look over at Mark who gives a nod of encouragement as the energy of the room is now much more vested in my presentation and less on me.

"The school secretary found someone who could help me and I waited in the teacher's lounge. Walking to the lounge I was taken in by the student artwork on display and the voices that I heard as music flowed out of classrooms and into the halls."

On the verge of laying out an opportunity that would turn the humdrum lives of my corporate teammates inside-out, I turn from them and look again, with pride, at the seemingly out-of-place blonde haired gentleman now standing next to the LCD projector.

"I would like to introduce Mr. Mark Tandem. He is the man who helped me find my way- a dedicated teacher who works at Dodson Street School, grew up in the area and just so happens to be the owner of the old shoe factory which was the site that I was investigating on the day I got lost. I invited him here today to contribute to the presentation and to answer questions you may have regarding the school, the neighborhood and the old shoe factory."

16

Mark welcomes the team with a flip of his ponytail and projects his first photo up on the screen in front of them. "Thank you all for your openness this morning. I thought I would begin by painting a picture for you of Dodson Street as I remember it from my youth."

A wide-angle shot of the neighborhood captures a well-kept school with a playground and grassy field in back. Just down the street are a deli, a drugstore and a hardware shop.

"Above all of the shops, were the apartments that were homes to many Polish immigrant families who worked at Tandem Footing. "

A visual of the shoe factory in its heyday goes up.

"Tandem Footing was my grandfather's shoe company and it employed a few hundred workers from the community in the factory building that you are considering for one of your business investments."

Pensively the team takes in the charming setting on the screen. At his side, I soak up the image of Mark who is so connected to the display of precious memories that have bound him in close proximity to the relics of his youth.

"Now, I would like you to see a similar wide-angled

photograph taken the other day of the same neighborhood."

Mark shows the neighborhood in its current neglected state and the room erupts in disheartened awe at the mere shell of a community that once was flashes by. He speaks candidly about the closing of the factory and the decline of the neighborhood and then the closing of the school.

He projects a photograph of some teachers situated in staircase form posing in front of a false library bookshelf backdrop, and carries on.

"Twelve years ago Dodson Street School reopened as a magnet school for gifted and talented children whose I.Q. scores are around 130. The teachers in this picture are responsible, in many instances, for not only the education of these kids but also for their health and wellbeing. The children come from all over the southwest side of the city and for many, although it may appear hard to believe having seen the earlier photo, our school is a daylight safe-haven. Most of the parents and guardians of our students understand that being accepted to Dodson Street School might serve as a way out . . ."

Mark hesitates, lip quivering in full vulnerability.

"out of their homes, out of their neighborhoods, out of a cycle that continues to repeat itself in so many families where the children end up in the same nowhere hell as their parents. For this, so many families of our students are grateful."

Mark clears his throat and continues.

"The city schools do provide a couple of busses with routes sprinkled within reach of most of our students' homes. So for their families, one of the biggest challenges is making sure that the safety of the children is not compromised getting to and from school. The rest is up to us."

Mark waves an open hand to the photograph of his colleagues on the screen and takes a deep inhale.

"After almost ten years, I still hold my breath checking off the names on my attendance sheet each and every morning."

Fire spreads in splotches from Mark's neck to his cheeks as he pounds a dedicated fist vehemently on the table.
"I am unable to give up on these children because I believe that so many others have."

The silence in the room empowers Mark as the professional hierarchy shifts a bit.

"You may be asking yourselves, "Why then, if the students

are so smart and so talented does this school appear to be so physically neglected? The answer is depressingly simple. These students score so well on the standardized tests that they qualify for acceptance to Dodson Street School but the scores do not qualify the school for the extra support or funding that could benefit their unique abilities. In fact, the input to output statistics and ratios show that Dodson Street School is clearly under funded. These children we teach are bright, extremely creative and carry so much potential that given current resources coupled with an even more nurturing environment they could launch new theories, compete in global studies, develop exciting technological procedures, become community leaders. . . but not without the belief, support and direction of equally minded, dedicated adults who. . . "

"I think I'd like to step in here." Interrupts A.J. Hoyt while gracefully walking toward Mark instinctively taking hold of the air in the room. "Thank you Mr. Tandem." She continues, giving him an excusing gesture while turning to her charges.

Glancing over at me, Mark sends an inconspicuous wink and an earnest grin. He tosses back his ponytail and takes a seat at the long table gathering another heavy inhale peppered, no doubt, with a rapid heart. A.J. and I take control of the meeting once again.

"It's time to see a new face on A.J. Hoyt Technologies. I want one that is more than dollar signs and high fives in the boardroom. Now I know that it was Alex who stumbled into this school and brought the idea to do something to my attention but in truth, I have been hoping for a long time to turn this company into a more holistic vehicle. I have plans. . . big plans and I want all of you to be a part of them. However, if you are not up for joining this radical movement, I also understand." Announces A.J.

"What sort of radical movement are you planning Ms. Hoyt?" Terry Blanchard inquires finally acting like less of a goon than before.

"Well Terry, in an effort to support the start-up of IDEA, which will be a furniture redesign business, we are going to purchase the shoe factory property and lease it to them for change as long as they hire and train as many parents and family members of the children who attend Dodson Street School as possible." She answers point blank.

"Forgive me for saying this but that doesn't sound too radical, Ms. Hoyt." Terry returns with shoulders high and brows higher.

"Oh Terry, I have only just begun." A.J. continues. "We will also be purchasing the buildings up and down Dodson Street, fixing them up and renting the apartments to student families and ground floor shops to other start-up businesses that need our support."

"Okay. . . now you've got me a little concerned."
Says Terry leaning back in his chair and loosening his tie.

"And most importantly, we will be moving our
offices to the hardware store across the street from the school
so that we have perfect proximity to mentor those children
and support the families in the neighborhood."

"Are you serious, Ms. Hoyt? I mean what kind of
profit margin would a move like this provide the company?
These kids sound really extraordinary but . . . seriously??? Is
there time for a vote? Do we have any say? Does anyone
else find this to be preposterous?" Terry's eyes plead out to
his colleagues to join him in his outrage but all are silent
except Juan Carlos who has been taking notes throughout the
meeting.

"I think this is brrrriliant!" Juan Carlos declares
rolling the "r" straight through the air like a slug to Terry's
gut.

"Thank you Juan Carlos and thank you Alex and
Mark for your candor and inspiration. This is going to be the
new face of A.J. Hoyt Technologies. We are investing in the
network of humanity and if you don't like it get out."

And with that I watch the tiny woman turn and exit the room.

22

I feel the eyes in the room again but now they don't seem to be digging at my gender identity. Instead, I feel daggers of blame from some and flames of hope from others. Change is a hard enough journey to embrace but as an ultimatum it can be quite a shock to the system.

Accepting my inherited position of leadership, I attempt to lighten the mood. "Can you believe it?" I say trying to make eye contact with the mix of disgruntled and intrigued colleagues at the table. "All this excitement because my GPS couldn't get me where I needed to go!"

Then as I glance over at Mark Tandem it occurs to me that perhaps that old GPS has directed me just where I need to be.

Chapter 1
The Jostling Begins

It has been eight weeks since the day I found myself
sitting at my desk and the phone rang from an outside line.
Normally, Juan Carlos intercepts calls of this nature but he
was in the john. It was Claudius, one of the guys from IDEA.
He was calling to see if I knew anything about real estate on
the southwest side of the city. IDEA is a new start-up in
which A.J. Hoyt Technologies is investing. IDEA reuses and
redesigns school furniture to be more suitable for use with
laptops and other contemporary learning tools. They needed
to lease an affordable factory and through research had come
up with an address in Chicago. Being top in-house research
analyst, I would normally pass this request off onto Terry
Blanchard, our team's V.P. of field support, but I was feeling
adventuresome. I told Claudius that I would look into it and
I jotted down the address and headed out of The Loop for the
afternoon.

Driving south on the Kennedy and then west on the
Stevenson expressways, I see my territorial comfort zone
shrink in the rearview mirror. Following the high-pitched
nasally directions from my portable GPS that I so lovingly
refer to as Dolores, my slick hybrid takes her lead and gets
off at the Austin Avenue exit and heads south. After

witnessing a few potential street corner drug deals and a flasher, I decide to turn off my Hall and Oates and instead concentrate on the directions from Dolores. The surroundings take on the feel of an urbanized western film, fast-food wrappers flying about like tumbleweed and weathered signposts dangling in front of abandoned convenience shops and liquor stores.

She sends me around in circles, up one ally and down the next. Frustrated, I whip out my phone to try and reach the property owner but there is no answer.

The only voice I hear is Dolores' annoying "At the next street turn right. Turn right. Turn right."

I want to smack her but decide instead to back track in left hand turns and get back to The Loop. In the midst of my great south-side rewind, I catch a glimpse of a pimped out lime-green Camry with tinted windows in my rearview mirror. It peels out of one of the empty industrial lots that I just passed and blasts up the road to where I am fidgeting with the steering wheel, unsure whether to take a left or keep on going straight. I hear and feel the bass pumping from the Camry and the closer it gets the more anxious I become. If I get carjacked here, I'm as good as dead. Just as the Camry reaches my tail, I floor it and launch my little enviro-car straight up the street gravel flying and the smell of burnt rubber filling the air. So much for the environment! I freak when the other car spits dust in my wake and races right behind me. I see an arm in black leather fly out of the passenger window and swear that it is flailing some sort of pistol. Holy shit! What's a suit like me doing in a neighborhood like this! The Camry is now practically next to me and I can see at least three faces, scruffy and laughing, baseball caps askew.

As both our cars fill the width of the street the passenger with the gun, points right at my face and I hit the brake. The punk squirts water at my window and the Camry trails off leaving me motionless and frozen in the middle of the road. Jerks! I am completely out of breath and shaking from the thought that I could have easily been another victim of gang violence. Thank goodness for the intimidating aura of my hybrid. Together we warded off evil!

Post-traumatic stress causes my bladder to go into emergency mode as the aftereffects of my lunchtime Big Gulp kick in and I lurch onward lost and looking for a sign of relief.

From the urban mire, I spot a tattered American flag flying on a rusted pole up the road. As I near, I see it is in front of a building that is branded in places where power washers have worked leaving ghosts of gang symbols and expletives. Bars on the windows suggest a prison or perhaps some sort of mental institution but my bladder doesn't care. I pull up in front and jump out. The sound of the fluttering flag applauds my bravery as I approach the entrance where a broken security doorbell dangling from the metal doorframe invites me in.

I thrust into the heavy metal handle and an explosion of funky pubescent body odor blasts my nostrils, lingering evidence of many young bodies telling me that I have entered a school. The strong scent ignites my gag reflux and I scan for a water fountain. Warm gritty water barely bubbles up from the cracked spigot but I dive in and the trickle down my throat gives me a slight sense of calm while the stench in the air begins to register familiar with me.

"Hurry up! I only got forty-five more seconds." A squeaky desperate voice shouts from behind me with a tug on my pant leg.

"Oh sorry." I say startled at the boldness of the child. "Where can I find a grown up?"

A scrawny black arm shoots out straight like a crossbar at a tollbooth pointing to the office across the way.

"May I help you?" a woman inquires as I scan the surroundings in disbelief. She rolls back in her chair and stands so that I can see she is just a little taller than the handle on the closed door behind her. Her hair is bluish gray and cut tight like mine. She is wearing a jade colored floral moo-moo and a heady scent of gardenia. She must bathe in the perfume. Her image rings of a lollipop munchkin from the Wizard of Oz. She is hardly a daunting gatekeeper but rather a comedic lively juxtaposition in the frame of the office; the walls, a putrid shade of faded gray and in some spots so deteriorated that the pipes show through, the blinds scarcely covering the barred up windows dangle by threads and an elderly man with hands covered in deep blue carbon is cranking papers through a ditto machine.

I feel like I have just taken a step back thirty years in time to my childhood grade school office and I want to raise my hand to speak.

"I'm lost and I desperately need to find a washroom." I admit as the woman sizes up my appearance and realizes that I am not going to kidnap anyone in the building. Normally first encounters with people cause my heart to race as I sense their need to try and figure out whether I aim for the men's room or the women's but this sweet old woman never gives my personal preferences a single thought. She escorts me to a faculty bathroom. Fortunately, it is unisex.

"Now," Says the woman as I dry my hands on the front of my pant legs because there were no paper towels. "Why don't you have a seat here and I will find someone to help you." I am directed to a wobbly wooden school desk where I do my best to sit and wait.

"Keep an eye on the place. I have the perfect person to help you." She says scurrying away like a little gnome.

I sit and wait mesmerized by the rhythm of the flickering fluorescent light above me and the beat of the thumping ditto machine across the room. A couple minutes later and I can smell her. The little gray haired gardenia troll returns wheezing as she tries to catch her breath.

I sit silently still anticipating that she will give me a delayed visual once-over but she seems unconcerned by my appearance and consequently I relax a bit. "Sorry to keep you waiting." She says, slightly out of breath. "The teachers' lounge is a fair distance for an old grandma like me. Anyway, I don't know the names of all the streets in the area so I thought it better to get someone from around here to help you out."

"Thank you, ma'am." I say as my eyes bug out at the sight of her going back to her desk where she begins tapping away at the keys of an old black typewriter. "I haven't seen an old dinosaur like that in years." I express in disbelief.

The woman looks up and acknowledges my comment. "Hey now, I am only sixty-two!" Embarrassed, I shake my head but before I can respond the room returns to its own pulse with the clink of a bell and the recoil swish of the typewriter.

A friendly-looking man with long blonde hair wearing khakis and a pressed blue oxford strolls in carrying a grade book and a set of classroom keys. He, too, carries his own strong scent, a magical potion of citrus and ginger. It makes me think of being at a spa and I begin to realize that personal odor must be a first line of self-defense for air-conscious adults in a school.

Seeing my tall, willowy figure dressed in corporate finery squeezed into a school desk he easily sums me up with objectivity and says with a chuckle, "You must be the desperately out-of-place lost soul. I sure hope I can get you where you need to be."

I immediately feel at ease when I hear his voice. Perhaps it is the thought of a human taking control of my whereabouts as opposed to Dolores.

"I can't remember the last time someone so polished looking came waltzing in here." He continues and as he speaks I can feel my guarded persona begin to quake. I hold my breath again, as I did with the secretary, awaiting the awkward moment that often occurs when people have a face-to-face encounter with me. The eyes of this man are not inspecting me at all.

Instead, his eyes just seem to be openly accepting me as a stranger in need. So few people besides my family and my roommates look at me with such simple warmth that I am almost startled. I nearly forget about Dolores and my failed mission but then pull a crumpled sticky note with the address on it out of my pocket and hand it to the teacher.

Reading the address on the note, a concerned look crosses his face. "You really shouldn't venture down to that end of the neighborhood alone. If you have a little time to wait, I would be glad to show you the building. I have the next class period off and then school is out for the day so if

30

you don't mind hanging out for a couple of minutes while I gather my things I could show you the location on my way home."

Hesitant to interfere with this amiable stranger's day but given that the surroundings are daunting, I nod in agreement.

"Why don't you come to the lounge for a coffee. I think there are some leftover bagels from lunch. I will only be a few minutes." Heading down the long corridor, I am saddened by the bleak surroundings. If it weren't for the enchanted sounds of a music class echoing off the tiled floor, I would swear I was headed to cell block A.

At the entrance to the teachers' lounge, he flips his hair back like a rock star and turns to me, "I'm Mark, by the way, if anyone should give you the third degree for being in the sacred teachers only zone, tell them you are just waiting on me. Don't let them give you a hard time about the coffee and bagel. The coffee is a nickel and the bagels were my treat today." Mark heads off and down the hall to collect his things.

I am slightly dazed by my encounter with Mark. He is unlike any professional man I have ever met. His look screams bad-boy but his actions speak saint.

Grabbing a steaming cup and a seat at the long cafeteria-style table I wait in anticipation for my intriguing escort to return. I notice that the soda machine in front of me only calls for forty-five cents. I mumble, "Well, I guess teachers have to get a break somewhere now, huh?"

"That pop machine is the only break we get around here, and sometimes even that darn thing is broken or empty." I whirl around shocked to hear another voice in the tiny room and recognize the old ditto machine man with the deep blue hands.

"So, you are waiting for your escort. It's a good thing. Nobody should be cruising around this part of town in a snazzy little ride the way you are. Especially looking as lost as you do. Mark will get you where you need to go. He's a long-time local in this part of town."

"Well, hello. Are you a teacher at this school?" I inquire of the old gentleman.

He shakes his head and sighs, "No, I used to be, years ago, but have since retired. I do my best to help out around here a couple days a week because I know how much they need me."

"What a good-hearted man you are."
"Well, it beats sticking around the house, looking at my honey-do list. Besides, I don't golf. I suppose you could say this school is my hobby."

"Don't most teachers retire and want to stay away from students?"

"I suppose but this place is special. Let me rephrase that. This place is a dump but these kids and these teachers are special. The powers that be, they just kind of forget we are out here. So, I do what I can. You know, I'm lining up my chicks for the pearly gates."

"Are you telling me that you are the only helping hand around here?" I inquire with surprise.

"You bet. Helping hand I am. They call me Paulie Blue Hands." He wiggles his indigo fingers at me in jazz hands. "There is an old office copy machine but it was constantly on the fritz. One of the repair guys got carjacked around the corner and that was it. Nobody will come down here to fix the thing. So, we pulled out the ditto machine because, at least, I know how to manage that when it breaks down."

I am in awe that in this day and age carbon papers still exist. Wasn't it outlawed?

"That's not all that's backward around here. You saw the typewriter in the office. We had a computer but just like the copy machine repairmen, no tech guys would venture out here to give us support. So, what's a secretary to do?"

I remember hearing the swish and ping in the office and am doubly shocked that it is used for school survival not just secretary whimsy.

"How can that be?" I ask. "There has to be electronic communication with higher administration in the school district."

"Oh there is. The principal owns a laptop that he brings back and forth from home. We'd be hard pressed to keep computers around here after hours anyway. Tempting fate, you know?"

"So are you here all the time?" I ask taking an overdue sip of my coffee.

"Not every day. I still have to tend to the ol' honey-do once in a while. I got to keep things calm on the home front. But you know, the teachers here they do so much more than show kids how to read and write. Helping them out is the least I can do." He says openhandedly. "Hey, speak of the devil. Here's our local Samaritan."

34

Mark enters the room loaded down with a stack of student papers and of all things an amazing vase full of flowers. I feel my cheeks flush as he speaks.

"Okay, thanks for waiting. I see you met Paulie Blue Hands. I hope he didn't bore you with the dramas of Dodson Street School. He is the resident historian, you know."

I assure Mark that, in fact, Paulie Blue Hands had been very informative about the sad state of help the school was in.

"I am upset to know that teachers like you are working so hard and receiving so little support. Why doesn't the city clean things up around here and make the area safer for the students and staff?" I inquire.

"Look, what's your name?" asks Mark.

"Alex. I work for A.J. Hoyt Technologies in The Loop."

He goes on, "Okay Alex of A.J. Hoyt Technologies. This is the real world. To be quite honest with you, the surroundings here are a step up for some of our students. We get kids from the projects along the lake all the way west to Cicero Avenue. There are a million sad situations that the city has to deal with in this little quadrant of Chicago and unfortunately, Dodson Street School is hardly at the top of the list."

"That's hard to believe," I say, "it's a school. There are a couple hundred children here, right?"

Paulie Blue Hands chimes in, "You got it, a couple hundred children who are doing real well on the Illinois exams and national tests. They're doing so good the school doesn't qualify for any extra funding or assistance from the state. Quite a double-edged sword, isn't it?"

Mark sweeps a lock of hair back behind his ear and looks at his watch and I feel a nearly uncontrollable urge to reach out and run my fingers through his silky tresses.

Seeing the time, he jumps and I blink out of my reverie.

"Look Paulie, I'm sure our guest has appreciated the mini-lesson on the ills of public schooling but we have to get out of here or I will never make it to the hospital in time. Let's go Alex of A.J.Hoyt Technologies."

Out in front of the school, Mark asks me to hold the vase of flowers while he arranges a sturdy spot for them behind the passenger seat of his Honda. "The sister of one of my students who was also in my class a couple years ago was

36

a victim of a drive by shooting yesterday. These are for her."
With a nod, I acknowledge the kind gesture and hand Mark
the beautiful flowers.

Mark circles the car and says, "Follow me just down
the street. I will give you a high sign when we reach the
parking lot of an abandoned industrial park. Next to the
parking lot you will see an old shoe factory, which is the
address that you have been trying to locate." He looks at his
watch once more and I thank him again for taking the time to
help me out."

With his window down, he starts his car and leans out
saying, "I can't believe anyone even knows the old factory is
still here. It's no wonder you couldn't find it. There are no
street signs over there or anything."

"How do you know it's there?" I ask.

"Oh um," He hesitates. "I just do. Let's get movin'. I
wish I could stay to get you out of the neighborhood and
back down to The Loop but when you are done, drive around
to the far side of the factory and there you will see Kedzie
Avenue. That will take you directly north to the expressway.
Whatever you do, it is best if you stay in your car."

I nod, remembering my close call with the lime-green

Camry, thank Mark, hop in my little hybrid and clear the bus lane in front of Dodson Street School following behind my huge-hearted, long-haired acquaintance.

****

Back in my office it's late in the day and I'm seated behind a recently earned oak desk that still smells fresh with lacquer. It's situated at an angle in the room so that I have both the vantage point of a million-dollar waterfront view and the millionaires that sometimes come walking in through my door. Today, however, my vision is adrift, all caught up in the ceaseless waves crashing on the break-wall out in the lake. Thoughts of the day keep riding like waves over and over in my mind, distracting my efforts to take notes on the shoe factory site. Then a call comes in from Juan Carlos. "A Mr. Tandem is on the line."

I can't place the name with any recent clients but pick up the receiver anyway and am pleasantly surprised to hear the voice that had been dancing in the echoes of my mind all afternoon.

"Hey there, it's me Mark. I just wanted to make sure that no search dogs were needed at the old shoe factory."

I let out a chuckle and confirm that all had gone fine. "In fact," I say, "the shoe factory has some really unique physical qualities that the folks at IDEA will admire if I can only convince them that the neighborhood safety will improve." Memories of almost being car-jacked by the squirt gun wielding punk send a chill down my spine.

"Well, I wish I had an answer for you there. I'm just glad that you made it back to work safely."

"I hope the hospital visit went well. You are a very dedicated teacher. Thank you for being so helpful."

"Have a nice weekend." He says. "It was great meeting you."

As I hang up the phone it occurs to me again that the whole time I was at Dodson with Mark, the secretary and Paulie Blue Hands, I never felt their eyes. Not once did any of them scan me or give me the usual visual assessment. To them, I was just a person passing through.

I pack up my laptop and head down to the car with a quick swing into JoToGo, grab a latté and The RedEye to check the Friday night movie listings. Chrissy and Janet are waiting at home for news on the evening's plan which I am supposed to drum up before walking in the door.

Living with roommates named Chrissy and Janet has

been quite a hoot. Aside from the customized doorbell we installed that chimes the show tune "Come and knock on our door . . ." we have all come to embrace the seventies sit-com cliché "three's company too".

We know how to give each other just the right amount of room and space. Chrissy and Janet are both incredible women, attractive, educated and unbelievably talented. The only area that they fall a little short in is financial. Their lives are evidence of hard work not always paying off. One time I found Janet sobbing on the kitchen floor.

"Oh Janet what happened?" I screamed thinking she sliced off her finger or slit her wrist because she was holding a knife in hysterics.

"I just can't take it any more." She bawled. She waved the knife around in the air some more and I saw it was not reddened with blood.

"What is it? What can't you take?" I asked her as I crumpled to the floor by her side. She handed me the collection bill that she had just sliced open. Her wages were going to be garnished. "Janet," I said. "Why don't you come to me, before things come to this?"

Then there's Chrissy who never, ever has her rent money on time. "I just need a couple more days, Alex. Honestly, I will have it for you before. . . " At first it was hard to accept these financial faults of my dear friends. I would wonder, "Don't all adults understand how to manage money?" Then I would consider the economic state of my city, state and country and accept my role in our threesome. I am the bank. It is plain and simple. I try not to let the inner-apartment financial bailouts interfere with the comfortable state of our triumvirate. They are my truest friends and they certainly pay their bank premiums by putting up with my peculiarities day in and day out. Besides, I know how hard they are trying to make ends meet.

Janet is working on her second screenplay while plugging the nightshift as a nurse at St. Joe's up on Belmont Avenue. Chrissy teaches English and coaches the dance team at Lincoln High around the corner from our place. I am jealous at times that they both contribute so much positive energy to the world around them. I do what I can to pay it forward but mostly I just make a lot of money.

Regardless, the weekend plans are always critical. I feel a bit of pressure, not wanting to pick a lame evening flick. After going through The RedEye listings while sitting in traffic, I decide to disregard the star ranking. It seems more the mood to forego a headliner and catch an old favorite at The Brew-n-View. Famous for its classics, fantastic pizza and ice-cold beverages, I am thinking that The B-n-V will be a sure-fire roommate pleaser. Casablanca is the chosen film du soir and nothing sounds better.

I look forward to the evening. However, thoughts of

my day are distracting - the oppressed neighborhood and Dodson Street School to the shoe factory and Mark. My memory of him standing ethereal in the afternoon sunlight, flowers in hand, next to his car in the school parking lot piques my interest. With hair cascading to his shoulders, sweeping so naturally behind his ear, and smelling so pure, I swear if he'd been in Berks and a toga, he seriously could have been body-double for Jesus.

I need to find out why he is teaching at Dodson. What is it that keeps him there? He seemed so out of place.

Stopping in at Dodson was like a trip to the Dark Ages. How could children and teachers who are making the grade be so overlooked?

My thoughts trail on, "Somebody should really do something." I announce to the interior of my car. But that's such a cop out. Janet and Chrissy would step up to the plate and figure a way to make things better at that school. Maybe I should live out loud a little more. Maybe I will plan a return trip. Maybe I'll do a little research on Mark Tandem.

My car veers to the off ramp and I pull to a stop at the light on North Avenue. The setting sun glinting off of the waves of Lake Michigan draws me from my focus on the brake lights of the car in front of me. I am mesmerized by the laser-like rays bouncing off the blue water. My palms sweat and my heart races. I am heating up and frozen in the same momentary lapse of concentration behind the wheel. Then it dawns on me.

"Dolores, maybe you did know where you were sending me!" I shout to the little black box on my dashboard.

Is this my calling? I know A.J. Hoyt Technologies could reach out to the community a bit more. We certainly profit from the city. I could drum up some kind of deal and use the company to give a little to Dodson Street School but that seems a bit trite. I feel something bigger brewing. The light turns green and I am still in a trance. The driver behind me honks. I snap to and accelerate. It's Friday at five.

Chapter 2
Three's Company

The sticky note is written in chicken-scratch. "Casablanca, Brew-n-View, Seven". I slap it on the fridge and throw on running shorts, an old Miami University sweatshirt and head out for a quick jaunt on the lakefront. Our place is only a couple blocks from the North Avenue footbridge and the beautiful vistas of Lake Michigan. The setting sun shimmers off the waves giving a warmth of excitement that makes early evening my favorite time of day. Running alongside the outbound traffic on the footpath that parallels Lake Shore Drive is liberating. There is a slight fish odor that takes me away from the Midwest and off on a Gulf Coast vacation. The wind coming off the lake, the water lapping in time with each breath, the exhilaration of being free of constraint while glancing over at commuters locked behind wheels in rush hour.

"Now this is why I love living here!" I say out loud, feeling rejuvenated after my unique day wrapped up a typical workweek. Disappearing into thought with the rhythm of sole to path, I begin to focus on the idea that A.J. Hoyt could be a source of new life for Dodson School.

If Mark Tandem and the ditto man had assessed and translated the financial dilemma of the school correctly, then the school staff and students are working wonders with very little support from the school board and surrounding community. Just thinking about the successes they could experience with some corporate backing causes me to pick up the pace. I sprint toward the jetty ahead.

New computers, supplies, teacher and student incentives, mentoring opportunities for the students to see life in corporate America . . . the possibilities running through my head are endless. I stop, out of breath at some piled up boulders and old cinder blocks leading out on a cement wall where the waves break and I close my eyes to the mist.

Stepping back from the water's edge, a loose stone breaks free from the jetty and I stumble and catch myself on a sturdier boulder. Realizing that the evening sun is retreating behind the tall buildings of the city, I brush off the dust of the fall and the discerning looks from concerned people on the beach and head home fueled with ideas of a new type of business plan for A.J. Hoyt Technologies.

Chrissy and Janet, all showered and full of chatter are sipping wine around the kitchen island when I sprint through the front door. "Well if it isn't our resident road runner! Why is your hair soaked? You never work up that kind of sweat." Chrissy teases me in a lighthearted tone, "You'd better hurry. Humphrey Bogart doesn't wait for anybody."

"Yeah, we were just placing a little wager that you picked up some gorgeous soul in the park."

Janet chides between sips of the favorite house merlot - only seven bucks a bottle and always in-stock for nights around the island.
"Nope, just consider my delay a result of fate. I'll fill you in on the way to the Brew-n-View." With that, I bolt down the narrow hall to clean up leaving Chrissy and Janet to polish off the wine.

Hopping into the cab, Janet overflows with excitement of news from her agent who thought he had found the perfect publicist to take a look at "Lost In the Louvre" her latest screenplay about a young Parisian woman who loses her mind in the Louvre while staring into the eyes of The Mona Lisa. Thus taking on the identity of Mona parading around the city of light as la grande femme de mystere.

Chrissy and I love the hysterical nuances and social irony set in modern-day France. Janet is so quick-witted with the pen. The story she weaves is absurd but realistic enough to be belly-achingly funny.

"So get this. My Mona begins appearing in the foreground of various prête-à-porter shows during spring fashion week in Paris. The paparazzi just can't seem to take a shot without her. Part of her mystique is that she lands tickets to all the hot spots in town and soon, all of Paris is bent on having photos taken with her. What do you guys think?" Janet asks anxious for our approval.

"Oh my gosh. That is awesome! It's begging for Hollywood!" Chrissy says with bright encouraging eyes. "Cha-ching." I react with a nod.

"My agent feels good about it too. We have a meeting with the attorney on Monday." She shares with high hopes and a deep anxious breath as we pull up in front of the obscure Brew-n-View.

Exiting the taxi, Chrissy leans over and inquires about my brush with fate that had gotten our evening off to a late start. "Oh yeah, that's right. Did you stumble into the love of your life en route to the footpath?" she asks me. "No, I had an awakening." I announce quickly sliding fare to the cabbie and hopping out of the car.

"What? Let me guess . . . you were struck down by lightening." chuckles Janet.

"No, I've got it," Chrissy replies, "Moses walked on Lake Michigan right in front of you and called you to service."

"Well maybe it wasn't that good of a visual but a little flame was lit for me today and I am pumped up about it." I say. "I'll tell you after the show." We enter the theater, buy our tickets, pizza, and beer and settle in to hear old Bogey saying, "Play it again, Sam."

"This is the beginning of a beautiful friendship." The film ends just as always but once again, as if we hadn't all watched it together half a dozen times before, we begin debating whether, in this day and age, Ilsa and Rick would have had a chance - given their personalities and circumstances.

Janet argues that Ilsa would have been the type to pursue Rick via e-mail. They would have set up romantic interludes the world over and the adventure of their meetings would have kept their love affair alive. She casts George Clooney and Uma Thurman in the roles of their lives. Ocean's Eleven and Pulp Fiction are a far cry from this type of romance.

Chrissy's claim denounces Rick as a pig and that Ilsa was too classy for and ex-boozer despite his hush puppy eyes.

I look at both women and say very sincerely, "I like to believe that, like all the best love stories, Ilsa would remain true to her marriage and her first love but for some added excitement Rick would end up with a breathtakingly beautiful African woman, maybe even a Zulu queen. Can you imagine, "Here's lookin' at you kid . . . in Swahili!?"

48

"Now that's an idea for my next screenplay. I love it. Let's swing into Sienna's for a drink. By the way, let's hear about the awakening. Did you discover the meaning of life?" Janet teases.

Out in the beer garden at Sienna's, I order a bottle of merlot. Fifteen dollars is a bit pricey for the same seven-dollar bottle that we stock up on at home, but the evening sky is clear and the scent in the air carries a slight hint of spring. I unbutton my jacket a little.

I feel my guard letting down. It doesn't happen in public often but when I am with Janet and Chrissy I can truly be myself. I know there are stares coming from across the room and they are checking me out. They aren't checking me out the same way Janet and Chrissy are being checked out but I don't care.

Removing the cork and filling up the glasses, I share the details of the days events; getting lost in the run down and dangerous neighborhood, stumbling onto some of the friendly staff at Dodson Street School, the scent of mildewed text books and the ditto machine. I explain how Paulie Blue Hands had explained the plight of the poor school whose students and staff were doing their best to defy the odds of their situation and then I describe Mark Tandem.

"I couldn't believe it! He took the time out of his day

to escort me to the old abandoned shoe factory and then went on to deliver flowers to a sibling of one of his students who had been a victim of street violence. He is an amazing person."

I feel heat rise unexpectedly to my cheeks and polish off my glass slowly as The Rolling Stones jam from speakers on the other side of the patio. The intimate conversation of a couple seated next to our little table fills my head along with the wine like helium as I float out of my seat a bit.

"I want to help that school . . . that community. I feel it down in my heart. Down at the lakefront I was overcome by desire to make a difference." I blink my eyes and my clarity returns. "This is what I am meant to do. I certainly have put in my years at Hoyt to round up the resources and manpower. I just need to establish a rapport with someone at the school."

"Why not Mark Tandem? It sounds like he's given you plenty of reasons to reconnect with him. But, you also need to go and visit with some of the students. Find out where they are coming from . . . their needs." Chrissy shares.

Coming from a schoolteacher her opinion means a lot. "Yeah." I agree. "I don't just want to be the money fairy."

"Go back Monday." Chrissy suggests. "They'll still remember you and thanking Mark Tandem can be the cover for your visit. Maybe he could introduce you to some students."

Leaning back in the wicker bistro chair, I look up at the white lights strung through the trees above the tiny table. The merlot bottle is empty. A gentle lake breeze rustles the cocktail napkins onto the ground. I am thinking to myself how different my life would be if all that mattered about this night had been scoring a pick up at the bar. That's just not for me. I am perfectly content chilling with Janet and Chrissy. I've got a good wine buzz going and the thought of returning to Dodson Street School has me revved up. It has been a stellar day. We tip our waitress and skip the cab. It's a great night for a late night walk home.

Chapter 3
Who's In Charge?

I love sitting out on the deck behind our apartment building. We have trees with branches as high as our railing. This afternoon I am noticing the first buds of spring as they begin to unfurl. It would be amazing to start fresh every spring like these flowering crabapples, revealing a whole new identity. I lean over the railing, look down the alley and see hints of green starting to appear in the postage stamp gardens nearby. It's not just the trees. Every living thing has a chance to start anew. Perhaps this is my time, too. I feel a little shiver as the day is fresh but still transitioning from winter and I find myself glad to be wearing, as always, my staple white Hanes, the second skin under my light cashmere.

I fluff up a weathered seat cushion and plop down on the lounge with my ever-handy digital pocket planner that everyone at A.J. Hoyt Technologies had been given as a holiday gift. Time ticks by slowly as I try to organize a five-day schedule. All I can think about is getting back to Dodson Street School but I also need to stay focused on IDEA. If I am lucky, they just might end up locating in the old shoe factory site, which would give me another reason to head down to that neck of the woods. The old factory appeared to have so much potential for IDEA. It also has worldly charm, historical value and is quite affordable. If only the neighborhood wasn't so sketchy.

I am glad for the reliability of my pocket planner where I see tomorrow's early morning schedule will be typical for a Monday. Coffee and biscotti with the team in charge of IDEA at eight, then at ten thirty a meeting with Houdini, my disappearing boss, to discuss a potential new client list and at eleven a trip out to do another check on the old shoe factory property site with a convenient visit to Dodson Street School and above all, a visit with Mark Tandem. Now that is a Monday both practical and predictable with just a hint of adventure.

Exiting out of the planner and setting it aside, I take a deep breath of the fresh spring air with eyes closed and thoughts focused on how the visit at Dodson Street might go tomorrow. It is impossible to hold back my ear-to-ear grin as I jump up and run to the kitchen to spend the rest of my Sunday evening whipping up some of my famously dangerous brownies.

****

"Zut!" I exclaim. Slightly preoccupied. The cup to mouth distance was a miscalculation. I find myself wearing hot latté and biscotti crumbs down the front of a newly acquired taupe ensemble.

"What's up with that action and what in the world is zut?" I hear from Terry who shoots me a quick glance and a smirk over his opened laptop.

"That action was a simple mistake and zut is French for "Shit it's Monday." I reply making every effort to justify the French and salvage the fabric while still grabbing sips of latté and avoiding a dicey confrontation.

"I am going back out to the shoe factory today to do another run by and check on the neighborhood." I tag on. "It was hard to get a good feel on Friday."

Jotting down some notes, Terry looks up and comments on my new taupe suit. "I didn't know Benny's Big and Tall was carrying the latest designers, Alex. That really shows off your . . . shape." He says with a smirk. "Oh and I do hope the shoe factory location is good because we are running out of time and options."

I nod at Terry and try to be the bigger person but just like always, it is in me to mess with him so I pull out a tinted cherry chap stick, a tiny pocket mirror and slowly and methodically moisturize my lips in his face.

Terry watches me befuddled and as I leave the meeting, he manages a barely audible, "By the way, Alex, don't drink and drive on your way out there. That suit wasn't meant to be spotted."

I head down the hall to have a powwow with Mr. Mackey. He is my direct boss and a company vice president, who I refer to as Houdini. I think to myself how I love this guy but he makes me crazy.

"How was St. Croix, Mr. Mackey?" I inquire upon entrance into the grand office of the company's most missing person.

"Have a seat, Alex." He replies all smiles and full of island color.

Staring over his shoulder at the cold blue waters of Lake Michigan, I envision him basking in a lounge chair on some white beach shouting out orders for fruity drinks to the local tiki girls. I snap to and realize that only the setting of this room, and possibly the temperature, at the top of the Chicago Works Tower, are different from my fabricated beach scene image of him. I gather my inner-islander and prepare to take his orders.

"My time on the island was marvelous. The snorkeling was unbelievable and we were even entertained by a beer drinking pig one night. But that's old news. Let's get on with our current situation here at Hoyt."

Unfolding a day copy of the Tribune business section, Mr. Mackey rustles it, pushes a three-inch stack of pink memos from Juan Carlos out of the way and shimmies down in his leather chair to absorb the print while simultaneously trying to conduct a meeting with me.

"I understand that the current project with IDEA is coming to a close and I want to make sure that we have our hands in the cookie jar for some activity in the near future. Any prospects?" He asks in an attempt to check up on me without any hint of a visual acknowledgement.

"Well, sir, I do have a list of four local start-ups and two businesses in Indianapolis that are looking to act in the next six to eight months and there is something else that I am investigating later today that has the potential to be a real unique opportunity if the cards fall straight." I answer, breath held tight with the hope that Houdini would just phase out the last part of my verbal prospectus.

"Good, Good. Now, I don't want any dead time. I know it's almost spring and Chicago can pose a world of temptation to the post-winter blahs. Your vacation time will come soon enough. Between now and then chop, chop and drum up some profit. Got it? Oh, by the way, have you heard anything about Tahiti? I'm thinking about booking a trip out that way for me and my gal."

"You'll have to brush up on your French, sir." I say.

To think that he's already plotting another escape sends me reeling . . . Tahiti? Seriously? Yet, he doesn't even want me to consider my own time off. Come on!

****

"A tuna wrap and a Fiji Water to go." I order at the counter of Eli's Deli. Strategic eating is a matter of importance given my earlier latté and biscotti bath. Tuna and water can't do much more fashion damage.

"Thank you. Keep the change. See you tomorrow, Eli." His food is excellent and the selections are always on the healthier side of fast food. After my partial breakfast, hunger is kicking in and I plan to eat on the road.

Instead of my GPS, the jabber of talk radio keeps me company in the car. On the Stevensen Expressway heading

toward the shoe factory, the newscaster announces that over
night another drive by shooting occurred on the south side at
Kedzie and Garfield Boulevard. I recognize the names of the
cross streets where the incident took place. It isn't far from
where I am headed. Double-checking the door lock I pull up
to a light at the foot of the off ramp, and am startled. A young
man runs up, sprays my windshield with a bluish fluid and
begins wiping it clean.

"Hey, that's okay. I don't want my . . . Oh what the
heck." I am too upset about the shooting to focus on digging
into my wallet so I grab some loose change from the cup
holder and toss it out the window to the guy as I speed off.

I retrace my path to the shoe factory and pull in to the
parking lot a little further than I had on Friday. I envision
the IDEA signage out front and imagine men and women
filing in happy to be employed and ready to work. The
feeling in my gut is good about this site and how it could
work for IDEA. It would be better, though, if I felt a little
safer.

As I back up I notice something glowing through a
barely visible window mostly concealed by overgrown
bushes off to the side of the factory entrance. I wonder if it is
a property security light. It would make more sense to

illuminate a more visible space. Strange, I think, if I ever I reach the owner I will inquire about this.

The clock on my dashboard displays 12:15. I assume that the school lunch hour is over and that there are only a couple hours left in the school day. Afraid that I will forget about the mysterious light in the window, I jot myself a memo and I work my way out of the lot. Down the road about five blocks or so I see Dodson Street School where once again my tiny hybrid pulls up into the bus lane.

Appearing as inconspicuous as a well-dressed corporate type can, I enter the school like a cowboy on an Indian reservation. The large metal doors push hard on the silver rod that links the madness of the surrounding world with the wonder and magic that I had heard goes on inside of this school.

In the main office, the school secretary's face peers up at me. She is wide-eyed and radiant with welcome. "Now what brings you back our way this morning? Did you lose yourself again in the spider-web of our neighborhood?"

I chuckle. "Well actually, ma'am. I was very appreciative of Mr. Tandem's kindness the other day. I have returned to thank him for helping me find my way on Friday.

By the way, I want to formally introduce myself. My name is Alex True."

"Well Alex True, I am Rosie Fishers. Now, why don't I walk you down to Mr. Tandem's classroom. I believe he has a free period right now. He'd be delighted to have a visitor."

I follow the trail of gardenia scent as Rosie leads me down a different direction than on Friday. It's a long corridor lined with rusted lockers and occasional school artwork. We arrive at a doorway and I hear beautiful piano music spilling out of the classroom. I enter, arm outstretched in thanks to Mark saying, "I want to thank you for going out of your way to help me on Friday. Here are some of my famously dangerous homemade brownies and a two-day supply of bagels for your staff lounge." Mark looks up from the papers on his desk and turns down the beautiful music coming from his IPod. He looks surprised.

"Brownies and bagels well, this is a fine day!" Mark takes a bite of a chocolate treat and melts deep into his swivel chair. He invites me to have a seat at an empty school desk. I feel his eyes on me and they are kind and appreciative. He is definitely happy to see me and I am humbled.

"Honestly Mark, you probably won't believe me when I say this but all weekend long I marveled over the kindness you showed me on Friday."

"Thank you." He says blushing with a hint of chocolate on his chin. "You are just lucky not to have me as a teacher. I make General Napoleon Bonaparte look like a puppy dog."

"He's up with that, for sure." A voice crackling in adolescence chimes in from a far corner of the room where a boy, that I hadn't noticed, appears to be taking a test. "Mr. T. busts my tail every day in social studies and gym class. It's cheap, I say."

The boy goes back to filling in an answer on the paper in front of him as Mark strikes back at the boy speaking very solidly, "Look Jamal, would you rather have your mama bust your tail if you bring home a lousy report card or would you like me to kick your butt? No complaining from you, sir. No way. You're skating on thin ice if you want to play in the game tomorrow."

"Sorry, Mr. T." Jamal says as he stands up to hand in his work. Mark gives him a high five.

"Good work, Jamal. Thanks for coming in at lunch to take this test. I'm sure you did fine."

Running out into the hallway, Jamal shouts, "Later, teach'!" and heads off to catch the remainder of the lunch period.

"He likes you." I comment watching Mark put Jamal's test in a bin labeled "Work to Grade".

"He's had it rough. He's lost his father and a brother in the past three years. His mother is barely keeping it together working nights at Taco Bell and cleaning houses in Beverly. Jamal's a good kid though. I've known him since he was in kindergarten. So many of my students are coming from tough circumstances. We try to make sure that they earn our love by pulling their weight in class and around the school building." Mark says taking another bite out of a brownie.

"What do you mean?" I ask curiously.

"We don't get a whole lot of support here. I think Paulie Blue Hands was moaning and groaning about it in front of you the other day. The kids here at Dodson achieve far above national and local norms on their standardized tests so we don't qualify for the aid that the substandard achieving schools do. So, we get less funding for extra programs. Books, even facility improvements have been denied because the kids are doing well." He pops the last bit of brownie in his mouth and continues his rant while chewing. "Isn't that a crock! Anyway, everybody pitches in to make up for the lack of help. The kids all give Rosie a hand in the office. You met her when you came in."

"Oh yes, she seems like quite a character. By chance is she Irish?" I comment.

"Irish and more. She's been working that front desk since I was a student here and is actually only earning part-time pay but putting in practically full-time days because she cares so much about these kids. It's not in the budget to give her more."

I am embarrassed and ashamed of my fancy clothes and my top-dollar salary. In comparison to Rosie Fishers, my contributions to society are miniscule and yet I have so much more.

Mark continues to explain how the school functions with so little outside support. "The students deliver mail, help run the ditto machine, help circulate books when the book-mobile arrives. The older students receive special privileges when they step in to assist in culture presentations and read-alouds with the younger children. It all works out. Most of the children cooperate well but only because they feel loved and often times safer here than they do at home. There have been a few who have tested the waters. We have had a weapon or two and some gang issues over the years but for the most part we all work together to keep our little ship afloat."

Mark tosses his hair back and gestures to the air. "I marvel at the abilities of these kids. Their interests and enthusiasm for learning supersede their plights in life. There are children here who think so creatively. I'm talking way outside the box and all I can do is hope that life doesn't come down too hard on them. You know, squash them out or suck them into thinking that they aren't worth anything. We all try our best to help them swim against the tide but you know . . ."

I do know, I think to myself as I am completely drawn into his space. He looks and sounds like an apostle trying to convince me of his vocation. I believe him. I can relate to the struggle. My childhood was an uphill battle as well. Me versus the mainstream - I think I have won or at least it's been a tie-game for a long time. He's working for these kids, building them up, so they can stand up against their own social norms of mediocrity, drugs, violence. His message is strong and I am moved not only by the words but also by him. His humility puts me to shame and something strange inside me wishes he would also take care of me.

The classroom is silent but I can hear students scurrying down the hall, which brings me back into the moment and to the reason that I am in his classroom.

"Well Mark," I say. "The information that Paulie Blue Hands shared on Friday was eye-opening. After hearing you describe the situation here at Dodson in greater detail today, I want to help. I am certain there is a way that life could be better for the students and staff of your school. Everyone's load could be a little lighter if you allow someone from the outside with the resources and manpower to come in."

Mark responds saying, "We've applied for some assistance in the past. Unfortunately, no volunteers will risk a trip out here . . . and to think, the staff, the kids, we stave off the dark side of these surroundings coming and going every morning and afternoon. The lack of interest in us, well, it's been disappointing but we keep on moving forward."

I wonder for a minute if the people back at Hoyt would be just as apathetic. Or, maybe I could convince them of the type of financial benefits that could come from investing in the lives of these exceptional, creative children.

I continue to strategize in my head thinking that we could commit to providing support and resources that these children might embrace and run with for years. We could sponsor them in their research and provide mentorships. We could help them explore theater and music by connecting them with local groups here in Chicago. We could train them on new technologies and challenge them to take those technologies further. I tell myself that the possibilities are endless. The wheels in my mind can hardly stop spinning.

I get up and move closer to Mark, leaning into his desk, and once again, turn inside out over the scent of ginger and citrus. "You know, I work with a team of people who just might accept the challenge to make an impact here. I, also know, that A.J. Hoyt Technologies has enough funding set aside for charity that could just as well go to Dodson Street School as any other organization."

The bell rings and students begin to scramble outside Mark's classroom. He rises, steps over to the chalk board begins writing a chronological time line and says to me, "I don't know what sweet twist of fate blew you in here Friday, but if you have the power to breathe some strength from the corporate world into our school, there will be a couple hundred students, several teachers and many families kneeling at your feet."

I turn to leave so Mark can begin his class and slide a business card across the top of a spiral grade book with a note saying "Be in touch soon."

"Alex True . . . brownie baker and business maker. I like that combination." He says while reading my card and gesturing a request for calm from the sea of examining eyes that shift from me to him.

"Hey guys, please take out your worksheet on early Greece."

I turn to observe his class through the long window next to the door and am dumbstruck to see him begin to write, what I believe to be my name on the chalkboard. He pauses after the first four letters and my heart stops for a second. Then he carries on, spelling out the remainder of his lesson topic of Alex-ander the Great. Embarrassed of my own pride, I head back down the corridor aroused that Mark paused when my name appeared on his chalkboard.

Thinking that this whole encounter is now more than a simple coincidence, I decide to elevate Dolores to the title of Her Majesty. Her inability to steer me down a clear-cut road to IDEA on Friday has sufficiently launched me off onto a path that turns me on in a way like I have never been turned on before.

Chapter 4

The Big Boy Bathroom

Back in the bus lane, my heart is pounding. I sit gathering my thoughts and emotions over the encounter with Mark Tandem in his classroom. The beguiling surprise on his face when I approached him with brownies, stirred up a thrill in me in a way that no other man's look has before. I could tell that he was happy to see me and that my killer chocolate thank you was a welcome addition to an ordinary day with his students.

Highly capable and creative they could do so much with their lives but they are trapped and tied to a destiny that needs to be defied. I relate to their circumstance so deeply from the experiences of my youth. I wanted out- out of a lifestyle that squashed my way of thinking, out of an environment where I wasn't fully appreciated, out of a community that looked at me to give answers about myself that I did not have. The roadblocks of being a social anomaly were as challenging for me to overcome as being entangled in the vortex of poverty.

The sense of urgency that I feel to help Mark and the students of his school is astonishing. For the first time in my life, I believe that I am experiencing some type of divine province. God has to be involved in this experience I am having. It just seems wrong to give all the credit to Dolores.

An acrid odor of burning fuel causes my nose to twitch and I look into my rearview mirror searching for answers. A massive yellow school bus is angling toward my car. So I snap to, press the ignition button and pull away from Dodson Street School. In seconds, the one sound that makes me panic chimes from somewhere within my dashboard announcing that both my fuel and my battery are just about up. Ugh! a double whammy in the hybrid. Why did I ignore the warning bells earlier? I have to find a gas station quickly. "Dolores, don't fail me now." I plead while typing a search into her and hoping for a nearby pump.

"Calculating. Calculating." I hear as Dolores' nasally salutation greets me in my panic.

"Turn right." She has me out on Dodson Street heading north.

"Turn left." I obey.

"At the next street turn left."

"Come on Dolores. Hurry!" I beg feeling pellets of perspiration rise on my upper lip.

"In one mile turn left." The warning chimes again.

"Zut! Dolores, you can't let me get stranded here. Don't fail me now." My feet dance frantically as if running with the car to keep it moving.

"Destination on right." Thank God I think to myself.

"I love you, Dolores."

I pull in to a Shell Station, jump out and embrace the pump with relief.

Going in to pay, the clerk gives me the type of stare that I had escaped all afternoon. Rudely conspicuous, he looks at me once checking out my facial features. Then scans my torso looking for bumps or bulges. Coming to his own conclusion he throws me a nasty capped grin and says, "Forty dollars, my luscious."

I hand him two twenties and ask for the key to the men's room.

Back behind the wheel I screech in the pleasure of my own secret power over people like that lame brained station attendant. Watching him squirm when he handed me the men's room key gave me the kind of thrill that has spurred on a selfish desire to maintain my unique style. It is a completely different sensation than the more humbled way I felt in Mark Tandem's gaze back at the school.

Hopping onto the expressway, I check the messages on my voicemail.

"Hi Alex. Southwest is having a sale on flights to Columbus. We miss you, dear."

I reply to the emptiness around me, "Aww mom, I miss you too."

Her voice triggers thoughts of my family and my hometown.

What a long way I have come since that day in June ten years ago when I packed up my Dodge Dart and told my parents, "I'm out of here!" At times, it seems like it was just yesterday. I summon the farewell conversation in my mind as if pressing rewind and play on a dvd.

My mother was doing her best to hold back her tears and despite my own excited anticipation, I felt sorry to be betraying her maternal grip.

"Did you pack your Bible?" She asked through choked words as she wiped away the tears that were streaming down her cheeks.

"Yes mother. I have it tucked away with my collections of sonnets and poetry."

"That's good, honey. If you get in a jam, you've got all the answers you need in there." She replied.

"What about your pipes, Alex?" My dad inquired peeking in through the side window of the Dart.

"I'm leaving the pipes behind, Dad." I replied.

"After all these years and all that training? Won't you miss them?" He asked.

"Look, Dad, I am starting fresh. The bagpipes were fun and quirky like me. We fit together here in Ohio. They were my ticket to college. They served me well but I am moving on without them. I did pack the kilt though. You never know, in a big Irish city like Chi-town, where or when a kilt might come in handy." I admit with a smile and dancing eyebrows.

My dad laughed at my humor and at the same time I recall seeing him, too, swipe a falling tear with his thumb.

Oddly, I never cried. It is so hard to explain why. I was, and still am, grateful for my parents. They supported me and loved me through all the ups and downs of my anomaly of a childhood but as soon as I saved enough money, I made it clear that I was hitting the road. It was all too wonderful to be launching off like a rocket into the unknown. I looked forward to going where the mainstream was less defined.

My dad handed me two crisp hundred-dollar bills and my mom handed me a cooler full of food.

"You have a full tank of gas, right?"

"Yes, mom."

"Call us when you check in to your hotel room. Okay?"

"I will. I love you. Bye." I honked the Dart horn twice as was the custom and didn't look back.

The sun was shining. Like good comfort food coming from my speakers, Hall and Oates were keeping me happy and the Dart was moving smooth as a skate on ice. Mom packed me a meatloaf and mayo sandwich, some carrot sticks and a sleeve of Chips Ahoys. I had a six-pack of RC and nobody to answer to. It was heaven for about four hours. Somewhere between Indy and the Chicago Toll way, I burned out on Maneater and opted for silence.

I stopped to stretch my legs in the booming town of Lafayette where I wandered into a Big Boy. A single line had formed in front of the bathrooms. I got in line. That was when my new life was born.

"You in line for the men's or women's room?" A crooked toothed, mullet wearing Dukes of Hazard wannabe asked me.

It wasn't so much the fact that the question was asked as it was the reaction it caused in me that had such an impact.

I looked the thickheaded guy straight on and said, "Whichever one you aren't going in to."

I watched him shrug and swagger into the men's room and went immediately to the women's not caring what the others in line thought or suspected. "Now, that was kind of cool." I said to myself in the stall.

Rather than feeling ostracized like I often did in my youth, the Big Boy's bathroom encounter introduced me to a whole new world of empowerment. My unique aura had finally given me an edge. I flushed the former Alex down the Big Boy toilet, washed my hands and looked in the mirror. Cropped dark hair, dark brows, unusually long lashes surrounding my icy-blue eyes, full lips, tall strong stature, sure enough I could work my way into any men's or women's room.

"Windy City here I come!" I remember screaming out the window as I pulled out of the greasy diner's parking lot. For the next two hours, I plotted in silence the manner in which I would present the new and improved Alex True to the world. Confident, friendly, impeccably put together but beguilingly and amazingly gender free in appearance.

The memory of the Big Boy bathroom forces me to flip down my visor and look in the mirror. Ten years later and I am doing a pretty good job at remaining non-descript. I could go for a little brow wax though. In the mirror, beyond my face, I see the decay of slowing industry behind me. It's sad. I think to myself, that everything has its prime. Factory chimneys emblazoned with gang graffiti indicating loss of control, rail yards with abandoned cars, apartment buildings lining the expressway that all once had their days. I wonder if I have had my time yet.

When my gaze leaves the mirror, I look up and over Dolores, through the windshield, beyond the stalled traffic to the thriving city ahead and the thought of an original watercolor painting that hangs in my apartment comes to mind.

I was inspired to purchase it a few years ago. It reminds me of that early evening ten years ago when I arrived in and fell in love with Chicago. A beautiful piece of the skyline at dusk, the clouds in a pinkish hue dance between the Sears Tower and The Hancock. A sentimental investment, it is the first view that I had of my new home as my little Dart worked its way up and over the skyway bridge crossing into the city limits. The shoulders of the city extended their arms and swept me in.

The taxi driver behind me lays on his horn as if I have the power to systematically force all the cars in front of me out of his way. The shrill distracts me and I bounce from my Dart of years ago back into my Hybrid. "Where are Hall and Oates when I need them most?" I ask Dolores.

I drum my fingers on the dashboard and fixate on the bright taillights of the Volkswagen that is finally moving ahead of me. My mind feels fried and fired up from the day. I would love to get home and sprawl out on the sofa with a bag of pita chips and a beer, but I remember there is one more place I need to be.

"Hey stone face, snap out of it!" The trucker yells

from his elevated perch alongside Dolores and me in the hybrid. I blink out of my daze, wave him off and press the accelerator. I need to hurry. Virgil is waiting.

Chapter 5

Soup Kitchen

"The bread slicer cometh!" I holler running past an old gray minivan with a large Jamaican flag painted on the door. Strange, I think but keep on moving. From the top of the basement stairwell at Pearson Street Church I see Virgil turn his bandana bound head from the steaming pot of boiling pasta. He gives me a thumbs-up. I whip over to the apron rack and tie one on over my business suit.

"So sorry to be late, Virg." I say heading over to the bread-cutting stand next to him. He sets down the spaghetti tongs and swoops me up in the familiar embrace that forces a gale from my chest. His massive tattooed mahogany arms done with days of fighting now find themselves the givers of bear hugs and warm meals.

Virg and I, we have good chemistry. He and I are so different we compliment each other like chocolate and chili. Imagine Mr.T with no gold chains. That's Virgil. I tower over him by at least a foot and tend to appear even whiter than I really am in his midst. There is no questioning who is in charge in this basement kitchen.

Virgil is my captain and I am his dinnertime copilot. The regulars call us Salt and Pepper.

Years ago when Reverend Hummel first invited me to assist at the kitchen, I didn't understand why. She knew me as a regular Sunday worshiper and we had chatted a bit over coffee after the church services. I think she saw that I needed to fit in somewhere in a way that I could not identify myself. A true preacher's gift, I suppose. She must have seen the same need in Virgil because she invited him at about the same time. He and I both make our Monday nights together a top priority.

Week after week, we slice and serve but we also receive. No judgments are dealt nor dealt with during the evenings in the church basement. I am just Salt. He is Pepper. The guests are hungry. Virgil and I are bound by our devotion to them and to each other. I love listening to the chatter and laughter of the men, women and children who accept me as part of their Monday night family. I have no idea where our well-fed diners go when they leave the basement. I don't even have a clue where Virgil goes. I have never asked where he lives. I know he is single. He picks up odd jobs around the city and he works with me on Monday nights. He is happy. He is my friend. That is all I need to know.

"Evening Peppa. Evening Salt." Johhny, a familiar recipient of our Monday Meals, greets us with friendly banter, a clean plate ready for a second helping.

"Hello, my friend. How was your day?" Virgil asks while loading his plate with pasta.

"Oh, this has been a fine day. See that nice lady over there? The one with the red flower in her hair? She picked me up in her van and drove me here like I was a king or somethin'. No sneakin' rides on and off The El for me. Tonight I arrived in style." He boasted, head bobbing, shoulders dancing.

"Who is she, Johnny? Do you know her?" I inquire curiously.

"I don't know. She just pulled up in that van of hers with the fancy painting on the door, asked me if I was hungry and told me to hop in. There was three other guys like me sitting in the back." He shared, eyeing his mountain of spaghetti.

"That's really a kind thing to do." I reply and weave my way through the dozen or so tables of nourished guests to the far end of the basement and approach the woman with the red flower in her hair.

"Excuse me, miss?" I gently tap her shoulder.

She turns and cracks a fleeting smile that disappears when she sees me instead of one of the other guests.

"I taut everybody welcome in da church." She claims in a defensive high-pitched Jamaican lilt.

"Everyone is welcome. I just came to thank you for bringing some guests. It is very kind of you." I reply noticing her face soften as she accepts my compliment. She fiddles with the tip of the plastic poinsettia tucked behind her ear. I can tell she is uncomfortable with the dialogue.

"I hear da food is good here. I tink so too." She states with assumed culinary authority, her seal of approval our golden fork.

"I will let Virgil know. He loves a compliment from a beautiful lady." I nod with a grin. "My name is Alex. You and you're your friends have an open invitation to dine with us every Monday."

She takes a moment to respond, looks me up and down, tilts her head, squints her eyes and begins to ask a question. I know where she is headed as her reaction to my physical presence is a normal one.

"You a. . ." She stops midway, blinks and replies instead, "Tank you, Alex. Dey call me Cherry, Cherry Bellafonte."

I am relieved to have dodged the pressing question she was about to ask as the extraordinary name twirls a pirouette from her lips instead, with a lingering rhythm, so hard to shake from between my ears, Cherry Bellafonte.

* * * * * * * * * * * * * * *

"Virgil, I think that woman will be back." I shout to him over the rushing water spilling into the tub of bubbles where my hands are scrubbing the crusted tomato sauce from plates and forks.

"What woman you talking about, Alex?" He throws back over the noise.

"Cherry. The woman with the plastic flower in her hair." I identify her more specifically. "She brought Johnny and some others in that Jamaican van of hers."

"I see. Well, like I always say, 'the door is open. The food is hot. We feed 'em all homeless or not'." He trails off and rests his large hand on my shoulder while I chomp down on a leftover slice of Italian bread.

"It's been quite the day, Virg. This is the first bite I've had since noon. It isn't much but boy does it hit the spot."

I notice Virgil examining me closely as I polish off the last of the bread and guzzle a glass of water to wash it down. "Yo Alex, you wearin' make up?" His odd question comes out of the blue and is suspended in the space between us. Before I can answer, we turn to the sound of heels clicking on the basement floor.

"I thank you but more importantly God thanks you both for another five star Monday night meal of service." Reverend Hummel praises as she extends a friendly handshake first to Virgil and then to me.

"It is our pleasure, reverend." Virgil responds.

"That's right, reverend. Salt and Pepper can really

serve it up!" I boast cajolingly.

Turning, to back out of the basement, she nods with her fist in a victorious wave, "Yes, yes you do! Good night Virgil. Good night Alex."

Back behind the wheel, I am ready to head home. It has been a full day and my blood is pulsing at rapid fire through my veins. I always leave the Monday night kitchen with a warm heart but this evening I feel that and more. My emotions are brewing inside of me. I am connecting to an unknown- Dodson? Mark? Both? As I go to adjust my rearview mirror I notice an uncharacteristic redness in my cheeks. I never wear make-up.

Chapter 6

Business Shmizness

It feels like I've reached a 5K finish line crossing the threshold of our apartment flush with elation and exhaustion.

"Hey Alex, how was your day?" Janet inquires as I drop my laptop bag and jacket on a chair and collapse into the sofa next to her. The lack of a response from me gives my well-tuned roommate plenty of information. She leans over and gives my scalp a tender massage. I melt.

Janet's presence soothes me. She always smells like warm vanilla in contrast to the essence of her mocha skin. Just being with her comforts my spirit like a freshly baked tollhouse cookie. I lay my head back on the throw pillows, close my eyes and drift into the drone of nonsense coming from the flat screen in front of us.

My other roommate, Chrissy is sitting at the table across the room grading papers. These days she is always grading papers, or dancing. The three of us met playing co-ed volleyball the summer I arrived in Chicago. We play on a team sponsored by a local bar called "After Ours". We play on most Thursday nights either on the courts of North Avenue beach or in the gym at Lincoln Park High.

"Hey Alex, are you okay?" Chrissy asks, perched from a stool in her makeshift office on the island in the kitchen. I open an eye and look at her. She then adds, "Are you wearing make-up?" With that question I sit straight up and turn to Janet.

"Will you feel my forehead?" I plead, wondering if, in fact, I am turning red due to an illness. Janet touches me with the back of her soft hand.

"No fever," She reports. "but I do know that if you experience something that ignites passion in your life the adrenaline can start to really pump and cause redness in the skin." Janet pinches my flaming cheek and gives me a wink. "I suspect that you, Alex True, are suffering from a case of aberrant exposure."

I roll my eyes and collapse back into the pillows.

"Wow, it sure is advantageous living with a screenwriter who moonlights as a nurse! It's constant Diagnosis Mystery around here." I joke toward Janet who I note is still wearing turquoise scrubs from a shift at the hospital.

Chrissy pipes up, "So, is it safe to say that your blush relates to your visit to Dodson Street School today?" She sets her work aside and walks over to join us on the sofa. Janet mutes the flat screen and they both stare at me, eagerly expecting information.

"Yes. It's safe to say so." I admit, unable to suppress the raw emotion flushing to my cheeks. "It's everything. Everything about this day was so effusive. I had an emotional connection with everything I saw and every person I met today, most profoundly Mark Tandem in his classroom. He is so unassumingly inspiring"

"You have to call him!" Both Janet and Chrissy implore of me in synchronicity.

"I don't have his personal number." I respond defensively. "Besides, this is business. I should call during business hours."

"Business, shmizness," Chrissy moans as she runs over to grab her laptop. "We teachers are always on the clock. I'll bet I find his number in a matter of minutes. Let's see here, Chicago Public Schools teacher directory. Yep, here it is. Sure enough, Mark Tandem, Dodson Street School. Here are his home and cellphone numbers. No address listed though." Chrissy quickly jots down the numbers on a piece of paper and slaps it on my leg. "Now go make a call. Tell him you want to visit again. Tell him he is causing you to overheat or something!"

"Darn Chrissy, alright already." I say snatching the paper with the phone numbers on it.

"Go Al-ex. Go Al-ex. Go Al-ex." Janet chants while pumping her arms, whipping her cornrows about and gyrating her hips as I leave my two cheerleaders to return to their show on the flat screen.

Chapter 7

A Close Encounter

I don't understand why I'm so nervous as the phone rings on the other end of the line. I keep telling myself that this is just business.

"Hello?" Hearing his voice on the phone draws a lump to my throat as I choke out a gravelly greeting.

"Mark, it's Alex True."

"Oh, hey there Alex. Are you lost again?" He asks me. I detect a little chuckle and the clink of glass on his cellphone.

"Am I catching you in the middle of something important?" I ask hoping not to be burdensome.

"Nothing more important than the last few sips of my ice cold Guinness." Mark replies. "Hey, how did you get my number?"

"I do research for a living." I answer back quickly. "Listen, I was hoping to set up a formal observation at your school. I would like to interview some of your colleagues, talk to your principal and spend time getting to know some of the students. Do you think that you could arrange a day for me to visit?"

The phone is silent and it makes me nervous.

"You can put it on the board, yesss!" Mark shouts into the phone.

"Mark? Are you okay?"

"Oh yeah. Sorry. I'm just catching a little White Sox pre-season action. That was rude of me. I just can't help myself when it comes to my Southsiders. Anyhow, I would love to set up a day of observation for you. How about this Thursday?" He offers.

Without even considering my calendar, I agree and make a mental note to reschedule all of my Thursday meetings. "Thank you, Mark. I can't tell you how much I am looking forward to returning to Dodson Street."

"No, Alex. I am the thankful one. See you Thursday morning."

"Until then, enjoy your White Sox. Good bye."

Sitting on the edge of my bed with the cellphone still in my hand, I am amazed at the ease with which Mark and I spoke. I also sense an increase of blood flow all over my body just as Janet had diagnosed. Touching the skin on my cheeks, I feel the inferno brewing on my face. I am a bit perplexed as I recognize the unsuspected physical power that Mark has over me. I walk over to my dresser and check in the mirror. Wow, a hint of extra color does do wonders. I wonder what a little eye shadow and lipstick would do? I've never really fussed with make-up. Oh well, it's been too exciting of a day to worry about my own appearance. I need to pull my thoughts together and start thinking about Dodson Street School's image instead.

****

"Good Thursday Morning Dolores! I need you today. I don't want to take the expressway to Dodson Street. I would like to take the locals." I say typing in a request that denies the quickest trip but opts for perhaps a more scenic route. "Dolores, you better have me going south quite a ways before you even think about sending me west, and that's all I know."

"Calculating. Calculating." Dolores responds addressing the new day in her emotion-free slightly annoying almost British tone.

This morning I double-check my gas tank and battery before leaving Lincoln Park. Both full. It feels good not to be heading into the loop first thing in the morning for a change. The energy on the side streets is more tolerable. I crack the window for some fresh morning air and breathe in the crispness tinged with a hint of espresso as I pass by cafés and drive-thrus offering commuters their morning fix. The blazing sunrise hits my eyes where the visor can't block it and I pull out my Ray Bans. The day already feels promising.

I have decided to leave extra early with plans of doing another swing by to investigate the old factory for IDEA before meeting Mark at the school. It is frustrating that I still have not been able to reach the owner of the property. So, I am going to take matters into my own hands. This time I want to get out and peek in the windows. I am wearing casual loafers that I can run in if need be and I've got pepper spray in my front pocket just in case things get real crazy. I remember the suspicious dim light shining in the front window from Friday's drive by and reach down to feel the security of the spray in my pants.

"At the next light, turn right." Dolores commands and I follow beginning to recognize abandoned landmarks that indicate proximity to Dodson Street.

"Arriving at destination." She says and I tap her on the head wrap her up in her own cord and shove her in the glove compartment. "Merci beaucoup, Dolores."

My heart is racing. This is not the typical type of research that I am used to. Peculiarly, I am armed with a weapon of sorts, albeit an aerosol but still I am way out of my comfort zone. I stop the hybrid in front of a sign covered with weeds and walk up to the front of the factory. The front door is padlocked. I walk over to the side and attempt to peer in the window where I noticed a light glowing the other day. There is no light but as I get closer, I can see through the overgrowth that someone has wiped away the filth from the glass in various spots creating peepholes for looking out. Crunching gravel startles me and I jump back from the window.

Turning around, I see a van pulling away from the opposite side of the factory lot. A wake of dust obscures my view but I am able to recognize a familiar painting on its side and the memory of Cherry Bellefonte returns to jostle my mind. I stand motionless wondering if the driver of the van saw me lurking around the front side of the factory. If it was Cherry, she might recognize me from the soup kitchen but from that distance I doubt it.

Then I begin to question the possibility of someone else still being on the property, possibly watching me from within the factory and the uneasiness drives me to sprint to my hybrid and drive off down the street to the school. My heart pounds wildly. I lift my foot off the accelerator and slowly press down on the break attempting a long crawling exhale as the car slows to a limp toward the parking lot at Dodson Street School. I try to compose my nerves and moderate my pulse putting the mysterious factory encounter behind me. I need to focus on the school visit now.

With a last minute check of my face in the mirror, I notice lip and brow sweat have gathered. I grab a discarded deli napkin, pat myself dry, take another heavy belly breath to calm down and think forward to the day ahead and Mark Tandem.

Chapter 8

Learning From The Kids

He's standing in the lobby. I see him through the glass window of the big metal door. Khakis, light blue collard shirt and a tie, he's animated, speaking to someone I cannot see. As I approach, he pushes the heavy door open to welcome me in. Standing at his side is a balding, portly man wearing a brown suit with a brown tie.

"We're so glad you made the trip down here to see us today. This is Michael Bluberry, our principal."

"Well, hello. It is such an honor to have you join us," he says, extending a stubby fingered hand and holding my grip a little too long. Given his bland suit and tie combo, I can tell he is not entranced by my fashion sense. It is, as always, the unspoken question of my gender that has him caught off guard.

I peel my palm from his nubby clutch and try not to break face over his uncommon name. "Thank you, Mr. Bluberry. I am excited to get to learn more about your school."

"Okay then, Mark and I have spoken to the staff and put together a schedule for you to follow for the next couple of hours. Feel free to roam about the classrooms and interact with the children as well. I think you will find many of them charming." He gives me a typed agenda listing the teachers and classes I am to visit and continues to drift in a gaze anesthetized by my aura.

Mark slices the awkwardness and interjects. "We gave you unscheduled time in the middle of the day to hang out in the lounge. The staff will be in and out during their lunch breaks which could be a good time for you to chat with them more casually."

"This is really great. Thank you. I should let you two get to work and I see that, according to my agenda here, I need to hurry off to Esther Crews' second grade class room." I am fully jazzed to begin my first official day at Dodson Street School.

Carefully, the door opens and I slip across the back of the room full of little people. They are seated on the floor in a circle looking at a beautiful poster of smiling barefoot children playing soccer in the middle of a dusty African village. Several students are raising their hands to comment on the poster.

"Why are the children smiling?" Esther, their teacher asks.

"Because they like to play soccer." Responds a very anxious volunteer. "I like to play soccer." He continues.

"Don't you wear shoes when you play soccer?" The teacher asks in continuation. "Why aren't these children wearing shoes?" She points to a little girl with many braids on top of her head.

"Maybe they don't have a shoe store near by," she responds.

"That could be." The teacher points on to a boy with two front teeth missing.

"Thooz are fo wich kidzth." He exclaims with a nearly incomprehensible lisp.

"You have shoes, Cordell. Does that mean you are rich?" She asks him calmly.

"No. I'm not wich. I got my thooz from Thanta Clauth," he admits proudly.

The teacher smiles and moves the conversation on to challenge her students once more. "These children are all smiling. Why do you think they are so happy?"

"They are happy because the sun is shining," one child says.

"They are happy because they are barefoot and playing with their friends outside," another contributes.

"They are winning," pipes up a boy who pumps his hands over his head victoriously.

"They just had a good breakfast," offers a final student.

I am consumed by the positive nature of the lesson. I want to slide off of the hard backed chair and into the circle of tiny bodies. What an image that would be! The lesson is a reminder of what consumed me so much as a child.

I remember marveling about those who lived life in different places and different time periods. Rural Africa, Shakespeare's England, Revolutionary France, the face of the moon, I was always journeying away from the suburban world that boxed me in. Paintings, books, recordings, movies, theater, other people's stories, they all intrigued me to no end. Right here in front of me all cross-legged and smiling is a cluster of bright-eyed children in a living poster. They each have a story of life much different from mine. I can feel that my journey with them is about to begin.

I glance at my watch and see that it is time to visit Lamar Wilkins eighth grade math class. I quietly ease out of the second grade and on down the corridor where the snare of a drum and methodical chanting is reverberating off of the cracked tile floor. As I work down the hall, I cross a patch that overwhelms me with the scent of ammonia and sawdust. A child must have gotten sick. I hold the elbow of my blazer to my nostrils and inhale the essence of dry cleaning to avoid the domino effect. It feels more like a tunnel than a school hallway as I try to keep a distance from the filthy walls of chipping paint and walk down its center. En route, I pass Principal Bluberry who is escorting a miserable looking boy from his office to the bathroom.

"Hustle on down there, Alex. You are missing quite the mathematics lesson." He mentions as I pick up the pace and scurry to the furthest door.

"Bip, bada, bada, bip, bada, bada, bip, bada, bada, bip, brroom, brroom. Bip, bada, bada, bip, bada, bada, bip, bada, bada, bip, brroom, brroom. Excellent James! Now that's rhythmic patterning." An enthusiastic Mr. Wilkins praises the boy standing before his classmates drumsticks mid-air.

From the rear of the room, I see only the backs of heads intently turned to the teacher and the drummer. The air of focus in the class is thick as this lesson connecting music and math carries so much meaning for the kids.

A girl wearing bright red glasses, a red dress and red sneakers raises her hand. "Mr. Wilkins, can I take James' pattern and set it to a ratio?"

"Yes, yes you can Bianca because mathematics is the basis of sound and sound has a very interesting mix of number properties that make us enjoy various rhythms and harmonies."

"Then Jay-Z must be pretty good at math, huh." She concludes.

I laugh with the class and Mr. Wilkins acknowledges me.

"Ah, you must be our guest from The Loop. Welcome. Are you a musician by chance?"

"Yes." I affirm with a nod. "Bagpipes."

Some snickers emit from around the room.

"Now there's an instrument that I am certain most of these students have neither seen nor heard." Says Mr. Wilkins as the attention in the room is upon me and I encounter the questioning stares of twenty-some sets of curious eyes.

"Don't you have to wear a skirt when you play the bagpipes?" A boy asks.

"Yes. During performances." I answer quickly hoping that the teacher takes back the attention of his students.

"Do you like wearing a skirt?" The boy carries on with a second question but Mr. Wilkins intercedes before I am uncomfortably cornered into a response.

"That's enough Deandre. Let's get back to our lesson. Now, let's consider sound frequencies." He says as I rise. I get the feeling that my presence is too much of a distraction from the powerful lesson, and move on to my next stop on the schedule.

I wonder what Mark Tandem is teaching his students today as I walk by his empty classroom. It is disappointing to see that his name is not scheduled on my list but feeling proximity to his professional universe is making me happy nonetheless.

In the hallway just outside the school office a display table of painted clay sculptures catches my attention. Next to each creation is an index card with a poem. They are haikus, simple and beautiful. I imagine the children connecting the essence of the clay with their descriptive words. It must be soothing for so many of them to feel the freedom to express themselves without the limits of their home lives impeding their voices. I consider the encouraging and nurturing nature of the two teachers I just observed and am comforted to know that their charges are in such inspired keeping.

At the entrance to the fourth grade room, I am greeted by the bow and the extended hand of a delicate woman with hair cropped as short as mine. Her skin is porcelain and her words have the gentleness of a birdsong.

"Welcome Alex True. I am Li Xhang. My students are coming from the gymnasium where they have been playing with Mr. Tandem and his class. Please come."

"Thank you Ms. Xhang." I follow her to a round table that is low to the ground and covered with rainbow fabric.

"Please sit." She instructs directing me to an equally low chair that I sit in. My knees rise high above the table and I am glad to be wearing pants of a loose fabric. I feel awkward like an NBA player at an ill-equipped press jaunt. Ms. Xhang pours a cup of tea from an electric kettle she has plugged in next to her fish tank. She hands it to me without saying a word, and returns to the doorway to greet her students.

"Ni hao, boys and girls. Please take out a pencil and your packet on the Aztec People," she says to her students as they file in marching slowly to their assigned table groupings. "Before we begin our lesson, who would like to share what you did with Mr. Tandem's class this morning." She pauses for a reaction and calls upon a boy wearing a faded Chicago Bears sweatshirt and jeans that hit far above his ankle.

"Yes Daniel."

"Well, first Mr. T gave us a sixth grade buddy. Then he made us ask each other questions like, what's your favorite season? Then we asked why our buddy liked that season. Next we had to ask of an activity that our buddy likes to do during the season. I like summer by the way." Daniel gives the class a thumbs-up and continues. "Then Mr. T made us count while our buddy did jumping jacks and windmills and stuff. Finally, he yelled at all of us for being too young to handle him and he started running around like a crazy person, tagging us in freeze tag. He was pretty fast for an old guy."

Daniel's classmates nod in agreement and praise of the able-bodied old teacher and Ms. Xhang smiles behind a cup of tea. "Yes, Mr. Tandem does have the energy of youth." She agrees.

I think about Mark playing in the gym with the students and imagine the joy he must spread and the example he sets being of such good nature and good health.

"Okay now," Ms. Xhang begins her lesson. "Who can tell me how the Aztec people shared their culture with one another?"

All the hands in the room are raised.

"Justice, why don't you answer." She suggests calling upon a frail girl seated at a table near the fish tank.
Barely audible, Justice's answer is practically a whisper.
"They shared myths."

"That is correct. Today, we are going to be just like the Aztecs and write our own myths with the friends at our tables."

The children look around at each other and fresh energy erupts in excitement for the proposed new task.

"First of all, we will practice creating a myth as a class." She says walking over to the fish tank. "A myth explains something that is often inexplicable, like where the marks on the moon came from or how the leopard got its spots. So, let's create a myth about Goldie. What can we try to explain about her?" A few volunteers raise their hands and Ms. Xhang calls upon a very excited boy across the room.

"Where does a goldfish get its gold?" He says jumping out of his seat.

"Excellent example, D.J. Can someone come up with a mythical explanation?" She asks.

"A sunken treasure!" A boy shouts from a distant table.

"A mermaid's yellow hair!" Offers a girl as she tosses her own pigtails about.

"Maybe the golden stars fell from the sky and landed in the sea where the fish swallowed them," answers Justice in an enchanted whisper once more.

I am delighted with their clever notions and want to add my own myth to the batch but stop myself by taking a sip of my warm tea.

Peering across the room over the dainty china cup I imagine so many of the innocent faces leaving Ms. Xhang's cozy environment for homes of much lesser beauty. I begin to understand why the teachers are so compelled to return day after day. These children are truly excited and appreciative to be in a school where the adults show such earnest affection for their learning and overall well-being. I had thought Mark Tandem's presence at Dodson Street School was a mismatch but now I realize, he has found himself in a perfect lifework.

The children begin working together creating myths with the other students at their tables and I walk over to observe Justice's group. They are listening intently to each other. They are not interrupting. I am completely impressed by their respectful composure.

"Why is the sky blue?" Justice quietly suggests to the children seated around her. They all smile and nod at the idea for their myth and Justice sits up a little taller in her chair with pride. In so doing, I notice scars that are the size and shape of cigarette butts up and down her arm. Alarmed, I turn and walk over to Ms. Xhang broken hearted.

"What an incredible group of children. Thanks for allowing me to observe your lesson."
I say gratefully.

"You're welcome. We're glad to have you here with us today. We don't have many guests."
Ms. Xhang replies.

"I couldn't help but notice Justice." I tell her hoping she understands both compassion and concern in my statement.

"Ah yes, Justice. She is one of our many survivors. I seat her near the fish tank on purpose. The sound of the water soothes her." Ms. Xhang shares quietly under the drone of the busy children. "She needs much encouraging. She is remarkably insightful though." She adds.

"I can tell." I respond feeling better knowing that her

teacher has such empathy. "Well, Ms. Xhang, I am going to introduce myself to some of your other colleagues now. This has been lovely." Leaving the class, I glance over toward the fish tank where I see Justice with her head laying across folded arms. She sees me looking at her and gives me a wink and a two-fingered wave.

Chapter 9

Dana Frinkle

The lounge is empty when I first enter. There are bagels out and a sign that says cream cheese in the fridge. I help myself to half of an asiago bagel and head for the spread. While reaching into the refrigerator, I am startled by a high-pitched voice.

"Hey there. You must be Alex True." An elf like blonde haired woman addresses me from the other side of the room.

"Yes, yes. Excuse me but I was helping myself to a swipe of your onion spread." I admit in reply.

"Go easy on the onions. They're liable to talk back to you in an hour or so." She says while putting down a huge stack of construction paper art projects and taking a seat. "I'm Dana Frinkle, first grade teacher extraordinaire."

"Nice to meet you Dana." I say thinking to myself how out of place the preppy little fair-haired woman seems. "Everyone I have met today has been simply amazing with the children here and I can tell by your nature that the first graders must just adore you as well."

"I like to think that they adore me as much as I adore them. They are all my children. You should see me at the end of each school year. I sob like a mama hen when they move on to second grade and fly out of my coop . . . and it's only the room next door."

I think I already like Dana. She is warm and spunky. It makes perfect sense that she would be teaching first graders. I purchase a can of soda and join her at the table.

"So, Mark has been talking about you all week. He is very excited that you are here today. How do you two know each other?" Dana inquires studying me quizzically.

"Well, it's funny you should ask. We don't really know each other at all. Can you tell me a little bit about him?" I ask her nonchalantly.

"I've worked with Mark a long time, over ten years now. I moved here from New York after September Eleventh. He was so kind to me my first year. I had been through a lot. He listened and took care of me when I really needed a shoulder to lean on. He is a really special guy." She shares as her cheeks fill with the redness that I too can sense developing in my face.

I ask Dana, "Did you know someone who died in the World Trade Center attacks?"

"Yes." She says as her eyes cloud over and her countenance changes to a pasty hue. "I taught first graders at P.S. thirty-three in Chelsea. Several of my students had family members who worked in and around the towers. It was awful." She admits with a sigh. "I finished the year and moved here to Chicago. I love the urban school setting but being in and around Ground Zero was just too much for me to handle."

"I can't even imagine." I say to her feeling completely naïve to the type of grief she must know.

"It has taken some time. That's for sure but these kids have helped me heal, the staff here has too. I am very close to all of them, Mark in particular. He grew up around here. Did you know that?" She asked.

"No. I would have never guessed it," I admit.

"Yep. He went to school downstate at the University of Illinois and came right back to this neighborhood. He's living proof that some people never have to travel far to have their life adventure. As for me, I wanted a big city life. I grew up in a small town in Kentucky. Strangely, I feel more connected with the pulse of life in a metropolitan setting." She admits freely.

"In that case, then, Mark must feel deeply connected to the pulse on Dodson Street. The children who come and go each day, the staff and then there must be a cultural piece that binds his allegiance. Maybe there's more to this neighborhood than meets the eye. Is Mark married?" I inquire sheepishly, not wanting to sound nosey.

"No, but I sure would love to be the lucky one," Dana confesses and I feel a stir in my gut that causes me to squirm in my seat. I undergo a familiar heat wave experience just thinking about Mark.

She carries on. "I have been hoping to win his heart for years now. He's just not interested in me in that way . . . yet." Dana says with a wink as she gets up all rosy cheeked and heads back to her classroom.

Sitting alone at the long table, I am coming to terms with the fact that thoughts of Mark Tandem are at the root of my facial hot spells. Hearing Dana describe her desire for him has caused my inner fire to swelter.

I take an oniony bite of bagel and Mark strides into the lounge. He looks at me and flashes a fantastic lopsided smile.

"Glad to see you found something nutritious in this sparse cave." He collapses in the wooden chair to my right and puts his feet up on the seat of the chair across from him. "I'm beat!" He continues. "Playing tag at forty is much different than playing it as a kid."

I see his pulse still beating in a vein on the side of his forehead and ask, "May I spring for a soda? You look like you could use a drink."

"Oh I could use a beverage but I was thinking something a little more rewarding and maybe after school hours. Are you up for it, Alex?" He asks.

"Umm, well sure. That sounds nice." I reply and our eyes meet and lock for more than a casual second.

"Your eyes are extraordinary." He comments. "They're Caribbean blue, both icy and warm. You know gentle like Ellen's"

"Ellen who?"

"Ellen, that really funny talk show host. I watch her reruns in the summer."

"You mean Ellen Degeneres? " I ask flattered and he nods. "Thanks." I say looking down at my bagel too self-conscious to get caught up in another locking gaze.

"Let's meet here after the final bell. I am looking forward to hearing the thoughts you have about Dodson Street School." Mark adds enthusiastically as he stands to grab a lunch sack out of the refrigerator. "I have to go help some students right now, Alex. See you a little bit later."

I am speechless. The present scenario that I have found myself in is turning my very controlled world upside down. Mark Tandem has invited me to get a drink after his workday. Albeit a casual work related outing, my body is reacting to the contrary. Now, I am perspiring for the second time today. My palms are moist and I am unable to catch my breath. I have to get up and move. I walk over to the barely cracked window, take in some outside air and pull the class schedule out of my pocket. To focus on the days real purpose would be a positive distraction. I see that Marion Jones is instructing seventh grade science and I decide to check it out.

Chapter 10
Lessons On The Environment

With her back turned to a room full of students, her head weighted down in lengthy dreadlocks, Marion Jones stands strong and as tall as I am. Her mere presence is a blanket of control over the students as they sit and wait for her command. She sets the chalk in the trough at the base of the blackboard and unflappably faces her eager charges. She is hard-core and I sense the students fear her by nature. Perhaps she is the mama of the school that nobody wants to upset.

She breaks her gaze from the sea of young eyes and sends a visual warning my way.

"Go ahead and perch yourself on my windowsill but don't even think about flittering about my classroom." The silent message is sent loud and clear with flaring nostrils, not exactly the warm cup of tea welcome I had enjoyed from Ms. Xhang.

"Boys and girls, our country is in crisis." She begins. "We are too dependent on one form of energy. What is it?"

The class sits motionless, each child afraid to react impulsively with the incorrect response for Ms. Jones.

"Come on now, you know this." She coaxes.

Hands rise slowly and she calls out, "Yes Gerardo."

"The United States is addicted to oil." He answers and Ms. Jones finally cracks a hint of a pleased smile.

"Excellent adjective, Gerardo. We are addicted and as many of us have seen on a very personal level, addictions are very hard to break. Am I right?"

Several heads nod in accordance to the personal reference.

"Can anyone tell me how someone can manage an addiction?" She inquires seeking the wisdom of her most observant deep thinkers. A moment passes in silence again and Gerardo raises his hand once more.

"The addicted have to change the way they think. They can't look backwards at the way life has been. They have to look forward." He explains beautifully. "Looking forward gives the addicted hope and those who care about them hope as well."

The room goes flat silent as Gerardo settles into his hard-backed chair and folds his arms. I am taken by the sincerity of his heartfelt words.

"Amen to that, Gerardo. I could not have explained it any better. So class, if the adults of The United States have an addiction, what should they do?" She challenges the class relaxing a bit onto the side of her desk as they ponder some more.

"We need to start to think differently." One child says.

"The government could offer money to people to stop using oil." A girl contributes bouncing around in her seat looking for peer approval.

"Somebody could offer the people something better than oil." Adds another child.

Ms. Jones strides over to the blackboard and underlines the word she had been writing when class began.

"What does this say?" She asks her students.

"Sustainability." They all reply at once.

"That's correct and sustainability is based on a simple principle that all we need to survive is available to us in our natural environment. Sustainability makes it possible for us humans to exist in harmony with nature. The amount of oil we consume these days disrupts the harmony of our planet." She explains searching the sea of faces for one who understands. "You see, for example, the automobile was not a bad invention. In fact, a car is a wonderful tool to use to help us survive but in some instances people have two or three cars and huge ones at that."

"Oh yeah, Ms. Jones. My uncle just got himself a shiny new black Escalade. Tinted windows too!" A boy pipes out from the back of the class.

"First of all, Terrence, you were not called upon and I don't appreciate that. Secondly, if he understood the principle of sustainability, do you think he would risk disrupting our environment just to drive around in a big gas guzzling status symbol truck?"

"Sorry Ms. Jones. I honestly don't think my uncle would care about sustainability. He just thinks about how cool he feels behind the wheel of his Es-ca-lade." Terrence ignorantly defends his uncle with a head bob.

Although I am not a teacher, I know what Ms. Jones is thinking. I can feel the power of flaming daggers that she launches toward Terrence as they singe the tips of the afros in the room. Her tolerance for rude behavior is nonexistent and in an effort to save the young boy from a verbal lashing, I take a chance and divert her attention.

"I drive a hybrid." I admit to the class. The children turn at once and notice me lingering in the background.

Ms. Jones wrinkles her nose and flips her dreadlocks over her shoulders looking at me like a fire breathing dragon. Just when I think my attempt to save Terrence has lead to my own untimely and painful demise, she puffs her cheeks out and surrenders her stronghold.

"Ah class, this is our very earth conscious hybrid driving guest who is here to see what life is like at our school." Ms. Jones softens her countenance slightly and gestures my way with her palm.

"Aside from being enamored of uncles who drive Escalades, can anyone think of something to share with our guest to show how we are trying to be sustainable at Dodson

Street School?"

"We collect rainwater in a barrel out back and use it to water your plants Ms. Jones." Says a proud girl certain of her response.

"Very good answer, Jaya."

"The eighth graders recycle old gym shoes twice a year and refit them on other kids in the building." Explains Gerardo.

"We recycle all our paper with Mr. Tandem. He has a big bin that slides in the back of his car and every Saturday morning he drives all our paper to the recycling station over on Fulton Street." Terrence shares with a broad smile making up for his love of his uncle's Escalade.

I smile back at him and am fully energized at the mention of Mark's name and the environmental example that he sets for his students on a weekly basis.

"I can see that you are all part of a school that cares so much about each one of you and the planet we all share." I say reassuringly.

"Now boys and girls, today we are going to focus on an alternative source of energy that is very sustainable. There are ways that it can replace oil. Let's investigate the power of wind energy." Ms. Jones announces as she plugs a small oscillating fan into an outlet on the wall and turns it on.

The attention of the students bounces from me back to the teacher as she demonstrates the impressive power of wind. The children are invited to stand in a circle and are handed various small objects to use in her wind demonstration with the fan.

As I look on, a startling yet familiar vibration jiggles my right thigh. In fear of distracting the lesson and receiving another death stare from Ms. Jones, I jump up and leave the classroom to retrieve the unexpected call that I am certain is coming from the office.

"Yes Terry." I say to Blanchard on the other end. "I am working on it. Give me another day and I will have some information for you about the factory." He hears me commit as I cringe into my cell phone thinking about how many times I have tried to contact the owner of the factory down the street. "I've seen it and yes the location is good for IDEA. Not too far from the expressway. I'm trying to get a read on the neighborhood right now. I'll call you back with answers."

That's not good. Terry is getting antsy and that leads to him becoming even more annoying real fast, I think to myself as I walk to the school office.

"Mr. Bluberry," I say peering around the doorframe into his cluttered domain. "I've had a great day. Your staff and students are magnificent."

"Well thank you, Alex. I happen to agree. According to these stanines that I have been milling over, so do their performance scores on the recent state tests. Once again, our kids as a whole are off the charts, above the ninety-fifth percentile." He shares proudly. "Too good, I might add." He confides.

"I realize your predicament, Mr. Bluberry. That's why I am here. It is a shame that your staff and students are performing so well that they don't qualify for the type of support that they deserve. It is my intention to share this issue with my colleagues at A.J. Hoyt Technologies with the hope that we can invest some of our time and energy in your deserving students and staff."

"We are all very appreciative of your kind efforts." He acknowledges and I get the sense that Mr. Bluberry is a big-hearted man in a tight corner. He is in a situation that calls for extreme measures but he is far from an extreme guy. He leans back onto the worn electric massage pad strapped to his chair and takes me in by way of a wondering gaze. Not intending to make me feel uneasy, he assesses my presence. I can tell once more that he is curious about me. He moves toward me folding his hands on top of the stack of test results and asks, "Why are you doing this?"

It's a fair question to which I don't give a fully definitive response. "Because it feels like the right thing to do." I confess impishly, hoping that my interest in Mark Tandem does not cause my face to combust into flames.

"I have to go and meet Mark in the teacher's lounge. So, if you will excuse me Mr. Bluberry." I say extending my right hand to his nubby grip once more.

"Have a nice afternoon." He replies absorbing me once more into a steady almost uncomfortable gaze.

"Hey there, Alex. You're going to have to wait a minute." Mark calls out while opening a can of Coke for Paulie Bluehands, who had apparently just nearly sliced off his blue and now red thumb in a paper cutter. It is wrapped in blood stained paper towels and Mark is helping him take some sips of soda.

"Don't mind me Fancy Pants. Just a war wound." Paulie Bluehands says to me fishing for pity.

"Oh my gosh!" I exclaim. "Can I take you to the hospital?" I offer feeling helpless and slightly relieved that the oncoming redness of my cheeks is going to be far out shown by the blood spurting from Paulie's thumb.

"No, no. Rosie is pulling her car up front. She'll run me over to the e.r. where my wife will meet us."

"Here Paulie." Mark comforts him, bearing the weight of the older gentleman and guiding him toward his ride. "Let me get you into Rosie's car. Alex, do you mind grabbing my bag of papers?"

I take his heavy canvas tote and follow the two of them to the front of school where Mr. Bluberry is standing with concern.

"They're waiting for you at the hospital, Paulie." I'll be by to check on you tonight. Take it easy and do what the doctor tells you." He says.

"You got it boss." Paulie says with a bloody thumbed wave from the car window.

As they pull away, Mr. Bluberry turns to Mark with worry. "He's a volunteer. The school system won't cover this injury. We can't really do anything for him."

"Oh yes we can." I interfere with confidence and the two men turn to me in hope.

"Don't worry about Paulie's medical expenses. Make sure he agrees to the best care for his wound. It's the least I can promise that A.J. Hoyt Technologies can do for you."

"Wow Alex, I know Paulie and his wife will really appreciate the help." Mark says to me and I notice his eyes, for the first time, taking me in . . . fully. With a note of appreciation in his voice he offers to buy me a drink at Floyd's.

Chapter 11
Mark Opens Up

Mark opens the door to Floyd's for me. I walk in, scan the room and am slightly confused. The entire place is decked in Chicago Cubs paraphernalia, which might not seem odd except for the fact that the south side is White Sox territory.

"Wow, I thought you were a White Sox fanatic. What are we doing here?" I ask wondering the obvious.

"Floyd was my grandfather's Monday evening fishing buddy. He closed his bar the first of every week from April to October so he and Gramps could reel in a few, rant about Chicago politics and place wagers on upcoming cross-town White Sox-Cubs games." Mark explained with a grin. "Although he lived south of the city, for some reason, Floyd's baseball allegiance was to the north side team. Everything in here is a plug for the Cubs except for these token pieces he allowed in for Gramps." Mark points to a black leather bar stool seat embroidered with a White Sox emblem and one matching pennant hanging above a photo of his grandfather and Floyd smiling ear to ear loaded down with fishing gear and a prize Muskie that, Mark said, they each claimed to have caught up in the North Woods.

"What a unique tribute to their friendship." I say noticing the same lopsided grin in the photograph that Mark shared with his grandfather. "I imagine you have many fun memories here."

"I have been sitting in front of the tap at Floyd's since long before I was of legal drinking age. In fact, I was just off training wheels when I rode my bike down to Floyd's one evening with Gramps walking by my side." Mark said. "I remember Gramps picking up a vanilla drumstick from a nearby ice-cream truck for me to lick while the old guys sucked down some cold ones and yucked it up right here with Floyd."

It was clear by the distant look in Mark's eyes that the thoughts of his past carried strong emotion and I commented on the special relationship that he must have had with his grandfather.

"His name was Otto Tandem, Gramps. I lived with him in a bungalow within walking distance of Floyd's. This neighborhood looked a lot different back when I was a kid." Mark sighed.

"How so?" I asked him curious as to how an area so bleak could hold so strong in his heart.

"Well, just down the block there was a grocer and the drug store with a soda fountain. We had a small hardware that always smelled of turpentine and next door was Benny's Deli, best stop for hot pastrami on rye. Besides Floyd's, the only place still open for business is Dodson Street School where yours truly was a student." He smiled, admitting his alma mater and ordered two Guinness beers from the tap. "The school was in much better shape back then. The parents planted a fairy tale garden out front that grew bean stalks for the children in late spring and pumpkins for us in the fall."

"Where did all the people who lived around here go?" I asked feeling sad for the demise of the backdrop to Mark's childhood. Just as he was to answer, my leg began to vibrate and I knew it was Terry calling me about the factory. "Excuse me for a moment. I have to take this call for work."

Out on the stoop in front of Floyd's, I pick up the call and Terry is going ape about the IDEA account being in stalemate because, he claims, I am inept when it comes to persistence.

"Well, thank you Terry for having faith in the one person who manages to save your ass every month or so with data! Go have a cocktail and relax. I am doing my best." Thank goodness I don't have to work with that buffoon in person. I think to myself. At least I can power off my cell when I want him out of my hair! Turning back into Floyd's, I realize that Terry does have a point. If we are going to move on the factory down the road, we have to get in to see it right away.

"Is everything okay?" Mark inquires as I go for a

long gulp of Guinness and absentmindedly spill some of the froth on my pants.

"It's just work." I confess. "I have been trying to contact someone for days. Do you mind if I make a quick phone call?"

Mark, ordering a basket of pretzels shrugs his shoulders in indifference.

"I am hoping to connect with the owner of the shoe factory that you drove me to the other day. I've reviewed all the public specs and it looks like a perfect set up for a business that we are investing in. It's called IDEA. They take outdated school furniture, redesign and recraft it for modern learning." I mumble pulling out a piece of paper with only a phone number on it. "Whoever owns this factory sure keeps a low profile. They've only listed a contact number."

"Well maybe the owner is some kind of public servant, a teacher or something . . . " and with that, a cell phone ring tone goes off playing 'Don't stop believin' by Journey. I know it as the White Sox victory jam. I hear it all the time in the city but he and I are the only ones in the bar. Mark takes a bite of a pretzel and reaches into his pocket to pick up the call.

"What?" I exclaim with a look of surprise as Mark chuckles into the phone held at his ear. "I am calling you? Why didn't you say anything?" Mark takes another bite of the pretzel and looks at me as I speak into the cell.

"I didn't say anything because I didn't know what to say." Mark returns the phone to his pocket and takes a swig of Guinness.

"There is a lot that might surprise you about me. Aside from your curiosity about my choice to teach on Dodson Street, you might find it interesting to know that I started attending Dodson Street School in kindergarten and went there all the way through until high school. You now know that I own a large abandoned shoe factory that I don't know what to do with that also just so happens to be located in the Dodson Street neighborhood. I love the White Sox who play on the same side of town as Dodson Street. I spend Sunday afternoons cooking with my mother while sharing stories about what goes on around Dodson Street." Mark lets out an exasperated sigh and apologizes for going a bit overboard with the self-divulgence.

Leaning toward Mark, I nod, chug some more beer and sit in silence. I think to myself that maybe there is a reason Mark hasn't won another heart yet.

"So, you own a factory. Huh?" I say giving him a slug to his slumped shoulder. He is embarrassed. I can tell he is not used to experiencing such outbursts.

"I'm so sorry." He says again, head hanging low over the beer mug. "Talking about my grandfather and the factory bring out a lot of pent up emotion."

"Maybe it would feel less harsh if you told me a little

bit more about your grandfather and your childhood." I suggest, interested in knowing more about Mark's life.

Our eyes lock once more like they did earlier in the day. He cracks a lopsided grin and flips his ponytail back.

"Maybe you're right. I don't want to bore you though."

"Come on Mark, you share and I'll share. There's got to be more to the story. You own a factory."

He finishes off the Guinness and sits back a bit on the White Sox stool. He is focused on the photo of his grandfather and begins to speak.

"The shoe factory was called Tandem Footing. My grandfather inherited it from his uncle who brought the trade over from Europe. He taught the art of working leather to Gramps who, in turn, stepped into the reins of the business." Mark waves at the bartender to order another round. "My mother and I lived with him just around the corner from here. She still lives there."

"Wow, Dana was right." I say as the next round of beer arrives.

"Dana Frinkle?" He asks.

"Yeah. She and I were talking about you in the teacher's lounge earlier today." I admit.

"Ah Dana . . . she is a piece of work." He says. "Don't get me wrong. She's amazing with her students but she is way, way too in to me." He slurps some beer. "I gave it a try with her once but she's too predictable, too preppy, definitely not my type."

I am unable to control a smile as I think about having such valuable private intel. To divert his thoughts from Dana, I ask, "So what does your mother do?"

"She's a nurse in the ICU at Loyola Medical Center. Her name is Mary Jane. We are very close, kitchen buddies, in fact. I even know how to bake her famous blueberry cobbler."

The thought of Mark with oven mitts on adds to the mystery of this renaissance man. He continues to reveal bits about his mother that reveal bits about him. "She knits sweaters and scarves and for my whole life she has had me deliver them to the local women's' shelter. She's a genuine neat freak, and to top off each day, has a cup of steaming hot Earl Grey with cream and two sugar cubes in the late afternoon at five fifteen."

"Your mother sounds lovely, Mark." I say intrigued by the influence she has had in his life.

"Oh she is. I have always appreciated my mother but I absolutely adored Gramps."

"I spent most of my free time with Gramps. On Saturday mornings I would be with him at the factory and he'd shout out an errand. 'I need you to run down to the deli for a hot pastrami on rye and a pepper and egg sandwich.'"

"You got it, chief." I would respond with a high-armed salute. I enjoyed the assigned responsibility and quick visits to the deli where Benny whipped up the most delicious sandwiches. Then I'd head across the street to grab a chocolate soda." Mark stopped and ate a few pretzels. "The truth is though, it wasn't just the two stops that made my lunch time missions so pleasurable, it was the break in the day devoted to shoes – shoe styles, shoe design, leather qualities and craftsmanship techniques, that I welcomed most."

Mark's face became pensive to the point of somber. "You see, Gramps carried on the family business of crafting upscale leather foot ware and hired and trained dozens of skilled European immigrants from the neighborhood to employ his techniques and shoe wizardry so that Tandem Footing was able to make a name for itself in the industry by providing quality, fashionable shoes that were considered, by some, artistic investments for the feet."

The bartender tops off Marks brew. He pauses, sips a froth mustache to his upper lip and licks it clean. I find myself intoxicated by both his actions and words as he goes on.

"Countless hours I would stand at my grandfather's side watching him whittle a heel or etch a design in the toe of an evening pump with one of his many treasured tools. I knew that I was being groomed to be future captain of the ship of shoes. As I got older, I acknowledged that it would

124

be a logical progression and it would ultimately be very gratifying to Gramps but the problem was that I found the prospect of foot ware – design, creation and consumption to be utterly mundane."

"Wow, Mark. I love nice shoes. I gotta' say, this all sounds very alluring." I comment thinking about the fine craftsmanship in my favorite pair of bucks that I happen to be wearing.

"Yeah sure. Who doesn't get into a good pair of kicks. But I'm talking at seventeen, looking at making shoes for life. That just wasn't for me." Mark admits as he slides a rubber band down his long ponytail and rustles his mane across his shoulders with a shrug.

"So Mark, what happened?"

Chapter 12

Otto Tandem

Mark swivels on the bar stool and turns to me head on. "I remember it vividly. I was so afraid to break his heart." He reflects. In his grandfather's voice, he continues his story.

"What do you have for me Markyboy?" Gramps asked me as I approached him in his office where he was seated behind his shiny walnut desk overlooking the factory assembly line floor of Tandem Footing.

"It's a letter, Gramps. I want you to read it." I replied hesitantly while stepping back a bit to create a physical chasm between us. The small room fell silent except for the whir of factory machinery behind the glass window. I can still sense the feeling of my moist palms, my parched mouth as I followed the steady rivet of Gramp's eyes back and forth down the stationary moving along like an old typewriter would sweep a fresh page. He spun his chair away from the desk and gazed out over the dozen workers below, then began the expected inquisition.

"Has your mother seen this?"

With a quick clip I responded, "No."

Going further he inquired, "Does she know about it?"

I replied, "No."

Trailing off Gramps sighed, "Do you have any idea how proud this will make her?"

As surprised as a grandson and heir to the helm of a ship of shoes that was about to be rocked could be, my barely audible "No?" was the end of the inquisition.

He took me in his arms and grabbed the microphone to make an announcement over the factory p.a. "Attention everyone. I have important news for all of you to hear." He piped out in his rough commanding voice. Work halted and eyes looked up toward us in the glass picture frame above them. "My grandson, Mark, is going to be the first Tandem to earn a college degree. My dear boy is off to the University of Illinois to become a teacher."

With that, a roar of hoots and hollers from the factory line of hard-working immigrants erupted. The men and women working the line had all watched Gramps and my mother raise me. They were a community of people who had come from across the ocean in search of dreams and understood the value of forging an authentic path and pursuing a college degree. At that moment, I knew that they were all vicariously living in my shoes. I was going to go to college for all of them."

"So you got your degree but what happened to the factory?" I demand fully vested in the heartwarming recollection.

"It was May before graduation just as I wrapped up

my student teaching stint in the sixth grade class room of a grade school down in Urbana. I got a call that Gramps was at my mother's hospital in the ICU. A factory worker had found him early in the morning crumpled on the steps of the entrance to Tandem Footing.

I flew straight up I-55 rushing the two and a half hour drive into less than two. I was panic-stricken when I arrived at the intensive care unit. Through the glass, I remember seeing in the dim lighting the familiar tuft of white hair among the fluffed down that cradled my hero. Hooked up to so many tubes and machines, like a marionette, Gramps' life appeared to be dependent of another being. It was hard to witness. I remember the nausea. My mother was there. We embraced and shared a tear-filled gaze mellowed even further, no doubt, by the reality that she had seen so many families in the same anguish.

Her father had lived a long and healthy life. My mother knew the love he felt for his family, his business and his community. It was a love that had sustained and driven him to keep forging on at Tandem Footing even in times of competitive mass production and discounted importing of foot ware. She told me that he had shared with her his feelings about keeping the factory open . . . keeping life, jobs and a purpose in the neighborhood. He had expressed with deep passion his hopes that I would follow in his steps and those of his uncle but he understood and admired the will I had to follow my own professional dreams also."

I sit silently and watch Mark's eyes well with tears as the memories flood but he does not let them fall in my presence. My tears fall instead.

"My mother told me that in the years while I had been away at college Gramps had struggled to employ his European craftsmen and women. They were being enticed by grander companies that offered better health care and benefits packages. They were companies with thousands of employees nationwide as opposed to his couple hundred local. He was up against plants located in more suburban areas outside of Chicago providing better schools, cleaner parks, more green space. It was a harsh reality with which to contend and he found himself desperate to keep the loyal employees he cared for and needed. Fear compelled him to entertain his workers with fishing outings, tickets to White Sox Games and gift cards to lighten their consumption loads. He even implemented more flexible shift scheduling and was considering an on-site childcare space. In my mother's eyes, her father had been forcing himself to scramble at a time when he should have been slowing down. With such a physical agenda at sixty-seven, Gramps' body couldn't keep up with his spirit."

I am now hailing for another beverage.

"Just a glass of water." I say needing to wash down

the saltiness of my emotion with something fresh.

"Outside his hospital room, I remember leaning in to my mother and whispering, "Can I go in?" She opened the door and slid a chair over for me to sit next to her father's bedside. I took my grandfather's hand and clung to its warm erratic pulse. I sobbed as I pressed my damp face to the cold white sheet.

"Markyboy. . ." a breathy, broken mutter bypassed the oxygen mask.

"Gramps, it's me. I got here as soon as I could." I choked out.

"I know . . . I've been waiting." Gramps replied with a dry medicated cough.

"Can I get you some ice? Water?" I inquired in desperation.

"No Mark but you can do something for me."

"Anything Gramps, anything you want." I pleaded.

"I am so proud . . . of you . . . finally a Tandem with a college degree. Teaching . . . a most admirable path. Use what the professors taught you . . . use what I taught you. Do something with the factory, Markyboy. I tried as long as I could. The neighborhood needs the life of the factory. Give it new life, young man. Use your teaching skills. Draw upon your spirit to set your course . . . " Gramps trailed off in a long whistling exhale. I looked across the room to my mother who returned the glance with a wise gentle nod, heartbroken. Seconds later, he placidly released my grip and slipped away before us, his countenance divinely serene."

At this point, I look over at the bartender who, like me, is emotionally undone. My mind is mush from Mark's tale and all I can say is, "Wow."

He takes a sip to wash down the emotion. "Have you ever gotten to know someone this quickly, Alex?" Mark asks me.

Quite truthfully I answer, "No. Never, but I am so glad. Your story explains a lot, your family, this neighborhood. Your grandfather had great vision for you. He loved you very much."

"Yes. I know and now that I know someone is interested in the factory, I feel that I have a chance to honor his dying wish." Mark confides in me hopefully.

"Let's go take a drive to the Tandem universe. I would like the owner of the old shoe factory to give me a tour." I amiably suggest finishing off my water. "I think it is high-time I get a closer look at the place. Do you have the keys?"

From his pants pocket, Mark pulls out a full chain and separates one extremely old tarnished key.

Chapter 13

Alex's Turn

"You carry that heavy piece of metal everywhere?" I ask amazed at the size of the old key that he had been hiding in his pants.

"Yep. Like an old rabbits foot." He says. "But we aren't using it until you hold up your end of the deal. I want to hear about you, Alex True."

"Okay, but how about on the way." I say as I try to carefully plan my own reveal. "I'm anxious to check it out."

"Sounds good to me." He says handing money to the bartender.

We step out the front door where the thump of dub step blasts from a jacked up big-rimmed Coupe de Ville parked just outside of Floyds. The windows are tinted. Mark pulls me back into the bar just as I am about to start down the steps.

"Let's wait a minute." He says.

"Why? What's going on?" I ask surprised of his sudden change in direction.

He stands and the silence around us is awkward.

In the distance the scream of a police siren trickles into the entryway of the bar and gets louder. We hear tires peel out and the whir of the cop car whipping by on the street.

"Okay. Now we can go." Mark says as he pushes the door open.

The buzz I had going fades with the brightness of sunlight and the harsh reality on the street. We both put on sunglasses and walk to the Honda. I open the passenger door and slide in to the car now toasty from baking in the rays. As Mark gets in to the tight space of the car I swim in his familiar and now comforting ginger and citrus presence.

Mark turns to me. "I'm not going anywhere."

"What?"

"Seriously, Alex. You owe me some info." He says.

"I'm from Ohio." I say in a very guarded manner looking straight ahead out of the windshield.

"What brought you to Chicago then?"

"Adventure. Change. Graduate school. U of C Booth School of Business." I continue to be somewhat dismissive in the sensitive interrogation.

"Okay then. How about A.J. Hoyt Technologies? How did you end up there?" He continues guiding the conversation as aware as a teacher would be that I am feeling vulnerable. "Try to expand beyond a word or two." He says inserting the key in the ignition.

"I was almost through with my second year at Booth and had picked up a job waiting tables at a bar in the lobby of The Intercontinental. My boss was out one day and it was dead quiet in the place so I pulled out The Tribune and started looking at the classifieds."

Mark nods, "Uh huh?" as he does a U-turn in the street.

"I thought I was alone and made some comment out loud about a job listing 'Not bad' or 'I like it' or something like that. I had been so focused on the paper that I didn't see a man slip into the booth near me and he replied, 'Well thank you'. He actually thought I was complimenting his tie." I said laughing at the thought of my tie-crazed boss years later.

"Let me guess. He offered you a job at Hoyt?" Mark says.

"Well, sort of. We chatted for quite some time. He was very interested in the fact that I was getting my MBA through Booth and especially that I wanted to be an analyst."

I also remember, how he cocked his brow when I stood up and went over to see if he wanted to order a drink. I think he was expecting a waitress in a skirt but I was wearing black pants. This part of the memory, I kept to myself.

"'No thanks,' he said to the drink. "I'm meeting my gal and heading off to Bermuda for a few days of sunshine and island drinks, but call my secretary and make an appointment with me at the end of next week. I like your spunk.' He handed me his business card and the next day I quit waiting tables."

"Were you confident that you would get the job?" Mark suggests as he pulls to a stop, out of habit, at a four way with missing signs.

"I was. I felt a connection with the man. Tom Mackey is his name. I spent the week gearing up for the phone call and then the day came. I reached Juan Carlos, his secretary, who said that he was on the look out for my call. He gave me two hours to be in Mackey's office with a full portfolio presentation."

Mark leans toward me and whips his wrist like a beater. "Go on." He says.

"My mother had recently been in town and purchased me a stylish navy blue suit for job interviews. I was smoothing out the lapel and caught a glimpse of a familiar sight."

As we pull up to the entrance of the old shoe factory, Mark asks, "What was in the lapel?"

"It was a piece of my mother's delicate linen stationary embossed with her initials at the top. To this day, I cherish the moment I unfolded the reminder from home. I can hear her voice as the memorized message comes to mind. 'Alex, my love, be authentic. Warm the room with your smile and remember how proud your father and I are of you. Good business people know a gem when they meet one. You are sure to be snatched away in an instant. We are always a phone call away. Love, Mom'"

"You have a wonderful mother too." Mark says.

"Yes, in many ways. My father is great, too. I wasn't an easy case to raise." I confess.

Dismissing my comment, Mark turns off the car lifts his sunglasses, faces me head on and says, "Well, you got the job. Didn't you?"

I peel my Ray Bans back to the top of my head and return the look, "Yes. I've been with Hoyt ever since."

"I think your mother knew what she was doing when she picked out that lucky blue suit for you." He suggests.

"What do you mean?" I ask.

"It had to have complimented those eyes of yours." He says getting out of the car.

I remain buckled in my seat as the weight of Mark's words bear an inflating impact so unfamiliar to me. A buzz returns to my head but I've had no alcohol. I tell myself to get it together though because this is supposed to be about business and not me.

How has the confusion in my normally level head become so tangled in a mental web with the mission to improve the situation at the school, the prospect of getting the shoe factory for IDEA, and with Mark?

I watch curiously as he crosses the weed-covered parking lot to an overgrown hedge. He twists and pulls to remove branches blocking the view of a brick beacon from the past. "Tandem Footing", Mark points and shouts aloud with his broad lopsided smile. His golden hair blows in the breeze and holds up the key to the factory waving me out of the car.

I think once more about the web I am in, and realize that not only is Mark holding a very important key . . . he is the key.

Giving an enthusiastic nod and a thumbs- up, I walk over to inspect the unveiled sign. We turn and start toward the steps of the door to the old shoe factory.

"You know Mark, I was here on a drive by this morning, before your secret identity was revealed." I told him.

He was listening but focused on entering the hallowed ground of his childhood.

"It's been years since I last entered the factory." He says.

I see how excited he is but also know that someone was definitely lurking around the factory earlier in the day. I have to say something.

"I think you should know that somebody has been in here." I tell him, trying to get his attention and now in slight fear for our safety.

"I can't imagine that. I do pay a fee to a surveillance service to keep an eye on the place." He replies defensively.

"All I know is that there was someone here this morning. They drove away in an old van just as I got close to the window over there."

For some reason, Mark is not as scared as me and continues to work the lock.

"I wish I had grabbed the mace that I keep stashed in the glove compartment of my car." I say.

He ignores me, determined and excited.

The key slowly turns and the heavy wooden door creaks open to a dark musty lobby lined with glass cases containing shoes of styles from years gone by. Across the entrance, a glass wall gives way to a factory floor that cries whispers from the ghosts of the many men and women who once crafted at the machines that now stand idle.

In the far corner is a stairwell that Mark waves me to climb with him. At the top, we enter the office and a heavy silence blankets the room. Mark inhales deeply the faint scent of leather that still lingers in the air. Eyes moist, he turns to me and with a lump in his throat expresses that he can sense Gramps there with us.

It seems like I have known Mark a lifetime now but it truly has only been a few hours. For some reason I feel our hearts beating together in the intensity of the situation. We are, however, each lost in our own thoughts. I am standing still and Mark is rubbing his hands along his grandfather's desktop. From somewhere within the factory we hear a door slam and our eyes connect in alarm.

"Oh no Alex, you were right. Someone else is here.

Let's get out."

I personally have never moved so quickly in my life as we bolt down the stairs, through the lobby and out the front entrance into the light of late afternoon. I am now perspiring for the third time in the same day, which is an Alex True record.

"Should we call the police?" I ask between puffs as we sprint to Mark's car.

"I'll take care of it when we get back to the school." Mark says thrusting his key into the ignition.

Speeding down Dodson Street, Mark runs the few four ways with non-existent stop signs to the school and is thinking out loud. "I will get this sorted out Alex. Don't worry. That factory is solid. It would be a great location for IDEA. I am just sure of it."

"I agree. Let's see what the police say. Okay?"

"Alex?" He says my name and pulls to a stop next to my hybrid. "Thank you for listening."

"You're welcome and thank you, too." I reply with a smile and a wink as my cheeks, already flush from the massive sprint and intruder scare, continue to heat up some more in his presence. Then, I look down at my watch and see the time.

All thrown off from the day that I have had I am confused and ask. "What day of the week is it?"

"Thursday."

"Oh no, I've got to go. I forgot. My roommates are waiting!" I exclaim climbing out of Mark's car and into mine. "Thank you for an amazing day."

Chapter 14
The Business Plan

Heading back up the Kennedy into town with thoughts and concerns, emotions and dreams a-swirl, I am hardly able to focus on the stop-and-go traffic of the expressway and nearly miss the Fullerton Avenue exit leading home. It is dark out and as usual for a night in Lincoln Park, the hunt for a parking space is the same challenge that always leads me to curse with internal road rage. After a quarter of an hour, I land a spot but realize I have missed the volleyball game.

My cell phone rings and I can see it is Chrissy. "Please come home." I plead. "I have a day worthy of the island." The kitchen island is our landing pad. The three of us cook and drink there. We work there. But most of all we solve the worlds' problems there. An offer to meet at the island is always an invitation by one of us in need of the rare camaraderie that we three share.

I am sitting on a stool sipping a glass of merlot, munching on hummus and pita crackers when Janet and Chrissy explode through the front door.

"What is going on, Alex?" Janet asks me with a wrinkle of concern in her forehead.

"Seriously, you haven't missed a game in years! Did everything go okay down at the school?" Chrissy inquires.

I pour each of them a glass of wine and invite them to listen to the drama of the inspirational day I spent observing the students and teachers at Dodson Street School that both started and ended with bizarre occurrences at, where else but, an old shoe factory. Not to mention the heat wave I experienced every time Mark Tandem's name was mentioned or whenever he got near me.

"He took you to his favorite bar?" Chrissy asks, wide-eyed, while pouring more wine.

"Don't act so surprised. This isn't the first time a handsome guy has purchased me a drink." I boast defensively. "In fact we sat together for hours. He told me all about his life and the relationship he had with his grandfather who owned the factory. Come to think of it, the whole point of going out after the school day was for me to share my class room observations with him and that never even happened."

"This is quite an interesting professional and personal circumstance." Chrissy says. "The question is whether or not to take it all to the next step."

"Yes, I know. All of the instances that took place today feel as though they are being directed by another source. It's as if God is setting me up for something and I just have to let it happen." I say to my two friends.

"This is a fabulous plot!" Janet exclaims. "I couldn't have written one like this if I had tried my hardest."

"I agree, Janet. Let's look at the big picture and try to connect some dots," Chrissy suggests, taking charge of my island night and giving me hope that my world is turning upside down for a good reason.

With my business sense, Janet's creative flair and Chrissy's awareness and connection to the social plight of families in the public education system, the three of us plot late into the night how it might be possible to convince my colleagues at A.J. Hoyt Technologies that an investment in Dodson Street School would not only be a positive humanitarian step but a financially lucrative one as well.

We consider the standardized test success rate of the student population to be, as it should, an asset.

"The children are gifted." Chrissy points out drawing upon her wisdom from many years of teaching experience. "If those students had the right resources and proper exposure to certain ways of thinking, they could be the ones to find cures for diseases, develop valuable software, solve world social crises."

"You know, Chrissy, you've got something there. Who wouldn't consider the notion of backing the next Steve Jobs?" I say holding up a glass to toast.

"Yeah, and if IDEA sets up shop in the old shoe factory the entire culture of the neighborhood just might shift adding inspiration and life of a positive nature to the area surrounding the school." Says Janet.

"Just as it was when Mark's grandfather was running Tandem Footing." I add, reflecting back to the memories that Mark had shared earlier in the day.

"You know what would really disrupt the thinking of my colleagues?" I interject as we all tap away thoughts into our laptops. "What if A.J. Hoyt Technologies supported the idea of truly raising up these kids by setting up an office in the neighborhood? I know it seems far fetched, but some of the best ideas are." I continue to talk and type. "We could work in tandem with the school at supporting the children in proximity as well as backing them with financial support. The children could be working toward future professions in companies that A.J. Hoyt Technologies will have stakes in."

"Oh Alex, that's brilliant. This sounds odd but I believe the process you are describing would be referred to as "professional germination"." Janet chuckles. "Thank heavens for my online thesaurus!!"

My neck is sore from leaning over the keyboard for hours and I look up at the clock on the microwave and realize that it is after three in the morning. Still in work clothes, stretching and yawning at the same time, I announce mental and emotional overload, "I had better get a few hours of shut-eye, you two. This is really turning into something. What would I do without my two roomies?"

144

Before going to bed, both Janet and Chrissy encourage me to invite Mark Tandem to meet the rest of the team at work for our next big meeting, which happens to be Monday. Since Mark is tethered to both the shoe factory property and Dodson Street School, he needs to be available to answer questions and give suggestions as to how we might be able to implement a plan of action.

Tossing the empty bottles of merlot out for recycling, Janet turns to me and says, "You know, if there is ever a need for a nurse down at that school, my hours are flexible and I would be so happy to be a tiny part of this project. I know it isn't much but healthy students breed success." Then, as the last lights above the island are turned out Chrissy says to me, " And I am always up for new curriculum, Alex. If there is an open teaching position, I am on it. As long as I can get some of those kids to dance with me." Chrissy leaps up in arabesque form, landing in my arms at the threshold of the kitchen. Holding on to her tightly, I begin to sob.

"We'll see how," I sniff, "you two feel," I blink away tears, "when your thoughts aren't wine induced." I choke out like a blubbering idiot.

Not sure if it is intoxication from the wine or joyful ebullience in reaction to the warmth of the heartfelt friendships but my healthy tears stain Chrissy's t-shirt, as Janet joins our embrace. No words are spoken and the three of us sleepily sidle through the narrow hallway to my room.

Morning comes quickly and despite the wine infused grogginess and minimal hours of sleep, I am up and electric with steam for the day. The apartment is silent except for the percolating coffee and the sound of neighborhood children playing out on the sidewalk. The smell of hazelnut helps to separate the cobwebs in my brain. My long legs sprawl out across the soft suede sofa and I stare up at the paddles of the ceiling fan rounding rhythmically in circles. My thoughts run around with the beat of the fan and I find myself excited for the unknown when the landline of our apartment rings.

Nobody ever calls us on that number so the sound is somewhat shocking and I jump off the sofa to answer it. "Alex, it's me Mark. I've had very little sleep." He says. "And if I sound crazy, chalk it up to fatigue and one too many Guinness." I laugh and feel my face blush, as I am genuinely glad to hear his voice. "I wanted to try to catch you before work to say how sorry I am."

"Why are you sorry?" I ask as a tiny pit of fear begins to rumble in my stomach.

"Well, I offered to take you to Floyd's to hear about your day at school and all I did was talk about myself and to top it off, I dragged you to the factory where we were practically murdered by an alien. Again, I am sorry." He says sheepishly.

"Are you kidding, Mark? It was a terrific day and the stories you shared about your grandfather were incredibly touching." I say. "My roommates and I were up practically all night talking about you. I mean. . ." I stumble with a slight gasp, "your school, the shoe factory, the whole neighborhood down there."

"Really?" Mark replies sounding intrigued.

"Yep, and we have devised an amazing plan that will knock your socks off!" I say trying to keep some levity in the conversation.

Mark and I discuss the issues, legal challenges, emotional and financial burdens that could counter this idea of a venture capital firm investing in a school of gifted students. In the end, we both agree that it is a groundbreaking plan for which we decide to pull out all the stops.

"Wow Alex," Mark confesses to me. "I'm flattered, impressed and humbled to know you."

"And I to know you." I respond sincerely. The silence on the phone emphasizes the distance between us and I realize that all I want is to be going back to Dodson Street School this morning but my life, my job is not there. . . yet.

"Mark, how did you get my number?" I ask curiously, before ending our conversation.

Coyly he answers, "You're not the only one who can do research."

Chapter 15
A Cup Of Tea With A.J.

"Radical thought requires radical action, Alex. You have to do this." Janet encourages me with all the gusto she can muster. "If you are going to throw something this big at your colleagues you need some serious muscle."

I agree with Janet's words but consider the potential ramification of losing my job into the equation.

"Just give her a call, Alex. She may be the founder of your company but she is also human." Janet's wise words linger in the air as she shuts the door and leaves for her shift at the hospital.

As I dance around the idea of approaching the boss of my boss, with whom I have never had a conversation, the day surprisingly fills with urgent phone calls. I speak with the representatives at IDEA and set up a meeting to take place at the old shoe factory certain that Mark will have the poachers evicted before show time. I also get in touch with local experts in the education of gifted children from the University of Chicago who share with me evidence of potential student achievement outcomes that I hope to use to entice my team of the risk to reward ratio involved in this type of venture. I plan to convince them that if given the proper exposure to advanced thought as well as the tools to experiment with and defend interesting ideas, the children at Dodson Street School just might become some of the next great leaders of our community. This is the type of business venture that could reap immeasurable rewards on many different levels.

The more time I spend researching and learning about education and kids and the plight of being a gifted child in an average world, the more my vision filters through clearer lenses. The confidence that develops in me gives me the will to make the call.

"Hello, Juan Carlos. This is Alex. I am interested in making an appointment to meet with A.J. Hoyt. Can you help me with this?" I inquire of our executive secretary extraordinaire.

"Yes. I am free this weekend. Oh, I didn't realize that she prefers meetings at her home. Whatever works for her will be fine with me. I will wait to hear back from you. Thank you." I say in a calm tone that does not match my rapidly beating heart.

****

Nervously approaching the lobby of the Carlyle, I nod at the doorman with a pleasant smile and approach the elevator. It appears that I am expected. I press the penthouse button and hear a subtle whistle coming from his lips that gives me extra confidence in the decision to wear my lucky Armani. The doors of the elevator open and I leap in to be hoisted up to the home of the woman whose power is paramount at A.J.Hoyt Technologies.

"Good afternoon Ms. Hoyt. I am Alex True. Thank you for allowing me to come and meet with you." I say extending a hand out to the founder of the company.

"Alex, please join me for some tea. I have been hearing wonderful praises of your hard work lately. What have you stumbled upon that warrants the ear of an old woman like me?" A.J. inquires as she guides me over to a bright yellow sofa in her tearoom.

"I have stumbled upon an opportunity that could change a community." I state bluntly looking straight into the eyes of the powerful gray-haired woman. "In a round-about way, I have discovered a new type of venture for A.J. Hoyt Technologies to facilitate. Our company has been a leader in the field of technology upstarts and innovative business launches for years now. Thanks to your persistence and business integrity we have also managed to give to the community in various monetary ways. I believe, however, that it is time for A.J. Hoyt Technologies to forge a different kind of path, a path of goodwill and good sense for the future."

"I'm listening." She says taking a sip from her beautiful fine bone china. I take a deep breath and continue.

"There is a neighborhood southwest of The Loop that has been forgotten. It was once home to a thriving Polish community with job opportunities and commerce. The people who once lived there worked hard and kept the streets safe for families. In recent decades, though, business trends shifted and the local shoe factory closed down. We have plans to place the firm IDEA into that old factory because of the affordability."

"Who would want to work in the type of forgotten neighborhood that you are describing?" She asks.

"I think that employees will come if we offer them incentives. Aside from bringing home paychecks, there is a grade school just down the road that educates about 200 children who are all there because they have potential that deems them gifted and talented despite all of the odds they face. Many of these children live with unemployed parents in homes and buildings between and around the old shoe factory. Some of them live a frightening bus ride away. I believe that providing employment for the parents and reviving the school will be an excellent investment in these children and a new type of venture for our company. The greatest financial dividends to A.J. Hoyt Technologies will be long-range but the benefits along the way will be palpable."

"You have my interest, Alex. Go on." A.J. says stirring a sugar cube into her tea.

"I believe that we can bring life back to this

neighborhood. I believe that we can bring hope and opportunities to these people. I believe that when we have the factory space occupied that IDEA will provide job opportunities. I believe that we can invest in the school and share our business success with the students and they can share their learning success with us. I believe that we can involve other small businesses and bring them to this disconnected neighborhood so that they can feel a part of life again. I believe, Ms. Hoyt, that we can be the start of change, an example for other major companies to step up and do what is good and right for those who are victims of life and economical circumstance. I do believe this and I know that the team I work with will embrace this plan when it is all said and done." The teacup rattles as I raise it to take a sip in an effort to calm a bit.

The silence of the room is overwhelming. The scent of fresh lilies from the end table combined with the emotion in the air bring about light-headedness soon broken by A.J. as she takes a sip of her tea and clears her throat to speak.

"It strikes me, that you have an even deeper connection to the situation. Tell me what is at the essence of your proposal, Alex."

I take a second to consider my words as a housekeeper enters the room. "How many for dinner, ma'am?" She asks with a hint of an Irish brogue.

"Just one and remember the salt restriction. Thank you, Fiona."

"Yes, ma'am." She replies and goes into the kitchen.

"Now tell me, I know the kind of investment research you've done in recent years. You've been all about the numbers and trends. And you have done extremely well, I might add. But this, however, this project is something completely organic. I want to know what is driving your desire to put yourself on the line with me today." A.J. demands with a just voice.

"I am a very complex person, Ms. Hoyt. It may appear that I am pulled together in a tight package but that's just a well-designed safety net. I still struggle daily with issues from my childhood that society was unable to accept. I was born different. God gave me choices that very few people get to make. Let's just say, my physique, my interests and desires were so unconventional that I felt trapped, unable to soar. Until I broke free of suburbia, I thought I might drown. This is my connection to the children and teachers at Dodson Street School. They are drowning in circumstances out of their control." I say biting my lip out of fear that I just exposed a little too much personal information.

"A very heart-felt mission, Alex. I admire your empathy for their situation. But, why should A.J. Hoyt Technologies be the company to step in? It is a huge risk."

I respond simply, "With all due respect, Ms. Hoyt.

Why shouldn't we take a risk like this? We have made the millions and will continue to do so. We have topped the charts and will continue to do so as well. We could set a new precedent for success that isn't just tagged with a dollar sign."

Hoping that the comments I make are not striking too sensitive of a chord, I stop speaking and add a couple sugar cubes to my tea. A clamor of pots and pans can be heard and the smell of homemade chicken soup floats into the room. I realize that this very important appointment is soon to end. Without saying a word, A.J. stands and walks to the immense window overlooking the pristine blue of Lake Michigan.

I slowly rise and go stand behind the woman who holds the fate of my dream. Looking down at the bustling street below, sidewalk and running path alongside the lake, joggers and bikers, fancy cars and shoppers carrying bags of treasures from a day well spent on the Magnificent Mile, it seems unfathomable that Dodson Street, only miles away, is most probably empty on a beautiful Sunday afternoon like this. No bustling. No treasures. A.J. turns to me.

"You know, Alex," She says. "The neighborhood in which I grew up sounds much like the one you just described to me. We were all children of immigrants who worked nearby. We relied on each other for food, clothing, medicine and support. Small stores lined the main street. I remember walking home from school with my brother and our friends. We'd stare into the steaming storefront window and wave to

154

our neighbor, the baker. He would motion for us to come in where it was warm and smelled of yeast and cardamom. He would ask about our parents and offer us freshly baked Pepperkakors to enjoy as we slowly weaved our way by each merchant down the street to our three flat. There was life and it was good."

We stand in silence, each with a vision of A.J.'s childhood stroll painted in our minds. She returns to the present and says to me, "There was life in my old neighborhood just like there once was around the old shoe factory that you described. Now, although I haven't been back where I grew up in years, I know there are only victims."

She turns away and crosses the room to an antique roll-top desk and flips to a fresh page of her agenda, makes a note and returns to me by the window.

"I like the idea of empowering a community. I love the thought of investing in children of immense potential. I will be at the meeting tomorrow morning to listen to and support your proposal." She says. "Does Tom know of your plans?"

"No." I reply. "He has been traveling quite a bit lately. He won't be at the meeting tomorrow."

"I see." She says. "Well, no matter. I have the ultimate say anyway."

My emotions get the best of me as her words fill my heart and tears gather on my fluttering lashes. She is not the lioness that I feared. A.J. Hoyt is compassion and poise all wrapped up in one very expensive but beautiful package.

"Thank you, Ms. Hoyt. Thank you so much." The simple words spill from my lips as she smiles and escorts me to the door. "Please, Alex," she says, "call me A.J."

I decide to walk home, through the Gold Coast and Old Town on up to Lincoln Park. The sun silently sets on this monumental Sunday as I try to predict the scene in the team meeting to come at sun-up. There will be questions galore, sighs of slight annoyance and perhaps a few raised eyebrows with the prospect of taking A.J. Hoyt Technologies and IDEA to a bygone section of the city under unknown terms.

I want to be ready to counter the bevy of legitimate concerns that the team will pose for liability and safety, longevity and sustainability and ultimately a general uneasiness that might be associated with the company's involvement in such an unorthodox business undertaking. Thankfully, I will be armed with facts and figures, forecasts and faith that with A.J. and Mark there to assist in the presentation, the seeds of hope for a new neighborhood and a thriving school will be planted.

Chapter 16
The Jostling

I realize that Mark needs some strategic support so I return to the head of the table before the sea of dumbstruck eyes. Pencils dangle from dropped jaw lips. Bewildered looks of accusation and confusion over his emotion linked to our out-of-the-ordinary Monday morning presentation drive me to corral their focus and take charge.

"Thank you, Mark. The opportunity for A.J. Hoyt Technologies to invest in Dodson Street School would be a professional challenge so worthy of our talents and our dedication. It would be an honor. If there has ever been a more diverse, skilled and open-minded group of people than this group here, I would like to meet them. It's already obvious that wheels are turning around the table and I am hoping that those wheels pick up speed here because we are pitching more than just one plan today."

"What the hell, Alex?" Terry pipes up. "Haven't we already heard enough?"

"Maybe you have, Terry," I shoot back. "and if so feel free to leave."

There is no movement in the room. So, I continue.

"Mark and I are proposing a change in business philosophy that could have great impact on how companies all over the country commit to their communities and measure their successes. When the school succeeds, the business succeeds. When the business thrives, so will the outcomes of the student population. In order to reach that point, however, it takes a community . . . families, businesses and a sense of hope for the future, around the clock and with the changing seasons. This is a massive pitch that will cause a shift in our lives as well as the lives of people we don't know yet but I can guarantee you that we will all benefit."

Deeply, and nervously inhaling with a concentrated look across the room, I make eye contact with A.J. Hoyt who responds with a relaxed nod and admiring wink to continue. The second half of our pitch today relates to the Dodson Street neighborhood as well."

Pointing to the colorful logo projected on the screen at the front of the room, I enthusiastically continue the involved pitch.

"As we know, the conception of IDEA-Innovative Design for Educational Advancement brings together futuristic and practical principles in furniture design for schools. The company takes in used school desks and chairs and redesigns them to be ergonomically effective for today's learning. The desktops are reshaped, raised and reconfigured to support proper posture and the chairs are adjusted with a few tweaks to provide comfort and offset potential physical strain."

"I could use an IDEA chair to release some physical strain right now." Lee mutters across the table, which leads to some welcome laughter.

I continue "In essence, they reuse and recycle and return the furniture to the schools that chose to hold onto, improve and modernize their mass furniture investments. IDEA is banking on the fact that schools have less funding for new furniture and are very conscious of future trends realizing that classrooms are taking on a whole new physical dimension with students being provided laptops and lessons being guided by technology driven instruction."

I see Lee and Pat nodding to each other from across the table with keen business eyes in agreement to the purpose of IDEA. I am encouraged.

"This company is truly devoted to brandishing a new direction in school furniture design. It is in the early stages of start-up and hopes to be wise about property selection. IDEA has requested that we locate them in an affordable factory space that jibes with its principles. It was while searching out a property for IDEA that I stumbled onto Dodson Street School."

Mark tosses his ponytail and gives me a thumbs-up. To me, it is a sign that he values the day I wandered into his school as much as I do.

I also see Juan Carlos wearing a big grin while fidgeting in his seat at the sight of Mark's and my private exchange. He bursts out, "I rrrrreally love this Alex! Drrrrama in the work place!"

Everyone in the room looks a Juan Carlos. It is very uncommon for him to do much more than take notes and refill drinks at our Monday morning meetings.

"Thank you Juan Carlos. We appreciate your enthusiasm." I say to him knowing that he needs to buy into the proposal as much as everyone else around the table.

"The site that we are purchasing for IDEA is just a few blocks down the street from the school. The property is an old shoe factory with the perfect layout and specs for the furniture re-production line. Access to the expressway for shipping and delivery is within minutes and if we set up a satellite office for ourselves across the street from Dodson Street School, the neighborhood will be in an upturn. The factory, itself, has been vacant for a number of years but is in good shape and has no immediate need for repairs or updates. In fact, the owner of the property is here today."

I turn with an open gesture to Mark Tandem who quietly stands and clears his throat. "Yes, The factory was left to me by my grandfather Otto Tandem, who owned and managed Tandem Footing his entire career. When he passed away, his dying wish was that I find a new purpose for the factory. It served as more than a place of work for the people in the area. It was, in all truth, the anchor of the community. If IDEA successfully manages to launch itself and its

160

philosophy in the old shoe factory and if A.J. Hoyt Technologies dedicates itself to Dodson Street School, your company will have facilitated and championed a new thought for modern day business. Your success will be waged in hope for a better tomorrow."

At that, A.J. Hoyt slowly rises from her chair and works her way up to where all of the eyes in the room focus on her commanding presence. Leaning forward in her navy blue Chanel suit, she plants her palms firmly, gold bracelets cracking loudly onto the table in the cleared space at its head and speaks with ultimate authority, "This is an unbelievable stroke of chance that we have before us. It has been a dream of mine that someday our company would be challenged with the type of opportunity that could change the face of common business practices. The right time and situation just hadn't come along until now. Last night, I contacted the head of the local school council of Dodson Street School and he gave us a go-ahead to begin working with the school under a trial basis for the next two years. He readily and regrettably acknowledges the council's lack of attention to the school claiming an absence of funding and state support due to the ironically strong performances of the students and staff. This is a case of true injustice unfolding in the hands of bureaucracy that Alex just happened to discover."

A.J. takes a sip from the teacup that Juan Carlos has gently slid in front of her. I am amazed with the intention of her words and zeal in her tone. Her efficiency and proactive nature explains a lot about her success.

"It is time for A.J. Hoyt Technologies to really look to the future and not just in the static but in the living. I am an old woman. I can see that our business is booming and growth is so positive that it is almost uncharitable. However, because I am old, I am also wiser than all of you. I can see that we need to become our own future. The school that Alex discovered, which Mark so beautifully described to us is a fountain of opportunity for us to invest in filled with young minds that have the potential to think the way all of you do. You are all quick and brilliant. You foresee change and push new ideas out into the world. I am supporting our suggested relocation to the Dodson Street neighborhood and am asking all of you to be a part of this effort. This move will facilitate our proximity to Mr. Tandem's school and we will adopt them. We will foster mentorships and provide for their needs. These children should be exposed to the finest and most current technologies and learning tools. We will make sure of it and years from now, perhaps we will inspire them to become a part of our team at A.J. Hoyt Technologies."

The room is silent.

I stand abruptly, trying to shake the stunned team to life and announce, "Well team, A.J. Hoyt, hereby directs us all to open our hearts, open our minds and open our eyes to a reality that we could improve and we could also benefit from.

Who knows, we might just end up discovering that this investment makes us richer than any other we have made."

A.J. continues to lead the charge. "As a team, we are going to rally behind Alex, with the guidance of Mark Tandem, to turn the situation at this school and in the entire neighborhood around. We will begin with some baseline statistics. I need a team of you to determine the schools and our present success levels with current raw data. This afternoon, another team will go down and visit the school, survey the neighborhood and develop a presence. There is a deserted storefront across the street that will no longer be empty. As of next week, this team is relocating to our satellite office on Dodson Street. Any objections?" A.J. scans the room, noting the puzzlement on the faces of her employees who are still in absorption phase.

"Excuse me A.J.," Terry Blanchard's hand goes up, not surprisingly, as he comes out of a haze of shock from such an unexpected unveiling, "but I have to inquire about security in the area. From what I can surmise, the neighborhood has been neglected for years. I find it surprising that you would want to risk the safety of your employees in this type of situation."

Acknowledging Terry's concern, A.J. nods and assures us that our security is her utmost priority in the process and that she will hire a full-scale firm to take on the area.

Terry stands down realizing that, aside from the team packing up and moving down to some ramshackle office building, it was in essence a done deal. The fact that A.J. was this involved meant that the project, or perhaps Alex True, had touched her soul . . .

Feeling a thwart of mixed emotion from both sides of the boardroom table, the overwhelming sense of support from A.J. and the apprehension of the team, I find myself momentarily frozen and only able to stare straight ahead into the caring eyes of Mark Tandem noticing that they are moist with heartfelt emotion. Trembling, I address my colleagues who are about to embark on a business and life adventure of an uncharted scale. In the arena of our field, some would claim the Monday morning declaration as a crazy plan . . . in the arena of life, however, it is more a leap of faith.

I escort Mark out of the offices of A.J. Hoyt Technologies and onto the elevator in silence. Pushing the button to the lobby, the doors close, Mark drops his briefcase and collapses against the back wall. I, unexpectedly, still overwhelmed and trembling, begin to hyperventilate breathless and heaving rapid breaths. Mark stops the elevator and has me kneel, helping to unbutton the top of my perfectly pressed shirt and cups his hands around my mouth in an attempt to gather puffs of air and calm my breathing. He too, kneels and waits, his own pulse rapid. Aside from the gasps of air and beating heart, there is no sound.

164

Together, breathing in syncopated silence Mark and I see our reflections facing back at us from the mirrored elevator door, two pillars supporting each other. We both realize that our lives have somehow become entwined and are at the foundation of a monumental shift moving forward in a bizarre free-fall state. We are falling together at the head of a cliff where any move or decision could change the course for so many other people.

Exhilarated, exhausted, emotional Mark withdraws his cupped hands and holds them around mine in a solid grip. He pulls them close and places them on his chest so that I can feel beneath the heat of his skin, the pounding of his heart. Its rhythm engulfing, unleashing an internal fire so intoxicating that I feel as though I have completely left my body. The essence of ginger and citrus inflate my lungs and I hear Mark whisper through his heart's pulsing beat, "This is real."

A startling voice cuts the electricity that hovers in the air of the stalled elevator. "Is everything okay in there?" pipes out one of the building security guards. Mark and I immediately jump to our feet realizing that we have been caught up in a seductive reverie and that reality is pressing buttons on the other side of the door.

"Yes. All is fine." Mark replies and just before returning the elevator to its duty, he turns, gently placing his hands on both of my heated cheeks releasing his lips passionately with an irresistible urgency that I have never felt before. The head-spinning swelling euphoria between us is short-lived as the elevator begins its descent and passengers slowly enter our hallowed space.

Upon ground level, the world is a buzz, echoing voices on cell phones, car horns honking out on the street, idle chatter carrying through the rotund lobby, I step out and into the chaos in a trance, flush with life and shocked with a look of bewilderment. Mark follows and casually puts his arm around my shoulder giving an awakening sturdy squeeze, "Hey, can I give you a lift down to Dodson Street? I hear you are going to be doing a little work in my neck of the woods." He says with a wink and a grin.

I snap out of the haze and smile back, "Um, well . . . you know, Mark, I think I should drive separately." My heart is pounding. My mouth is dry. What am I saying? Of course I want to jump in his Honda but I feel too out of control. I muster up some lame excuse. "We might be down there long after the school day ends this afternoon. I'm going to need my car."

"Okay. I see." He deflates and steps away from me. "Come by my classroom if you find you need a break around three o'clock." He says coyly turning toward the public parking garage entrance.

"Hey Mark," He whips his ponytail around and looks back at me as I manage to shout, echoing him from a few moments earlier, "This IS real."

Chapter 17
Looking Into The Bean

I stumble across the lobby, shoot out of the revolving door like a pebble from a sling, launch into the movement of the sidewalk and join the beat of the other business people in an attempt to get some emotional and physical control. Caught up in the rhythm of the sound of footsteps on cement, I go forward mindlessly, lost in the moment that was, just a few minutes earlier, one I have longed for in so many ways for my entire life.

I have always enjoyed the anticipation that comes with meeting someone on a first date, going all out to put forth the best initial impression, waiting for that long kiss goodnight that means "I can't wait to see you again." But it has never happened. Not once, when the timing and setting and date seemed perfect had the earth quaked, like it does in the movies at the end of a perfect evening. But now, in the middle of the biggest and craziest morning of my life is the earth starting to rock and roll.

Thinking out loud, "My mother always said, "When you least expect it, expect it!" I laugh, touching the lips that had just touched Mark's, feeling his warm trace. I look down at the palm that just touched Mark's chest believing that the pulse in my veins belongs to him. The cheeks that Mark had so gently held are warm and wet with streaming tears as I march on, unaware of time or even where the sidewalk is leading. At last, the glistening sun reflects off of something massive and breaks my euphoric zombie walk.

Looking up with surprise, there in front of me is the famous giant mirror-like Cloud Gate statue that the entire city refers to as The Bean. My slightly distorted reflection is staring straight back wearing the same beautiful beige suit, sporting the same tightly coifed stylish hairstyle and aside from being strangely stretched and more curvy than normal, looking relatively the same as it did at home in the mirror earlier this morning. Except, I can see that my Caribbean blue eyes, that Mark compared to Ellen's, appear to have an inexplicable twinkle. I move as close to the big shiny bean as possible and can't deny it. There is an actual twinkle that was never there before.

Is this what falling in love does to you? I wonder and gasp a bit, teeter back and turn to see a group of high school kids laughing about ten feet away. Curious to be the source of the laughter, I lean up to the sculpture again, see the twinkle and then spot the group of kids bouncing the sun's rays off of a hand-mirror causing my eye twinkle in the big bean. I bow and applaud the gawking group and laugh hysterically at the poetic prank that will forever be my own private treasure. Coming off Lake Michigan on a breeze, my heart sweeps up its new journey and ties it in a bow to be opened again later.

As I arrive back at the office the sensation of a gentle vibration hints that someone is checking in. The text is from Chrissy who, I assume is having a humdrum lunch in her teacher's lounge and wants the scoop from my morning meeting. All I can think of for a reply is,

"TTYL w/ merlot. Meeting- excellent! Tandem- amazing." There are not enough words in text-speak to even try to describe the morning's events – pitching to the team, Mark's heart-felt presentation, A.J.'s commanding declaration, the frozen, dumbfounded and maybe slightly inspired faces around the table, hyperventilating in the elevator with Mark and above all the kiss. Nope, no text would do this morning justice.

Chapter 18

Powwow At The School

I am anxious, hesitant to pull open the door and enter the school. It is important for me to be as focused at this staff meeting as I was back at Hoyt. So, I take a deep breath and hope that I am able to behave like myself around Mark. Rosie is seated in the front office. The door is open and I can smell her gardenia scent as she waves me on to the meeting. The students have gone home for the day leaving the building lifeless like a carcass that has been bled out. It is quiet, except for the clap of my heel on the tile. I walk on.

I turn a corner and follow my nose to the scent of freshly brewing coffee and find the teachers seated around the long table listening to Principal Bluberry. I take a seat in a chair near the door and catch the tail end of his message.

"Paulie's doctor was able to mend his thumb but I am afraid he will be out of commission for a few weeks. His wife wants me to thank you all for the beautiful flowers and Paulie says that the time off will do his skin good. He is looking forward to not having to explain the reason for his blue hands all the time." He shares, receiving a chuckle from the group in front of him.

With all that is going on, I am glad to be reminded to follow up with the hospital. I want to be certain that Paulie's medical services are covered by A.J. Hoyt Technologies.

The chair that I am sitting in creaks as I adjust to it and the heads in the room turn to notice that I have joined their afternoon powwow. Mark says nothing but I see the redness in the skin of his neck smolder up to his ears, which makes me feel a secret, private connection to him across the table.

I am seated closest to Marion Jones, who surprises me with a beam of warmth that I did not receive in her classroom. She waves for me to move closer to the group and places her hand on top of mine, a motherly welcome. Essence of lavender emanates from her wiry dreadlocks and her aroma helps me to relax. I wonder if it has the same effect on her students, a subliminal strategy perhaps.

Mark clears his throat and gestures a hand my way.

"I believe that most of you have had the pleasure of meeting Alex True."

As always, I am über-conscious of formal group introductions. I have freshened up and dressed down a bit from the morning meeting, one less button fastened at the collar, no blazer, rolled up sleeves. I appear to be prepped less for center stage. Even still, the spotlight is on me and I graciously nod to the group.

"Alex is a research analyst with the venture capital firm A.J. Hoyt Technologies. In case you aren't sure, a venture capital firm invests in, sometimes long shot, business opportunities that analysts like Alex identify as excellent generators of revenue and cultural impact. Believe it or not, our school has become a component in a very interesting financial and cultural equation." Mark explains to his surprised colleagues.

"What role exactly does our school play in this type of business deal?" Dana Frinkle inquires eyeing me suspiciously.

"Well, the good thing is we aren't being asked to do anything differently than we already have been. A.J. Hoyt Technologies is going to support our curriculum needs in ways that we have not been supported. They will provide us with computers and training in new technology practices so that we can better instruct our students. The plan is that A.J. Hoyt Technologies will, without a doubt, be very present in a nurturing way that fosters the best out of our kids. They will be offering scholarships and arranging mentorships with other companies that they invest in. The connection that our students will have with A.J. Hoyt Technologies will go far beyond the walls of our school. To top it all, they are settling in on another deal to bring a company into the old shoe factory down the road which will bring life back to the neighborhood."

Mark's enthusiasm is palpable. He is animated and confidant in such a different manner than he was in the boardroom earlier in the day. I like seeing both sides of him.

He knows how to work an audience. Perhaps that is the key characteristic of a strong teacher.

"How did Alex pick our school?" Ms. Xhang asks calmly in a tone that lays like silk over Mark's lively explanation.

"It appears that divine intervention has played a role in bringing me here." I interject wanting to relieve Mark from having to field an awkward question. "To be honest, Ms. Xhang, I was lost. I had been out and about looking for the address of an old factory space in the area for an investment. I came in to your school for some help. And look where I ended up." I say smiling broadly to the contemplative faces that fill the room. "In all truth, I couldn't be happier. In fact, you will be seeing a lot more of me in coming days and, I imagine, for a very long time. At this very moment, there are members of my team in the old hardware store across the street. We are purchasing it as a satellite office with the belief that close proximity to our venture will enhance the experience and the value of our claim. We want to help bring this community back, and become a part of it."

"Don't take offense, Alex, but this sounds like a p.r. stunt. Are you running for office or something?" Dana digs.

I am hurt but can't show it. "No. I am not running for any office and no this is not a stunt." I defend.

Michael Bluberry offers his review of the situation in an attempt to assuage Dana's concerns and any others.

"When Mark called me the other evening on the phone and explained this to me, I thought that we were going to be dragged through some disappointing, Pollyanna-type proposal to save the school by check writing big wigs wanting to fulfill a charity claim for their company's credo but as I've seen the activity across the street today and having received a few uncustomary calls earlier this afternoon from some inquiring local business minds, I believe that this is the real deal. I can't say that I have ever heard of a company investing in a school like this before but if all bets are on, we are headed for the big time with A.J. Hoyt Technologies. For the next couple of years we are going to be linked with them at the hip."

Mark looks at his unassuming boss accepting that he is, as anyone in his position would be, excited that someone is stepping in to improve life for him, his students and staff.

Dana speaks up again asking the obvious, "So, there is no doubt that a company like A.J. Hoyt Technologies will have the means to improve the environment down here for us but what on earth can we do for A.J. Hoyt? I have a hard time thinking that we won't be asked to put more into this deal." She says while heads around the table teeter.

"Listen everyone," Mark says weighing in on his

colleagues. "We've got some of the brightest, most creative students on the south side of Chicago. Their minds could go places we can't even imagine if given the right tools and most current instruction."

"Are you implying that we aren't doing a good enough job?" Dana speaks out again.

"No. Nobody is saying that Dana. We could all do even better. We don't even have computers for the kids yet. That's almost a crime." Mark points out and the look on Dana's face seems to soften.

"A.J. Hoyt is definitely in this for business. They are hoping to foster great minds, and to place those great minds in to even greater learning institutions as they grow older, and in the end have them trained to work in the many businesses that they have invested in both locally and globally." It is really an incredible gift.

"You all need to consider the opportunity that we have here. This is no fly-by-night declaration like we are used to hearing from our higher-ups. This is, like Alex said, divine."

Marion stands and shakes her dreadlocks out over her shoulders above the table. She pumps her fist and with a furrowed brow looks at each teacher. "I don't know what you all are thinking but I know what I am and I'm on board with this. If there are already people, and white people at that, working on settling into the old hardware across the street then this is more than just a fleeting promise. It's more than anyone has done for us since I've been at Dodson. We are up against so many odds here. I think it's crazy to question Alex's motives. These kids and this room full of teachers need all the help we can get!"

"I'm glad you feel that way, Marion." I say as I back toward the doorway. "It's time for me to join my colleagues across the street and to let you all discuss this amongst yourselves. If you have any pressing questions or suggestions, Mark knows how to reach me."

At that, Dana gives me a smirk and a cock-eyed nod. Mr. Bluberry and the other teachers stand and applaud in thanks. On my way out, I stop in and chat with Rosie in the office. She has a pile of medical forms that she is trying to file away and a long list of families to call that are delinquent on their student's physicals.

"It's never ending, Alex." She says to me holding up the back stack of yellow cards.

"I can only imagine." I respond to her still in awe of the typewriter on the desk in front of her.

"How did your meeting go?" She asks. "Mr. Bluberry is beside himself about all that is going on. He filled me in over lunch."

"I think it went well." I say peering through the window over her shoulder at the activity across the street. It amazes me how a few people standing on the sidewalk and some parked cars have already begun to enliven the neighborhood.

"I can't tell you how much this means to all of us." Rosie says as I turn to leave.

"You don't have to, Rosie. I already know." I say. Before crossing the street, I decide to stop into the faculty bathroom across the hall.

In the third stall, I am zipping up as I hear the door open and two women walk in.

"I don't care what you say, Marion. Something about Alex True makes me uneasy. She's too pushy." The voice belonging to Dana Frinkle says.

"She's too pushy? She's too pushy? What are you talking about, all this she's too pushy? Alex, ain't no she, he's definitely a he. I could tell when I touched his hand at the meeting. It was rough like my boyfriend's. Besides, he's wearing a suit." Marion says.

I am dying in the stall. It's one of those moments that I wish I could record because I would love to play their conversation over again and again. I also make a mental note to get some more Lubriderm.

"No way. I know Alex is woman. She's after Mark. I can taste it in the air. The way she was watching him during the meeting today. This is all some kind of effort to move in on my guy." Dana rants.

"Now listen, Dana. Man, woman, alien, no matter, I can tell that this whole deal with our school and A.J. Hoyt is not just about somebody getting laid. It's about people helping people." The water faucet turns on and hands are washed. "See you later, Dana. I'm heading home to my man."

"See you tomorrow, Marion. Tell Orlando I say hi." Dana says and goes into the stall two down from me.

I flush and leave the bathroom without washing my hands.

Chapter 19

The Suits Arrive

I feel like some kind of groupie approaching the small crowd on the sidewalk in front of the hardware store. The faces prone to downtown high rise Loop comfort seem a bit out of their element but also interested in the plans being described by a man in charge who is wearing a yellow construction hat.

"We will install the security tomorrow as soon as the electricity and water are turned back on. The plan is to have one large welcoming room with cubicle-type offices around the perimeter and a massive drafting table in the middle for meetings."

"How long will it take before we can actually work here?" Dannie asks.

"I've got guys in there now and we've got orders to work non-stop to completion. So, I would imagine you could have furniture delivered the day after tomorrow." He says.

"Wow, now that's efficiency at it's best." Dannie says.

"That's what happens when you take direct orders from A.J. Hoyt." He acknowledges to Dannie and the entire clan of suits on the sidewalk.

Terry is glaring at me with daggers from across the group. So I divert my gaze from him and check my cellphone. There is already a message from Mark. I lean over to Pat and whisper in his ear, "Hey, I need to get back to the city. Is everything going okay here?" I ask.

"Besides Terry being a pompous ass, all is going just fine. Go on ahead and go, Alex. I am really excited about all of this." He says and turns back to the man in the yellow construction hat.

I inch my way off the sidewalk and back across the street to my car. It feels good to have Pat on board. He's a great team player. Now, to see about Mark.

I dial.

"Alex?" My heart skips a beat at the sound of his voice.

"I saw you called."

"You left our faculty meeting so quickly today."

"I know. I'm sorry. I really felt you all needed to talk without me being there. How did it go after I left?" I ask.

"Really well. Everyone is excited. Well, except for Dana for some reason. Mr. Bluberry is just walking on cloud nine over the whole deal. It's great to look out and see life across the street. The next few days are going to be exciting around here." He says as my thoughts drift to Dana in the faculty restroom.

"The next few days? How about the next few years, Mark! This is a permanent maneuver. You better get used to seeing life across the street." I say.

"Where are you right now?" Mark asks.

"I'm in my car heading back to the city." I say.

"Oh." The other end goes silent and I sense with a thrill that Mark was hoping to see me.

"It's my night to serve in the soup kitchen at my church and I need to get a jump on the traffic." I share with him while pressing on the break in the rising gridlock.

"Sure." He acknowledges. "I totally understand. Listen, my friend Liam is a cop and I asked him to look into the trespassers at the shoe factory."

Grateful that he had tended to the matter quickly, I respond, "Really?"

"Yep. He found evidence of some poachers, sleeping bags, some clothes. No drugs, no weapons. Not much. He told me that he gathered it all up and replaced a broken lock with a new one on one of the loading dock doors."

"Well, that's good. So, whoever it was can't get back in."

"Yeah. He is upping surveillance and has given me a few names of off duty cops to stand guard at night. I want to make sure that our mystery resident gets the picture that I am not managing the Dodson Street Ritz Carlton."

182

For some reason, I can't get the image of the van with the Jamaican flag out of my mind. Is Mark displacing Cherry Belafonté?

I laugh at myself and share with Mark that his efforts would look good to the folks from IDEA. Any attempt to present a stable and secure property is always added value.

"I will be bringing Terry Blanchard down to walk the factory in the morning. As difficult a colleague as he is, he is our best when it comes to closing a deal. He wants to map out the space prior to the final sell to IDEA."

The thought of Terry potentially tripping over a Jamaican woman sleeping in the factory makes me ill. There's so much a stake and Terry is one person who, given his judgmental nature, could put an end to all of the good that is happening.

"I am anxious to hear what Terry thinks. Do you mind giving me a call after the walk through?" Mark asks.

Do I mind? I ponder the question and realize that Mark still isn't sure where he stands with me, even after our moment in the elevator. I feel equally unsure as our professional and personal lives are drawing closer. It's best not to stop and think too hard as our worlds are a swirl and the slightest derailment could send either one of us reeling off like a stray firework.

"I'll call you as soon as I can."

"Thanks Alex. Enjoy serving at the soup kitchen."

Chapter 20

Cherry

"She's back!" I say to Dolores as I pull up behind the van with the Jamaican flag painted on the side and throw my hybrid into park. The paint job is too unique to be on any other rickety van in the city. "What was Cherry Belafonté doing all they way down on Dodson Street the other day?" I ask Dolores not expecting a response.

I see her sitting at a table in the far corner with a group of regulars. They are listening to her tell a story and laughing as she gestures wildly. Virgil waves a ladle at me and I run to wrap on an apron.

"How you doin' today, Alex?" He asks me as I fall in synch slicing bread to his stirring of the pot of spaghetti.

"You know, Virg, I am doin' great."

"I can tell, my friend. You are just as red faced as you were last week. Either you are fallin' in love or you are spendin' too much time at the make-up counter in Carson's." He says with a wink.

"You know I don't go for makin' myself up, Virg."

"I know that. That's how I know you're falling'"

I continue working the knife through the soft bread, lost in my own thoughts. I've never fallen before. The sensation is extraordinary, if that is what is happening to me.

I have spent so much of my life working to develop such a strong exterior that I have most certainly deterred potential suitors, until Mark. What lead him to become attracted to me? And not the suspiciously sweet Dana Frinkle?

I am pulled from my slicing reverie as Johnny places his plate on the table and greets Virg and me with a hearty, "Well howdy do, Salt-n- Pepa?"

"You certainly are cheerful this evening, Johnny." I comment while serving up some bread.

"You know what? I's in a great mood. That Cherry lady, she done picked me up an' brung me here again. Save me from hoppin' the tracks. She did." He tells us with a monstrous broken toothed grin.

"Hey man" Virgil says to Johnny. "Not many folks can say they got a free ride these days. Good for you." He looks over at Cherry Belafonté and I see Virgil assessing her like a gambler rubbing his chin before placing a bet at the tracks. "What's she telling you all about over there?" He inquires one eye on Cherry and the other on the steaming pasta.

"She talkin' 'bout the boy she take care of. Some little Richie Rich." Johnny skirts back from Virg and me to the lively table and settles in to Cherry's tale.

I can see that Virg is now beyond curious about the unique Jamaican woman and I too find myself drawn to her deep and sinewy chatter. I, however, have a secret connection to her, one that she is not yet aware of. It is not only our shared proximity in the soup kitchen that draws me toward her but also my awareness of the presence of her van on the property of the old shoe factory that has me intrigued.

Together, Virg and I meander through the tables and over to our most animated dinner guest. Again, I see a plastic red flower tucked behind her ear. Her lips stained the bold color of a fire engine flap away in entertaining fashion.

"Da boy, he done sit der 'til his momma come home. I say No peas, no plays. Den his momma, she give me mo' dollas fo' bein' strict wit' da boy." Cherry nods and her flower flops up and down. "Easy money."

Virgil pulls up a chair and I lean against the wall. The last of the guests finish off their meals and Cherry carries on telling simple stories about the boy for whom she cares. The backdrop of her black patent leather skin, her full red lips and the bright flower peeping out of her hair pulls us in like magnets to metal. I can see that Virgil is mesmerized by her exotic presence.

I, however, can not avert the juxtaposed image in my mind of her wild van with the Jamaican flag pulling up to a brownstone on the Gold Coast in the morning and then, from my own assumptions, pulling in to the loading dock at the old shoe factory at night. What an extreme existence, that shall no longer be. Cherry Belafonté can no longer stake unlawful

186

claim behind the filthy windows of the empty building on Dodson Street.

Something, however, inside me feels sorry for her. She brings our homeless guests here and asks nothing in return but perhaps a free meal. She makes them laugh and feel included in life's happenings. For a woman who has so little, she appears to be amazingly content. I look over at Virgil. His legs are straddled over the seat of the chair and his chest is leaning on its back. His arms are dangling, muscles bulging out of his tee-shirt sleeves. He is broad jawed and dewy-eyed caught up in Cherry's magical yarn.

"Hey mon, da food. It was good." Cherry says to Virgil and his mahogany cheeks fire up to burgundy from her compliment.

"I'm glad you enjoyed it." He replies getting up to approach her with an outstretched hand. "My name is Virgil and my friend is Alex."

"Ah yes, I knows Alex from da week before." She says remembering our prior acquaintance. At this point, I am sure that she has not made an association with our near run-in at the shoe factory and I am glad.

"Cherry," I say. "You've done something real kind this evening."

"I know dat. Dey already tell me so." She replies graciously.

"What inspires you to bring them to our church?" I

ask curiously.

"God tells me. 'Tis a good ting to do." She admits batting her eyes and bowing her head in honor.

I see that Virgil is completely moved by her sincerity. He cups his enormous hands around hers and says in nearly a whisper, "You are a beautiful woman, Cherry Belafonté."

I watch my friend fall as he has claimed I, too, have fallen and I wonder if I look as he looks, soft and vulnerable. I realize how unique it is to witness love blooming and to experience it just the same. I am honored to watch Virgil tumble and hope that Cherry sees my friend for all that he is good. That is what true love does and it is with such admiration that I view Mark Tandem.

Chapter 21
Old Shoe Factory

We pull up to the shoe factory in separate cars. Terry plows his big black Suburban right up next to me in front of the old Tandem Footing Sign. The overgrowth has been cut back and it appears as though Mark has hired someone to come and clean up the landscape. I walk over to the entrance and wait as Terry finishes up a phone call from the front seat of his car. I notice that the windows to the building have been washed and the large handle on the front door is polished. It is as if a breath of life has been pumped into the place.

"So, nice neighborhood you dragged us down to." Terry barks stepping out onto the cracked pavement in his very pricey leather loafers.

"Give it some time, Terry. If history repeats itself, the place will be hoppin' in no time." I reply in an attempt to carry out an upbeat endeavor.

Terry watches me carefully as I pull out the key to unlock the enormous wooden door. He laughs as I jiggle the handle and the door doesn't budge.

"This is a man's job." He scoffs at my failed attempt to enter and pushes me aside. "Let me get us in."

As he works the tired handle, I turn to the sound of

tires on gravel. I immediately think of Cherry Belafonté and panic. That would be a really bad scene. Instead a long black limo pulls onto the property. Both Terry and I look at each other skeptical of the mysterious arrival. The car pulls up and a driver steps out to open the passenger door. To our disbelief, A.J. Hoyt steps out, thanks the chauffer and greets us nonchalantly. "Good morning Alex, Terry." She nods and files up to enter the building with us.

Sun shines through the clean windows and the lobby feels less antiquated than it did when I came in with Mark. The cases of shoes catch A.J.'s eye and she wanders over to inspect the display.

"My father wore this pair. I haven't thought of his shoes in decades. He only wore them on Sundays, at weddings and at funerals. Come to think of it, I think the box he stored them in was a Tandem Footing box." A.J. said connecting to days long ago.

"Isn't that something?" I say looking over her shoulder at the sharp shoes under the glass.

"Hey, we aren't shoe shopping here." Terry says as he opens a giant metal door to the factory floor and waves us through.

The smell hit us first. The air was heavy with a fermented richness that stopped all three of us in our tracks. It was the grittiest blend of yeast and honey and allspice and earth, so thick it was like gel going into our noses.

"What is that?" Terry whines, nose pinched and squinty-eyed.

"My guess is that decades of leatherwork has left its mark like sawdust in a mill." A.J. answers.

I stride past them and stand in the middle of the factory looking up to the window of the office where Mark had taken me, where Otto Tandem announced to his workers that his grandson would be going to college. I imagine being a hard-working Polish immigrant down below hovering over a machine that cut the leather for a shoe he could never afford. I wonder what it felt like to hear that a young man like Mark would have the opportunity to pursue a life that the factory worker could only dream of. I wonder.

We tour the entire floor, noting the old machinery that would be shipped off to auction and taking measurements of the space for the new equipment to be brought in for IDEA.

"This is surprisingly perfect, Alex." Terry says and I note that he is rubbing his hands together making friction with his palms like he rarely does when he gets excited.

"I told you it was great!" I say to him.

"I know you did. That's why I had to see for myself." He says as rude as ever. I just roll my eyes and walk over to a door in the front corner. I open it up and see a folded blanket and a plastic poinsettia plant on a table in what appears to be a break room. Apparently, Mark's officer friend forgot to gather everything.

I shut the door and join A.J. and Terry in the lobby once again.

"I feel good about this you two. Nice work, Alex. The rest is up to you, Terry." A.J. says. "Close the deal." She turns and walks away leaving us to stand side by side in the front door. We watch her driver open the door to the limo and guide her in.

"Imagine having the power to control situations the way she does?" I say in awe.

"As of late, Alex, you do." He turns his back to me and walks away without even a whiff of good-bye.

His oversized Suburban peels out of the lot spitting dust like an obnoxious smoker blowing smoke in my face. I wave it away and work toward my car. A siren wails out of nowhere as I climb in and a cop car pulls up next to me at frightening speed. My heart is racing and I roll down my window. The officer glances in to make sure I am not packing any heat.

"Are you Alex True?" He asks.

I am surprised. "Yes."

"I'm Officer Liam Flannery. I've been ordered to escort you to the expressway. You are not to be here without proper security." He says.

"Did A.J. Hoyt send you?" I ask.

"No. I am a friend of Mark Tandem's. He sent me."

Chapter 22
It's Not Oprah

I find myself spending more and more time down on Dodson Street. I am up and out of the apartment earlier than ever traversing the side streets of Chicago in the pink hue of dawn. Dolores sits silently on the dash, a statue for worship waiting to dispatch. I bounce in a triangle from the satellite office of A.J. Hoyt Technologies, to the factory to the school; the proximity of my new endeavors to one another is advantageous. Being a part of the new life and energy on Dodson Street is invigorating.

The children jockey for window views to witness the transformation of the old hardware store across the street. First come the power washers, the window cleaners and the locksmith. Then arrive the cleaning services and furniture movers. A rumor starts among the older students that Oprah is coming to town but that is put to rest at a school assembly on the third day of the excitement.

Principal Bluberry takes the microphone and asks all of the children to settle down and listen to the very important message that Mr. Tandem is about to share. Mark steps in front of the crowd of eager faces and greets them with a respectful bow.

"Good morning boys and girls."

In unison, the entire student body replies, "Good morning, Mr. T."

"Many of you have noticed that there is something exciting happening across the street." He says.

"You got that straight, Mr. T." Jamal pipes out from the back of the gymnasium.

"Well, some very important people have heard what wonderful children you are and they want to come and work closer to you. In fact, they want to get to know all of us and share what makes us such hard-working, special people." Mark explains in the simplest of terms. Glancing out, he spots my team members from A.J. Hoyt Technologies standing along the wall next to the doors. He notes Terry, A.J. who surprisingly is wearing a denim dress and white sneakers and then he sees me.

We transfix, lost in each others eyes, caught in a private moment on a public stage. The room goes silent and Mark rests the microphone on his chest. Through the speakers in the corner of the gym I recognize the same beat that I had felt under the warmth of his skin in the elevator. Everyone else hears it too, especially Dana Frinkle who gets up from her chair and storms out of the gym leaving her students to squirm on the floor. Sensing an awkwardly public intimate moment, Michael Bluberry clears his throat and puts his hand on Mark's shoulder.

"To emphasize Mr. Tandem's message, I would like to point out that some of those very important people are here in our school today and they want to spend some time getting to know us."

An outspoken sixth grade girl named Latasha shouts and asks if they all work for Oprah. Mark chuckles and acknowledges her inquiry but explains that there are a lot of people in Chicago who like to do nice things for good people and that Oprah is just one of them.

"How many of you like coming to school here?" Mark asks and most of the children raise their hands.

"How many of you would like it more if we had computers in the classrooms?" Mark shouts into the microphone.

Cheers from the children!

"How many of you would like it more if we had a playground and grass to play on?"

More cheers from the children!

"How many of you would like it more if you came to school and saw other people working in a safe neighborhood at stores, cafés and businesses that are helping the economy of Dodson street to grow back the way it used to be long ago?"

Cheers and a standing ovation from the children and the staff. The enthusiasm of hope fills my heart as big as the gymnasium.

"Okay, please everybody settle down and take a seat." Mark says as the teachers all wave their arms to the revved up students. "The adults here with us today look like visitors to you but in time they will be familiar faces. They work for a company called A.J. Hoyt Technologies and they are putting great faith in all of you. They want you to keep doing your best. They want to help you share your creative ideas with the world. They want to work with you to explore places and things you would have never thought possible. They are going to give you the tools to succeed beyond your dreams because you all deserve to be given the greatest chances that life can offer."

"You sound like a preacher, Mr. T." One of the older boys shouts as Marion Jones hushes him.

"I'm no preacher, Miguel, just a teacher who believes in all of you." Mark says handing the microphone back to Mr. Bluberry.

"Okay boys and girls, we have one more surprise. Our friends from A.J. Hoyt have brought us all pizza to celebrate this special day."

Wild cheers from the children!

"Please follow your teacher back to class and lunch will be brought to you there." He concludes.

The children and their teachers exit the gym shaking the hands of each member of the team from A.J. Hoyt

Technologies as if going through a receiving line at a wedding reception.

Having our team scatter about in the classrooms is a wonderful experience for the students and the staff. The children are able to speak openly with pride about their accomplishments and dreams. We, especially A.J., find their confidence, knowledge and communication skills to be impressive given the broken homes from which so many of the children come.

Mr. Bluberry invites A.J. into his office and they establish a chain of command for this new business arrangement. They realize that they are going to be working together closely and spend the afternoon walking the halls and sitting in on lessons, joining in with reading circles and even putting on smocks to paint with the kindergartners.

I realize now why A.J. chose to wear denim.

Terry and the others are in and out of the school and the offices across the street trying to get a handle on the new situation and establish a comfortable presence with the children.

I decide to spend some time with the sixth graders. In Mark's classroom, Jamal approaches me, "Excuse me, but was it when you and Mr.T met that all this stuff started happening?" I nod with a smile and sit down next to him and try to explain in more depth what is going on. Jamal smiles and understands and says, "I can't wait to get home to tell my

Mama."

With her math book in hand, Latasha wanders over and sits near us at an open desk. She sizes me up and down and says, "You sure are tall. How tall are you?" Grateful that that's all she wants to know, I chuckle and say, "Six feet and I wear a size twelve shoe."

"Dang. My sister's that tall. We call her the jolly giant. You and Mr. T are the tallest white people I ever seen face to face."

I turn and smile at Mark realizing for the first time that he really is quite tall. He comes over and joins the conversation introducing me to Latasha and sharing that it was her sister that he was taking flowers to on the day we first met.

Tears begin to gather and a lump swells in my throat as the realization of the seriousness and fragility of the situations of these children becomes more personalized.

Latasha hands me a tissue and says, "It's okay. My sister is going to be coming home soon and they caught the guy that shot her. He's bad news and they hauled him off for a long time. You know anybody who been shot at?"

Seeing that I have no words for Latasha, Mark steps in and puts his hand on Latasha's shoulder and says it is time to wrap up the math assignment and get ready to clean up for the day. Latasha thanks me for spending time in their classroom and obeys her teacher's direction. Mark hands me a water bottle and steps to the front of the room.

To close out the day, he reminds his class in a manner different from the all school address that they had better continue to study and work hard at school because the people from A.J. Hoyt are counting on them to do their best.

He says, "If you continue to show us excellent effort and commitment to your education, then you will experience far more than the pizza party we had today. Your families will be curious. Please give them this letter from Mr. Bluberry and tell them that they can contact us with any questions. There will be other people around the school and throughout the neighborhood. They work for a security company and have been hired to keep all of us safe. Tell your families that this is going to be a different place from now on. It is going to look and feel as wonderful as a fine school is meant to."

With that, the dismissal bell rings. The students grab their belongings and head for the door. Jamal lingers at Mark's desk, waiting for the last child to leave. He salutes Mark and they give each other a fist pumping, shoulder banging, neck rolling secret handshake good-bye.

Heart full, I smile, wink at Mark and walk off with the sea of exiting children down the hallway taking in the excited chatter of the day's events, smelling wafts of Rosie Fisher's floral scent mixed with the now very familiar heavy adolescent body odor that I have come to accept as an acquired taste- like a fine merlot.

I realize that this is the first time in a long time that the heavy metal doors will be opening out on a sign of hopefulness for the future of Dodson Street and the school community. I pass the big yellow busses as they fill up with sweet smiling faces and hope that the children will all make it back safely for a new day and vow to try unstoppably to work with Mark and A.J. to develop this venture into a commitment for life.

Chapter 23
Chillin' At Floyd's

It feels like my career as a research analyst is taking a turn. Perhaps it is better to call this professional metamorphosis that I am experiencing an evolution. Some people believe that living is a fluid existence- ever changing and hopefully constantly improving. If this is the case, then my life is in heavy flow right now. I have gone from researching high end and often high tech business prospects to investigating and purchasing learning tools to inspire grade school children so that they think more scientifically. I have gone from making money for A.J. Hoyt Technologies to spending it like nobody's business. It is an extraordinary sensation to leap from extremes.

"Our accountants are monitoring the expenditures of this project. So far, we are working within reason of the forecasted budget. It's the dividends I'm after, Alex. Just spend wisely! We must facilitate their creative and intellectual desires. Look what they have already been able to do with so little. Now let's give them a chance to fly. Find out what those teachers would love to have and grant their wishes." A.J. commands to me without even the slightest hesitation.

"Okay, A.J. I know that your generosity is very much

appreciated." I say to her as I place a massive order for I-pads.

"I'm not just being generous, Alex. I am doing what needs to be done. I am also banking on the long range benefits." She says with a wink and scurries off to meet with a friend on the Chicago city planning committee.

Juan Carlos comes to my desk and says that I have a call. I am surprised, though, as the phone number has just been set up for the office.

"This is Alex True."

"Hey there Alex True. How's about meeting me for a drink right after work today?" I hear the friendly voice of Mark Tandem asking.

"What are you doing calling the office line?" I inquire.

"Just testing it out. Wanting to see if you guys are official over there."

"Oh we're official, all right. A.J.'s moving full-speed ahead. She's calling in massive favors with her friends on the Chicago City Council. There are all kinds of permits being waived and mountains being moved for her. Thank goodness for Chicago city politics!" I acknowledge knowing the harsh reality of the power of money.

"I can't say I mind at all." Mark replies. "Listen, would you like to grab a beer at Floyd's this afternoon? My friend Liam and I grab a cold one every now and then. I thought you might like to join us."

"Officer Liam?" I inquire sounding as if I know him better than I do.

"Oh yeah, I forgot about that. I guess you have met him, in a way." Mark says.

"He seemed like a decent guy." I surmise. "At least he made a good escort."

****

"Two Guinness, Jimmy." Mark calls out to the newest bar tender at Floyd's Tap.

"Make that three, my friend." Requests Liam as he slides up to us at the bar taking of his blue uniform hat.

"How have you been, Mark? I haven't seen you since the Sox swept Detroit pre-season a few weeks back."

"It's fair to say that I've been busy." Mark answers. "Let me officially introduce you two. Alex meet my old pal Liam." He takes a nice long well deserved swig of his favorite brew and watches as we shake hands.

"Good to meet you, Alex." Liam says paying little attention to me, and getting lost in the baseball game being played on the screen in front of us. As the innings pass I become a spectator at the bar observing the two friends as they sit complacently sipping away, side by side watching two different games on the various televisions that embellish the place. It occurs to me that this is how they unwind. Finally feeling the beer and the ambiance taking the edge off his day, Mark turns to Liam.

"What's new with you?"

"Not too much. Same old beat, same old characters up to no good. Hey have you heard anything about what's going on over by your school? There are some pretty heavy-duty studs patrolling the area. You'd think they were guarding Fort Knox. When I asked for i.d., it was legit. The only thing is they can't disclose whom they work for. " Liam says taking another sip and tossing down some peanuts.

"Oh yeah, man. I know all about it. The security detail is for me." Mark confirms grinning at his buddy.

"What? Are you kidding me man? There have to be at least a dozen guys posted around the clock in an eight-block perimeter of your school. What makes you so important." Liam inquires more seriously with a punch to Mark's shoulder.

"I'm a teacher." Mark replies turning back to the White Sox game with a smirk and another swig.

Chapter 24

Jamal

A fresh day and I cross the threshold at A.J. Hoyt Technologies satellite south-side office. The funky smell of day-old pizza mixes with the odor of ancient turpentine. It's unassuming and definitely not a corporate fragrance. It surprises me pleasantly to see my team and A.J. herself sitting on desktops laughing, telling stories of the day before and eating slices of leftover cold pizza. Styled up inner-city farmer chic, A.J. in yet another denim get-up, bright red crocs dangling above the floor, crazy multicolored beaded necklaces cascading in layers down her chest, spots me through her bright yellow cat-eye glasses as I enter. She hardly seems the same sophisticated corporate mogul who led the charge in the boardroom a while back. She weaves her fingers straight back through her striking grey hair and shoots her arms overhead and in victory style shouts to me like a swimmer emerging from a deep water dive, "I feel so alive!"

Unsure how to respond to this proclamation, I grab a plastic cup of soda and walk over to toast A.J.'s bold business leap of faith.

"Oh honey, you don't need to toast me. This is your doing. I have been praying for something exciting to pull me away from my tea and crumpet lifestyle for years. I feel like a kid in a candy store right now. There are a thousand ways that we can implement our company resources and our success to improve the situation for the kids and staff across the street. I think that when it is all said and done, we are going to benefit from them in more ways than you or I can even imagine."

Still dumbstruck by A.J.'s unbridled enthusiasm, I reach out a respectful handshake and with a coy grin say, "I have already felt the benefits." Thinking personally about the consuming tingling sensation that sweeps my core at the mere thought of anything related to Mark Tandem. Handing out more slices of the day old pizza and sensing a comfortable casualness amongst the otherwise stuffy corporate group, Terry Blanchard as abrupt as ever, takes the opportunity to pose an intimate question of our commander in chief.

"So A.J., since this morning has gotten off to the unconventional start of cold pizza and soda, I'm thinking office casual is the new norm. If that's the case, may I be so bold as to float you a personal question?"

In accordance, A.J. releases the smile of a Cheshire cat.

"Okay then," Terry inquires, "why do you go by A.J.? Why the initials?"

"Really Terry? Is that your prying question? And I thought you were a cut-throat." She says with an eye roll and a laugh. "Anyhow, in graduate school I decided that business people, especially men, would take me more seriously this way than if I went by my given name Agnes Justine. My sweet parents blessed me with the names of both of my grandmothers but really the combo is hardly going to win dukes in a fistfight. So, I decided to match my identity with my title. I wanted to win in a man's world so I chopped up my name a bit and voilà forty years later here I sit. I have probably knocked the socks off more unsuspecting clients and potential partners over the years that have expected a man to do the job but have gotten a woman than I care to count. Just look around at yourselves. Your business cards are just as deceiving. We have Terry and Alex, Jamie and Pat, Lee and Dannie. There is no way to tell on paper who of you is male or female until communication becomes face to face . . . and in the end, does it really matter?"

The burgeoning office sits in quiet as we down pizza and ponder A.J.'s words. I notice Jamie, Pat, Lee and Dannie as they innocuously scan one another visually. None of them seem unnerved and then their eyes land on me. I squirm with an uneasy feeling, certain that their thoughts are challenged by A.J.'s words- Male? Female? Does it really matter?

The intimacy of our unique setting tugs at a chord in my heart that wishes these people knew me better. Surface relationships are safe but something in the moment is leaving me exposed and not in control of their perceptions. They should know that I am an enlightened human. There's so much more to me than meets the eye and I love that about myself. To those who really care, I am like a mystery gift to be unwrapped. I have wonderful friends and an active life outside of venture capital. I am deeply committed to my family, my church and I am falling, falling for a man who has opened my mystery. My colleagues should know these things about me but our business and at times, my pretense, has kept us isolated from any deep rapport.

To my surprise, breaking the awkward silence, Terry walks over and puts his hand on my shoulder. I see in his demeanor a side of him that tells me too, that perhaps there is more to him than I have ever known before. The harshness in his countenance appears benign and I wonder if our new venture on Dodson Street is bringing out the best in him. I thought I sensed an uneasy mellowing in him as we toured the shoe factory and am relieved as he comes to my rescue.

"Look Alex," he says. "I can see that you really want to manage our efforts with Dodson Street School. Why don't I take on IDEA? I scheduled a meeting with their executive and legal teams for tomorrow. Let me handle them while you continue to work the stats up at this end of the street."

My response is a wide smile and a grateful nod as his gesture sets a kindhearted tone amongst our previously unsettled faction, for only a minute though. We all hear commotion on the sidewalk out front and the door flies open to a deeply bronzed Tom Mackey. He blows into the office donned in a tropical shirt and Polynesian lei.

"What on earth is goin' on here? I leave for a couple of weeks and the whole company goes soft? The driver wouldn't listen to me when I told him he was headed the wrong direction. And now look where we are . . . What the . . . what is A.J. wearing and why is she here? Am I being "punked" or something?"

Fumes pour from my utterly confused, jet-lagged boss. I bite my lip realizing that he is one person that I had not factored into the equation of the day.

"Can somebody please explain to me what I am doing in a dilapidated old building on the south side with the chairman of our company dressed like the farmer from American Gothic and my team feasting on cold pizza?"

A.J. pipes up and says, "You know Tom, I will take it at as a compliment that you think I resemble a masterpiece. As for you, you look more out of place than anyone here Mr. Tall Dark and Jet-lagged. Now, if you will take a seat have a slice of pizza and relax a minute we will gladly inform you of the most exciting venture in A.J. Hoyt Technologies history and you have Alex to thank."

I bow my head, slightly embarrassed and blushing from A.J.'s compliment.

"What? Alex, when we last spoke you didn't mention anything out of the ordinary." Tom says to me.

"This has all happened so fast, Tom. You were leaving for your trip when I was considering the plan. I went to A.J. because I felt she would be most responsive to the situation." I explain.

"What is the situation?" Tom demands. Sitting down next to him, I explain the entire series of events that led to us eating cold pizza in the old hardware store on Dodson Street. Tom sits motionless, almost catatonic as his smooth, predictable, easy business future transforms.   "I'm not sure I am cut out for this." He says to me. "We are a venture capital firm. We invest in companies whose plans show promise. We do not become the ones responsible for the promise." He shot back.

A.J. walks over to us and takes Tom's hands in hers. She looks at him through the bright yellow cat-eye glasses like a mother would look at her difficult child. "Listen Tom. Change is good. This is a new adventure for all of us here. You're going to have to reach down into your soul a little bit to feel the benefits at first but trust me this is going to be great for our business. It is going to be great for our spirits. It is going to be great for that school across the street and all of the children and their families as well. Besides, how many tropical islands can you visit before they all start to look the same?"

Again Tom, looking catatonic, just stares at A.J. as if he doesn't recognize her while she is speaking.

"Listen, go home get some rest and come back down here bright and early in the morning. Alex will give you a neighborhood tour." A.J. suggests walking Tom to the door. She thanks the driver for following her earlier instructions so well. "It had to have been tough fending off a ranting sun-quenched jet-lagged big-wig in the back seat all the way from O'Hare Airport." She slips him a fifty-dollar bill and sees Tom off at the curb.

Back in the office, A.J. announces to all of us that her day on Dodson Street is winding down as well. She wants to head home, get some rest and return early for another day of organizing and planning for the success of Dodson Street School and A.J. Hoyt Technologies. She announces to Lee and Dannie, our heads of marketing that they had better come up with a logo to represent this new venture because she plans to put it on the school front, the hardware store we are currently in, tee-shirts for the students, letterhead and any other form of communication. She wants it to be bold and symbolic of hope and worth.

Me, Terry and all the rest of our team watch as our fearless leader turns, walks back out of the office entrance and gets into the backseat of her town car.

"What do you think about all this, Terry?" I ask Terry with a new found comfort.

"I'm a skeptic, Alex. I didn't like this idea from the beginning but I do like the idea of keeping my job. If A.J.'s wanting to gamble, I'm going to play."

With that, I feel the tightened chest and stomach muscles that had been in anxious knots all day loosen and relax . . . just a little bit.

The day ticks away filled with phone calls and e-mails and investigation. No time for a proper lunch. There is no place to pick up a sandwich around here anyway. In my research I learn of opportunities in which the students can enter nationwide competitions that relate to creative application of ideas. It impresses me that a few major corporations have stepped up to offer ways in which developing minds can share their inventions, their poetry, their writing, their music, their art. I am happy to know that other corporations are venturing into the capital of children. No doubt that they, too, are offering such opportunities in the hopes of unveiling the next new great idea in their industry. Great minds lead to great possibilities.

Rays of late afternoon sunlight bounce off the windows of the school and across my desk distracting me from my work. I follow the path of light and catch Mark alone in the empty school parking lot carrying a brightly wrapped gift to his car. My heart soars at the sight of him and without hesitation I salute my diligently working team, leave our office and head across the street.

"Hey Mark, wait up. Where are you going? Would you like to come over and check out what we have done to the old hardware store?" I call to him walking quickly toward the parking lot.

"Well hello, again." Mark replies back with a broad grin.

"I would love to. Just let me put this gift in the car."

"Who's the lucky recipient of that lavish box?" I inquire curiously.

"It's for Jamal. Well, actually it is for Jamal's mother. Today is her birthday and he really wants to give her something special. So, I told him I would help him out a bit. I am going to drop it by his home after while."

Speechless and yet so moved by his compassionate ways, I gently take Mark by his free hand and release a long slow kiss on each knuckle. He takes care of so many. All I want at this moment is to take care of him. Slightly caught off guard, he gasps for air and then pulls me closer. We stand breathless, face-to-face, lost in gazes burning deep, melting into each other. A longing power within forces me to thrust forward into Mark unleashing a savory exchange of heated kisses. We cave onto the hood of his car in uncontrolled passion engulfed in desire for each others lips and tongue, neck, earlobes... and.

The sound of a police siren in the distance pulls Mark out of the entangled embrace and into the reality of being in the parking lot of his school. He runs his fingers through my tousled hair and says breathlessly, "Look what you've done to me."

I stare back happily and take Mark's hand again, unfold all five fingers and find an opening in my suit coat, place it where Mark can feel the wild beat of a heart that is falling madly in love.

"Ahh, not now." I whisper and reach down for the cell phone that is gently vibrating in my pocket and am surprised again to find Terry nervously questioning me on the other end.

"Yes, Terry. I am fine. I'm in the lot next to the school helping Mark Tandem load up his car. Sorry to worry you. I will call you later." I retort returning the phone to my suit pocket.

Overhearing the exchange, Mark asks me, "What do you mean, you will call Terry later? I thought we were going over to check out the new and improved office of A.J. Hoyt Technologies."

Stepping around to the passenger side of Mark's car, I open the door and get in replying, "You know Mark, I want to see the look on Jamal's face when he sees what you have done for him. I would like to come along. We can check out the new office digs tomorrow."

We drive east toward the Dan Ryan expressway, passing under train tracks and by busy liquor stores, a currency exchange, a boarded up grocery and a health clinic. We turn down a street that appears forgotten, even more so than Dodson Street. Bedraggled adults lurk on vacant stair steps like ghosts with emptiness in their eyes. Unlike any area I have ever driven through in my beloved city, this neighborhood causes me to become anxious thinking about the children that had been sent home from their nurturing school to such a horrendous environment. I grab hold of Marks hand to steady my nerves just as he pulls his hatchback up to the curb. He turns off the engine and looks over at me. "We're here."

I unfasten the seat belt and get out without saying a word. I don't have any words to say. The hollow neighborhood, the decrepit building, the waiflike older men and the dreamless younger boys in hooded sweatshirts concealing their images sitting idle on concrete stoops make me want to cry. Wandering thoughts of hopelessness and despair paint permanent mental images of the destiny awaits Jamal. I follow silently up the steps past the men and boys who, like statues, don't even flinch as we walk by.

Winding up a barely lit stairwell past crooked mailboxes, cracked and broken light fixtures, Mark and I reach the third floor and knock gently. From within, a fine scent of pasta sauce permeates through the crack under the door as Jamal's familiar voice shouts, "Mr. T, is that you?"

The door flies open and again Jamal flings himself

into the arms of his adored teacher. Slightly hidden behind the brightly wrapped gift, I feel a little out of place but am soon welcomed with a friendly "Yo." I hand the gift over to Jamal and he welcomes us into his tiny home. It is stark, adorned with a few furniture pieces covered with loose floral fabric. The only picture in view frames a much younger Jamal grinning toothless from ear to ear.

"Thanks so much for bringing the gift! You wrapped it so swanky, Mr. T." He says running off to give the pot on the stove a stir.

"I'm making my mama her birthday dinner. She loves spaghetti and I love to make it! I am the best spaghetti chef in the building. Wanna' try some?" Neither Mark nor I could deny the enthusiastic offer and accept the meal from the sixth grader graciously.

"This is delicious, Jamal." I compliment after the first bite. The sauce is spicy and sweet. The noodles are even al dente. I am impressed.

"Thank you. We love the Ragu." Replies Jamal flashing a bright ear-to-ear grin. Mark smiles back, proudly grabs his student and rubs a fist around his scalp of matted out-grown preteen hair. Side by side on the sagging old sofa, the two horse around giving shoulder slugs, joking and laughing as I look on admiring their comfortable presence together. How could one man be so lovable, caring, outgoing? Jamal leans his head on Mark's shoulder and looks up at the ceiling.

"Thank you both so much for coming by. Not just for the present but for being here. It feels like me and mama have a real nice family with you two here."

Mark and I smile at each other and then there is a knock at the door. "That can't be mama. She's got a key." Jamal stands and walks to the dead bolt. "Who's there?" He hollers.

From the hall outside the tiny apartment booms an ever feared, "It's the Chicago police. May we come in?"

Two large black police officers enter the apartment and remove their caps.

"Is this the home of Estrella Benson?" The one officer asks Mark.

"Yes, it is. This is her son Jamal. I am his school teacher."

"May we speak with you for a moment in the hallway sir?" The officer asks Mark motioning out of the room.

Jamal and I sit alone listening to mumbling voices on the other side of the closed door. Jamal is wringing his wrists. His brow is furrowed as his eyes are squeezed tight. My heart has stopped in shock and fear. I am frozen and unable to go over and sit next to Jamal. He is so alone even with me in the room.

The door opens and Mark enters. He looks right

through me, empty and pale. His eyes are moist. Jamal doesn't see Mark as he kneels at the base of the sofa but he knows he is there.

"Jamal," Mark says softly pulling the boys face to his. "Look at me, son. It's your mama. She was crossing the street and was hit by a van just a few blocks away from here. They tried to save her but there was nothing anybody could do."

"No, no, no, not my mama. Not on her birthday. I didn't even get to give her that pretty present." He sobs. "Where is she?"

"They took her to over to Cook County hospital." Mark answers.

"I need to see her. I need to see my mama." Jamal cries.

So we take him to say goodbye.

Chapter 25
Sitting In A Pew

I blast through the door of our apartment. Chrissy is sitting on the sofa, school papers strewn about, her laptop grade book open in her lap. It is late, almost eleven. She sees my bloodshot eyes and my cheeks caked with dried tears, and says nothing as I crumple down next to her. She strokes my hair and tries to calm me with a tender hush. My sobbing is inconsolable. After a while, I sit up a bit and look at Chrissy with bleary eyes.

"It was just awful. I can't even believe this day. I am a wreck." I confide between heaving gasps.

"What happened?"

Trying to muster up words to describe the situation that had just unfolded, I stammer with the story of Jamal's mother's birthday gift, the special dinner and the policeman's knock at the apartment door. That is when I lose it again and fall into the cradle of Chrissy's arms shaking uncontrollably.

"It was a hit and run, Chrissy, on her birthday." I choke out. "To make matters worse, I think I might know who did it."

"How on earth could you come to that conclusion, Alex? You don't know anyone who would be driving down in that neighborhood." She rebukes in my defense.

"There was an eye witness." I say. "The van that hit her had a Jamaican flag on the side door."

"Okay?" Chrissy poses in query.

"I know a Jamaican woman who drives a van of the same description."

"Who is she?"

I hesitate, uncomfortable placing a name with a crime and then I tell her, "Cherry. Cherry Belafonté. I know her from the soup kitchen at church."

"Does she volunteer with you?"

"No. She drives around the city and picks up homeless people from the street and brings them for dinner."

"Wow. That's admirable. She doesn't sound like someone who would be involved in a hit and run." Chrissy surmises.

"I know, but there's more." I feel sick exposing that I know more about Cherry than I should but it is by chance. "I am pretty certain that she has been a poacher and of all places, I think she's pitching camp in the old shoe factory that belongs to Mark's family. I saw the van there."

"Oh no. That's not good at all." Chrissy confirms. "But it would explain why the van was down in the area where Jamal's mom was hit."

"I know."

We sit together for some time and then Chrissy asks me, "Where is Jamal now?"

I sit up and shudder, "His mother was all he had. He didn't have anywhere to go. He's with Mark at his house. The poor child is in shock. He's so scared and sad. It is just awful."

Chrissy walks over to the island and grabs our only bottle of whiskey. She dusts it off and pours me a shot.

"Here. You need this." She says.

I toss it back and swallow hard. The heat burning down my throat equals the burning in my eyes.

I let out a sigh and close my eyes.

"What's going to happen to him?"

I look exhaustedly into Chrissy's warm eyes and reply honestly, "I don't know."

"What are you going to do about Cherry Belafonté?"

"I don't know."

****

"Walk Like an Egyptian" the upbeat and much too early ringtone goes off waking me to a pounding head in a fully dehydrated state from all the tears shed. On the other end of the line is Terry who just picked up my text from the night before.

"I am so so sorry about this Alex." He says clearing his throat at a loss for any other words. I am in awe of his tone as I am just getting used to seeing and hearing Terry's more sensitive side.

"It's just tragic, Terry. I can't believe Jamal is going to be alone." I say choking back tears.

"Look Alex, I am surprised you went to this child's home." Terry says expressing concern for me for the first time since I have known him. "I mean really, we are all working in unchartered and unsafe waters down on Dodson Street even with the crew of security that A.J. has brought in. What are you thinking venturing off the grid like that?"

The phone is silent. I hesitate and then freely admit to having gone to Jamal's home because it meant more time with Mark Tandem. Silence envelops the phone once again until I inquire if Terry has lost the connection.

"No Alex. I'm here, just speechless." He admits and I wonder if my expressed interest in Mark feels like a curve ball being thrown at Terry. He continues, however, without a word of judgment. "I am trying to imagine how hard it must have been for you to see Mark go through all that with Jamal last night. I am truly sorry. Will you be coming in to the office this morning?" Terry's empathy shocks me further but I am grateful for it. "Yes. I will be there. I am going to check in with Mark and Jamal and then I'll be at the office."

Terry is glad to hear that I am able to remain focused during such a difficult time and he reminds me that he has the meeting with IDEA at the old shoe factory later in the morning as well.

"Thank you, Terry, for understanding, and well, for everything." I say and hang up.

I reel back on the bed with tears welling and stare up at the blank ceiling wondering how life can be so full of twists and turns. It is hard to get a handle on the events of the last twenty-four hours. I can't imagine what the next twenty-four hold in store. It is painful to imagine Jamal without his mother and it is impossible to imagine doing anything or going anywhere without Mark Tandem.

Anxiety takes hold of my gut to the point of nausea and instead of grabbing breakfast, I grab the car keys and venture down to Pearson Street. It has been a couple of weeks since visiting with Reverend Hummel and I really feel a need to check in with her. Pulling into the lot of the Pearson Street Church, I begin to calm down immediately. The nerve tying knots that had been working overtime in the last day start to ease just a bit as God's presence takes center stage.

The pews in the church are padded with soft red velvet cushions, sunlight illuminates the sanctuary through stained glass designs that dance on the walls and ceiling and warm my troubled core. I inhale the sacred incensed air into my lungs as the church bells ring with the strike of the hour, the whole world seems to slow down for a moment and I retreat into the holy space.

With eyes closed, thoughts of simpler times fill my

mind. Memories of going to church and Sunday school and brunch afterward with my family force a hint of a smile.

"I have wondered about you, Alex True." Reverend Hummel says tenderly settling into the pew next to me. In an instant, my heart expands and tears flow simultaneously. The reverend says, "Don't say a word. Just pray."

So I do as I am told and Reverend Hummel places her hand on mine. Together we sit in peace and I pray for Jamal. I also ask for guidance to help find justice for his mother whose death is linked to the driver of the van with the Jamaican flag. The litany of prayers goes on for Cherry, for Mark, for Dodson Street and for the common denominator to them all- for me. With another chime of the bells outside, I turn to Reverend Hummel, give her a warm embrace of gratitude and say, "Thank you. I needed to be here with you this morning."

"I am always here," She says placing both palms over her heart. "and here." Then she makes a fist with her right hand extending her thumb and pinkie like a phone along her cheek and reaches into the pocket of her blazer with her left hand. She places her business card next to me on the seat of the pew. "When you are ready to talk, please call."

Her gentleness grounds me, and leaves me feeling cared for in a way that is both spiritual and motherly. I nod and muster up a fractured, "Thank you, reverend. I will call."

As I step out of the church with a clearer head, a sense of urgency comes upon me. I am overcome by the realization that the last time I walked out of this church, I was thinking about Virgil and Cherry Belafonté and here I am again in anguish over thoughts of her. There is so much that needs to be done down on Dodson Street today but it will all have to wait. I need to find Cherry.

Chapter 26

Virgil

"Reverend Hummel, it's me Alex True." I say into my Bluetooth not five minutes after leaving the church.

"Oh hello, Alex. I had a feeling I'd hear from you sooner than later." She answers.

"Well, I really do want to talk with you but not right now. Instead, I need to get ahold of Virgil. It's an emergency." I plead as Dolores and I sit in traffic on Lake Shore Drive. She gives me an address and a phone number. I call. There is no answer so I type the street number into Dolores and take off to find my friend.

I pull up to a three flat with an open metal gate out front. There is a sidewalk that leads around back to a garage where gospel music is pumping and I hear a familiar voice belting it out in harmony with Yolanda Adams. The music guides me to Virgil. I see him as he ducks behind the hood of and old van just as I round the corner. Tools are lined up neatly at his feet and he bends down to grab a monkey wrench. His eye catches me. He drops the wrench and freezes as the music plays on with out him. The smell of oil and gasoline singe my nostrils and make me think of the old auto shop in my high school.

Virgil shakes off the shock and his big, black, oily body jumps over the tools to engulf me in a greasy embrace. "By golly, Alex, what in heaven's name are you doin' here?" He steps back and looks at me, assessing my bloodshot eyes, my uneasy countenance, my stifled breathing.

"Is somethin' wrong with the reverend?" He asks me wide-eyed with concern.

"No Virg. She's fine. She gave me your address though."

"Is something wrong with you?" He asked. "Did somebody hurt you, Alex? I swear on my Christian mama's grave that if somebody hurt you I just might have to use these guns of mine." He says rubbing his massive muscles up and down in a protective threat.

"It's not me Virgil. You need to help me find Cherry."

"Cherry?" He questions and his eyes lighten up.

"Yes. I think she is in trouble." I say and confide in him the news about Jamal, Jamal's mother and the van with the Jamaican flag on the side door. The color in Virgil's face turns from mahogany to muddy gray as he takes my arm and walks me around the open hood to the side of the van where we see the Jamaican flag that the police are searching for emblazoned on the door.

"She told me that it wasn't running right. So I said I would check it out." Virgil says shaking his head. " I just can't believe this. It's been years since I've had any kind of doins' with the cops. Are you sure, Alex?"

"I'm sure. There was an eyewitness and the description fits. I also know that Cherry's van has been down in the area of the hit and run in recent weeks. I've seen it there." The silence between Virgil and I bears the weight of an avalanche. I can hardly catch my breath as I gasp for Virgil to lift the heaviness.

"Well, there's only one thing to do." He confirms as he closes the hood of the van and turns off his Yolanda. "Let's make the phone call."

The police arrive within minutes of our call. I can see the concern in Virgil's eyes as they question him about Cherry and the van. Virgil tells them that she is working and doesn't know where or how to reach her but that she is returning by bus later in the day to pick up the van. I hear him tell the officers that he doesn't believe that she is responsible for the hit and run.

Then one of the officers says to Virgil, "We need you to come down to the station with us. We have some more questions for you." I feel sick as I look at Virgil and I can see a ghost from his past sweep across his body. The tension in his arms and neck shows that he does not wish to return to the clandestine past that he has worked so hard to distance himself from. He picks up a rag from the top of his toolbox and begins to wipe the grease from his hands. I watch as he twists it with the madness of a man wringing the neck of a chicken. He grunts and grits his teeth. The police wait and he whips the wretched rag at the wall of the garage. He slumps his shoulders and goes with them out to the street.

As he is getting into the squad car, I tell Virgil that I will meet him at the police station. He nods, sinks back into the seat and they drive away. Two officers and a detective are running tests on the front of the van and I walk away in a daze wondering what I just did to Virgil.

My phone vibrates in my pant pocket. I see that Mark is calling.

"How's Jamal?"

"He's resting. How are you?" Mark asks.

"I don't know if words can describe how I am feeling right now." I confess fighting back tears once more.

"I know what you mean. It's been rough."

"Mark?"

"What is it?"

"I have something I need to tell you." I say hesitantly. "I found the van . . . the van that hit Jamal's mother."

"Oh my God. What? Where are you?" He nearly screams into the phone.

"I am headed to the Seventh District Police Station on West Sixty-Third." I answer matter-of-factly.

"Are you alone? Why are you going there?" He asks me in increasing panic.

"I'm going there to be with Virgil." I tell him.

"Who on earth is Virgil?" He asks me exasperated.

"He's my friend. We volunteer together at the soup kitchen."

"And . . . "

"And he was working on the van that hit Jamal's mother." I say.

"What the?" The phone goes silent in the melee of our discussion. "What on earth was your friend doing working on that van?"

"I'm not sure, but I believe he is in love with the woman who drives it." I tell Mark as I hear the click of Mark starting his car.

"Who is this woman?" He pleads.

"Cherry. Cherry Belafonté"

Chapter 27
Tell Them

Mark and I both pull up to the Seventh District Police Station at the same time. He is out of breath and perspiring. I am out of breath and gasping for air. Together we enter the station to find Virgil sitting next to an officer who is tapping away into the system on a desktop computer.

"Hey Alex." Virgil says to me seeming more under control than I would have expected. "This is Officer Jones. He is just taking down some information. I wish I knew more about Cherry but we are just in the early stages of getting to know each other. Didn't you say you had seen her somewhere nearby?" He asks me.

I feel a lump in my throat as I realize that I must divulge the secret information that I have withheld from Mark. "I think," I begin to explain hesitantly. "That she has been trespassing on the grounds of Tandem Footing. It is an empty shoe factory off Dodson Street."

"What?" Mark exclaims in disbelief. "Why didn't you say anything to me?"

"Because I wasn't sure. I saw the van there the other morning when I went to check on the property but I didn't see who was driving it. I also didn't see anyone in the building just in the lot."

"How do you know she drives the van that hit Jamal's mother? How does Virgil know her?" Mark asks emphatically.

"She brings homeless guests to our soup kitchen in that same van. She parks it out front of the church on Monday nights."

Nobody says a word. The only sound in the room is the tapping of the officer's fingers on the keyboard and then a dispatch comes in.

"They're bringing in Ms. Belafonté and they've got fibers that match the victim's clothing on the front bumper of that van." Says the officer as he steps away from his desk and pours himself a cup of caffeine.

The wait for Cherry's arrival is interminable. Mark and I do not make any eye contact. We stare at the tiles on the floor and listen to the nervous rock of Virgil's squeaky chair as we tolerate the annoying slurp of the officer's coffee. Mark lets out an exhausted sigh and announces that he needs to make a phone call.

"Who do you have to call?" I ask.

"My buddy, Liam."

"The cop?" I ask.

"Yeah." Mark says as he turns to talk to his friend in private. It seems odd that Mark can't wait to talk to him but then again, so much of this day seems odd. Mark's hands are shaking when he returns. He sits and plants his forehead into

232

his palms. He whispers to himself and I barely decipher the words, "This is a disaster."

"What is going on Mark? Is there something Liam knows about Cherry?" I ask in a whisper.

"I was just trying to make a little extra money. . . to help cover the property taxes on the factory. . ." Mark whispers as if he is having a dialog with himself. "Oh shit. I think I'm gona' puke." He blurts out and runs to the nearest men's room. I can hear him convulsing over the toilet as the door slowly shuts behind him.

My palms sweat as my own heartbeat launches in the confusion. Virgil looks at me and I shrug my shoulders in ignorance as Mark reappears from the men's room and stops at the drinking fountain.

"You okay, man?" Virgil asks and holds out a stick of gum to Mark. He scoots his chair a few feet away from us to get a better view of a couple of prostitutes bickering in the opposite corner of the station.

"I don't know." Mark says pealing off the silver wrapper and popping it in his mouth. He chews it real hard to get the juices flowing and confesses that he might know what Cherry's van was doing on his factory property the morning I saw it there.

"I figured she was a squatter, just using it as a free place to call home." I say quietly to Mark.

"That's probably true." He agrees. "But she is also

running stuff."

"What? What the hell does that mean?" I ask.

"Liam and I had a deal." He whispers more softly so Virgil can't hear.

"You made a deal with a cop?" I ask as thoughts in my head start to spin.

"I needed the money and Liam promised that nobody would ever know."

"Know what?" I demand as wild scenes from The Godfather flash through my mind.

Mark is about to divulge his sin when a husky Jamaican trill blows through the glass door entrance.

"Virgeel. What day doin' to me? Virgeel innocent I am. You know, mon." She shouts filling the lobby area with her Caribbean spirit. "Tell dem Virgeel. Tell dem. I was wit you, mon. Last night. You done take me to Kentucky Fried, mon. You drove me. We sat hours eatin' dem biscuits an' honey."

Virgil nods his head agreeing with Cherry as they take her into another room. The officer asks Virgil if he can prove that they were together at the Kentucky Fried Chicken during the time of the incident and the look on his face goes blank. After a moment, Mark and I notice Virgil reach for his wallet. In it he pulls out a small receipt with a victorious smile and says, "Here is your evidence."

Mark and I both buckle with the news. "Well, if Cherry wasn't behind the wheel then who was?" He asks me as if I would know.

"I think that Cherry should be brought out here." I suggest to the officer. He calls for her and she is brought back into the area where we are all seated. She takes the chair next to Virgil, smooths out her skirt, crosses her legs, arches her back proudly and adjusts the red plastic flower behind her ear.

"Now dat you treatin' me like a lady, I might be answerin' dem questions betta'." She says in the full elegance of her dialect.

"Ms. Belafonté, your van was involved in a hit and run accident that killed a woman yesterday evening. Virgil, here confirms that you were with him at Kentucky Fried Chicken and not in your van at the time of the accident. Is this correct?" The officer asks seeking clarification.

"Dat is so. I feelin' great sadness for da woman." Cherry says conveying her grief.

"Who then was behind the wheel of your van?" He asks her point blank.

"Maybe Mista Johnny. He done sleep in da van all day long. I work as a nanny 'til late in de afta' noon. He like de sofa in de back." Cherry explains. Virgil and I make eye contact at the mention of Johnny's name and we both know.

Cherry continues. "Virgeel done ask me to go to

dinna. I left da van and done go wit Virgeel. Dem keys is always beneat da mat on de floor. When I return de van done been bout' where I left it but Mista Johnny he gone."

"I see." The officer acknowledges the veritable story and continues to type away into the system on his computer. "Can anyone here provide information on the whereabouts of Mister Johnny?"

Both Virgil and I respond, "He comes to the church soup kitchen on Monday nights." Then I add, "But Cherry brings him."

"Yes dat es true. I pick up Mista Johnny on da Sout end of State Street. Dems his neck o da woods." Cherry confirms.

"Okay. Ms. Belafonté your van is being impounded as evidence. You are going to have to pay a fine and go to court for operating an uninsured vehicle. We will also need to have you come in and identify Mister Johnny. So, please leave your contact information and we will be in touch."

The four of us rise to leave the surreal scene. Virgil takes Cherry by the hand and pulls her close as they exit ahead of Mark and me. I watch as he opens a cab door for Cherry and acknowledge him with a partial wave as he climbs in. I turn to Mark, he gives me a hopeless stare and slumps down on the step of the police station. His shoulders heave as he puts his head in his hands once more.

"I just needed some extra money." He sighs.

"Tell me what Liam got you into." I say as I collapse on the step next to him and contemplate the possibility of our whole world unraveling.

"He was paying me cash to store his stuff." Mark says.

"What kind of stuff?" I ask.

"I never asked but I think I know."

"Okay, so. . . " I pry.

"Confiscated stuff. Stolen goods, things he impounds. I think he's on the take but I don't know for sure. He just told me that he was giving Cherry cash to deliver for him."

"Oh my God." I respond in shock.

"He told me that she had no idea what was in the boxes though. She was just the runner. He's paid her a few times to haul stuff over to some shop near State and Roosevelt South of The Loop."

"That's probably where she picked up Johnny."

"What a mess." I admit.

"Is there anything still stashed at the factory?" I ask nervously.

"No. Liam told me he unloaded all he had. I don't even want to know if he just moved it or if he really did dump it all. I just wish I never agreed to the deal in the first place. Jamal's mom might still be alive." Mark says as his posture goes limp over his knees.

"Don't do this to yourself, Mark. It was an accident

and you have no control over the fact that Johnny stole Cherry's van." I say trying to lift some of Mark's burden.

We sit in silence as a few people file by us and into the police station. I decide that none of my colleagues can know about Mark's deal with Liam. It could jeopardize our entire project. The thought of keeping all this to myself is heavy but I will do it in order to protect Mark.

"I am so sad." He says.

"Me too." I agree. On so many levels am I sad. This news of Mark's deal with Liam makes me wonder what other secrets Mark is hiding and then I realize that he might be wondering the same thing about me. He turns to face me, and several strands of his hair fall across his face. He juts his lip out and blows them out of his eyes with a defeated breath.

"I am exhausted and devastated for Jamal." He says. "Finding Johnny won't bring his mom back. All night long, I held him and he just begged for her. Of all the parents at our school, she was the one who always took the time to pitch in, come to his plays. She brought leftovers from Taco Bell to his class. She did everything she could to show us her appreciation for helping her raise her boy. I just can't believe she's gone."

"I know. I am so sorry." I say.

"If only I hadn't cut that deal with Liam." He mumbles again.

"Listen," I say. "You learned a serious lesson about Liam. I can only imagine how it must feel to trust a good friend and then see this kind of thing happen."

"This just sucks." Mark admits. "But I know I need to move forward, for Jamal."

I toss his sweaty tangled hair out of the way and lean my head into his.

"I think you need to go home and get some sleep." I say knowing that fatigue can be treacherous when emotions are running hot. "Get some rest. Eat a warm meal. Take a shower. You'll be able to deal with all this much better." I take Mark's fist and brush my lips across the outer side. "I'll check in with you tomorrow."

A nerve jarring cacophony comes from across the street where two teenage boys are kicking an empty can back and forth as they meander down the empty sidewalk. We hear them laughing and one shouts out, "Check out the two dudes gettin' it on over there in front of the police station!" They point at Mark and me and the words hit like a bulls-eye to a target.

"Don't pay any attention to those punks, Alex." Mark reassures me. "They don't know what they're seeing."

"You can say that again." I reply, turn to him once more and plant an impassioned kiss on his lips to spite our onlookers.

"Ewe, nasty business!" Squeal the naïve youth across

the way. Their reaction fills me with that twisted pleasure I find when watching others squirm beneath my guise. Mark however, looks at me and benign to my hidden intention grabs my waist and pulls me close with no ploy to cause any reaction in anyone other than me. His breath tastes of cinnamon gum. I devour the spicy flavor and forget about the ruckus coming from across the road and Mark's secret.

Chapter 28
Going For A Walk

"Great news!" Terry exclaims bursting through the door of our new office. "They love it!"

I see Claudius Parker and Bev Davies trailing in Terry's wake. Claudius and Bev are the two who pitched IDEA to us and we bought their enthusiasm hook, line and sinker.

"We are just swinging by after a morning down at the old shoe factory and with just a few upgrades and other adjustments it should be ready to go!" He continues.

"It has great proximity to the city and the expressway and," Claudius clears his throat like a drum roll to carry on. " . . . to Dodson Street School."

"What are you saying?" I ask grateful that no evidence of Liam's wrong doing was discovered on their tour of the factory.

"What Claudius is saying is that we would like Dodson Street School to be our first official account. Let's call it neighborly good will." Bev says with a wink.

"We'll take their existing desks and chairs and redesign them for all of the amazing technology that we hear the school will be receiving." Says Claudius.

"You can't afford to do that for free." I say, pointing

out the simple economics. "We are banking on IDEA to be making money on the front end, not giving it away."

"Relax Alex. Shit, I can never tell which side of the fence you are on, both literally and figuratively?" Terry yaps at me.

"That was uncalled for, Terry." I strike back at him trying to keep my professional cool. "Listen, I just want everyone to succeed these days. Tell me your plan, Claudius."

"It's simple, really." He says. "Terry suggested it. We do the job for the school and word gets out. We figure with all the plans you've got for the school that there will be a lot of attention drawn to it and that leads to great p.r."

"He's got a great plan from a marketing standpoint." Dannie chimes in from his drafting table in the corner of the big room.

"Then I guess I jumped the gun." I say apologetically. "It appears I'm on both sides of the fence, Terry." I throw back a jab at his rude humor and attempt to make up for my anxious leap at Claudius and Bev.

A.J., who has been quietly studying building specs strewn all over the table next to me, removes her glasses from the end of her nose and gets up. She walks over to Claudius and Bev.

"Thank you both for your generosity. Welcome to the neighborhood." She says shaking both of their hands.

242

"Thank you A.J." Bev says. "Is there a chance that we may take a look at the school? We would like to see just what they have and we want to meet our new neighbors." Bev and Claudius look at me for direction but my emotions are so raw that I just can't force myself to go into the school yet.

I look at Terry and think what a fool he can be and what a fool I was to think that his recent kinder self was anything more than a passing phase. Then like a chameleon, he surprises me again.

"Why don't the three of us finish the neighborhood tour?" He offers to Claudius and Bev. "I'll introduce you to Mr. Bluberry the school principal. He will be thrilled to meet his new and very generous neighbors."

A.J. and I say goodbye to them and return to the long table covered with papers and maps. Juan Carlos runs over and hands her a pill and a glass of water. I realize the frequency of her medications has increased and decide to ask, "Are you okay?"

"What do you mean?" She responds.

"The pills, A.J. You're taking them more often."

She brushes off my concern by turning a question to me. "Do you have a big family?" She asks me out of the blue as she swallows more water to wash down the pill.

"Well, I have my parents and brothers back in Ohio." I answer popping my brow to her curious inquiry. "Why do you ask?"

"I just hope you make an effort to stay in touch with them. That's all." She says and I wonder if the diagnosis behind her pill taking is causing her to evaluate life for some reason. There is definitely more to her question than meets the eye. So I close my laptop and set it to the side, turn in my chair and look directly into her eyes. "How about you A.J.? Does your family stay in touch with you?" I ask knowing very little of the family that she never references.

"Ahhh. . . the heirs to my throne. . . I only hear from them when they need something. They're so busy with their own families, their own successful careers." She says lost in a distant haze. "Juan Carlos helped me become "friends" with my grandchildren on Facebook just so I can watch them grow from afar but honestly, they don't have time for me. They don't know anything about my life right now." She says as sadness crosses her face.

I find it hard to imagine that the children of this remarkable woman are so disengaged from her world but then I wonder, too, if somehow on her climb to corporate power and wealth if she failed in the role of mother.

"I'm sorry to hear that. They don't know what they're missing." I place my hand on her shoulder. "Look at it this way," I say, "You don't have time for them either with the school and the neighborhood taking off. There are a lot of other people who really care for you and need you now."

244

She smiles, shakes off the emotion and sits up straight and strong planting her glasses at the end of her nose in a take charge way.

"Okay, enough wallowing for now. Let's get to it. I want new doors, new windows, fresh landscape and a sense of connectedness with the school and this old hardware store." She snaps as I whip my laptop back open and start typing away.

"How about a brick crosswalk connecting the entrance of the school with the entrance of our front door." She proposes, hoping for more of a campus feel. "I also want to know if the team has made any progress on a new logo for us to share with the school."

My list of responsibilities from A.J. grows and I am thankful that the items on the list are all achievable with one exception. "If you don't mind me saying, A.J., I believe that the children should create the design for the logo. We could have them submit entries and then have a company wide vote." I suggest.

"I love it!" She exclaims adjusting her purple cat-eye glasses and straightening out the sleeves of her even brighter purple cardigan. "You have wonderful ideas, Alex."

Before being able to thank A.J. for the kind thoughts, the office door blows open scaring us both. Tom Mackey arrives like a bull in a china shop, dropping files and screaming into his Bluetooth.

"Where is my new desk?" He asks between huffs and puffs and yeses and hell no's. I escort my boss to a corner desk with a different kind of window view than he is used to. His new vista is Dodson Street School and the surrounding vacant buildings- a far cry from the shore of Lake Michigan. The only water in his sights on Dodson Street will be the water cooler in the corner.

"I think you are going to grow to love it here, Tom." I say. "Just think how much you'll save on parking alone!"

"In fact," adds A.J. "you are going to come with me right now. I want you to meet Michael Bluberry and the rest of the staff across the street. We need to announce to the students that there is going to be a little logo contest that Alex and I have been planning."

With A.J. and Tom out of the office, it is quiet enough for me to work on the to-do list from A.J. Arrangements are made for new door and window measurements to be taken, ordered and installed. Check. The landscape firm agrees to be out next week. Check. Then, brick pavers are going to be laid straight across the street joining the two front doors. Check.

I stare out the window at the little school and wonder how Mark is managing with Jamal. I decide to call Rosie Fishers to see if she knows anything about the poor child's situation.

"He's at Mr. Tandem's home right now. He is staying there with Mr. Tandem's mother until a relative can be found. Mr. Tandem is here at work. He felt he needed to come in to be with his students today." I can't believe what she is saying considering how strung out he was at the police station yesterday.

"Thank you, Rosie." I say and hang up the phone visualizing Rosie sitting in that dreary office with the broken window blinds tapping away at her typewriter . . . and that archaic ditto machine. I shout to the empty office, "We are going to replace that ditto machine! No more Paulie Blue Hands! I am ordering them an office computer, a fax machine, a copier and some decent window treatments! Check!"

Juan Carlos peers in from around the corner and asks me, "Are you okay in there, Alex?"

"Yep, I'm fine. Can you get me an office supplies catalog? I have some shopping to do." Juan Carlos brings me the catalog and a cup of coffee.

"I can place orders for you Alex. Just tell me what you need." I jot down the items for him to order and decide that it is time for some fresh air. Cup of coffee in hand, I head for the door feeling a need to explore the surroundings a bit and knowing that the security team is scattered about and on post makes the thought of a neighborhood stroll appealing.

Temperatures are unseasonably cool for early May so

I throw on the light tan topcoat that goes so beautifully with the days ensemble of taupe and yellow silk. My wardrobe, which I snagged straight off Ebay, is the only thing light about me today. Inside I feel heavy. I have never been so close to witnessing tragedy as I did with Jamal last night. Somehow, I have managed to pull it together as I notice my impressive figure taking to the broken sidewalk in the reflection of the storefront windows.

The foot tour of Mark Tandem's universe takes me past building after empty building, but the feeling is different here than the feeling that I got driving through Jamal's neighborhood. There are no people moping about, no empty eyes or stone faced hopeless creatures. The area has been truly vacated by all life form except for the children and staff at the school. Even the air lacks the life that the scent of early spring brings. There is no essence of wet grass or budding leaves. Instead, I breathe in a cool, old dustiness from piles of gathered trash packed into the alcoves of doorways and windows along the street.

As I wipe away city grime to peer into store windows it feels more like looking into exhibits in a museum. A deli with its once busy counter sits empty, hollow with ghosts of a busier time. A one-time pharmacy all gated up houses old faded cardboard displays of Pepto-Bismol and Exlax. I can see the tattered red leather topped swivel stools at the soda fountain and imagine Mark as a young boy ordering a root-beer float or a vanilla coke. As I forge onward, touching the door knobs and cool brick entrances to Mark's past, a sense of hope begins to override the weight of filth and despair as I think about the plans we have for the neighborhood.

Looking a few blocks south, the parking lot to the old shoe factory is just visible but something directs me and I turn down a different street where a building stands with a neon light on in front. It's Floyd's Tap. I chuckle and remember Mark bringing me here and spilling his soul over some cold pints of Guinness.

Just beyond the pub I am surprised to see a couple of neatly kept bungalows. As I approach even closer, an older woman walks out of one to pick up a newspaper. I nod and she asks me, "Are you lost?"

I stop and explain about A.J. Hoyt Technologies venturing with the grade school around the corner and the woman says, "Oh you must be Alex True. I've been hearing about you. My name is Mary Jane Tandem. My son is Mark."

I freeze. The prospect of meeting Mark's mother is not even on my morning radar. I knew she lived close to the school but never imagined this close. There is no pre-scripted dialogue or even expectation for this moment. I hold out a hand to her and say, "Yes, ma'am. I am Alex. It's a pleasure to meet you."

Still at a loss for words, I stand and stare at Mary Jane

noticing the striking similarities that she shares with her handsome son.

"Would you like to come in? I have a cobbler in the oven and it is just about ready to come out." Still baffled, I look on down the street as if accepting the offer for blueberry cobbler might throw off some important mission but then some force within me accepts the kind invitation.

Following Mary Jane up the cement steps of the front stoop and into the solid brick bungalow, I have the sensation of entering the scene of a fairy tale or a dream. The exciting thought of a thousand treasures from Mark's life hidden inside is captivating. Mary Jane turns to me and quietly whispers that Jamal is sleeping upstairs and immediately, the fairytale vision takes a different turn.

"How is he doing?" I ask feeling just heartsick for him.

"It's hard to say. He's been asleep all morning. Mark has called to check on him every hour but honestly I have had nothing to report. I am waiting for social services to come talk to him." Mary Jane explains leading me through the front living room to her pale yellow kitchen where the homey smell of her cobbler takes the edge off of the sadness of the discussion.

Mary Jane takes her teapot off of the stove and places two cups on the kitchen table. She motions me to take a seat and she pours us some tea.

"I have certainly heard your name often lately." She tells me while stirring some cubes of sugar into her cup. "More so than anyone that Mark has spent time with ever before."

Thinking that the spoon spinning in her tea would actually distract me, Mary Jane shoots me a motherly glance that is coated with questions I am all too familiar with. I imagine her wondering questions only a mother would wonder, and then some.

Feeling a heated rush to my cheeks, I quickly take a sip of the tea and hide for a moment behind the cup.

"I think it is amazing what you have convinced your company to do. More big businesses should consider venturing with schools the way that you are with Dodson Street School. It's really wonderful."

For the first time, I am hearing outside praise for the personal energy and emotion that has gone into this project.

"Thank you Mary Jane. I can't take all the credit. Your son pleaded a very convincing case to the rest of my team. Those children are fantastic and the staff works so hard. Who wouldn't want to venture with them?" I admit openly. "It's funny but I can't even envision my life without Dodson Street School in it now."

I set down the hot tea on the red checked tablecloth and turn as I hear the creak of footsteps in the other room. "Jamal." I whisper in urgency getting up and running to the child standing in the doorway. Jamal holds onto me like he will never let go.

"My mama, my mama." He shudders into me and I feel his pain pierce my gut. Mary Jane hands us each a tissue and guides us to the sofa in the living room where Jamal rests his head on my shoulder. An empty silence nearly suffocates all of us until the oven bell in the kitchen goes off.

The woman from social services arrives, and I take it as a cue to return to the office.

"It was good to meet you Mary Jane. I wish that the circumstances had been different." I say while giving Jamal a final embrace. I turn from the kitchen table and head back through the living room toward the front door stopping only briefly to admire the collection of framed school portraits of Mark that line the wall up the staircase.

Chapter 29

Assault

Out on the sidewalk in front of the Tandem's bungalow, I have a dying urge to phone home. Something about my earlier heart-to-heart conversation with A.J. and being with Mark's mother in their family home coupled with the emotions of the last twenty-four hours causes a pang of homesickness that I haven't experienced in years.

"Hi Mom, it's me. I'm okay, well sort of . . ." stifling a sob I begin to reconsider this phone call. Much of the emotion that I had unleashed with Chrissy comes forth again. My mother listens as the story unfolds between sobs across the miles. With the cellphone to my ear, I walk and talk rambling aimlessly in a haze of fatigue and drama. A car drives by but I don't look up. I hear the repetitive thump of base and then a door slams. I am oblivious and continue to walk and talk.

"I do need to see you and dad. It's been far too long since your last visit." I say into the phone longing to be consoled by them in person. "Call me with your flight plans. Thanks for listening. Love you." I hang up.

I'm not sure where I am. Another car door slams. I turn to the sound and see a lime-green Camry. I remember my frightening car chase on the day I discovered Dodson

Street School and that same sick feeling returns. Two people are on the sidewalk twenty feet from me. We make eye contact. One of them is short with long black greasy hair and a red bandanna tied in a knot on his forehead. His jeans are sagging low. He walks toward me with a low bounce. The other is my height. She has a huge bust and is the width of a linebacker. She sneers at me and rubs her palms together. I look down at my stylish shoes, step backward and whip around in a high-paced panic march that turns into a sprint away from them. I am not fast enough.

The female linebacker grabs my arm and yanks me back. I fall into her cushiony chest and she pushes me to the ground. Her friend pulls a toothpick from his mouth and flicks it on me.

"Nice day for a walk my friend." He says, sucking spit through his front teeth. "You look like a vanilla ice cream cone."

"Mmmmm." She moans. "I need to get me some vanilla ice cream."

I try to get up but the stubby dude pushes me down with his big work boot. Please God, don't let them kill me.

"What you got for us vanilla?" He asks.

"Nothing." I snarl, reach into my pocket and pull out a ten. "That's it." I fling the money onto the sidewalk.

"What you mean, you got nothin'. That suit you got's worth more than my ride." He says kicking the dirt with one

254

foot like a bull preparing to charge. His breath smells of cigarettes and alcohol.

I manage to get up slowly. They watch. Then the big woman grabs my wrist and looks me in the eye, "Give me your coat, sugar. I need me some vanilla."

In this moment I come to the abrupt realization that although God gave me some tools to do a man's job, in this case, I wilt and scream like a defeated feline in a cat fight. "Just take it!"

I whip off my gorgeous coat and throw it at her, turn and run.

"Help! Help!" I scream. I can hear their laughter in my dust. "Help!" I cross diagonally through a four-way intersection and the blast of a siren stops me in my tracks. The car pulls up and a man jumps out flashing a security i.d. I recognize it. He works for the firm that A.J. hired.

"Are you okay?" He asks as I am practically convulsing on the pavement.

"They, they, took my coat." I barely choke out.

"Who? Where are they?" He demands.

I point in the direction that I ran from and try to catch my breath as he pulls out a walkie-talkie.

"Sloan here. I need back up. We've got a two-four-zero. It's someone from Hoyt." He pipes into his dispatch. "Four blocks south and west of the red zone."

My hands are bleeding. My pant leg is torn. My

pride is shattered.

Another car pulls up. Terry gets out of the passenger side, sees that I am upright and rips into me. "What the hell are you thinking, Alex?"

Of all people to come to my rescue, why him?

"Not now, Terry. Just take me back to the office." I say.

He walks me over to the car, opens the back door and I slide in. He sits in the front next to the hired hand.

It is silent for only a moment and then he says, "I predicted something like this would happen. This whole project is just pushing too many limits. You could have gotten killed, and over what? Some pipedream?"

"I am not in the mood for this, Terry. You know what these last two days have been like for me. Get off yourself and get off me." I shriek at him with a fierce intensity that I wish I had used with the muggers.

Chapter 30
Questioning The Venture

"Oh my God. Alex are you okay?" A.J. asks and moves as quickly as she is able to meet me at the door. "Look at you. You're bleeding." She takes the cardigan off her shoulders and shrouds me in cashmere as if it is a blanket- like a mother does when one of her own is hurt. This gesture reminds me that she has children and grandchildren, although she never speaks of them.

I just stand, frozen stone cold like a statue while Juan Carlos wipes the blood from my hands with a wet napkin.

"Rrrreally Alex. What were you thinking, all alone like that?" He asks.

I still have no words.

He pulls a chair over and forces me to sit. He pours me a glass of water and pats my face with another wet washcloth.

Finally, I speak in staccato form. "I needed . . . fresh air. Went for a walk. Found the home where . . . Mary Jane Tandem is taking care of . . . Jamal. We drank . . . tea. We cried. The social worker came . . . I left . . . called my mother and . . . walked and talked and walked." I take a sip of water. "I didn't know . . . where I was. The car . . . pulled up. Two gangbangers charged . . . pushed me down. They took my coat. I ran . . . screamed for help."

"How awful, Alex." Lee says. "Now, I'm afraid."

"No kidding." Terry chimes in. "I knew moving us down here was a bad idea from the get go. It's just too dangerous."

"Hold on." I say catching my breath to smooth out my speech. "I know the neighborhood is bad but people get mugged up in Lincoln Park and out in the burbs. It was my own fault." I exhale, deflated in front of my colleagues. "I was dumb to go out like that alone."

"You aren't dumb, Alex." Dannie says. "You've just been through so much in a day that your judgment is off. It could have happened to any one of us under the type of stress you've been through."

"I still say, I told you so. This was bound to happen and I bet it'll happen again. Who knows, one of us might get shot next time." Terry belts out in fury.

"Fine. Terry, if you feel that way, I'm going to put you in charge of making sure it doesn't happen." A.J. fires back at him.

"Wha, what? What are you talking about?" Terry asks in panicky hesitation.

"I'm putting you in charge of improving security measures in the neighborhood. I'll double your raise every six months if there are no reports of criminal activity." She throws out.

"Whoa. . . " Dannie exclaims.

"You've always liked a challenge, Terry. This will be the biggest one of your career." She says but I can tell that as she looks at me she is teetering on the inside.

"Don't think about me." I tell her. "You are doing the right thing. The children, this neighborhood, this whole project is a very positive investment. You can't question your decisions just because I got a little scuffed up. This is a bump in the road."

A.J. walks over and to the window. She stands silently staring at the school across the street. Her fists are on her hips. I can tell that she is weighing her options to either fold in fear and defeat or fight for what we have started.

Juan Carlos puts down the glass that he is holding for me and looks at his watch. "Oh Shheet!" He jumps and runs to his desk. He pours another glass of water from the cooler and goes over to A.J. by the window. She takes a pill from his hand and swallows it. Watching her take the medicine makes me even more afraid.

"Look," I say attempting to belittle my incident. "I'll be fine everyone. I appreciate your concern but please get back to what you were doing."

The mood in the room shifts from shaky to supportive as my words reignite the torch of progress. Dannie goes back to his drafting board and Juan Carlos reaches for a ringing phone. Terry storms off to make a private call and I stand and announce, "I am going home . . . to sleep. . . for a long time."

"Would you like my driver to take you home?" A.J. asks.

Something inside me doesn't feel like fighting traffic so I accept her offer. "Sure, that would be great."

"Very well then. I'll let him know." She says. "Oh, listen up everyone, before Alex leaves I want you all to know that I am having Terry up the security immediately. I don't want anyone else to have to go through what Alex did today."

"Thank you." I say and I go down to the town car.

The soft dark leather seat engulfs me tight like a glove. The scent of rich leather is intoxicating, reminiscent of the old shoe factory and Mark, who knows nothing of my day. I must call him. I reach for my phone but exhaustion takes over and before I can dial, I fall asleep.

Chapter 31

Sleep

The landline startles me awake. Our apartment phone rarely rings anymore. It is almost foreign to my ears. Ouch, how did I get here? My arm aches as I reach for the receiver.

"Hello?"

"This is Officer Quinn of the Chicago Police Department. Is this Alex True?"

"Yes, it is."

"How are you? Are you resting?" He asks.

I sit up and look around with no sense of time or day first thinking that the officer is calling about Jamal's mother or Cherry but then the pain in my wrists is a reminder that he is calling to check on me. Oh my God, I was mugged!

"Yes, officer. I've been resting. Come to think of it, what time is it?"

"Two o'clock."

"What? I slept for an entire day. Zut!" I shout with surprise into the receiver.

"Relax, Alex. You've been through a lot but we need you to come in and file a report."

"Okay." I say. The thought of a second trip to the station in two days is unfathomable. I hang up the phone and notice a glass of water and peanut butter and jelly sandwich on the nightstand. My stomach growls and I devour what is left out for me. I get up and wash my face and notice that aside from my sore wrists and achy arms, I feel rested for the first time in weeks.

Out in the kitchen on the island is a note next to my cellphone. Janet and Chrissy want me to call them at work. I don't feel like talking to them now. So, I send texts to check in. I only want to speak with Mark.

I curl up on the sofa and dial. He picks up right away.

"Alex?"

"Oh Mark, I'm so embarrassed." I say.

"What? You were mugged. There's nothing to be ashamed of. If anything, I should be sorry because it happened in my neighborhood. But let's not talk about what happened now. How are you doing?" He asks.

"I'm okay. I guess. A little scraped up and surprisingly well rested. . . I think I was out for at least twenty hours."

"I know. I checked in with Janet and Chrissy a couple of times. They were very shaken up by what happened. A.J.'s driver helped them get you in and settled. You have some pretty special roommates." He says.

He called to check on me more than once. The words echo in my mind. "I wish I could see you now." I say. "How are you? How's Jamal?"

262

"I'm wiped out but okay. Jamal is with the woman from social services. He's about the same." He says. "It's just killing me to think about how quickly my students seem to grow up these days and now that his mother is gone Jamal is being forced to leave his childhood behind even sooner."

I feel a lump in my throat remembering the sweet boy resting his head on my shoulder at Mary Jane's. "Well," I say. "Maybe we can do something to help him make the most of what is left of his childhood."

"We'll see. I can only do so much as his teacher." He says in a disappointed tone.

"Speaking of school, are you going in tomorrow?" I ask.

"Yep. In fact, I'm sitting at my desk right now. Remember, you slept through an entire day." He says with a lighter air.

"That's right. I've got to get it together. I'll be down on Dodson Street right after I stop into the police station tomorrow morning." I say.

"Sounds like a plan. Get some more rest, Alex."

"More rest? . . . I feel like Rip Van winkle!"

"See you tomorrow." He says and hangs up the phone.

I return to my room planning to lie down for just a moment but am woken by the alarm sixteen hours later. Holy shit! I slap the buzzer. I am Rip Van winkle!

Chapter 32

Moving Mountains

"Well look who's back!" Tom shouts out warmly from the table where he is seated with A.J., Juan Carlos, Claudius and Bev.

"Sorry to be a little late. I'm coming from the police station." I admit with a sigh as I join the group.

"No worries." Tom says with a distracted headshake. "We're all just glad you are okay."

"What fun am I missing here?" I ask intrigued by the many maps and blueprints scattered about in front of them.

"We are trying to get a grip on the prospects of the neighborhood here." Tom says waving his hands about in frustration. "A.J. is hell-bent on saving the world or something."

"I'm going to pretend you didn't just insult my intentions, Tom. If you weren't such a mastermind, I'd demote you to the mail room." A.J. says and whacks Tom over the head with a rolled up blueprint.

"Hey watch it you old bat!" Tom jabs back in jest. "I've forgotten what it's like to work with a dragon lady."

We all laugh and I admire the type of working friendship that only comes from shared histories.

A.J. points to a building on one of the surveyed maps and announces, "This building has space for fourteen apartments and that one across the street has space for ten."

Claudius chimes in, "Our goal is to hire around two hundred for two shifts. If they live close by, they won't have to worry about transportation."

I can't believe what I am seeing and hearing. A.J. is actually planning to renovate the buildings to house the workers of IDEA.

"Terry, did Michael Bluberry say how many families have students at the school?" A.J. asks.

"I believe I have jotted down here that he said there are around a hundred and thirty five. They have a few sets of siblings." Terry replies scrolling through notes he had typed into his Blackberry.

"That's a sufficient pull for the workforce we are hoping to hire. We need a few weeks to get things set up in the factory and then we can start looking to interview and train our lines." Claudius states with an intention that means business.

Bev explains a first quarter timeline to the group seated at the table. They plan to spend the early part of summer taking in used school furniture from around the Midwest so that it can be redesigned and returned by the end of August. She continues saying, "Wouldn't it be wonderful to hire some parents whose children are students at Dodson

Street School. Those children could say, "This is the desk my mama made." -or remade as is our company theme." All the heads at the table nod, faces grinning.

There is the sound of constant tapping as Juan Carlos is in a frenzy taking notes on his laptop. His notes, however, won't capture the awe that I experience as I witness all that is taking place before me.

I consider the magnitude of effort and state directly to A.J., "This is more than a simple venture of a business and a school. This is conscious community redevelopment. A.J. you're not a developer." I think to myself how much A.J.'s reputation is influencing quick action in the city. Permits and favors are pouring in left and right to expedite A.J.'s plans. It's advantageous being in Chicago where money and power can move mountains. . . quickly.

"And your point is?" She demands peering over the purple glasses that are sliding down her nose.

"My point, well, I have no point except that when I came to you with this idea I never intended for you to risk everything, to invest so much time and energy. These years are meant for you to enjoy." I declare, a little ashamed of bringing the older woman into this, even though it was necessary to call upon her.

"Look Alex, I am enjoying myself. I have felt more alive in the past few weeks than I have in years. Nobody is holding a gun to my head to get me to come down here each day. I love it. I have the resources and the time. Quite honestly, when I heard about the drive by shootings that the children have been dealing with and how Jamal's mother had to work two jobs to barely survive and was killed coming home from the second one, and then when you were assaulted just blocks from the school, I realized that there is a bigger issue at stake here."

The entire room goes silent and all eyes turn to A.J. who, surprisingly with tears in her eyes says, "You, Alex True, are the reason I am here. As young as you are, you came to me as old as I am, unafraid of taking a chance and believing in a mission of good. I am grateful you did that. But the other night when I went home after you were attacked, I thought about all these terrible events and I wished to myself that you had only come to me sooner. Maybe we could have spared so much pain. Maybe we could have given Jamal's mother a chance to share one more birthday with her son."

I scan the faces of the executives at the table. Not a dry eye can be seen.

"Well then," I announce. "I guess it is fair to say that venturing with this school is going to involve much more than prepping the kids for tests and quizzes."

"I believe so and now, if you will allow the Mastermind to speak," Tom clears his throat and shimmies up in his chair. "If we are going to come out on top in this business deal we have to consider the whole package. Just like we have always made sure our corporate employees and their families are taken care of so must we do the same for the students and staff across the street. Happy, healthy students going home to happy healthy families are going to perpetuate a more vibrant and hopeful future for us all."

"Thank you Tom. If you're feeling it then that says a lot for the rest of us. I am willing to put it all on the line here. Heaven knows, at this age, my days may be numbered so let's get to work." A.J. commands and the reference to her own mortality feels like a knife in my gut.

I join the visionaries at the table feeling overwhelmed with pride for this woman and her company.
Knowing fully that just as she nurtured her venture capital firm into being a thriving example of successful leadership in the business world she will also do whatever it takes to work every inch and angle to help provide the Dodson Street School teachers and parents with opportunities necessary to help the children rise up and improve their odds so that together A.J. Hoyt and Dodson Street School will be leaders sharing success in academics and in life.

Chapter 33

An Invitation

"Okay guys, this note needs to go home and be signed by a parent or guardian so that we can all go and support Jamal at his mother's funeral. Remember that we are all one big family here and when one of us hurts," Mark pauses for a response from his students, "we all hurt." I hear them chime in unison from my seat in the back of the class. It's an ever-familiar mantra that Mark insists they understand in an effort to instill empathy for the much too frequent sad situations.

Mark sits down, elbows on his desk, palms rubbing his weary eyes and waits patiently for students to come up to his desk one by one, to take permission slips and return to their desks where only a few have backpacks to organize for home but most shove the notes in their pockets.

"I know it has been a tough couple of days for all of us, but don't forget we have to keep moving forward. You have standardized testing tomorrow. So get plenty of sleep tonight. I will bring in bananas and apples for a mid-morning power snack. These tests are especially important this year as you are not only representing yourselves but you are also representing our school and our new friends at A.J. Hoyt Technologies."

I can see that Mark is trying so hard to hold himself

together but he looks emotionally drained and sounds exhausted as he tries to wrap up the day with his class. The students rise. "Word up, Mr. T." Shouts out a boy in the back of the room with a wave and the rest of the students begin to make their way toward the door.

At the sound of the dismissal bell, they all file out of the room except for Latasha. She remains in her chair staring out the window. Mark slowly gets up from behind his desk to check on her when he notices tears streaming down her cheeks.

"Latasha, what is it? Are you thinking about Jamal?" He asks her and pulls up a chair to be a little closer. She sits in a silent trance, frozen to her seat. "Latasha, the bus driver is waiting for you. Are you okay?" He tries again to encourage her to open up.

Turning to Mark, she whispers, "I'm so scared, Mr. T. I don't wanna' go home. I don't wanna' end up like Jamal's mama. I don't wanna' get shot at like my sista'. I just wanna' sit here and wait for tomorrow."

Mark takes her hand, empty for words, lost in heartache for her, for Jamal, for the dozens of wonderful children seated on the school busses in the bus lane in front of the school at that same moment waiting to be taken home to neighborhoods of uncertain safety and potential harm. As they sit in stone silence, I slip away and Mr. Bluberry enters the room putting a hand on Latasha's shoulder. Without a word, she rises at the guidance of her principal and allows him to lead her to the bus that will be taking her where she doesn't want to go.

Back in Lincoln Park, I lumber up the landscaped sidewalk to my comfortable apartment and think about Latasha and her agonizing walk to her home. I picture her hesitant to step off of the bus, looking over her shoulder every jittery step of the way past abandoned buildings and slum dog street urchins. She deserves better. I want better for her. In my gut, I feel an urgency to kick A.J.'s plans into higher gear.

****

It's been another heavy impact day. Exhaustion and drained emotions collapse my body under the spinning ceiling fan, the sofa swallows me and I fall asleep on the couch. I am not sure how long I have slept and am startled awake in the darkness by the sound of my ringtone, "Walk like an Egyptian".

"Hello?" Dry and cracking from fatigue, my voice carries the heft of knuckles dragging on dessert sand.

"Alex? Is that you?" Mark inquires from the other end of the line.

"Mark? What's going on? I, I fell asleep and . . . "

My voice trails as I come to.

"I'm just checking in. You snuck out before I could say good-bye earlier today. So, I thought I would call." He admits ardently.

"I'm a little groggy but otherwise fine. How are you?" I ask more concerned for him now than ever.

"I just woke from a long nap as well." He says to me and I hear a light slurp of something. "Ouch. That's hot!"

"What?"

"Just a little tea and cream burning my lips. That's all." He tells me and I imagine Mary Jane in the kitchen of her bungalow brewing a pot for her son, adding an extra sugar cube or two.

"How's Jamal?" I want to hear that he's sitting in that same warm kitchen eating blueberry cobbler with Mary Jane but instead Mark informs me that he has been taken by a woman from social services.

"She took him down to her office and then they went back to his apartment to gather some of his belongings." The pit in my stomach swells at the thought of Jamal being forced to go with a stranger at a time like this. "My mother really laid it on the line with me earlier. She doesn't think I am equipped to deal with his grief right now. I suppose she is right." He shares. "Social services will be bringing him back here tomorrow." He explains. "He will be staying with us until they can find one of his relatives. I just can't believe that there's nobody out there for him. The social worker is going to meet with my mother and I to help us understand the best ways to support him."

"I would think you would just keep on loving him the way you normally do, Mark." I say in a complimentary way.

"Speaking of my mother, Alex. . ."

Oh no, here it comes. He knows. He thinks I was stalking his home. He's calling to insist I keep thirty feet distance. Another reason why I should have never taken that walk the other day.

"She is beside herself that you were assaulted leaving her home. She wants to do something for you. I suggested a cobbler. What do you think?" Mark asks.

"Sure. I would like that very much but she shouldn't feel bad." I say.

"She liked you, Alex."

"She did?" I reply a bit surprised that it mattered so much to him what his mother thought of me.

"She found you to be charming. Charming and sophisticated to be exact."

I wonder if he can feel the heat of my cheeks through the phone. I've never imagined myself being painted with this type of description. It's usually that I am "interesting" or "tall" or "unusual looking" when others attempt to gently describe me. I am flattered by his Mary Jane's words.

"I found your mother to be lovely as well." I assure

Mark. "And she pours a delicious cup of tea."

"You can say that again." He slurps once more and I can sense his lopsided grin on the other end. "I am not even going to ask you how you ended up sitting in my mother's kitchen the other day but I like the visual."

I am relieved to avoid explaining my stupidity for the umpteenth time as the wounds on my wrists are enough of a constant reminder. Thinking back to his shady deal with Liam, I decide that we all do stupid things every now and again.

"I don't need to know. I am just glad you two met." He admits. "I think it's time I invited you to go on a proper date. May I take you to dinner?" The invitation comes as quite a surprise given the nature of the recent events. Mark's voice carrying a formal invitation causes an even more fleeting rise in my pulse.

"Oh Mark, I have been thinking of you all day. I would love to see you. . . go on a proper, date that is. . . a rendezvous so to speak."

"That's perfect then. I'll pick you up Friday at seven at your place and we can go out somewhere up in Lincoln Park ... an official rendezvous as you say." We hang up the phone and I fall back into a more restful slumber under the breeze of the ceiling fan once more.

Chapter 34
Café Bernard

The doorbell rings and I can hear Janet and Chrissy scramble to answer it. They scuffle over the handle and the door flies open with schoolgirl excitement that causes Mark to jump.

"Hi, Janet and Chrissy?" He greets them with a broad friendly smile. His sweet and spicy scent of citrus and ginger enters our apartment. His long wavy hair the color of sand is still slightly damp and tucked behind his ears. Warm and friendly, his eyes shaded bluish grey arrest my roommates with their first impression.

From around the corner of the bathroom, I am entertained as both Chrissy and Janet do completely obvious double takes at the door noticing the dark, freshly pressed denim, handsome wing-tips and light-blue oxford. The man at the door is far from the grade school teacher who hangs out with his mother that they had imagined. To complete the package, in his hand is a single red rose.

I quietly enter the room where the three stand waiting. Tonight, I decide to dress more casually. I want Mark to know that I have more than suits in my wardrobe collection. I am wearing a black cashmere v-neck and designer jeans.

Simple and, to quote Mary Jane Tandem, sophisticated.

"This is for you, Alex." Mark says. "You look amazing this evening."

We stand face to face. Our equally tall elegant forms balance each other out.

"Wow, you two are almost the same height." Janet says, no doubt, what Chrissy is also thinking.

"And to think you two thought I would only land a player from the NBA. . . " I chide in a fun-loving way, giving Mark a squeeze.

"Well, come on Mark, you must play a sport." Chrissy inquires in reference to his stature.

"A little volleyball back in school." He answers, which is all it takes for Janet and Chrissy to be won over by my newfound love. Janet mentions that we need subs from time to time in our Thursday night volleyball league and that they would love to have Mark fill in if he ever has the time.

He thanks them and puts his arm behind the small of my back in a gesture to politely proceed with our evening.

"Where to on our rendezvous?" I ask Mark emphasizing the letter "r" like a true Francophile while sliding into the passenger seat of his car.

"Well, your French reference brought to mind a little French joint over on Halsted. Would you be up for an appetizing meal? Steak frites, perhaps?" Mark asks me.

"I think that sounds fantastique monsieur." I reply having fun with my college French.

"Then Café Bernard it is. I think we could both use a cozy quiet evening of fine food and wine." He says pulling away from a prime curbside parking space and making an anxious, hovering driver ecstatic.

I appreciate the playful banter we share. Maybe it is the quick pace of our time together or the events of the past days but our emotional guards are down and it is evident that we both share confidence in our budding affair.

The café is lively. Dim and warm, shadows dance in the amber light to the songs of Joe Dassin playing low in the background. Our waitress is discreet offering delectable steak frites and glasses of Burgundy that go down like velvet. For Mark and I, however, neither the ambiance nor the food is responsible for the magic playing in our hearts.

"I was shocked, at first, when my mother said that she met you the other day. It makes me happy though. If only the circumstance had been different. She would have taken you out in the garden and told you stories for hours. She is wonderful. I do wish that my grandfather had had the chance to meet you too. He would have adored you." Mark shares, openly leaning forward and taking hold of my hand in the center of the small table. "He would have loved your passion and your openness. Gramps would have admired the manner in which you follow your heart." He moves even closer and takes my other hand.

Eyes moist in reaction to the candor of Mark's words, I gently express regret in not having met Otto Tandem but imagine that Mark must have inherited a lot of his grandfather's strong qualities and by the look of the fine shoes he is wearing, a great sense of style.

"These are my grandfather's greatest work, the wing-tip that won him praise around the world. He even shipped this shoe to the King of Norway." The waitress comes by leaving a small plate of macarons. I take a bite and being quite the fashion guru comment again on the workmanship and design of the wing tip.

"Oh yes, to the discerning eye they are works of art. Fortunately, for my grandfather, people chose to pay for quality back in his heyday. In fact, my mother and I had the most amazing massive marble replica of this wing tip placed as the headstone to his grave." He shares proudly but then recoils to heartache at the imminent prospect of attending Jamal's mother's funeral at the same cemetery in less than a week.

"I know what you are thinking Mark. I think we need to help make arrangements so that Jamal's mother is properly honored. I have a friend who is a minister. I am sure she would perform the funeral." I offer as we both witness tears welling in our eyes, wondering how and when we will find the strength to help Jamal bury his mother.

"I wish our evening didn't have to end like this, Alex. Honestly, I have enjoyed every second with you." Mark confesses looking at me and blinking between the tears.

"I know. Me too. We just have to keep things in perspective." I suggest as the waitress quietly hands Mark the bill.

"Thank you Alex for seeing me tonight. I'm afraid that early next week I will be caught finishing up the standardized testing that we have scheduled for the fourth through eighth graders. Then there's the funeral. I have made some arrangements but if your friend could come and say some kind words, that would be nice. I will have to see how Jamal is doing but I would love to take you out again soon."

Walking to the car, his words linger in my thoughts and are of such mixed emotion involving his responsibility to his students, caring for Jamal and his mother's funeral to looking for some time when we could be alone again. I am touched and graced to be so valued in his precious time.

"Well, we'll always have Paris, or at least Café Bernard." Mark says innocently as he slides behind the wheel enchanting me with his reference to my favorite film. The stirring citrus and ginger scent draws me close to him and sweeps me into a rush of intoxication. He winds his arms around me and I shroud him in hot, tender kisses tinted with the sweet taste of fine Burgundy wine.

Outside the car, night's blanket of darkness offers privacy as we savor the impassioned touch, taste and sound of our desire, sharing a release both exhausting and joyful.

Chapter 35
E.Q.

"The work vibe down here is just so much different than up in The Loop office." Dannie says to me. He is leaning against the window, cross-legged next to my desk sipping a coffee.

"I know. How many years have we worked together?" I ask him.

"At least seven or eight, I think." He says.

"That seems about right. Seven or eight years and this is the first time you've ever come to hang out in . . . 'my office'." I say making quotation signs with my fingers.

It doesn't feel like a hardware store anymore even with the unmistakable odor of turpentine in the air.

"I suppose the lack of walls is an open invitation to get to know each other better." Dannie says to me as I lop to and fro in my leather swivel chair.

"Did you hear that the security guys nailed some dope dealers they spotted just around the corner last night?" He asks informing me of something I didn't want to hear. "And one of the guys has a little sister in fifth grade across the street."

"How'd you hear?" I ask.

"Juan Carlos told me."

I wonder to myself why A.J. didn't share this with the rest of us. Maybe she will. Maybe she won't. She might not want to throw us off the driven course we are on. But she should know that we are smart enough to recognize the growing number of men patrolling the area.

"Thanks for letting me know." I say not wanting to make a deal of it for A.J.'s sake.

"What are you working on now?" He asks.

"I'm trying to figure out how to measure the success of our efforts on Dodson Street." I answer.

"That's easy. Look out the window." He says.

We both look across the street and see that a landscape crew has been out to dig up beds all around the perimeter of the school. They have taken away unnecessary blacktop and cement to allow for more green space and an eco-friendly playground.

"We are hoping that the environment will inspire." I admit with pride over the work that had begun. "We also hope that tools will inspire." He nods. "Juan Carlos has placed multiple orders for the school from iPads and Smartboards to science equipment and sports equipment."

"Yeah," He adds. "and IDEA is redesigning the furniture, too."

"All of these things are meant to inspire the students to think outside of the box and to provide them with the tools to realize their creative potential but they don't help me measure success." I say as I chomp on the eraser of a pencil.

"Good point, Alex and that's my sign to head back to the drafting table because I have no clue how to help you with that one." He says, unfolds his legs and taps the top of my desk with his knuckle. "Good luck, my friend."

I never knew how sterile my work life was until I started working in this hardware store. Dannie would have never socialized with me up in the Chicago Works Tower. I guess it's like what we were saying about the school-Environments do inspire.

"Tom?" I ask, using my boss' first name in a more relaxed tone than ever.

"Oh hi Alex, I didn't hear you walk up he says taking his ear-buds out of his ears and spinning around to face me in his chair. "I'm trying to learn French on line."

French on line? He can't be serious. At work? I'll give him a little French on line. I try to muster up some gritty street French to throw at him but he beats me to the punch.

"Comment allez-vous?" He rises and does a lilted wrist bow as if I am royalty.

Unsure how to respond to his quirky gesture, I cut to the chase, "I need a measurement tool."

"I see. What do you want to measure?" He asks.

"Progress." I say.

"What kind of progress are you looking for?" He digs even deeper to get me thinking.

"Progress in the community. Not just academic progress so standardized test scores are only part of the quotient."

"Okay, go on. . ."

"I want to measure growth on an even more holistic scale." I say to my boss who is now deep in thought. He always rubs his eyebrows with his palms when he is coming up with something ingenious.

"Okay," He says. "It's clear that we are doing a whole lot more than banking on a few great minds to launch our company into the financial ozone. A.J. is looking at an even bigger picture. She is connecting us to a developing community where we will foster children and families to find contentment in who they are and what they have to offer to the world." His words start to swirl in my mind. Like pedals on a bike they take me to my next thought.

"Happiness." I say.

"You think?" He questions.

"Yes, I need to measure levels of happiness and confidence which means I have to find an evolved measurement tool. Academic intelligence tests only take most students down the hallway and past the school office. To predict and determine success beyond those heavy metal doors and out in the real world is the true deliverable for the students, the faculty, the families, for all of us."

"I knew hiring you years ago would make life more interesting for me, Alex True. And look where we are now. My number one research analyst wants to measure happiness. If anything, it will get us a by-line in The Tribune business section." He gives me a thumbs-up and pops the buds back into his ears.

I return to my desk in the corner of the giant office space and determine that he must get paid these days to just count his stock options or something.

Now, I must figure out how to measure happiness. There ought to be a measurement tool.

****

"Hi Mark, I thought this was your free period. I hope you don't mind me calling but I need your help. I want to measure the well being and societal preparedness of your students. What kind of educational measurement tool is there for this?" I rattle off in a business-paced machine gun manner.

"Well, I'm very well. Thank you. How are those crystal blue eyes of yours?" Mark chides in response to my high-strung address.

"Sorry Mark. I am just really managing a lot over here and I think I am on to something and I need your help. I am fine by the way, and you?" I express in a calmer tone.

"It's been hectic today. I am okay though. Jamal has been here and that's really tough. But to answer your question, I think you want to measure E.Q." He says.

"What is E.Q?" I reply.

"Well, E.Q. is a person's emotional intelligence quotient as opposed to their intellectual intelligence quotient. Some theorists believe that higher levels of E.Q. are better indicators of achievement in the real world." He states.

"I see." I respond intrigued.

"The efforts your company is making to improve the quality of life and connectedness of our students and staff will have a positive impact on their E.Q., without a doubt." He says sounding like a university professor. "What's more is that being the ones to make these efforts will most certainly impact the E.Q. of you and your colleagues as well. You will find that connecting with others on a level that is more organic than the material driven connections made in typical business situations is very fulfilling."

"That's it. That's it. We can get a baseline E.Q. measurement of the entire school and company population and see where all of our scores go over a period of time. The data should be interesting to follow." I shout into the receiver.

Mark gently interjects saying, "Well, in theory Alex, I think you are spot on. The problem is that there is no real standard for measuring emotional intelligence. There are behavioral assessments that measure individual strengths but to ascertain emotional growth, I think we would need to have a shared creed that we strive to meet."   I am silent after Mark's last comment. Quickly jotting down thoughts on a sticky note so as not to forget the idea of a shared creed. "You have helped me so much, Mark. Thank you. Personally, I think my E.Q. is off the charts right now. And yours, Mark Tandem, the way you read people and understand your presence and purpose, your E.Q. must be sky high."

"Oh, I don't know about all that. My emotions are in tact but they sure have taken quite a ride lately." He admits in unspoken reference to Jamal's situation.

A cloud blankets our enlightened dialogue and matters at hand take the conversation focus in a more poignant direction. "As for Friday morning, I have Reverend Hummel scheduled to meet us in the cemetery at nine o'clock. Does Jamal need anything?" I ask as the conversation goes sideways.

Both Mark and I know that Jamal needs so much, most importantly his mom. "I think he will be fine. He is staying with my mother and me for the time being. We are going to just have to take this one day at a time." Mark says with hesitancy, stressing so many unknown factors between the lines.

"I'm glad you were able to take my call, Mark. Just hearing your voice is making my heart race in ways I can't even explain." I confess quivering from head to toe with a long heavy inhalation.

"I'm glad it worked out too. If only Paulie Blue Hands wasn't sitting across the table from me in the faculty lounge here. . . well, I better stop before I get started. The bell is about to ring. So, I should get going. I will see you at Oak Woods Cemetery in the morning." We hang up our phones and I remain seated and satisfied behind my fancy oak desk enjoying private thoughts of Mark as I rock back and forth in my leather swivel chair.

Chapter 36

Creed

The sun is setting behind the apartment buildings that line Lake Shore Drive and a pink hue bounces off the cool sand of the volleyball courts as After Ours plays our first game of the beach volleyball season. Janet, Chrissy and I are delighted to be out together for some fun after the recent weeks of early mornings, late evenings and my intense dedication to the venture of A.J. Hoyt Technologies and Dodson Street School and Mark Tandem.

"Mine!" I call out claiming the lofty dig from several inches above the setter and slamming it down on the opposing team. "Wow, did that feel good!" I declare in a cathartic manner.

"Best stress relief in town." Chrissy says giving me a pat on the back. "One more point and we've got our first match of the season to celebrate."

"Mine!" I call out again using my more than six-foot advantage to level the middle blocker on the other side right in the chest.

"Yes, Alex! You are limbs of steel tonight! Well played my friend." Janet cheers from behind me as we fall in to line up and shake hands with the other team. We gather our belongings and head toward the North Avenue Beach footbridge and on into Lincoln Park.

The scene is familiar. The barstools at After Ours are full and like every other Thursday night a few tables in the back sit waiting for our volleyball team that represents the establishment.

gathers our orders for the bartender.

"Tomorrow's the funeral, isn't it?" Chrissy asks.

"Yeah." I sigh with a heavy nod.

"I think I would like to be there, Alex. Even though I don't know Jamal, I feel strongly about this whole situation. I want to come, for you." She says tenderly to me handing over the beer.

Sliding up in a seat next to Chrissy, Janet jumps into the conversation. "What are you two chatting about?"

I am still silent with surprise from Chrissy's desire to attend the funeral. So Janet looks to Chrissy for a response. "Well, I just told Alex that I want to attend the funeral for Jamal's mother in the morning." She says to Janet.

"I'll be there too. It is unimaginable to think of that poor boy waiting for his mama on her birthday like that and . . . " Janet trails off as the reminder is too much to bear.

"Thank you both. It means a lot. If you have time afterward please come back with me to Dodson Street."

Janet and Chrissy agree to clear their schedules for the day and to be available to me if I need them.

290

"Is there anything else we can do for you, Alex?" Janet asks me as we get up to leave the bar and head home.

"Well, Janet, you are so good with words. I need some help putting together a creed for the school. It has to be something that the students, staff and employees of A.J. Hoyt Technologies share and strive to live up to."

"I see." Replies Janet pulling the door open for Chrissy and me.

"Well wait a minute Alex, I too am good with words. For goodness sake, I'm an English teacher." Chrissy says staking a claim on her professional training.

"Oh Chrissy, I'm sorry. I would love both of you to help me come up with a creed that we can measure ourselves by. I don't want it to involve success through academics or economics. I want it to be a statement from which we can grow together in a positive and outward manner, you know like your E.Q." I suggest assuming that emotional quotient is a mainstream reference.

"E.Q.? What on earth is E.Q.?" asks Janet quizzically.

"Mark described it as much more powerful than I.Q. which is the measure of our intelligence. E.Q. is the measure of our emotional readiness for success in life. I think that I would like the creed to be more about emotional preparedness than academic potential. That way, the corporate fraction of this venture can follow the same claim."

I explain as we walk home hoping that between the three of us we are able to brainstorm a worthy idea that children and adults will embrace.

After tossing phrases and goals around, we spin out a worthy canon.

"That sounds perfect!" I announce to Chrissy and Janet putting down a gnawed upon pencil. "I can see it now engraved above the entrance of the school and at A.J. Hoyt Technologies. Listen to this.

"Show that you care deeply about your community. Live Authentically."

I love it! It is a very evolved creed. I think we can also measure growth according to it." I smile wide fulfilled that the three of us have come up with something important enough to be engraved in stone.

"Now I need to present this to the school community and the rest of my team at A.J. Hoyt Technologies." I announce thinking fondly of the framed linen note that sits on my desk at work, my mother's words, and the role they have played in influencing the determination of this creed- a simple heartfelt handwritten message that has reminded me to remain true to my spirit, my own personal creed I suppose.

I have tried and continue to strive to live up to my mother's guiding advice. Living in a society that runs on the surface has made it tough at times, as face value is so two dimensional. I have found a way to get by though. I have allowed certain people to get to know me for who I am, below the surface. They have touched chords in my authentic spirit that help me achieve success and happiness. In a deeper sense, they have helped me to get to know myself. My family, Janet, Chrissy, A.J. Hoyt, Tom Mackey, the students at the school and Mark- I am realizing that as I live a little more openly each day I am feeling more connected to the world. I have dreamed of this epiphany my entire life.

I hope that the students and staff at Dodson Street School and my coworkers will experience the joy of feeling connected. Through the synergy of our lives coming together, we will promote true success in one another. We will care deeply for each other. What appears to be a capital venture on the surface is turning into much more. We are becoming a community.

As I say goodnight to Janet and Chrissy and thank them for their support, I envision the note propped on my desk. "Authenticity defines a person." Thanks mom.

Chapter 37

A Final Hug Goodbye

The bright yellow school bus pulls up to the gate of Oak Woods Cemetery. The sight is a contrast that makes me sick. I watch as the students of Mr. T's sixth grade class somberly file off dressed in their church clothes. Knobby ankles pop out from too-short pants on the boys, many of the dresses wrinkled and worn from frequent good-byes like this- a family member, neighbor, friend.

Behind the bus a half dozen cars pull up for the mid-morning burial. From the final car come Mark and Jamal walking slowly toward us in the crowd of people who have come to honor his hard-working loving mother. Alongside his teacher, Jamal is stone faced appearing to be in shock from his despair. Mark holds his arm around him and brings him to meet the pastor.

"Jamal," I explain gently. "This is Reverend Hummel. She is a good friend of mine and I invited her to come and honor your mother. Is that okay with you?" Jamal nods his head and Reverend Hummel extends her hand to his.

"Jamal, I have been hearing some very special things about your mother from people who knew her. Tell me about your mom." she says kindly with the deepest of sensitivity.

Jamal takes a moment and looks over to the people who are quietly gathering at the site.

"My mama," he hesitates. "She was saving up. She wanted to take us to see the ocean. Her whole life she wanted to see the ocean. She always talked about getting there. Heading out on a big bus. We would play gin rummy the whole ride there. She wanted to swim in the ocean with all the secrets it keeps. All the sunken treasures, The Titanic, stuff like that. We watched all those shows on the Discovery Channel together. It was going to be our big adventure. It never happened." Jamal's voice trails off and tears begin to stream down his face.

Reverend Hummel thanks him for sharing such special thoughts and guides him over to the burial site.

I stand on one side of Mark and Jamal. Michael Bluberry is on the other. Behind us are Jamal's classmates and A.J., Terry and the rest of the venture capital team, Janet and Chrissy. From the gravel road I see two more figures approach. Virgil and Cherry walk slowly, hand in hand. That is all.

I wonder how a boy as wonderful as Jamal has gotten along with basically nobody besides his mother acting as an influence in his life and then the reality of the sheer value of Mark Tandem and the other caring, intelligent, disciplined teachers at Dodson Street School really hits home.

"Ashes to ashes, dust to dust. The Lord bless her and

keep her, the Lord make His face to shine upon her and be gracious unto her and give her peace. Amen."

Mark bends down handing Jamal red roses to place on his mother's casket as it is being lowered into the ground. Through blurry tears we watch Jamal give his mother a final hug goodbye.

As the busload of students drives away, Mark takes Jamal by the hand and asks to go for a walk. He invites me to join them as they follow a winding path of headstones and statuary. The silence of the cemetery is a reminder of the peace that Reverend Hummel promised would be waiting for Jamal's mother. It feels like the peace of a thousand promises as we wander in the warm sunshine.

Mark speaks softly, "This is it. This is the Hall of Shoes." Still holding Mark's hand Jamal glances up with a confused look on his face.

"Whatcha talkin' bout' Mr. T?"

"This is it . . . The Hall of Shoes . . . See all those track shoes on the ground over there? That's where Jesse Owens "The Buckeye Bullet" Greatest Olympian of all time is buried." Mark says in an effort to ease the mood. "I also call this The Hall of Shoes because of what comes next."

"Wow! Check that out Mr. T. It's a giant workin' man's shoe. How'd you know it was over here?" Jamal asks in wonder.

"I know about The Hall of Shoes because my grandfather is buried beneath this giant shoe." Answers Mark with a smile.

I keep my silence but walk over to Mark's other side and take his hand. The three of us stand admiring the monument to Mark's grandfather for quite some time. It's a massive shining wing tip made of dark tan granite to match the leather color of his grandfather's famous style pleaser. Mark lets go of my hand and kneels at the base of the enormous shoe.

Jamal and I watch as he smooths his hand down the toe box to the sole and opens a one-sided dialogue sharing briefly about the changes at the shoe factory and asking for grandfatherly guidance.

"Gramps," He whispers. "Mom and I miss you so much. We're doing well though. I want you to know that we've got a business moving into the shoe factory. They won't be making shoes but I figured you'd understand. I've met someone special too, Gramps. I can tell you all about that later. Do me a favor, watch over my pal Jamal here. He could use an extra guardian angel."

Mark wraps himself over the round polished granite trying to hug life into the stone. Certainly the coolness of its touch is an absent response to the warm embrace he longs to feel.

Breaking the silence Jamal asks, "You think my

297

mama could have something cool like that on top of her?"

"Sure Jamal. What did she enjoy most?" Replies Mark rising up and out of his private reverie with heaven.

"Well, she liked spaghetti and tacos." Jamal says in a serious tone that quickly turns into hearty laughter mixed with some tears.

"Maybe we should take a little time and think about some of her other favorite things." Redirects Mark taking Jamal's hand again and turning to head back to the car.

Chapter 38
Newsroom Madness

Chrissy and Janet are waiting patiently, seated on the hood of my hybrid when we return from our walk to the big shoe. Without saying a word they get into the car and wait for me to take the wheel. Chrissy speaks first, "That was really tough, Alex. Reverend Hummel did a great job honoring Jamal's mother in a way that all of those children could understand. What a strong little boy to be all alone like that."

"We're going to make sure he is not alone." I assure her.

I drive Janet and Chrissy in silence across the south side of town over to Dodson Street. Moving through the neighborhood, I am surprised to see new building permit signs hanging in the street front windows from the IDEA factory all the way up to the school.

"This is amazing." I exclaim interrupting the noiselessness of our ride. "A.J. isn't fooling around. It usually takes months for a permit in Chicago. Look at all these signs."

"What's going on?" Janet asks.

I think to myself, "A.J. is cashing in on some serious

IOU's with the city." But then I give Janet a different response. "A.J. wants to offer affordable safe housing to the families of the children who are attending Dodson Street School. She's working with some developers, and apparently pulling huge favors on someone in city council, to renovate these old properties in the hopes of providing a stronger more positive neighborhood environment."

"She's like a grey-haired super hero!" Janet says in awe.

"Seriously, I know." I agree. "She is also working closely with IDEA in hopes that they will provide as many factory job opportunities for parents of Dodson Street School students as possible." I explain as we pull up to the lot next to the new offices of A.J. Hoyt Technologies.

"Aren't you glad you planted the seed in A.J.?" Chrissy asks.

"I really am. On so many levels." I answer turning off the ignition. "A.J. regrets that this idea to venture with the school didn't come to us sooner. Even though it was an accident, she believes that Jamal's mother would still be alive if we had only acted quicker. She's compelled to do what it takes to provide more hopeful opportunities to the school community as soon as possible for fear of losing another life to the misfortune of circumstance." We climb out of the hybrid just as two large office supply trucks rumble down the street.

300

I open the door for Janet and Chrissy and the office is a fury of energy. Papers flying from Tom Mackey to Juan Carlos and back again for signatures, phones soliciting attention at hips, from desktops, in ears, A.J. commands orders for work to be picked up, passed out, performed.

"This is more like newsroom madness minutes before going to press than a venture capital firm." Janet exclaims.

From the chaos, Tom Mackey shouts, "Can somebody please open the windows? Another minute of this lingering eau de turpentine and I'll start foaming at the mouth."

I cross the large busy office space and unlock the window nearest Tom. With a strong heave up, a soft and promising spring breeze swirls past me and Tom causing heads to raise and notice Janet and Chrissy standing in the entry way.

Tom's eyebrows pop at the sight of my gorgeous companions.

"Alex, you never told me you kept such intriguing company." Tom says gliding smoothly over to the two beautiful women at the door. Knowing fully the history of Tom Mackey's bravado and womanizing island escapades, Janet takes command of the greeting and extends her hand with a smile and a firm handshake.

"I'm Janet and this is Chrissy. We live with Alex." Tom shakes hands with both women who very courteously turn on their heels and leave him at the door to stand by me as I am speaking with A.J.

"These are my two wonderful room mates, Janet and Chrissy. They came down today for the funeral and since they have taken the day off of work I invited them to come check out Dodson Street. If it weren't for these two, I would never have had the nerve to speak with you about taking a chance with the school." I explain to A.J.

"Well then, I personally owe you two a basket of gratitude. This venture has given me a new reason for living." A.J. says putting her notebook down on the long table covered with papers, applications and blueprints. "May I offer you ladies an apple or a pear from the fruit bowl?" Accepting the offer, Janet and Chrissy each select a piece of fruit and take seats at the table amidst the chaos.

"Alex, I see the office supply truck has pulled up across the street. Why don't you leave your friends here with us and go supervise the delivery. I am certain that Rosie and Paulie Blue Hands could use your help. They've been holding down the fort while Mr. Bluberry attended the funeral with the sixth graders."

****

"Wait, wait guys out with the old then in with the new." I holler in quickstep over from the office to the occupied bus lane in front of the entrance to the school. "Let's get that old weathered office furniture and equipment out first."

"How was Jamal at the funeral this morning?" Rosie asks looking up from a stack of attendance cards.

"He hung in there, Rosie." Her scent fills the tiny office like flowers at a funeral parlor. "It was gut wrenching though. How did the morning go for you?" I inquire anxiously glancing out the window at the waiting truck in the bus lane.

"It was just fine. The first graders invited all of us outside for their butterfly release, which was as sweet as pie. Several of those little ones cried as their winged friends took off to the heavens and then I couldn't help myself either. Thinking about Jamal and his mama and all . . . Thank heavens I had a hankie with me. Even ol' Paulie got choked up." She shared reaching into her pocket for another swipe with the hankie.

"Well speak of the devil . . . do I have a treat for you my friend." I stroll over to Paulie who is walking down the hall toward the front office giving him a pat on the back.

"Whatcha' got up your sleeve for me, Alex?" Paulie asks suspiciously knowing that I have been full of interesting surprises lately.

I roll Michael Bluberry's chair out of the principal's office and into the lobby of the school and kindly guide

Paulie to take a seat. Then with authority of a great orchestra leader I proceed to conduct the men from the office supply company to haul away everything, except Rosie Fishers, her attendance cards and moist hankie, from the school office. The old furniture is set out on the curb of Dodson Street for IDEA to pick up too worn out to redesign but worthy of being passed along to someone else in need.

Sitting empty, I step into the office with a big broom and sweep away dust and grime that has gathered for years. I set down the dustpan and get the attention of a few children who, on account of all of the commotion, have gathered by the washrooms "Drum roll please everyone." I hail to the wide-eyed onlookers. "Okay guys, bring it on in."

First rolling off the truck comes a beautiful desk for Principal Bluberry, dark wood with sturdy handles. Then comes a smaller but more detailed, feminine styled, oak desk. Rosie gasps when she sees it and claps with glee. Two leather swivel chairs are pushed into the school and finally I turn to look at the old kind-hearted fellow seated in the tattered chair and exclaim . . . "No more Paulie Blue Hands!!!!"

The children cheer from the washroom and Rosie jumps for joy giving Paulie and me high-fives and hugs as a fabulous state of the art copy machine along with reams of paper are rolled into the school.

"Wow!" Says the new machine's commander in chief. "Does this mean you can call me Paulie No Hands now?"

Rosie, Paulie, the children and I laugh and dance around the entry to the school excited like children on Christmas morning.

"That was so much fun." I say taking off my black blazer and collapsing into a chair next to Janet back in the office with Chrissy and A.J. who are talking intently at the other end of the long table.

"It sure is great to have these fresh minds in here today, Alex." A.J. announces putting her hand on Chrissy's forearm. "Your friends have unselfishly offered to join up with A.J. Hoyt Technologies in the next few weeks. Chrissy needs to finish up her school year and Janet is going to put in her two weeks notice at the hospital and then they're all ours."

"What?" I say in surprise.

"At least for the summer," Chrissy says. "Janet and I have so much experience in our backgrounds that we want to contribute to your development process for next school year."

Stretching a stellar grin from ear to ear, I grab both women and hold them close. To the three of us it is another familiar embrace holding a tight seal to our loyalty.

"I can't believe this is all happening." I exclaim stepping back and looking at the women who believe so deeply in the venture.

"What exactly will they be doing?" I ask.

Resting her black reading glasses on the end of her nose, A.J. flips the page of a legal pad, glances at her notes and says, "Well, Janet is going to set us up for an on sight nurse and nutritionist." Looking over the top of her glasses she confirms, "You can't have a healthy venture unless the people involved are fit. She is also going to set up an after school care program so that our students are safe and cared for until their parents can pick them up."

"It's all right up my alley." Janet confirms.

"But what about your writing, the screenplay?" I ask in concern.

"Don't you think there will be material around here for me to write about?" She answers with a smile.

I raise my brow with an obvious nod.

A.J. continues. "Chrissy is going to be the academic liaison between our company and the school. She will offer support in and out of the classroom looking for ways to enhance the learning experiences of the children. She will also be developing a dance program within the school that I am sure will be well received."

"Oh yes," chimes in Chrissy, "I can already picture it. We'll have classical ballet, jazz, tap and hip-hop. I can even work in a little break dancing. Every kid wants to learn to moon walk."

"But what about your job up in Lincoln Park?" I ask.

"Let's just see what happens over the summer." Chrissy says. "I've got tenure with Chicago Public Schools. Maybe I can put in for a transfer."

The office fills with upbeat chatter as heartache and heaviness from the early morning lightens little by little. With the day wearing on the offices at both A.J. Hoyt Technologies and Dodson Street School inflate with hopeful prospects of better days to come.

Chapter 39

They Found Johnny

The final days of the school year are upon us. Mark and I find it hard to get together with all of the deadlines and duties that engulf the month of May. It's a phone call here, a lunch there, an outing with Jamal. When the pace slows down and I have moments alone, I miss him terribly. I imagine his long beautiful hair in my clasp, the smell of his cologne. It sends me soaring fortunately we both understand the nature of our present lives. For a teacher at this time of year, the chaos is temporary.

Unlike life in the business world that never slows down, the academic calendar has a finish line, so to speak. It is interesting to straddle both worlds and to see how my professional existence has become like a bike. The school and its energy are like the gears stopping, starting, slow and strong controlling the front tire while the back tire of business spins faster and faster.

"Yes, I know Whitney Young is an amazing high school. Okay, The Illinois Math and Science Academy too. Thanks Michael." I hang up the phone with Michael Bluberry and think to myself that he just doesn't get the fact that I am a research analyst. I do my legwork.

On my desk in front of me, I am looking at a dozen applications for Chicago area high schools to which we hope to send our students. We want to narrow it down to three or four of the top schools to which our students will go in clusters. The plan is to chart their progress and maintain tight reigns on them, which will be easier to facilitate as several of their parents have taken jobs at IDEA and are moving into the renovated apartments up and down Dodson Street. If we can keep the children at just a few of the same high schools then we plan to provide transportation to and from each one. I am amazed at A.J.'s intent on the behalf of each child and each family. It is powerful to see the families jump on board.

I dial the cell phone of Mrs. Jackson. Her daughter is one of the eighth grade students we have slated for Whitney Young.

"Hello?" She says.

"Mrs. Jackson, this is Alex True over at Dodson. I am calling to confirm your daughter's intentions to attend Whitney Young High School."

"Are you asking me if my child wants to go there?" She asks me.

"Yes." I say.

"Hell, yes. If that school is good enough for Michelle Obama, it's got to be good enough for my baby."

"Glad to hear it, Mrs. Jackson. You will be receiving

a very important form in the mail from us in the next few days. Please keep an eye out for it. Have a good day." I say putting down the phone to move on to my next task.

Lost in the simple rhythm of stuffing envelopes for each soon-to-be eighth grade graduate, I am startled by Juan Carlos.

"Someone is here to see you, Alex."

I look up toward the door and see Cherry. She approaches me with her arms outstretched and embraces me with a heave of emotion.

"Aleeex, Eeet ees goot seein' ya. Virgeel and me, we done mees ya' at dee soup keechin'."

Awkwardly, I respond in kind and pull back knocking the red plastic flower out of her hair.

"Oh Cherry, it is good to see you." I say picking up the flower and attempting to tuck it back behind her ear.

"Let me do dat, Alex." She says taking the flower and weaving it a bit through the nap around her ear.

"What brings you here Cherry?" I ask as the memory of seeing her at the funeral brings a lump to my throat.

"Eet ees Meesta Johnny. Dey find heem. He gone to jail now." She says with a look of anguish over the unfortunate outcome from her attempt to care for the homeless man.

"Oh my gosh. They did?" I say in disbelief. I had assumed that Johnny might just disappear to another city and become lost in a sea of regulars at a different soup kitchen somewhere.

"Yeah, dey done seet and wait Monday to Monday. He not showin' for dee pasta but fo last night. He come. Virgeel and me, we done panic we do. Den dey cuff em at dee table. Eet be crazy at dee keechin'. Dee odas, dey done run out dee door. Me and Virgeel, we be cleanin' up all de night long but we pray fo dee leetle boys mama."

"Thank you for coming to tell me Cherry. It won't take away the pain but Jamal should know what has happened."

"Dat ees so, Alex." She says as her bright red lips turn to a pout. "I ees soo sorry."

"You had no way of knowing that Johnny would take your van." I tell her as a vision of the flag painted on its side pops into my mind. "What are you doing now that your van is gone?"

"I ees lookin' fo work. I lost dee job fo dee reech boy. Now, I look around. Virgeel too. He be lookin'." She shares with me and thinking of Virgil, I realize how much I miss him.

The calmness of the office is a reminder that much activity is taking place down at IDEA and I suggest to Cherry that she and Virgil apply for positions on the assembly line.

"Ah yeah, de 'ol shoe factory. Dat I know." She naively admits and my suspicions of her wrongful presence on Mark's property are confirmed.

"Tank you, Aleex." She says as her eyes brighten and her shoulders whip back into their proud Caribbean stature. "Life ees gona' be betta."

Chapter 40

Undecided?

"Mark, I like how you've decorated." I say admiring the shades of gray that cover his walls and the select pieces of furniture in his Bridgeport apartment. The smell of herbs and baked chicken fill the air.

"Thanks. It's hard to go wrong when you are working with such a simple pallet." He says.

"The flowers are beautiful." I add, wondering if he always has fresh peach colored roses in the middle of his dining table or if he set them out for me.

He smiles and says nothing but hits a button on his stereo and Stevie Wonder's voice adds even more color to the mood.

"I wondered how long it would take you to invite me to your place." I say as I kick off my shoes and take a seat on his sofa.

"Well, doesn't everyone enjoy a little mystery?" He says sliding up next to me. "I know I do." He takes my cheek in his palm and turns my face toward his unleashing a kiss. "I think," He kisses me again. "Your mystery hides behind those amazing eyes of yours." He takes his thumb and outlines my brow.

I am flattered but his comment also makes me

nervous as the thought of revealing too much about myself causes me to feel naked. I do want him to know everything about me. So, I pursue his lead.

"It's fair to say that mystery is what you get when you're spending time with me." I say.

"I like that, you're different from anyone I've ever met." He whispers in my ear. "That's what makes you special."

His warm breath brushes over my neck like velvet. I am in heaven. "You're smooth, Mark." I whisper back.

"Thanks, I shaved just for you." He says.

"No, I mean your words are smooth." I reply. "They're just what I need to hear." I lean back into the cushion of the sofa and notice the title of the only book on his coffee table. It is leather bound with gilt inlay print.

"Pericles," I read aloud. "It's my favorite of Shakespeare's romances. Do you always keep a copy on the table?"

"No." He answers and says nothing more.

"What?"

"Open it up." He suggests and hands me the beautiful book.

On the inside cover is a hand-written message that I read aloud, "To Alex. Your childhood passion for Shakespeare is just one of the many qualities that intrigues me about your spirit." Then I hesitate as the next words

314

jump off the book onto my lips. "Love, Mark." I am stunned by the weight of the two words. I sit speechless and stoned by their magic.

Mark fidgets on his half of the cushion and asks, "Do you like it?"

"How did you know?"

"That you love Shakespeare?" He clarifies and I nod.

"I hung on to every word you said when you pitched the Dodson Street venture to your colleagues down in The Loop." He answers and I am still at a loss for words. I flip through the delicate pages recognizing familiar scenes and lines, realizing that it has been a long time since I took time to enjoy Pericles.

"You know, he never fully gives up hope in this play." I say stumbling for just the right words.

"I know. I read it. It's a wonderful love story."

"Thank you, Mark. I am truly touched." I say replacing the book on the table and wrapping my arms around his neck. I straddle his torso and pull him close. All I can think of are the two words at the end of his written message. He loves me.

I have waited all my life for this and worried just the same. I figure it's now or never. So, I roll across his body and sit at his side again.

"You know I'm different." I say point blank.

"Yeah, so?"

"No, I mean really different. Inside and out." I admit and hold my breath unsure of the type of reaction he would have.

"Whatever makes you different makes you interesting to me. Besides, how different can you really be?" He asks.

"I'm . . . I'm Undecided." I say and hope that the carefully chosen word defines my lifelong dilemma.

Mark takes my hand in his. "What a gift to be given the power to chose your gender." He says with deep sincerity. "Let me help you figure it out."

He takes my hand, guides me through the living room and opens the door to his bedroom. It is dark but I can feel a shag carpet beneath my feet. Sir Duke is playing softly from the speakers in the other room. He begins to unbutton my shirt, slowly. I pull his t-shirt up over his head and lay the side of my face on his chest. I can hear his heartbeat and I know I am no longer undecided.

Chapter 41
Lessons From A.J.

So much is heating up on Dodson Street. It could be the warmth of the early summer sun bouncing off the pavement or the students' anticipation of vacation but the air up and down the block is electric. We all share an attainable goal toward which to strive in our new-shared creed that graces the entrances of the school and business offices respectively, "Show that you care deeply about your community. Live authentically." I already feel a developing sense of allegiance to my coworkers, the students and school staff.

"Hey, A.J." I say. "I finished the data collection and we have a baseline measurement for our initial E.Q."

"Tell me what you've got." She says to me.

"The results of the first round data intake show that the students and staff at Dodson and our staff here at Hoyt have much room to grow." I answer.

"That doesn't surprise me." She says. "The whole point of this venture is to raise the happiness quotient of all involved. Happy smart people breed success. It's a community mission."

"It helps that we all share an attainable goal." I say in reference to the shared creed that graces the entrances of the school and business offices.

"I like that a lot, Alex. You should be proud you came up with it. 'Show that you care deeply about your community. Live authentically.' It is what every person on earth needs to be reminded of." She says.

"I can't take all the credit. Janet and Chrissy helped me come up with it." I admit.

"All the more fitting that it was a group effort." She adds.

"Did you hear that the kids are already beginning to use the iPads? They came in just in time. Nothing like some incredible technology tools to keep them dreaming of school all summer long." I say.

"That's exactly what we want to have happen." A.J. nods. "Now come with me across the street. Let's announce the winner of the logo design contest."

****

"After all the votes were tallied, the winning artist is . . . Latasha in Mr. Tandem's sixth grade class with her marvelous winged dragon- a symbol of confidence, determination, courage and intelligence." A.J. announces over the p.a. system. A loud roar of cheers erupts from Mark's room.

Latasha comes running into the office screaming, "Woo hoo! Where's my prize?" Mr. Bluberry hands her an ipod Shuffle and a twenty-dollar itunes Card.

"Listen up everyone." A.J. wraps up her announcement. "We will be having shirts with our new dragon design made for everyone to have at the start of the next school year. Thank you all for participating."

"Great job, A.J." Mr. Bluberry compliments on her enthusiastic address to the school. "Want to stick around and lead the pledge of allegiance?"

"No thanks, Michael. There are some principal privileges that can't be passed along." She says as we leave the office to go back across the street.

"Have you spoken to Terry lately?" A.J. asks me.

"No, not for a few days. Why?" I ask holding the door to open for her to enter our office.

"He has been working so hard with IDEA that I think you should check in and see the progress they have made." She suggests. So, I hop in my car and head down to the factory.

"Hey Terry." I say walking up to where he is seated at a makeshift desk in the corner of the entryway to the factory floor.

"Well look who's here. It's the company cage rattler in the flesh." He says looking up from a stack of job applications.

"How are things here?" I ask Terry, brushing off his rude greeting.

"Well, despite all doubt on my part, IDEA is making strides toward a planned busy summer of redesigning school furniture. The doors are open for business orders and many parents of students from the school are scheduled for job training." He says with a snort.

"The opportunity to provide eager parents with solid work is a key factor in the success of this whole venture." He says. "So, I am making sure my end of the project flies. Success here at IDEA leads to more dollars in my pocket." He says and gets back to the stack of applications. "And," He adds, "no crime, more dime. . . in my pocket that is."

"So far, so good since you've been in charge of safety around here. No more muggings." I say in a complimentary way.

"Nope. Not going to happen. We've got new cameras installed at various check points and I just gave an okay for the security agency to hire a handful of guys who just came back from serving in the middle east to patrol the neighborhood. For them, this job's a piece of cake." He boasts.

"I hope you're right Terry. It's nice you could get those men working." I say.

I know that in A.J.'s eyes none of this is about fattening Terry's wallet. She has put him in charge of safety issues and getting jobs for the parents of our students because those are two areas that are critical to the success of the overall project. Terry may be a jerk but he always gets the job done. A.J. knows that if our students see consistent work ethics in their parents then a powerful wheel will be set in motion, as the cycle of dependence on the government for everything is broken.

"Hey Alex," Terry looks up as I am turning to leave.

"Huh?"

"How's Jamal?" He asks and I am surprised by his concern for someone other than himself.

"Social services has granted Mary Jane Tandem temporary custody until they find a stable family member who will take him in." I say. "Keep up the good work Terry."

As I drive back up to the office I marvel at the determination A.J. is showing to procure a community so children and their families can exist safely without fear. Jamal's story is a driving force but there is something more.

She has been working around the clock to oversee building upgrades and renovations to entice occupants to open shops and rent out apartments. She is intently focused on bringing start up businesses to the storefronts of the neighborhood to offer more employment opportunities and enhance the community feel.

"She's moving so quickly and calling on so many favors, it's as if she is playing with borrowed time!" I shout

out loud to myself noticing that in no time at all several apartments have been prepped and wait to house those who will take jobs in the neighborhood. She has reviewed applications for tenants of families whose children are enrolled at the school. She told me she is looking particularly closely at those who will commit to a safe and healthy community for the children.

It's no wonder, I think to myself, that Brenda Swenson has found A.J.'s involvement in the school and neighborhood project to be intriguing. I've always liked her personal interest stories on WGN. Back at the office, I park and get out. I can see Brenda and her crew setting up in the front lobby of the school below the emblazoned new creed. I walk over and watch the interview.

"Good afternoon Chicago. Today I am here with A.J. Hoyt the name synonymous with worldwide success in venture capital. Her name is a moniker in the city for the contributions of millions of dollars to our various museums and for funding a wing at The Chicago Medical Center. These days, however, she is most likely to be found in an old abandoned hardware store across the road from Dodson Street School here on the south-side of town."

She turns to A.J. "Prior to this current project, had you ever spent time down here on Dodson Street?" Brenda inquires.

"Quite honestly, no. I found out about this neighborhood through a," A.J. hesitates, "friend who stumbled upon the school."

"Just how bad was the situation before you set up shop on Dodson Street?" Brenda continues.

With a tear in her eye A.J. responds candidly, "To me this is a difficult question to answer but I'll do my best. It makes my heart ache to know that for many years now, the teachers and staff at Dodson Street School have been neglected, ignored by the powers that be. They were underfunded and under resourced while the teachers and students were working hard to achieve far above local standards. The staff is the most dedicated group of professionals that I have ever known. They find it deep in their hearts to go beyond curriculum and provide support for the children in ways that," A.J. chokes up, no doubt, with thoughts of Jamal, "most of us barely show to our own children. The adults in that school are truly selfless. Before we stepped in, the teaching materials were out of date. There were very few supplemental materials, no classroom computers. They were working in the dark ages with a ditto machine.

I know that their situation is not unlike so many others in Chicago and in other cities across the country but for some reason my friend brought the plight of Dodson Street to my attention. I like to believe that it was God who really brought us all together."

I think to myself chuckling, it was actually Dolores but nobody really needs to know that.

Brenda pauses for a moment and looks around at the colorful student work hanging in the hallway. She notes the sparkling clean floors and the throbbing beat of a copy machine coming from the office. She looks out the window and sees flowers blooming in big planters near the bus lane and smiles at the sight of the "fairy tale garden" plaque just to the right of the entrance of the school.

"Well, A.J. it appears that your company has made sure that this school is taken care of for the time being but how do all of these physical improvements insure a better life experience for the students and staff in the long run?" She asks.

"That's a fair question. To quote a favorite author "What is essential is invisible to the eye."" A.J. says with a glimmer thinking back perhaps to her high school French class.

"The Little Prince" Brenda acknowledges with a smile

"Yes. Antoine de Saint-Exupéry reminds us all that it is the time and energy, the hope and love that we put into nurturing that is most essential. I am hoping that if my employees work within close proximity that they will not only become role models for the students but we will actually become part of their social fabric."

"I see. How are you doing this?" Brenda asks.

"We are reaching out to the entire school community by providing the adults opportunities to work nearby, giving them affordable and safe homes for their families, offering community-wide incentives to reward and grow their spirits and safely strengthen their hearts with hope that in time we will break the unhealthy cycles that these children, at Dodson Street School, would most likely have been thrown into."

"What an undertaking." Brenda responds.

"So, to answer your question fairly, there is no guarantee that life will not be tough for these children and their families but there is a guarantee that without our efforts to be present and actively connected to them that the chances for them to thrive would be much less. The physical changes we have made to this school were well deserved. The emotional and social support we are providing is essential."

"Are you saying," Brenda continues. "that your entire company has transplanted itself from The Loop to Dodson Street? That seems a lot to require as an employer. How has all of this gone over with your staff?"

"You know, at first, I got some pushback from a few who, naturally, questioned many aspects of this extreme move from issues of personal security, to performance expectations and beyond. I can honestly say that after the months that we have spent down here on Dodson Street my staff, as a whole, has been just as productive and dedicated as ever. Our numbers are high. Productivity is good. We have simply picked ourselves up and dropped ourselves off in a new neighborhood."

"Sounds like gentrification."

"Call it what you will. But I like to think of it more holistically. Putting business aside, knowing that our presence is powerful enough to revive the spirit of a neighborhood has not only given my staff a boost in purpose but I have seen some of my stereotypical stone cold corporate types reach into themselves because they actually see needs daily that they can fulfill in the school across the street. People who just did their jobs and hurried home at the end of the work day when we were set up down in The Loop are sticking around and going over to help with tutoring, planting the fairy tale garden, interviewing families for the apartments that we are renting out, serving lunch over their noon hours and beyond. It has really been incredible because the opportunities for my staff to reach out in ways that they are comfortable are so accessible and nothing is negatively impacting their work performance. In fact, the intangible rewards far exceed any bonus I might give in a paycheck because they are not temporary."

"Wow, that's an impressive lesson to share." Brenda says reflectively.

"In fact, just yesterday my vice president and I purchased homes around the corner near where a few long time residents have continued to stake their claims despite the difficulties that the neighborhood has experienced. We want to be closer to this community that we are fostering. We want to be here to see all that changes around the clock. We want to be available. These families, the students, the staff at the school, they are all becoming my second family and I hope that as the school takes on its new life that my staff might consider the benefits of moving their families down here to Dodson Street so that they can experience the wonder of being a part of something so beautiful."

In the unlikely position of being a speechless reporter, the interviewer goes silent. Brenda searches for words to say to reflect her awe and to show to the world that if a seventy-something year old woman with wisdom and financial backing can reinvent her purpose on earth, so could the thousands of home viewers who are watching this interview.

A.J. looks the curious reporter in the eyes and says, "I have lived a long time. I have written a thousand checks to the needy and I have finally learned that there is a big difference between charity and participation. I now choose to participate."

Brenda says nothing. She realizes that A.J. Hoyt has just given the last words of the interview.

Chapter 42

Parents

"Did you see A.J.'s interview?" I ask Mark.

"Yeah," he replies reaching across the front seat with a kiss and a warm embrace as I jump in.

"She did great didn't she? I mean really, she captured this whole thing in a nutshell. She really is amazing." I rave in accolades.

Mark turns the key and stops for a second. He looks to me and says, "There is only one thing that bothered me about her interview. She never mentioned you, Alex. This is all happening because of you."

I can feel myself blush as I shrug my shoulders and say, "I don't mind. If it all continues to go well and A.J. Hoyt Technologies manages to be successful and grow as the school improves along the way, then that's all I really care about."

Without a back comment Mark starts the car and we drive along in silence for a while heading toward O'Hare.

"I am so excited for you to meet my parents. You are going to love them and they are going to adore you."

"I have no doubt." He says driving on in the late afternoon Saturday traffic.

"Let's go right to Twin Anchors from the airport. My parents have been talking about those ribs since their last visit. I can send Janet and Chrissy over to put our names on the waiting list." I offer in an attempt to avoid an hour-long potentially trying sidewalk wait.

"Mmmmmmm yes, tantalizing ribs. That sounds perfect!" Mark groans licking his lips.

****

"So Mark, Alex tells us that you went to the University of Illinois." My father offers up as a conversation starter while our mouths water amidst the scent of savory Chicago barbecue.

"I sure did. First in my family to be accepted to a university." He responds.

"That's quite something. You should be very proud." My mother compliments with a genuine grin.

"Oh I am. But I have to pay tribute to my mother and grandfather who helped me get there. When I was very young my mother went to school at night to earn her nursing degree and my grandfather took care of me. Then as I got older, she worked nights and weekends so that she was home when my grandfather worked and she worked when my grandfather was home. I always had someone taking care of me, making sure I studied, did my homework. I am very lucky." He admits.

"You would really enjoy Mary Jane, mom. She is a wonderful woman." I add encouragingly.

"Well, I hope to meet her someday."

"How about this weekend? I can see if she is free?" Mark interjects excitedly knowing that aside from taking care of Jamal her Sunday would be rather quiet.

"We would love to meet your mother." My father quickly responds wide-eyed as a steaming hot plate of juicy ribs is delivered to the table. Knowing my father, I wonder which excites him more, Mary Jane or the ribs.

****

As we stroll down Sedgwick toward my place after dinner, we split into twos. The sidewalk is too narrow for a four-person span. Mark and my father walk side by side and get into a healthy discussion over baseball. Mark's adored White Sox have just beaten the Cleveland Indians and my father has some healthy opinions about the outcome of the game. Just within my earshot, I hear my father relive some moments of the game.

"The Sox should never have pulled off that win." Says my father. "They don't have the depth. They are just consistently lucky."

"You think so? I don't know Mr. True. Your Indians do have some depth and big hitters but we've got the hardware to prove how good our team is. It hasn't been that long since the Sox won the World Series." Mark emphasizes with his arms taking a bat swing to the air.

"You got me there, Mark." Confesses my father with a healthy punch to Mark's shoulder.

Walking hand in hand my mom slows our pace so we are just far enough behind them and says to me, "I saw the way that you and Mark were looking at each other during dinner. This is serious isn't it Alex."

"Yes mom. I have never been so comfortable with a partner as I am with Mark. He is everything I have waited for my whole life. We are very much in love." I admit squeezing tightly the hand that has always been such a guide and comfort.

"Oh honey, I am so happy for you. I have prayed that you would find that special someone." My mom says. "I always hoped that your lifestyle would lead you down an honest path to true love."

"Oh mom, wait 'til you see what Mark and I have going on down on Dodson Street tomorrow. You will really feel love overflowing." I confess proudly.

"Your father and I can't wait." She says as we come to the building where my roommates wait bottle and corkscrew at hand.

****

A familiar heavenly aroma of freshly baked blueberry cobbler dances from open windows welcoming my family as we work our way up the sidewalk to the front door where Mary Jane, in blue jeans and blue t-shirt decorated with hummingbirds, is holding the front door open wide. She greets us with a friendly smile.

"Welcome, welcome. Please come in. Mark is out back playing catch with Jamal." She says leading us into the tidy living room where I then introduce all of our parents.

"May I offer you some tea or lemonade?" Mary Jane asks clasping her hands and smiling with delight.

"I would love a glass of tea, Mary Jane. Thank you." My father replies.

"Me too." I say.

"Let me help you in the kitchen." My mom offers as she followed Mary Jane out of the room leaving my father and me behind.

"Take a look at these pictures dad." I say pointing at a couple of old framed photos of Mark. In one, he is about fifteen years old. He and his grandfather are wearing fishing waders, both smiling ear to ear with pride for their catch of two equally large trout. In the other photo Mark stands in cap and gown, towering over his mother who is beaming with pride on the day of his college graduation.

"His grandfather raised him with his mother." I remind my father. "They all lived here in this house and Mark's grandfather, Otto, owned a shoe factory just a few blocks away. It was called Tandem Footing."

"I see." My father acknowledges. "That explains why they live here. I was wondering what would influence someone to live in such a dwindling neighborhood."

"What do you mean dwindling, dad? This area is on the rise. Just you wait. We will give you and mom the royal tour a little later. You won't believe the changes that have taken place in the past few months. We'll show you what we've been up to. Soon it will have a vibe that rivals the good ol' days when Mark was a young boy hanging out at the old soda fountain in the drug store and riding his bike every day over to Dodson Street School." I shoot back with a slightly perturbed air.

"I'm sorry. It's just surprising to me to be in such a nice home having seen the neglected surroundings. It appears that the neighborhood is struggling." My father explains attempting to eat some crow.

"As we know so well, appearances can be deceiving." I state with my fingers running through my short locks as I straighten the collar of my pale pink oxford in a mirror hanging above a bookcase in the corner of the room. Mary

Jane reenters with tea and lemonade.

"Your mom is serving up the cobbler. She will be right out. Did I hear you explaining some of these pictures to your father?" She asks.

"I did my best." I answer. "I just love the shot of Mark and his grandfather.

"So do I." Comes a voice from the doorway. Mark is in a White Sox t-shirt, faded jeans and some old Chuck Taylors looking completely comfortable and casual with Jamal at his side. "Mr. True, this is Jamal. He was just working my arm out in the backyard."

Extending his hand with a warm friendly smile, my father leans down and says, "It is a pleasure to meet you, Jamal. This is my wife, Mrs. True. We are visiting from Ohio."

Jamal shakes both hands and asks them very seriously, "Do you like the Indians or the Reds?"

"We're Indians fans when it comes to professional baseball. But have you ever heard of The Ohio State Buckeyes? We love to cheer for them in football and basketball." My mom declares with scarlet and gray pride.

"Of course I've heard of The Buckeyes. They're part of the Big Ten. Mr. T. went to a Big Ten school. That's what I want to do when I grow up." Jamal shares, which brings a smile to Mark's face. "I am going to go grab some lemonade from the kitchen." He continues and leaves us adults to continue visiting in the living room.

"What a wonderful boy." My father compliments fully aware of the tragedy that had taken place in his life, and seeing the important role that The Tandem's were filling.

"I agree." Says Mark. "He has taught me so much."

Hearing these words makes my heart soar like never before at the notion that Mark could be so humble as to accept lessons of life from a young and vulnerable child.

"That is why I love you." I openly yet quietly whisper, taking hold of Mark's hand, squeezing it tightly a sight that our parents savor.

Still holding my hand, Mark suggests, "I know it's a Sunday, but let's drag ourselves into work. We can show off all that has happened because Alex, here, got lost a few months back and stumbled into Paulie Blue Hands."

"Paulie Blue Hands wasn't the only one to win my devotion. Mark." I say with a hip jab as we meander out the front door into the sunshine and down the sidewalk hand in hand, our parents and Jamal in tow.

Chapter 43

Mid-Week Wedding

"A summer wedding on Cape Cod!" A.J. exclaims.
"Massachusetts, yes it's a fine state for all types of weddings.
Very progressive. I know the perfect spot. Please let me
make a call."

I agree to her request to help with the very
spontaneous nuptials that Mark and I are planning.

"We want to be married before the school year
begins." I say to A.J. who is already on her phone with
someone on the east coast. "Here's my credit card number.
Just hold the space. It will be a small group." She says to
the person on the other end.

"If you don't mind having your wedding mid-week,
there are still a few open dates in August." She says.

"No, I don't mind at all." I respond completely open
to anything that A.J. has to offer.

"Good. I have a friend out in the town of Chatham
and she can get you all set up for the most beautiful
beachfront ceremony you could ever imagine." A.J. says
beaming- the prime example that every girl no matter how
young or old loves to plan a wedding.

"Where is it?" I ask.

"A charming little hydrangea covered resort called Chatham Bars Inn. Here, come pull up the website." She says.

"That's gorgeous." I say drooling over the oceanfront vistas and gray-shingled buildings. Mark will love it! But I can tell from here that it's going to be way out of our budget." I say.

A.J. looks at me funny. "Why do you think I just gave them my credit card number?"

"No. A.J. I can't let you do this. It's too much." I plead.

"Stop it right there." She says. "I never got to plan the weddings of my boys. I want to throw at least one wedding in my lifetime besides my own. If you like the idea of having your wedding there then let me give it to you as a gift."

I look at the pictures again on the computer screen and imagine the warm ocean breezes as we say our vows barefoot in the sand. I accept A.J.'s generous offer and call Mark and my parents right away.

****

"It's even more beautiful than the pictures on the website!" I exclaim running barefoot through the sand holding Jamal's hand. "Come, come stick your toe in the water. Your mom would be so excited for you."

Jamal and I stop just short of ruining our wedding clothes in the froth of the waves as they tickle our toes and crackle like Pop Rocks on the sand.

"Listen," Jamal says. "They're telling us the secrets." He points to the waves building and rolling several feet ahead of us. "Just like mama said."

I put my arm around his waist just as Mark walks up and tells us that the ceremony is about to begin.

A white trellis that is flounced with voluptuous hydrangeas of antique blue and faded raspberry frames us. It is mid-day and the lobster boats are drifting by us on the Nantucket Sound. The rigging on their boats clank like chimes in an organ. It is the music of our moment.

Mark is wearing an Armani day suit, a surprise gift from A.J. and I am in light blue silk a gift from my mother. The salty fish smell of the sea is an intoxicating cologne that we both share.

"Until death do us part." I repeat after the reverend nods our union and steps away so that we may consummate it with a kiss.

"I can't believe we did it!" Mark says to me with tears in his eyes as a light wind blows strands of his hair across his face.

"Here," I say and tuck the loose strands behind his ear. "Let's pose for the photographer. I want to capture this moment forever."

A waiter in a white tuxedo hands us each a glass of Proseco and we toast to our family and friends, especially A.J., who have all come to share in our joy.

Chapter 44

Porch Swing

"I can't believe we just did it!. The Cape was the perfect place for our wedding. My parents loved it. Your mom loved it. A.J. was out of her mind over it. The plane ride alone launched Jamal to the moon. I just can't believe we did it!" I clamor on and on in sheer disbelief that in a few weeks time Mark had proposed and a wedding had been planned and our life journey had taken off.

"My father never even hinted that you had asked him for my hand when they were up visiting in Chicago." I continue, looking down admiringly at the shining platinum bands that have bound us eternally together.

"Yes, I know. I bribed him to keep silent with tickets to a White Sox game against the Indians next season. He said he wouldn't even mention a word to your mother if I could promise him seats behind the dugout." Mark confesses proudly.

"Now that was a good bribe. He will hold you to those tickets for sure." I say as we rock back and forth on the porch swing that hangs from the timbers of our new address.

"I knew from the moment we kissed in the elevator that we were meant to be together." Mark admits nuzzling into my tousled hair.

The two of us in t-shirts and shorts, flip-flops brushing along the floorboards of the porch with each swing. The summer evening is closing. In the light pink of the hour a cricket's song keeps rhythm with the drum of the swing and for the first time in months I experience serenity.

"What's with the big smile?" Mark asks me.

"Oh, I was just thinking back to the beach at Chatham Bars Inn. Your mom and my mom were holding hands during the ceremony. My dad held Jamal's. Janet, Chrissy and A.J. were beaming. The sun was dancing over The Cape. It was just a perfect moment . . . just like this moment right now." I share, pulling him closer.

"I agree, perfect was as perfect is."

"I can't believe that A.J. insisted on throwing our wedding." I admit in wonder.

"Are you kidding? She was thrilled. From the minute I told her we were going to be married on The Cape, she practically begged to make the call. Although she acted coy by waiting to hear it from you." Mark explains. "She said that her family had spent several summers at Chatham Bars over the years and that it would be her wedding gift to us. I figured, why not? I trust her." He continues.

"So you knew all along that she was going to offer to host our wedding?" I ask.

"Yep. I talked to her right after I asked your father for your hand." He admits.

"Really?" I respond a bit surprised. "Wow."

"Do you remember the day of her television interview?"

"Uh huh." I reply sleepily.

"Well, I was irritated that she took all the credit for everything that has been going on down here. Right?" He reminds me.

"Uh huh." I nod almost in a comatose state from the syncopated motion of the swing and the song of the cricket.

"Well, I went and spoke to her about it." He says admittedly having gone behind my back.

"You did what?" I pop up out of the lull of the swaying motion and sit tall next to Mark. "I told you I didn't care about getting any credit."

"I know but I do. I care about you. Besides, I could sense in the interview that A.J. was dancing around the obvious. So I confronted her, gently of course." He concedes.

"What did she say then?" I demand curiously.

"It was actually quite sweet. A.J. wanted to protect you. Well, us really. She could see that there was a lot more happening between you and me than just a business venture and improving social climates. She said that the kind of love that she sensed between you and me was unique and it needed to be sheltered from any negative outside forces . . . like the media. She intentionally put up a barrier so that our love could be free to grow with as little distraction as possible given the circumstances that already challenge us. A.J. IS an evolved woman for her time." Mark says with gratitude for the clarity and thoughtfulness of our kind friend.

"I can't believe you didn't tell me all this before we got married, Mark. I would have surely spoken with A.J. and thanked her." I say, wishing that the clock could be turned back just a little.

"I wouldn't worry about it. She is beside herself. She told me that she feels like she has a front row seat at a movie theater showing a great romance film every single day. For her, we are entertaining and exciting. As if to say that developing this neighborhood and the school isn't enough for an older woman, throw in a daily dose of romance and she's living on the set of a real soap opera minus the detergent commercials." Mark pokes lovingly about A.J.'s enthusiasm.

I laugh at the thought of A.J. having arrived at the office each day in anxious anticipation for the next episode of "The Young and The Restless".

"You know, she really is one of the most incredible women I have ever met. Here she is pushing eighty and in a short span of months, she has orchestrated an entire neighborhood overhaul and social development plan, thrown a wedding and moved herself from Michigan Avenue to a bungalow off of Dodson Street. I hope we have half her energy when we are her age." I add.

As dusk begins to fall, lights are turned on in the newly occupied neighboring apartments across the street. Workers from IDEA are changing shifts and some are coming home for the night. Barbecues are firing up and the air absorbs the perfume of suppertime. We swing back and forth to the faint tunes of vintage Earth, Wind and Fire that pump from an open window nearby and a young family walks past as the parents attempt to wear out their children in the night air.

"This is really something, Alex. My old neighborhood is coming back to life. Gramps would be so proud." Mark expresses with the ease of a teacher floating on the waves of well-earned summer.

"Uh huh . . ." I mumble trailing off into a sweet porch swing slumber.

Chapter 45
Going Public

"Twenty-four hours to go." I announce hearing my echo bounce down the empty hallway. The opening bell is soon to ring in the new school year. I am inspecting the work of a slew of summer services. All of the walls are freshly painted. The floors sparkle with polish. Each classroom is set up with re-designed furniture that IDEA has delivered and a brand new desktop computer waits on each teacher's re-designed desk. The tech team from A.J. Hoyt Technologies just finished setting up a joint network to ease communication within the school and A.J. Hoyt Technologies while an electronic security firm has rewired the alarms and tested the new safety bell at the front door.

New textbooks and workbooks sit on shelves that previously held old and tattered musty versions and new equipment waits for use in the gymnasium. I keep running down the check-off list that has been growing all week long.

A parent of one of the students has been hired to be the school groundskeeper and throughout the summer he watered and maintained the freshly sodded playfield, took in the fairy tale garden harvest and oversaw the installation of our new playground. Trees were also planted and he watered those. I insisted that the school makeover be as evident on the outside as it is on the inside.

"This is not only to encourage strong performance but to reward it. The students and staff here at Dodson Street School deserve to feel pride for the place where they come every day." I explain to the groundskeeper. "I trust that you want the same for them too."

In just a few minutes the teachers will arrive for the first time since June and I am beyond excited to see the looks on their faces. The transformation of not only the school but also the entire neighborhood is epic and speaks volumes for A.J.'s determination and influence to move mountains in a city that easily gets caught up in molehills.

A coffee shop that sells sandwiches has been open since the first of August and has already done great business with all of the workers servicing the school, the men and women from the private security team who patrol the neighborhood and the new residents of the community who enjoy having a place to mix and mingle during the day. We continue to wait for a hardware shop to open up and have heard rumors that a hair salon will be coming soon too.

There is an air of well thought out control for the decisions that A.J. has made and the assistance and care that she has provided to the business tenants and new apartment tenants who fill the once abandoned spaces surrounding Dodson Street School. No doubt the teachers are going to be impressed.

346

One by one as they pull into the freshly paved parking lot, I see their expressions of disbelief as they rubber neck the area.

"Unbelievable Mark. Can you even handle this?" Dana Frinkle says running up and giving him and overly friendly welcome back hug that I just happen to catch.

"This is fabulous A.J. How on earth did you manage to get all of this work done in just a few months?" Asks Ms. Xhang.

"Let's just say that I know a few wonderful people who needed work and we needed workers. So, it all came together like in a very timely fashion." A.J. explains brushing off the true extent of her tireless hours of work that were interrupted only briefly by a weekend wedding in Cape Cod.

Janet and Chrissy eagerly join the crowd of excited staff that grows in the front lobby as the teachers share embraces and introduce one another while waiting for instruction from Principal Bluberry.

"Good Morning everyone. Welcome and welcome back to a new school year. As you may have noticed, we have experienced some physical enhancements around here in your absence over the course of the summer." Mr. Bluberry announces gesturing at the freshly painted walls and the glistening floors. "I am personally overjoyed at the extreme generosity that A.J. Hoyt and her employees have shown to our school community. She and Alex saw a need early last spring and in a matter of months have selflessly given their hearts to make life better for the families of Dodson Street School. Please join me in thanking A.J., Alex and the rest of A.J. Hoyt Technologies staff for their tireless efforts on our behalf." Mr. Bluberry hands A.J. and me each a dozen multicolored roses and embraces us while the staff cheers.

I stand tall before the eager group of teachers dressed in my summer suit with the bouquet of flowers in my hands. I am glowing with joy at all of their happy faces, and savor each and every appreciative nod, finally locking gazes with the one who matters most.

Mark's chest inflates with pride as he watches me accept the praises from his colleagues that have gathered to start anew. The risks that we took and the strides that we made all came down to when I listened to my heart and followed my instinct. Mark is undoubtedly the proudest in the room. Full of emotion he comes up to me with an embrace that rivals the kiss we shared on the beach at Chatham Bars Inn.

The room goes uncomfortably silent, as not a sole would have expected such a bold gesture from anyone on the opening day of school, most specifically Mark Tandem. Turning to his coworkers with his arm around me, he sees nothing but dropped jaws and bug eyes in reaction to his momentary lapse in professionalism. For a moment the room waits in a frozen state as the crowd is rocked from complete elation to total shock in a matter of seconds. Thankfully, A.J. breaks the silence.

Dressed in her strongest red business suit, bright purple glasses and hair styled to perfection A.J. steps over and puts her arm around Mark's waist.

"Well," She says. "The truth is that Alex sure knows how to take a leap of faith. Along with drumming up the idea to develop the Dodson Street School Community, and convincing me that it was a project worth believing in, Alex managed to fall in love with a wonderful man. I would like to formally introduce all of you to Mark and Alex Tandem."

Again the room is painfully silent as the flabbergasted staff continues to process the news. Thankfully after a couple of seconds, Rosie Fishers claps, followed by Paulie Blue Hands, Mr. Bluberry, Janet and Chrissy, Ms. Xhang, Ms. Jones, Mr. Wilkins, Debby, Marian, Lamar, the new groundskeeper and my coworkers from A.J. Hoyt, everyone except Dana Frinkle who crumples onto the bench next to her.

"Well now, we have a new school year to celebrate and a new marriage. All is good. Let's head down to our redecorated teacher's lounge for a complimentary breakfast provided by Sweet Pea Café, one of A.J. Hoyt Technologies venture capital investments and a new neighbor across the street." Suggests Mr. Bluberry inviting his staff to relax and catch up for a bit before attending to the back-to-school tasks at hand.

In the lounge, A.J. holds up a bright blue t-shirt emblazoned with Latasha's dragon. "I am happy to say that each of you will find one of these on your desks when you arrive in your classrooms later. There is also a box in each room containing one for every student. Please tell your students that these are not uniforms but shirts to be worn with dignity whenever they want to or whenever the school has a special spirit day. We are all now officially the Dodson Street School Dragons."

A few whistles and cheers come from the happy group of teachers as they accept the new title and toast each other with their coffee cups, gently transitioning from lazy summer days into the hopeful high paced beat of a new and already very exciting school year.

Chapter 46

Farewell

"Okay Jamal. Now you have everything you need in your backpack, right?" Mark asks while pouring him a second glass of orange juice as he sits at the kitchen table eating a bowl of cereal.

"Yep." He replies between slurps.

"Because I won't be your teacher this year you are going to have to work real hard at keeping organized. So, use that assignment notebook at school and we can go over it each night when you get home. Okay?" Mark suggests knowing that a year ago Jamal was heading back to school under his mother's wing and that he was most likely flashing back to thoughts of her.

"Okay." Jamal says looking up into our eyes as Mark and I have managed to take him in as a foster child.

There is a knock at the front door. I go to answer it and return to the kitchen with Mary Jane who is carrying her camera.

"I came to wish my favorite seventh grader good luck on his first day." She says giving Jamal a big squeeze.

"But things won't be that much different. Same school and all." Jamal says shrugging his shoulders in indifference.

"You may think that now but just you wait. I hear there are several new students in the seventh grade and we have some new adults working in the building too. I think you are going to be in for a big surprise, Jamal." Informs Mark.

"Listen, you three. I didn't lug my camera over here for nothing. Let me get a photo of this auspicious occasion will you." Mary Jane pleads heaving Jamal's backpack over his shoulders and lining us up on our front porch side by side with Mark and I towering over Jamal in the middle.

"Now this is one for the memory books. Smile, on three, everybody. Say cheese, one two, and three . . . " Mary Jane takes the photo and wishes us all a fine day as she strolls on down the street back to her home.

The sun is shining down a late summer heat as we head toward school and work on Dodson Street and the three of us observe the first bus load of students pulling up in front of the school entrance. The teachers are standing in great anticipation along the sidewalk holding signs that welcome the children to their various grade levels. Most of the students are not paying attention to the signs that the teachers hold but rather the sign, or evidence that someone has swept in over the summer and completely beautified the school. There are hoots and hollers coming from all the children as they peer around at the new playground and the playfield. I am ecstatic watching from a distance.

Taking the scene in from another vantage point is A.J. who woke up extra early to be at the office for the big arrival. According to some neighbors, she stopped by Sweet Pea Café for hot tea and a scone and headed up to take a perch in the front window of her offices.

The coffee shop owner was sweeping his sidewalk and he waved to her as she lifted the windowpane so as to hear the rumble of the busses coming down the street and the chatter of the children as they walked down the sidewalk toward school.

I can imagine her savoring the warmth of her tea along with the joyful noise of healthy laughter and glee coming from young friends reconnecting under the giant sunflowers and beanstalks of the fairy tale garden. She was probably reflecting back to her own innocent joyful childhood experiences on the first days of school seventy some odd years before.

She wanted the same for these children who deserved all that the first day of school is meant to be. As the opening bell rang and the students filed into the building behind their teachers, the coffee shop owner noticed that A.J. had disappeared from the window.

****

"Oh no. No . . . " I enter the office and run to A.J.

lying below the open window. Touching the side of her neck, her pulse is weak. I quickly dial my cellphone for an ambulance and try to bring her to consciousness.

"A.J. It's me Alex. What happened? Are you hurt? Hang in there with me. Medics are on the way." I plead to her in panic, taking her cold hand and hoping that someone else will show up to work early too.

For what seems like an eternity, nobody comes through the door and then I hear the sound of an ambulance. The medics come running up the stairs and are followed by Mr. Bluberry and Mark.

"Alex, what's happening?" Mark shouts.

"I don't know. I walked in the door and she was lying on the floor barely breathing." I answer in extreme fright.

"She has had a heart attack. We need to get her to the E.R. now. Out of the way people, NOW!" The medics take charge and wheel A.J. out and into the ambulance. I jump in with the stretcher and Mark runs to his car.

"Mark, you follow the ambulance. I will go back and have Rosie contact A.J.'s family." Mr. Bluberry calls out as he runs back into the school.

The painful whirring of the ambulance siren throbs in my head as we rush north to Loyola Medical Center. All I can do is hold A.J.'s hand and pray that she makes it to the E.R.

When we pull into the hospital, Mary Jane is there waiting at the curb with a medical team ready to go.

"Mark just called, Alex. I ran over from ICU and rounded up the best we've got. Go try and reach her family." Mary Jane commands with a sharp urgency that I have never seen from her.

Shaking from shock, I move robotically to the waiting area and dial Tom Mackey.

"She was just lying on the floor, barely a pulse. The window was wide open. I think she went in early to watch the children arrive on the first day. I don't know why she was alone. You know A.J. She does what she wants." I shout tenuously into the cell phone completely terrified. "Rosie Fishers is trying to reach her family. You need to get here now, Tom. Please hurry and call Juan Carlos. He can contact everyone else." I continue with the intensity of the moment stealing away all my breath.

Mark runs through the door and sees me gasping for air.

"Hold my hand." He says as we slowly kneel together down onto the cold tile. Mark cups his other hand over my mouth to gather air and stop the hyperventilation and we pause in the anxious fury to gain some control.

Mary Jane comes around the corner with a grim look. She sits down next to us and speaks in a soft gentle voice.

"They have stabilized her but she has had a severe

heart attack. Has A.J.'s family been reached?" She asks.

"Yes. Rosie has been in touch but none of her children are in Chicago. We are all she has right now." Mark tells his mother.

"Well then, I guess it would be best if you two come in and sit with her." She tells Mark and me.

As we enter the room, I begin again to gasp for air, at the sight of the tubes and machines that pump and ping to keep my dear friend alive. Mark takes my hand again, turns and says, "Listen Alex, you have to get a hold of yourself right now. A.J. needs you to be strong."

With a deep heavy, slow attempt to inhale I muster up courage and take the chair at A.J.'s side. Sitting there, I focus with gratitude and admiration on the beauty and love that has poured out of the strong heart of this woman over the recent months. To me, it has seemed as though we have known each other and worked side by side for years when in truth our time together has only been a blip on the screen of her life.

Lying helplessly in the hospital bed is a woman who had been a young determined scholar, devoted wife and mother, a driven businesswoman and leader of a corporate empire. Yet, at the end of it all she chose to step out of her deserved glory, start anew, and follow her spirit. It is this spirit that we share that is far above charity down on Dodson Street. A school, a group of teachers and their students, families, business employees, an entire neighborhood and a couple in love are all thriving on account of the fact that A.J. Hoyt had decided to believe in her spirit and participate in life even up to this end.

The doors open quietly and Tom Mackey enters with Juan Carlos. In the dimness of the room, I see that even Tom has been brought to tears by the sight of his business mentor and friend. I feel a slight movement from A.J.'s chilled clasp and whisper to the others in the room.

"She's awake." I announce as she flutters her lids to try and break free from the blanket haze.

"Alex, is that you?" She forces out long and wheezing.

"I'm here, A.J. Don't you worry. Your kids are on their way. Just rest." I tell her as my body shakes in uncontrollable tremors.

"It was so beautiful. The children. . ." She trails off trying to catch a breath through the tube that is providing her oxygen. "It was so beautiful. The sun was shining. . . the laughter. . . I saw Jamal smiling. . . I am so happy. You are so happy. You and Mark. . . my family too. Tell my children I love them. . . I love you all. . . Stay strong with our dream. Tom, well he has. . . a good heart too. Work together . . . " She trails off peacefully into profound silence that resonates through every heart in the room.

****

"I know this isn't your style but this is to be a celebration." I say spreading his gorgeous Armani across the bedspread. "If there was ever an occasion to pull out all of our bells and whistles, this is it. Look Mark, I'm wearing my best." I do a catwalk strut from one side of the bedroom to the other in the pale blue silk of our wedding.

"I know, I know. It's just that putting this on. It reminds me of The Cape and the morning that A.J. surprised me with it. I miss her too."

"I know you do. It pains me everyday to think that two full school years have gone by without her here. Then I tell myself, she's all around us, and I feel better. A.J. graced us with her love and spirit in so many ways that she will always be a part of everything we do." I say in comfort sitting down on the bed next to Mark as his head hangs low in his hands and I try to remind him of the joy that A.J. would want him to feel while wearing the handsome Armani suit.

"You're right Alex. This day is all about A.J. " He agrees holding tight to the pale blue tie that goes with the ensemble she had given him for our wedding day. "I'll be right down. Go check on Jamal."

Walking up the street toward the school, we are amazed by the television cameras, reporters and throngs of people, students, staff and families who are gathered in front of the school on Dodson Street. Facing the crowd is a podium stationed next to a monument draped in bright purple fabric.

I step up to the microphone and welcome everyone. "Thank you all for coming to celebrate a woman who took what God gave her and made the most of her talents to become an incredible mother, wife, business and community leader and friend. A.J. Hoyt believed that life was full of risks that needed to be taken and she took them. She would encourage all of us to do the same. Today we are here to honor her spirit in this community with a dedication. Jamal and Mark, could you please unveil the remembrance."

I stand tall and proud considering the risks that A.J. chose to take for so many people that she didn't even know but cared for nonetheless. The purple shroud is lifted for all to see the brilliant brass lettering attached to a magnificent stone wall. In large letters it reads *A.J. Hoyt Academy of Excellence.* Also attached to the wall are plaques denoting the pride of the community- two back-to-back State Science Olympiad Championships. Applause lasts for minutes as a sea of camera fire erupts from behind massive lenses.

The first shift of workers from IDEA is given the morning off and the entire factory joins in on the celebration in front of the school. I see Virgil and Cherry with an ever-present flower sticking out of her hair. They wave and approach me through the crowd.

"Aleeex, you done a goot job hee." Cherry compliments as Virgil takes me in his massive arms. The heft of his squeeze forces tears from my eyes. Words are snuffed out by the undeniable physical testimonial of our emotional embrace that tells the world we have both spent much of our lives carrying crosses, in one form or another, that seem to have been lifted. The release of tears is cathartic and as I step back from my dear friend I see that he too has rivers rolling down his cheeks. Cherry moves me aside in her brusque yet caring manner and cups his face in her hands, touching her bright red lips to the stains on his cheeks.

"Alex, this is all 'cause God has an amazin' plan for us my friend." He chokes out between Cherry's kisses. I nod with a quivering smile of gratitude.

We have sent the children back to class with their teachers. I have said good-bye to Mark and Jamal. The factory workers have returned to IDEA. My colleagues have gone back to their desks to pick up the work left from the day before. The photographers and reporters have gone and most likely are sifting through shots of the day and writing up titles for the story of the school and the successful capital venture of A.J. Hoyt Technologies.

No doubt they will mention the capital gains that we have seen that have been linked to every single decision A.J. made in her final days.

360

Thanks to her internal wisdom and drive, she instigated the rebirth of a community that will sustain itself with the pillars of her company as a foundation. She integrated a strong business model for other companies to follow if they feel the need to reap the true benefits of participation in capital ventures.

It is safe to say that A.J. Hoyt Technologies is stronger and more fluid than ever both financially and internally. The newspaper articles to be written will remind us all that successful business decisions, like those made by A.J. Hoyt, are ultimately about disruptive positive change.

The ardent autumn sun shines down. I am alone and I sit on a bench next to the Fairy Tale garden where the sunflowers bend low over my head. I close my eyes to the sunlight and it warms my face. The smell of freshly cut grass fills my lungs. I ponder those stories that the reporters will write, I realize that there is another wonderful story that could be printed but won't be.

It's an interesting story about a unique human being who had passed through much of life undecided- teetering between roles of physical and emotional identity, allowing only the relationships of a few people to fill the empty spaces of the desire to belong.

Due to God's timing and hand, or the power of Dolores, many lessons were learned. She now lives life confident in her chosen role caring deeply about a wonderful man, a beautiful boy and an entire community - living authentically.

Acknowledgements

To those in my community who have helped me learn and grow as a teacher, student, friend, daughter, wife, mother and writer while *Educating Alex*.

Especially . . .

Grace, Katie and Aunt Jackie- uniquely different, beautiful women who connect the art of writing with the spirit. Thank you all for helping me find my voice.

Kathi and my other Katie - both with eyes and ears of steel to read drafts and listen to my musings of teaching and social conflict. May your patience never get rusty.

Gier, Tina and her late-husband Art- who with extraordinary business minds gave me friendly lessons on disruption theory, germination of ideas and synergy in business. You all left indelible marks in the fabric of this story.

My parents- relentless readers, listeners and leaders of my thoughts and opinions on education and social norms. Many thanks for being the most important educators in my life, still teaching me today!

To my children- three loves of my life your inspiration keeps my world balanced. This story grew up with you . . . maybe you will find a friend within.

Tim- my knight, you tell me when to put down the

pen, rest and have a glass of wine, knowing that the story will still be waiting for me in the morning but alas . . .

It's done.

Cheers!

Book Club Guide

I dream of joining a book club and hearing thoughts and ideas generated from the themes of *Educating Alex*. Please consider contacting me to join your book club. Visit **positivelypressed.com** to try and set something up.

Book Club suggestions for *Educating Alex* . . . one maybe two bottles of merlot!

(It's a long book, you deserve it.)

Discussion Topics

1. Given the theme of non-descript gender, was it easy or hard to connect with Alex True throughout the story?

2. At what point did you begin to have a sense of what Alex's gender choice would be?

3. Do you think that Alex's reaction to the situation at Dodson Street School was inspiring? Would you risk it all to try to help improve life for someone else?

4. Can you relate to Mark Tandem's devotion to his students? Do you know any teachers who are as dedicated to their students as he is?

5. What motivated A.J. to act so intently upon the venture with Dodson Street School? Did she have a sense that this was her last chance to make up for years of materialistic living? Did she have an organic connection to the similar setting of her youth when she heard how the neighborhood had faded out?

6. Why do Rosie Fishers and Paulie Bluehands continue to show up at Dodson Street School day in and day out with so little compensation? Do you know anyone like them?

7. What will happen to Jamal?

8. Is the possibility of businesses germinating young minds and communities for future economic profit positive? Are there negative sides to this model?

9. What are Alex's biggest lessons in this story?

10. Does gender identity really matter when love is true?

About the Author

Katie McKinney Fox is an Ohio native but has spent the last twenty years teaching school in and around the city of Chicago where she lives with her family. She enjoys yoga, dark chocolate, a fine glass of wine, music from the seventies and everything French! This is her debut novel.

22770868R00199

Made in the USA
Lexington, KY
13 May 2013